AMSTERDAM

The Golden Age 1275–1795

RENEE KISTEMAKER AND ROELOF VAN GELDER

AMSTERDAM

The Golden Age 1275–1795

ABBEVILLE PRESS · PUBLISHERS · NEW YORK

On the jacket: Detail of *View of Amsterdam,* Jacob van Ruisdael, c. 1675–1680; Cambridge, the Fitzwilliam Museum.

Frontispiece: Amsterdam houses facing the Amstel.

Text by Renée Kistemaker and Roelof van Gelder. Captions, chronology, and sections on windmills and costumes by Mondadori.

Translated from the Italian by Paul Foulkes.

First American Edition

ISBN 0-89659-405-X

Library of Congress Cataloging in Publication Data

Kistemaker, Renée.
 Amsterdam.

 Bibliography: p.
 Includes index.
 1. Amsterdam (Netherlands)—History. 2. Amsterdam (Netherlands)—Description. I. Gelder, Roelof van. II. Title.
DJ411.A55K5 1983 949.2'3 83-8776
ISBN 0-89659-405-X

© 1982 Arnoldo Mondadori Editore S.p.A., Milan. English translation © 1983 Arnoldo Mondadori Editore S.p.A., Milan. Published in Italian under the title *Amsterdam, 1275–1795, Buono Governo e Cultura in una Metropoli di Mercanti.* All rights reserved. No part of this publication may be reproduced, stored in a retrieval system, or transmitted in any form, or by any means, electronic, mechanical, photocopying, recording, or otherwise, without prior written permission of the publisher: Abbeville Press, 505 Park Avenue, New York, N.Y. 10022. Printed and bound in Italy, by Arnoldo Mondadori Editore, Verona.

Contents

A village becomes a trading city

The landscape in which Amsterdam arose

From the air, the province of Holland in the western Netherlands resembles one single city. The spread of towns that together form the so-called Randstad—Amsterdam, Haarlem, Utrecht, The Hague, and Rotterdam—are constantly growing toward each other. Between them the familiar pattern of green pastures, ditches, and ponds remains just barely visible. The landscape of Holland was created by man. The speed at which this happened is amazing: in 500 years a muddy and inaccessible stretch of fen developed into one of the most urbanized parts of Europe.

About A.D. 1000, little of this was yet evident. Behind the line of dunes along the North Sea lay a wild area of fenlands, intersected by rivers and small water courses. The place was inhabitable only along the coast and on higher ground along the rivers. These limited living areas were insufficient to accommodate the growing population, for, during the 11th century, settlers moved into the fens in order to cultivate the marshes.

These farmers dug drains toward the interior, starting from a small stream. Between the drains stretches of land arose that through burning off and draining were made ready for cultivation. From about 1200, simple small weed dikes provided protection against water on higher ground. In the drained areas, the fens began to sag because of the drainage, so that the land came to lie lower, which meant that the ditches had to be made deeper. During the 13th century, the arable land was already so divided by this process that it hardly was possible to cultivate fields. From about 1150, while engaged in arduous draining operations, the farmers had to fight against severe flooding, which was due as much to the rise in sea level as to the sagging of the soil. Vast portions of reclaimed land were lost again. Meres developed, like those of Beemster and Purmer; the Zuiderzee grew to a considerable inland bay; and Holland was almost cut in two by a giant arm of the sea, the Ij, running from the Zuiderzee to the dunes. The worst danger had to be staved off by better dikes. With dams consisting of turf stacked like tiles, the inhabitants tried to protect the water courses that were linked with the sea.

By using simple, small sluices they were able to regulate the removal of drainage to the sea more efficiently. To keep up so risky a form of settlement required good organization from the beginning. To this end the farmers worked together in "neighborhoods," tightly knit groups designed above all for the maintenance of waterworks. By about 1300, the draining of the fenlands of Holland was complete. Everywhere the flat horizon was dotted with small villages and towns. Ditches, pastures, and fields, small winding dikes, and here and there, small woods of alder or willow formed a delicate landscape.

It is not known precisely when a settlement first arose by the mouth of the small river Amstel. Excavations show that by 1225 the place was inhabited. In the immediate surroundings there were already other settlements such as Sloten, now a suburb of Amsterdam. About 1270, a dam was probably built in the Amstel, near the settlement, in order to protect the land behind it against seawater from the

7

Ij. Shortly afterward, in 1275, the name of the settlement first appeared in a written document: *Amestelledamme*. Tradesmen lived there—a blacksmith and a shoemaker, farmers and sailors—in simple half-timbered houses of wood and clay, with roofs of reed, all materials that could be found in the surrounding countryside.

Sovereigns and municipal administration

The desolate fens in the western Netherlands belonged partly to the counts of Holland and partly to the bishops of Utrecht who had extensive secular holdings in the Netherlands and were the central power there until the 12th century. Holland, by contrast, was a newcomer on the political scene. In the course of the 12th century, the young county gradually grew at the expense of Utrecht. The struggle took place mainly in the border regions, including Amstelland, the area in which Amsterdam arose.

Amstelland belonged to Utrecht and covered a parcel of land astride the river Amstel. It formed a special legal entity nominally administered for the bishop by the rulers of Amstel. Among these, Gijsbrecht remains a well-known it tragic figure, thanks to a play by the 17th-century poet Vondel: by playing off Holland against Utrecht, Gijsbrecht tried to make Amstelland independent. This was too ambitious a task, and after the spectacular murder of the count of Holland, Floris V, the house of Amstel was relieved of its authority in 1296. The same count had accorded certain privileges to the inhabitants in a document drawn up in Amsterdam in 1275: for their goods they were allowed free passage on the waterways of Holland. This document, in which the name of Amsterdam occurs for the first time, was already an attempt at currying favor with Utrechtian Amsterdam. In 1317, the counts succeeded in permanently annexing the small city to Holland. It is no accident that it is referred to as a city: shortly after 1300, Amsterdam received some privileges set down in a civic law. This guaranteed it a secure measure of autonomy from the count. In feudal Europe, the first largely independent cities arose beginning in about the 11th century. A system of administrative, juridical, and economic privileges collected into a civic

law protected the city against interference from its rulers and competition from the country. In the rather static agrarian society, the cities became islands of progress, economic prosperity, and freedom. Northern Italy, Flanders, and northern Germany were important urbanized areas. The counts of Holland soon grasped that their territory was agriculturally poor and without minerals, and that this would have to be made up for by means of trade. From the 13th century onward, therefore, they tried to stimulate trade, and the granting of civic rights played an important part in this endeavor.

The first civic law consisted in part of a codified common law. Afterward, Amsterdam received some new privileges. The penalties for killing, disturbing the peace, and causing injury were mentioned in separate clauses. Another series of regulations dealt with the protection enjoyed by citizens when staying elsewhere. In spring and at harvest time, citizens could leave the city for six weeks to work on the land. The exercise of jurisdiction, maintenance of order, and everyday administration of the city were in the hands of the mayor and a few jurymen. Offi-

Amsterdam is not very old, compared with Mediterranean cities. Venice had conquered Constantinople before Amsterdam appeared in documents. Little archeological evidence remains of early settlement. Below, a 14th-century shoe; below right, a terracotta of the same period. Above, the landscape of Scharwoude, north of Amsterdam. It is in this sort of terrain that the first inhabitants settled near the city's later site.

cially, they functioned in the name of the count, who, indeed, had appointed them. A particularly important privilege was the right to make new laws or hold elections, which were, likewise, the tasks of the mayor and jury.

According to another regulation, the citizens had to give the count military assistance at his request. In that case, the jury and council gave them permission to leave the city. The privilege of supplementing the civic law gradually shifted power from the city's ruler to the citizenry. In other words, the city acquired ever-greater autonomy in administration, jurisdiction, legislation, and finance. This development readily can be observed from the shift of power within the administration. In the first civic charter, the mayor and jury together formed the administration. During the 14th century, the jurors included many Amsterdam citizens, which shows that in making appointments, the count took note of the citizens' wishes. Regarding the appointing of a mayor, the counts largely reserved this right for themselves until well into the 15th century.

About 1350, the councilors, who also were mentioned in the first charter, were given a more definite role: They were charged with public works, finance, supervision of the church, and the care of widows and orphans. These councilors were typical city figures who represented the interests of the citizenry.

In 1400 Amsterdam received an important power in return for helping Count Albrecht van Beieren: henceforth, the college of four councilors would sit for one year. Their selection was strictly defined and put wholly into the city's hands: the count had no influence at all on this. At the time, the councilors received their better-known title of burgomasters, namely, masters of the burgh or city. Their power grew very quickly during the course of the 15th century. In everyday administration they acquired the additional task of accepting new citizens and were entitled to raise the excise tax. This was important in giving the city an independent budget. The defense of the city also was their responsibility. From their original tasks, jury and mayor retained only jurisdiction.

During the 15th century, a third institution de-

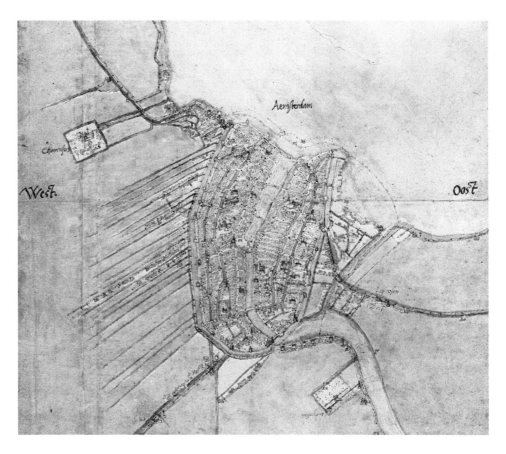

veloped in civic administration, the community council, which represented the wealthier and more influential citizens. By 1416, the city administration was already consulting these citizens when important decisions were taken. From this group there developed a closed administrative college, which in 1417 reached its final form by a privilege from the Duchess Mary of Burgundy, the sovereign at the time. The thirty-six members were selected for life and new ones were chosen by co-optation. The council acquired the right to compile a yearly list of people who might be nominated as jurors by the sovereign, but it had no influence on the nomination of burgomasters, who in turn were not accountable to the council.

By about 1480, Amsterdam had attained complete administrative, juridical, and political autonomy. The degree of independence from the sovereign and the surrounding countryside was considerable. In the case of Amsterdam this revealed itself especially in the independent position of its burgomasters, which was unique in comparison with other cities. In the same period, the civic administration had grown

Map of Amsterdam dating from about 1560 (Haarlem, Rijksarchief). Note the enclosing medieval wall. The town lies on the two banks of the Amstel and on the Ij. It later expanded east, west, and south, gradually pushing the walls further out and tracing canal belts of increasing radius.

into a free and uniform enterprise, an urban patriciate consisting mainly of merchants. Only occasionally were newcomers able to penetrate the system. Thus, the greatest part of the population had no influence on the way the city was administered.

Amsterdam as a trading city: A new generation of traders

By 1300, the inhabitants of Holland could no longer survive solely by raising crops and cattle. Given the abundant water in the area, the next obvious means of existence were trade and fishing. Compared with other European countries, both the rise of cities and of trade was a late development in Holland. When, from the 14th century, its inhabitants began to participate in the north-south trade between Novgorod, Lübeck, Bruges, and in the east-west trade between the German states on the Rhine and England, there already existed a much older trading tradition along these routes. The Hollanders took advantage of this and added their own elements. They were soon to play an important role, and by the end of the 15th

century Amsterdam had surpassed the other towns of Holland as a trading city.

In the Early Middle Ages, the Friesians, who now lived in the northern Netherlands, had been taking an active part in the trade between northern German regions and the Baltic on the one hand, and with England, in particular, on the other. From the 11th and 12th centuries, cities like Utrecht and Tiel, which lay along the major rivers, as well as Stavoren on the Zuiderzee, developed into important staging posts in the northern trade. Merchants from these cities maintained contacts with rising northern German cities like Hamburg and Lübeck. Trade was still on a modest scale. Small, shallow barges conveyed goods over inland waterways. Large stretches had to be traveled overland in carts. In the field of transport, the development of the cog, a fairly large and seaworthy vessel with a mast, was a revolution. Now, for the first time it became possible to ship large quantities of goods—for example, grain—across the sea. A swift cog had a capacity of 100 tons and a crew of about 13. In the 13th century, merchants from northern German cities like Ham-

The Zaan, north of Amsterdam, a typical landscape of the province of Holland. It demonstrates some basic facts of life in that region: control of waters and low-cost energy from windmills for drainage and industry. Flooding from rivers and from tides, which are held back only by a thin strip of dunes, were a constant challenge. Right, the flood of November 18-19, 1421, in a picture of The Life of St. Elizabeth of Hungary, *on whose name day the disaster occurred. The picture is by an Utrecht painter around 1500.*

burg, Bremen, and Lübeck traveled in large numbers to the south, where from mid-century they had a vast depot in Bruges. This meant that goods were brought there in order to be sold. Groups of merchants from these cities had united into a Hansa, a league for defending common interests and rights. Moreover, there were members who were merchants from Prussian, Westphalian, and Rhineland cities. The *mercatores in hensa Theutonocorum* shipped goods to Bruges, among them amber, grain, beer, furs, and timber. To the north they could take cargoes of French salt and wine, English wool, Genoese velvet, Venetian brocade and spices. Through Italian traders such goods likewise reached the stores of Bruges.

From the 14th century, eastern Netherlandish cities like Kampen, Deventer, Zwolle, and Zutphen took part in this trading movement. They more or less joined the Hanseatic League, which had, meanwhile, grown from a society of merchants to a league of cities. The river Ijssel on which they lay was a link in the inland waterways for the north-south trade. In addition to these routes, east Netherlands traders sailed around Denmark to the Baltic, the so-called "round-land" trip. Within this trading area, everybody had to abide closely by the strict regulations of the Hansa, which had now become a monopoly. One could only call in certain harbors, and goods could be sold only on the market in Bruges.

As newcomers, the west Netherlands cities of Holland took their first careful steps in trade in the 14th century, with strong support from the counts, in whose trading policies Dordrecht on the Meuse was the first to become involved. A compulsory market established there was bound to give an economic stimulus to this city on the trade route between Germany and England: for goods carried over this route a toll had to be paid in Dordrecht, which, in the 14th and 15th centuries, made the city into one of the most important trading posts in Holland.

Shortly after Amsterdam finally joined Holland in 1317, the count established a beer toll there. On all beer imported into Holland a toll was imposed in Amsterdam and Medemblik. This was done chiefly because Amsterdam lay at the mouth of the inland

Witnesses of history:
Opposite, frontispiece of
Jacob van Oostsanen's
genealogy of the counts of
Holland and two Dutch
coins (top, from 1359-1404,
and bottom, from
1482-1494, where,
significantly, a ship
appears). Bottom left, the
Privilege of Count Floris
(1275) where the city's
name first appears. On
this page, top, the
Kalverstraat miracle in
1345 (the consecrated host
unscathed by fire), in an
embroidered tapestry
(16th-17th century). Right,
the seal of Count William
IV (1342) and wooden
statues of William VI
(1404-1417) and Jacob of
Bavaria (1417-1433).
(Amsterdam Historical
Museum)

13

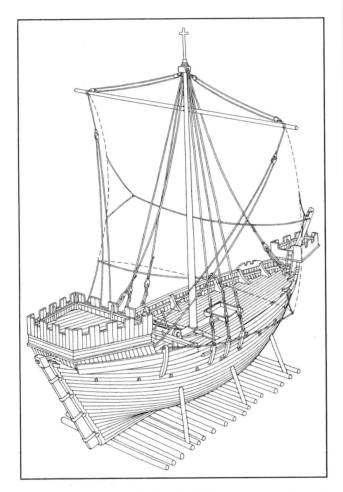

waterway through Holland. This route had the advantage of being deeper than the older waterway via Muiden to Utrecht. The trade route through the Utrecht region, indeed, declined in the 14th century. Beer, popular because water was rarely potable, was introduced into Holland mainly by merchants from Hamburg.

With the toll, Amsterdammers came into contact with the Hamburgers and, through them, with the north German and Baltic trade. At the beginning, Amsterdam fishermen and farmers served as shippers for Hamburg merchants. Next, they discovered Prussia, a large grain producer, and the important region of Skane in southern Sweden. Like other Hollanders, the men of Amsterdam at first worked mainly as shippers. Because of their low freight rates, they soon became feared competitors. Moreover, the Hollanders hardly bothered about the regulations of the powerful Hanseatic cities. They went to "cliff" harbors outside the league's control, which gave them a free hand in pricing and enabled them to take their goods wherever they wanted. Lübeck especially was angry about the transport of Prussian grain to the southern Netherlands, where, at that time, these imports were essential for daily bread. However, in the 14th century the cities of Holland were not yet strong enough to challenge the powerful league. In case of conflict with the Danish king, who controlled the sound between Sweden and Denmark, the cities of Holland fought alongside the

Hansa. Besides routes to the northeast, the Hollanders took the road to the west after 1350: from time to time traders from Amsterdam called at English ports, where they acquired anthracite, cloth, and lead.

After 1400, the trading activities of the Hollanders grew rapidly. From the Baltic they took away grain, timber, skins, meat, flax, tar, pitch, and beer, partly as shippers and partly on their own account. In order to ensure cargo for the trip out, they went to the west coast of France—among other places, to the Bay of Bourgneuf—for salt, important for preserving fish, and wine. The vessel for overseas trade was still the cog, somewhat enlarged in the 15th century. The trade expansion of the Hollanders naturally met with opposition from the league. Lübeck, in particular, made repeated attempts to keep the inconsiderate new carriers out of their trading area—but in vain. The Hollanders fought several trade wars with the Hanseatic League, emerging as victors. Amsterdam merchants sailed as commanders of the war fleet. The league wrought its own doom: its system of trading was too rigid and old-fashioned, and in practice it was impossible to adhere to the rule that goods must be sold on the market in Bruges. The temporary shift of this market to Dordrecht in the mid-15th century merely played into the hands of inland transport, and therefore of trade, in Holland. At the end of the century the league's predominance was gone. The towns of Holland, with Amsterdam at the head, had secured their position in the Baltic. This is clear from the figure for tolls imposed by the Danish king at the sound: In 1497, seven in ten passages were by north Netherlandish shippers, and of these 78 percent were Hollanders, predominantly from Amsterdam and from Waterland, the region to the north, where many sailed on behalf of the city.

Trade with England continued. This was concentrated in the Zeeland town of Middelburg, where wine and cloth were very important. In the north the Norwegian trade developed especially after 1443, mainly in timber and stockfish. The Hollanders' own export goods were cloth, dairy produce, and North Sea herring. About 1400, the great herring catches from the neighborhood of Skane fell off, so that North Sea herring trade became much more impor-

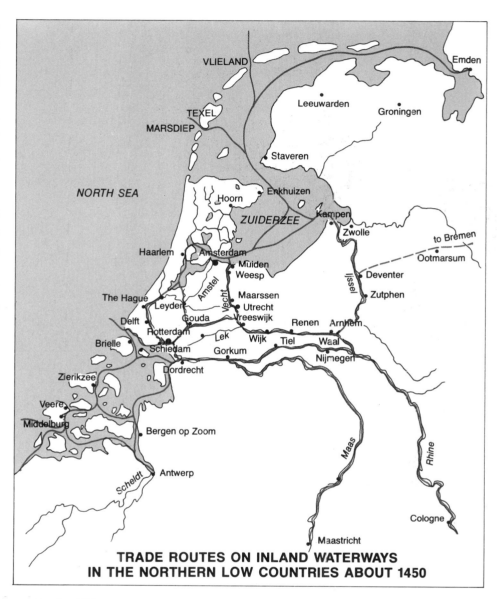

TRADE ROUTES ON INLAND WATERWAYS IN THE NORTHERN LOW COUNTRIES ABOUT 1450

tant in the 15th century.

Inland trade was almost as important as the North Sea trade. Through Amsterdam the Ij led toward Haarlem over natural waterways to Dordrecht, and then farther south. In Dordrecht shippers checked the east-west flow of goods. Another considerable trade route extended across the Zuiderzee to Deventer, where several great yearly markets were held. The Amsterdammers brought their export goods of cloth, stockfish, dairy produce, and herring, taking return cargoes from the German hinterland. An export register from the mid-15th century shows this trade to have been especially lively and of great importance to Amsterdam's economy.

How was the city's trade organized at that time?

Internal waterways of the northern Low Countries round 1450. This network, where the Scheldt, Maas, and Rhine rivers run into the sea, was the key to the commercial growth of cities. Bruges was foremost at the time.

LAND AND WATER

The fertile fields of Holland have been reclaimed from the sea and from inland waters. The present-day state of affairs, which is the result of a long historical process, is well illustrated in *figure 4,* which shows a diagrammatic cross-section of the area between the North Sea and the Ij, on a parallel bisecting Amsterdam. The vertical dimensions are exaggerated in relation to the horizontal dimensions, but this helps to give us an overview of the coastal strip of dunes, the stratum of peat lying above the sand, the dikes, embankments, and canals, and the different levels of the areas that have been reclaimed. The dotted line is the *NAP (Normal Amsterdams Peil),* the normal level of Amsterdam. The sea rises above and falls below this level with the tides.

In about 1540 the area belonging to the province of Holland to the north of Amsterdam (1) was punctuated by lakes and pools. The inland waters were separated from the Zuiderzee by dikes, and the land itself was protected by embankments, but it would have taken just a few breaches to turn all these interconnected lakes and pools into a single inland sea.

The huge task of reclamation and drainage was undertaken between 1540 and 1650. The land surface increased by 52.7 percent. This gain is clearly shown in *map 2* and *table 3,* which indicates the reclaimed areas in the two districts

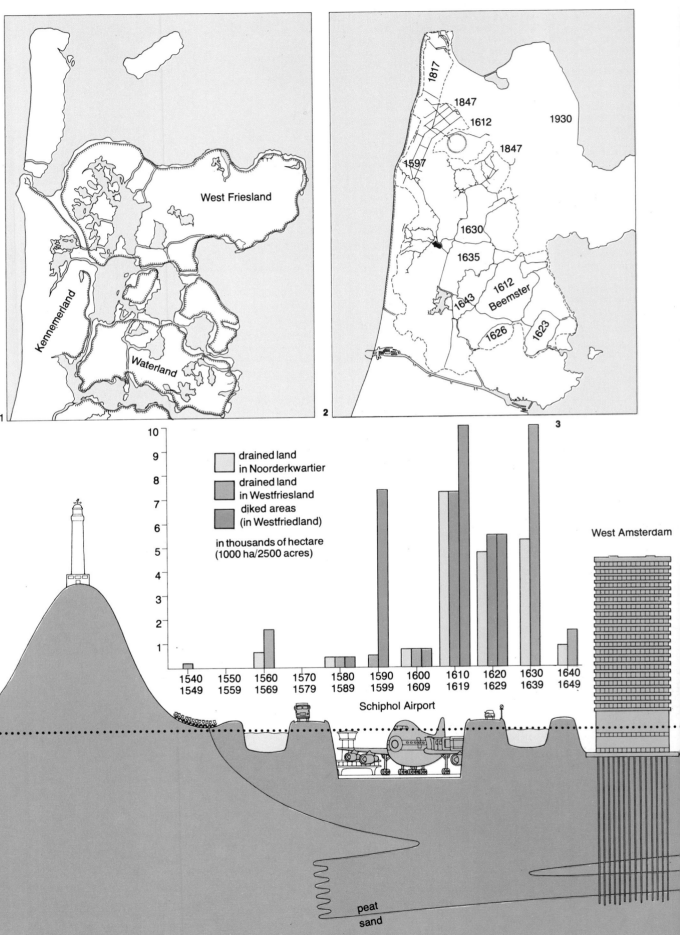

drained land
in Noorderkwartier

drained land
in Westfriesland

diked areas
(in Westfriedland)

in thousands of hectare
(1000 ha/2500 acres)

| 1540 1549 | 1550 1559 | 1560 1569 | 1570 1579 | 1580 1589 | 1590 1599 | 1600 1609 | 1610 1619 | 1620 1629 | 1630 1639 | 1640 1649 |

North Sea

West Amsterdam

Schiphol Airport

peat
sand

West Friesland

Kennemerland

Waterland

Beemster

1
2
3
4

Noorderkwartier and West Friesland, which formed the northern part of the province of Holland. Approximately 67,000 acres of water were transformed into arable land. Among the factors that made this transformation possible were the existence of a central government body responsible for inland and maritime waters; the use of the *bovenkruier*, the octagonal windmill with the upper rotating part; and the accumulation in Amsterdam of capital to be invested. After a preparatory phase that dragged on for more than a century, under Charles V the central government body responsible for inland and maritime waters came into being. The flow management of these waters and the upkeep of the dikes were no longer in the hands of local bodies. If it had been otherwise, the major waterworks of the later half of the 17th century would not have been possible. The windmills being used in the second half of the 15th century for draining the polders were fixed constructions with ordinary blades set to the direction of the prevailing wind, and their effectiveness was limited. Much greater potential was offered by the *bovenkruier* and its use in a series called a *molengag* (6), whereby the wheels that raised the water were at different levels. The increase in height was in the order of one *el* (27 inches) for each wheel.

A fine example of land reclamation was the drainage of the Beemster, an inland lake covering 17,500 acres, and 11–12 feet deep. Authorization was requested from the States of Holland in the spring of 1607 by 15 associates (five influential merchants, three burgomasters, six people with jurisdictional posts in The Hague, and one goldsmith).

An embankment was thrown up around the edge of the lake, and a canal was dug to the Zuiderzee. The embankment was constructed in 500 lots of 250 feet each. Two builders provided the windmills, initially 16 large and 8 smaller ones (in the end 43 were needed). With the embankment ready in January 1609, work started on removing the water. A breach in the embankment because of a storm in the spring of 1610 meant that everything had to start again. In March 1611 the bed of the lake came into view and people hurried into the polder to catch any fish that were still alive there.

The drainage operation was completed in March 1612 and celebrated by a banquet held in a tent erected on the mud. As is evident from the plan (5) the polder was laid out with roads, canals, embankments, and was then parceled out and distributed by lottery. In 1642 the land that could be cultivated accounted for only 10 percent of the total area. But there was also livestock, and holiday places sprang up, too, with villas, gardens, and orchards with exotic species of trees. In 1640 there were already 52 manor houses or country residences, 141 houses belonging to burghers, and 207 farms.

5

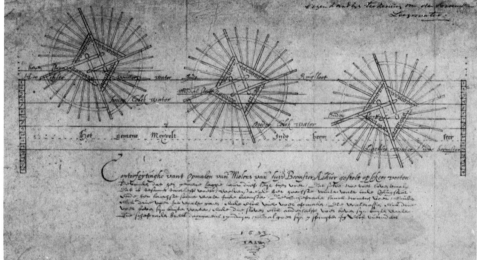

6

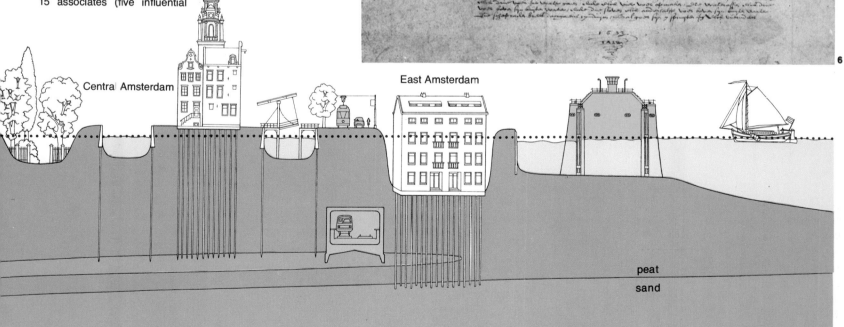

Amsterdam burghers
around 1500. An
upper-class family
portrait, the van Korsgen-
Elbertsens, from the
chapel of a monastery,
painted by Jacob
Corneliszon van
Oostsanen (Amsterdam
Historical Museum).
Right, the city's coat of
arms on the portal of the
old hospital. The right to
cap it with the imperial
crown was accorded by
Maximilian I, count of
Holland by marriage to
the heiress of Burgundy.

Compared with Bruges, the major west European
emporium until about 1500, operations were rather
simple. Merchants worked mostly in groups of two
or three, probably on the basis of kinship. Fathers
and sons, brothers and cousins traded together.
Since a merchant could not be away from home too
long and wished his interests to be looked after in
several places, he had his out-of-town factors or representatives. The landlords of several hostelries in
the respected Warmoestraat were factors for their
fellow countrymen in north Germany. Conversely,
Amsterdammers had their attorneys in German
cities. In the 15th century, merchants kept their own
books in their own offices in the high fronts of their

medieval houses. Goods were stored in the cellars or attics of the dwellings. While, in the 14th century, shippers were both transporters and merchants, in the course of the 15th century this changed: shippers increasingly acted on behalf of merchants.

Trade was well regulated from about 1400, because members of the city administration were mainly merchants. It was vital for them to attend to matters of trade, even with regard to foreign policy. In the struggle for supremacy with the Hansa, Amsterdam did her utmost to win, and she quickly became a true trading city. Along with trade, in the 14th and 15th centuries several industries developed concerned with the processing of raw materials that

the merchants brought to the city. Soap works, textile manufacture, and shipbuilding gained some importance in the 15th century. The cloth industry was quite important, although the cloth, of heavy wool, was not as good as that from Leyden. It was a kind of cottage industry, the draper as employer making sure that the many preliminary processes could be accomplished by workers in their homes. For the spinning stage, one looked for workers in the country. Fulling, a heavy and tiring task in which the woven cloth gains in volume, sometimes led to strikes. It was the only activity in this period for which some labor disturbance is recorded. Shipbuilding mainly involved repairing ships that win-

Houses on the Nieuwezijds Voorburgwal, in a drawing by C. J. Visscher, about 1650. In spite of the late date, this is a good picture of medieval Amsterdam. The buildings were of wood, which allowed lighter construction on the soft soil. After the fire of 1452, when two thirds of the houses burned, side walls had to be in masonry.

tered in Amsterdam. In addition, a few new ships were built at this time. As in the other two industries, the workers here were highly trained. Trade and industry went hand in hand: a soapboiler might well be a trader in potash, one of the basic materials of this industry, and a shipbuilder might trade in timber.

The bakers, blacksmiths, carpenters, and shoemakers who had settled in the city ensured that everyday life ran smoothly. From 1350, guilds began to appear, and, in the next hundred years their number grew. In general, the trades and some parts of industry were organized into guilds. The leaders were nominated by the city administration, and rules settled the distribution of raw materials, periods of apprenticeship, length of the working day, and training. Members had to be citizens of the city and to have passed a master's trial. The religious character

of the guilds was strong: the brothers had to accompany religious processions, on pain of a fine; every guild kept an alter in one of the churches. About servants, porters, and apprentices next to nothing is known.

In sum, we might characterize Amsterdam in 1500 as a medium-size trading city. Compared with Bruges (40,000 inhabitants in the 14th century) and Antwerp (about 40,000 in 1520) Amsterdam in 1484 was rather small. Its advantage over those markets was its active trade, the merchants themselves shipping the goods they imported, and the low freight rates due to the low wages the people were willing to accept. In the 16th century, competitors had to take careful account of these two facts if they were to avoid being completely overtaken by the industrious Amsterdammers.

Life in a medieval city

A true river city, Amsterdam arose at the mouth of the Amstel, near the Ij. About 1225, the first inhabitants lived on an artificial rise, or mound, at the water's edge. About 50 years later, both sides at the mouth of the river were probably inhabited. The city grew in several stages, until in 1425 it reached the size at which it would remain until about 1700. The spread occurred as the defensive canals and walls around the city were shifted farther east and west. Thus began the system of parallel canals. On the other hand, building land was gained on both sides of the river by artificially raising the land some 100 feet. This reduced the mouth of the river by almost 200 feet. It was further narrowed by certain official prohibitions. On these new extensions, warehouses and dwellings for merchants were advantageously situated on the inner port, or Damrak. The speed at which the city was extended is closely linked with the economic rise of Amsterdam in the 14th and 15th centuries. The earliest houses were built with simple materials that were available in the neighborhood: reed, alder branches, and loam. They were flimsy buildings, at first with only one room, in the middle of which a fire was kept. As early as the 14th century some houses were built of timber, which was expensive since it largely had to be imported from other countries such as Norway. These houses, too, were still rather unsolid: in fact, a regulation stated that in case of fire the owner had to pull the house down with a fishhook to prevent the flames from spreading. The danger of fire was, indeed, very great: in 1452, two thirds of the city burned to ashes. To prevent such disasters, the city administration ordered that henceforth walls had to be stone-clad and roof coverings made of slate or tiles. Bricks were costly, for brickworks lay on the big rivers of South Holland, and, therefore, the bricks had to be carried a long way. Those who were unable to pay for this could even apply for subsidies. While, in the 14th century, the city was still fairly sparsely built up, the ground was soon filled in the 15th century. Large plots behind houses were split and the lines of buildings became more continuous. Stands of trees and vegetable gardens were gradually shifted out of town. Space could also be gained by building upward, and so dwellings gained an extra floor.

The shortage of building land also might have been one reason for the administration's reticence in 1494, when approval was sought for the building of a 16th nunnery in the city. The others had been founded mainly in the last decades before 1400 and in the course of the 15th century. Together, they occupied about a third of the city's land.

The Dam was the center of the city. About 1400, a town hall was built, and, from the 15th century, there was another important building, a weighbridge, where goods over 50 pounds had to be weighed. One of the two parish churches, the New Church, was quite near the Dam, only one block of houses away. In the 14th century, there was already a weekly market: on Mondays dairy produce such as butter, cheese, and eggs were offered for sale by outsiders and by Amsterdam citizens. At first there was a cattle market as well. Along the Damrak, the inner port, there were sellers of apples, wooden ware, greens, and obscure remedies. In the locks of the Dam there was a lively fish market, and, in the 14th century, the fish merchants belonged to the respected citizenry.

Hardly any medieval portraits of Amsterdammers have survived. Judging from those few pictures that do remain, and taking into account the results of excavations, it is clear that even the rich wore extremely simple garments. Adornments turn up now and then, but gold and silver hardly ever. Heavy cloth—often black, but also bright orange-red and blue—was used for both male and female outer garments.

In a population of approximately 4,400, about the year 1400, everybody must have known almost everybody else, at least by sight. Even at twice this number in 1494, when about 8,000 people lived in the city, a common acquaintance must still have been the case. The problems of a metropolis did not yet exist. Amsterdam was a rather small-scale community, young and energetic. The foundations for the explosive growth of the city in the 16th century had already been laid, both in trade and in administration.

Right, a detail from one of the Seven Works of Charity *("feed the hungry") painted about 1500 by the Master of Alkmaar, from St. Laurence's church in Alkmaar, shows the atmosphere, life, and types of people of late medieval Holland, as does the wooden figure of a milk girl, opposite (Rijksmuseum). Around 1500, Amsterdam had about 8,000 inhabitants, a small young community, already showing signs of sudden future trade expansion and urban growth.*

Europe's grain market

Ancient red brick houses reflected in the canals of old Amsterdam. Intense mercantile activity enlivened this area as early as the 16th century. Two hundred years later Daniel Defoe, in A Plan of the English Commerce *(1728), wrote that the Dutch must be taken for what they are: a link in the commercial chain, agents and brokers of Europe, buying to sell, importing to export, most of their vast commerce consisting in getting supplies from everywhere in order, in turn, to send supplies everywhere.*

Commerce and trade until the revolt

About 1480, the countries of Western Europe began to grow in population and their economies expanded, a process that was to continue until the early 17th century. This first renewed growth in numbers brought about major changes. These developments ended at different times in different countries: in Spain they lasted until about 1580; in Holland, until 1650.

Other general features of the 16th-century expansion were economic differentiation and specialization: an unprecedented accumulation of capital led to a large investment in farming and in trading ventures by the Portuguese, Spanish, and English. Throughout the century, money lowered in value, a decline that lasted until the 17th century. This inflation was caused primarily by the rise in population and by the vast spending of the German Empire, France, and Spain on such things as military equipment. The flood of silver from South American mines made this possible. Technical developments that greatly influenced everyday life included the large-scale application of printing for industrial purposes and the regular use of windmills for land reclamation. From about 1500, Western Europe saw the emergence of several distinct economic areas that were linked with each other but functioned largely independently. During the 16th century, the economic balance shifted from the Mediterranean to the Atlantic and to the centrally placed Netherlands.

One of the economic centers of Western Europe was the Mediterranean region. In Northern Italy there were many cities whose production of luxury goods was well developed. The merchant fleets of Genoa and Venice went after imports from the Eastern Mediterranean, where spices, silk, and porcelain were brought to such large cities as Constantinople and Alexandria along the caravan routes from the Far East. Venetian galleys carried these goods through the Straits of Gibraltar to the markets of Bruges and Antwerp, where the Italians came in contact with products from the northern regions.

Another trade route led across the Alps to southern and central Germany, a second trading area, where the powerful banking firm of Fugger in Augsburg and Nuremburg had a monopoly and acted as moneylenders to the German emperors. The Fuggers derived their main income from Bohemian silver mines and from Hungarian copper. The latter was in great demand for the making of weapons. The interests of the Fuggers stretched as far as northern Germany. German merchants brought copper to the market in Antwerp and bought luxury goods, such as spices imported by the Italians and, chiefly, by the Portuguese.

The Baltic, likewise, was a separate trading area, although it was much less able than the Mediterranean countries to stand on its own, economically. For salt, wine, and textiles, the Baltic and north German regions had to rely on imports. During the 15th century, Holland, and above all Amsterdam, succeeded in winning an important position for importing such products. The main exports were grain and timber, which, earlier, were in short supply in the Netherlands. In contrast with the transport of goods from southern regions, the trade between the

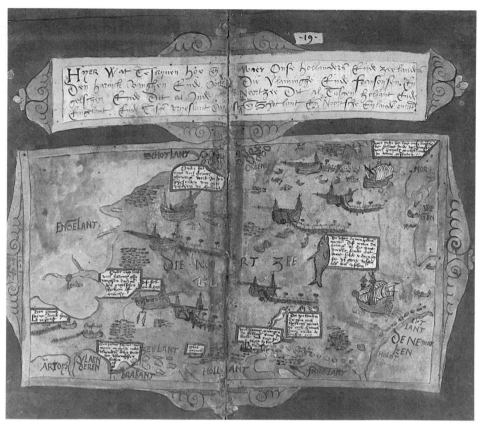

In 1384, a Zeelander, Willem Beukels, discovered or invented a way of preserving herring by salting them in wooden barrels: attempts of this sort date from the 12th century. In the 16th century, Holland's herring fisheries grew through the efforts of sailors from Waterland and then from West Friesland, who sailed in the service of Amsterdam merchants. Above, map of herring fisheries in the North Sea, from the Vischboek *by Adriaen Coenenz (1578). Right, frontispiece of a sailing manual (1558, the first of its kind) painted by Cornelis Anthoniszon.*

a trading city. In the course of the 16th century, countries like Spain, Portugal, and Italy were no longer able adequately to supply their increased populations with grain. Rye was the main component of their diet. They could not as yet fall back on potatoes, which became widespread only in the 18th century; as to alternatives such as rice, far too little was being grown. To avert the threat of starvation, southern countries had to resort to Baltic grain. In this period, the landed aristocracy of Poland transformed that country into a huge agricultural region, where impoverished peasants worked as serfs and raised crops of grain on land belonging to nobles. In Polish ports, chiefly Danzig, merchants from Amsterdam or their agents organized transshipment directly to the clients' locality or to their own city, where it was kept in numerous stores. In about 1560, the city, proud of the imperial crown above its coat of arms, a privilege granted by the Emperor Maximilian in 1489, grew into an international grain market. As in the previous period, political stability in the sound was vital for the grain trade. In 1543, led by

Baltic, north Germany, and the Netherlands primarily was in mass-produced products. The value of the goods themselves was much smaller than that of luxury goods, so that shipping costs had to be as low as possible. As early as 1500, the Hollanders were able to fulfill this condition.

Finally, we must mention the transatlantic trade of Spain and Portugal. After some 75 years of trading on the west coast of Africa, the Portuguese in 1480 became the first to sail around the Cape of Good Hope, thus opening the sea route to Asia. Henceforth, the trade in spices and pepper was largely in Portuguese hands. They brought their goods to Lisbon and to the world market in Antwerp. The Spaniards mainly obtained silver from South America.

In the sense of economic units, Antwerp, Lisbon, and London were the foremost centers in the 16th century. Antwerp had succeeded Bruges about 1500. Only in one thing was Amsterdam a greater market than Antwerp: namely, grain for the Netherlands. The growing population of Europe was highly important to the further development of Amsterdam as

Lübeck, the northern German cities tried for the last time to subdue the Hollanders, and failed. A year later, by the Treaty of Speyer, the Danish king agreed to let the Dutch sail freely through the sound into the Baltic. Even so, the threat of closure remained: for example, in case of war between Denmark and Sweden. As during the Middle Ages, the policy of Amsterdam aimed to keep the sound open—if need be, by force of arms.

Bad harvests made the regular transport of grain impossible, because of the great fluctuations in sup-

Salting the catch, from the border of a map of Holland by Claes Janszon Visscher (1608). Since herring had disappeared from southern Swedish coasts, fishing gave rise to a lively export trade to the Baltic, which involved salt supplies from Portugal, and timber for barrels from the Baltic coasts.

ply. Shortages and the merchants' passion for speculation then raised the prices, making grain too expensive for the poor. Even in ordinary times, the grain trade was quite profitable, since merchants bought in Danzig for half the price at which they later sold the grain. Dutch city authorities fixed the price and weight of bread, and this was the same in Amsterdam. When harvests threatened to fail, the city bought up imported grain in order to have cheap bread baked for the needy. Grain exports were prohibited in such periods, although this did not prevent

resolute grain dealers from sending their ships away in good time: for example, a certain Jacob Fick, tipped off by a relative in the administration, stored away great quantities of grain. In years of genuine shortage many could not afford bread, and people in Amsterdam starved, as did the inhabitants of the industrial regions in the south of the country. Periods of social unrest, of course, coincided with grain shortages.

Amsterdam's development as a grain market obviously favored trade in other traditional products such as timber and dried cod. The trading area remained the same as before, except for Lisbon, which was added during the 16th century as a supplier of salt, pepper, and spices. The range of goods likewise remained the same. However, the volume of shipping increased because of the grain trade. In cheap transport Amsterdam had a great advantage over Antwerp, where trade was much less active. Merchants from all over Europe took their goods, particularly luxury goods, to the Antwerp market, and yet the city had no merchant fleet for merchandise. If merchants, for whatever reason, stopped visiting Antwerp, trade would be finished. In Amsterdam, on the other hand, development was based on shipping. Because labor from Holland was cheap and ships not too costly, freight rates could be kept low throughout the 15th century.

In the 16th century, the merchant fleet of Holland was expanded. In 1500, the whole fleet of the northern Netherlands was about 60,000 tons: by 1570, it had grown to 23,000 tons. By 1565, Amsterdam had a fleet of some 500 large ships. After the cog, the hulk became the main merchant vessel, varying from 40 to 100 tons. The bigger ships needed crews of 20. Until the late 16th century, freighters hardly differed from fishing vessels. By then, fishing, especially for the North Sea herring, had increased considerably, which was important for the development of the merchant fleet. Herring became an important export to the Baltic, since shoals of herring around southern Sweden had vanished. When ships were not needed for fishing, they served as freighters.

In the early 16th century, Amsterdam merchants mainly employed shippers from Waterland. Later,

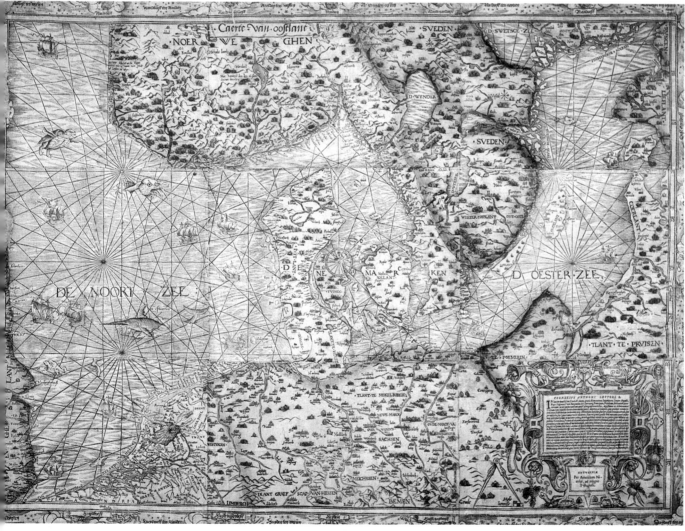

Opposite, view of
Antwerp, 1518-1540
(Antwerp, National
Maritime Museum). About
1500, Antwerp had
replaced Bruges as the
mercantile center of
northern Europe. The
foremost world market,
Antwerp, in turn, declined
when the traffic on the
Scheldt went to
Amsterdam after the
Seven Provinces became
independent. Left,
Holland, North Sea, and
Baltic countries in
Cornelis Anthoniszon's
map of 1543. The Baltic
route was vital for
Amsterdam and hinged on
the Sound between
Denmark and Sweden,
which had to be kept open.
Above, Amsterdam in
about 1547-1550, from a
drawing by Antoon van
den Wyngarde.

Social panorama of a growing city: the nameless. Below, fishermen and farm workers in the countryside, from a plate by A. Arentszon called Cabel *(1585-1631, Rijksmuseum). Right, furniture makers at work, from an anonymous plate (1565, Gouda, Catharina Gasthuis).*

they also used shippers from Friesland. This period saw the rise of Hoorn and Enkhuizen as trading towns. Both were on West Friesian territory, on the Zuiderzee. Freighting was enhanced not only by the growing merchant fleet, but also by the flexible organization of trade. In Amsterdam, the method of financing enterprises had not really changed from the Middle Ages. Relatives and friends continued to collaborate in partnerships for shorter or longer periods. Partnerships sometimes changed membership. Only rarely did a single merchant fill a ship. The load consisted of many things, since few traders were specialized. Even those who were called "grain merchants" or "wine merchants" invested their money in other goods if this was likely to fetch

120-ton caravel. Share shipping gave a broad base to the merchant fleet of Holland.

Although the organization remained the same in form, it began to show more capitalist features. Amsterdam merchants became entrepreneurs, hiring shippers who were no longer independent. Yet there were still no signs of vast commercial enterprises and of large capital. Shipping regulations were few, compared with other and more developed ports. Only under Emperor Charles V did the authorities establish rules for the equipment and safety of ships. Crews, armament, and tonnage were fixed. The first printed charts appeared in 1532, a great boon for seafarers. The Amsterdam painter and surveyor Cornelis Anthoniszon published one of the earliest such

a good profit. Import and export registers for 1543–45 preserved in Amsterdam give a good indication of how the loads were made up.

A merchant rarely owned the ship that carried his goods. As in the 15th century, shipping partnerships remained the best way of spreading risk. This became more important when the ships increased in size. For merchants and citizens alike, shares in a ship were a good investment. As an example, let us take an Amsterdam merchant of 1569. Besides unspecified shipping shares, he held the following: $\frac{1}{8}$ of a 200-ton caravel, $\frac{1}{8}$ of another caravel, $\frac{1}{16}$ of a single-master, $\frac{1}{16}$ of a 180-ton caravel, $\frac{1}{24}$ of a 200-ton caravel, $\frac{1}{16}$ of a 180-ton caravel, $\frac{1}{16}$ and $\frac{1}{8}$ of a 100-ton single-master, $\frac{1}{8}$ each of a 220-ton and a

maps for the Baltic in 1543. Shortly afterward, he added a manual of instructions, the oldest-known Dutch guide of this kind. The first part concerned navigation, and the second part was a coastal chart describing coastline and currents, with coastal profile drawings. Such charts first appeared in the 16th century.

Town and country

Amsterdam merchants relied on sailors from the countryside. During the 16th century, Amsterdam and the other towns of Holland increasingly dominated the economic life of the surrounding areas. Small enterprises and tradesmen in the towns did not

tolerate rural competitors, who generally paid lower wages and enjoyed open regulations. Moreover, the towns resented the fact that the country was free from municipal taxes. An extreme attempt at controlling the country was the 1531 ordinance on external trade, granted by Emperor Charles V at the request of the towns: no new enterprises were allowed to be established in the country. In practice this measure could not be enforced. To attain their goal some towns nevertheless bought up surrounding estates on which they could then impose city regulations. Amsterdam did this early and on a large scale.

In this period, the plain of Holland became more specialized for city markets and for exports. In the area of today's province of Holland, cattle and dairy

were established more quickly and efficiently than elsewhere in Europe. Suburbs grew up around Amsterdam and other big cities, typical urban outposts on the plain. Trades that carried with them the danger of fire or that spoiled the surroundings were relegated to this area in the 16th century. The vegetable gardens of city dwellers, storehouses, and rope works are shown outside the town walls on maps of the period.

Industry and guilds

The growth of special types of enterprises linked with Amsterdam's large-scale trade, such as soap works, drapery factories, oil mills, and shipyards,

Social panorama of a growing city: the moneyed. Left, E. Gerbrandszon and wife, perhaps by Dirck Jacobszon, about 1550 (Amsterdam Historical Museum). Some decades later, Descartes wrote of the "great city" where "nobody lives who is not devoted to commerce," and where all are "inspired by personal profit." Top, Pompejus Occo (1483-1537), banker, merchant, and humanist, by Dirck Jacobszon.

Right, St. Anthony's Gate, assembly room of Amsterdam city architects, a warm late-16th-century Dutch interior, typically decorated with visible bricks.

products joined shipbuilding and navigation as the major industries. Thousands of heads of cattle were driven overland from Jutland every year to be fattened in the Netherlands. Cheese and butter from the plain were important exports from Amsterdam. In Holland, south of the Ij, large brickworks and limekilns were set up, for in these times of growing population the towns had to be able to build many houses. Thus, bricks were often carried as ballast on ships for the outward trip to the Baltic.

The cultivation of flax and hemp developed next. These were raw materials for making linen and rope. Around Leyden and Delft, horticulture expanded and vegetables were grown for the town markets. With a good network of natural watercourses, links

can only be guessed at. Besides the repair of ships wintering in Amsterdam, the building of new ones seems to have proliferated especially after 1530. During the difficult decade of 1568–78, this industry lay in abeyance. Shipbuilding was confined to an area east of the city, outside the walls. When war threatened, the wharves had to be abandoned for military reasons.

The manufacture of drapery had never been as important as in Leyden, and during the late 16th century it was probably on the decline. The dyeing of uncolored cloth, particularly from England, was an Amsterdam specialty, as was the finishing of fabrics. The soap works were a trade rather than an industry and presumably they did not produce much. The

Illustrations from Tre navigationi fatti dagli olandesi e zelandesi al settentrione della Norvegia, Moscovia e Tartaria *("Three Journeys by Sailors from Holland and Zeeland to the North of Norway, Muscovy and Tartary"), Venice, 1599.*

These are the trips to the Arctic Ocean made by the Friesian Willem Barents in 1594-1597, touching on Spitsbergen, Bear Island, and Novaja Zemlia. Around 1600, new routes were explored by Dutch sailors. Barents's last trip in search of a northern

passage to the East ended in tragedy, but Cornelis Houtman succeeded in rounding the Cape of Good Hope, laying the basis for supplanting the Portuguese on the spice route.

making of rope and of sail doubtless grew with the increase in shipbuilding.

During this period, trades tended to become more specialized and independent. A shoemaker was no longer a tanner as well. From the original guilds, which sometimes combined the most unrelated trades, special guilds developed. In 1542, the coopers left the guild of blacksmiths; in 1551, clogmakers and surgeons split up. In 1579, the masons' guild gave rise to the guild of St. Luke, which also encompassed the painters' guild. Ever more precise regulations were adopted by each guild concerning training, the sale of goods, the distribution of raw materials, and working hours. The guilds closed, which had an economically curbing effect. However, in a period when vocational training did not exist, this ensured that the technical knowledge of the membership was preserved. Since the Amsterdam administration still appointed the heads of the guilds and took a hand in their affairs, city control of the quality and quantity of goods offered was guaranteed. Thus, in the event of damage to wholesale trade, which was not within the jurisdiction of the guilds, the city could intervene. As far as possible, the council's ordinances protected trade against outside competition.

Fairs and weekly markets enabled farmers and foreigners to trade their goods in small amounts. As Amsterdam grew, so did these events, and the license fees beame a considerable source of municipal income. In the early 16th century, weekly markets were held each Monday, and fairs in the spring and autumn. The supply of goods from outside the city and off-market sales were a constant worry to the local "middle classes." At the guilds' request, the city had continually to counter the street vendors and the uncontrolled sales of food, chairs, shoes, and the like. The religious character of the guilds continued until 1578. A contemporary tells us that they formed a colorful part of religious processions. "The column began with each guild in full spendor, under its own banner or sign held high, on a long staff, and carried before it. . . . The masters carried lit wax candles in their hands, handsome young girls in attractive costumes represented Our Lady, Mary Magdalen, St. Barbara, and St. Margaret . . . children dressed up as angels and devils formed various groups.''

About 1560, Amsterdam was thus far behind Antwerp, but it was the largest city in the northern Netherlands. The Florentine scholar and nobleman Ludovico Guicciardini (1521–1589), a merchant who lived in Antwerp, described the town, comparing it with Venice: ''From the Netherlands, France, England, Spain and Portugal, Germany, Poland, Livonia and Norway, and Sweden, large merchant fleets enter the city, up to 200 or 300 ships; most of them are loaded in Danzig and Reval.''

Population

Unlike other places in Europe, where, in the 14th and 15th centuries, populations had decreased partly because of the Black Death, Holland continued to grow; this was especially so in the 15th century, and more in the cities than on the plain. An official census dated 1514 shows that 51 percent of the inhabitants lived in towns or urbanized areas. Barely a century earlier, the figure had been 36 percent. In Holland, the growth was even more rapid in the 16th century than before—until it stopped, about 1650. During this period, the population had trebled, with a more rapid increase in towns than in the country: 1 percent as against 0.7 percent a year. In 1622, 59 percent of Holland's people lived in towns.

Amsterdam was among the fastest growing towns in Holland. In 1514, it counted 13,500 inhabitants, less than Leyden (15,000) and certainly Utrecht (30,000). Antwerp was well ahead with 40,000—the same number as London. Fifty years later, Amsterdam had become the largest town in the northern Netherlands with 30,000 inhabitants, continuing to grow after 1580, but Antwerp with its 100,000 inhabitants remained ahead. Other places in Holland that expanded equally fast were industrial towns like Haarlem, Leyden, and Delft; Dordrecht, however, declined. It was typical of Holland's landscape that cities and villages were spaced out at regular intervals. Each town was surrounded by its own plain. The distance was small enough to engender a mutual influence between the town as market and the plain as supplier and buyer, so that town and plain formed a unit.

The population grew along with the economy, a connection that cannot always be fully explained. At any rate, immigration played an important role in this growth, even before 1580. People came partly from other towns and from the plain of North Holland and partly from north Germany—among them, merchants who belonged to the wealthy class in Amsterdam. The immigrants from Holland were

Mother-of-pearl lid of a box, showing a reception of sea travelers (1596-1597). It evokes the atmosphere around 1600 and Dutch attempts at gaining a place in the great road to riches of the time, the Indian route. In 1595, seven Amsterdam merchants had founded the Company of Distant Lands. Of four ships and 240 men sent east in 1595, only three ships and 87 men returned in 1597; the modest cargo of pepper from Bantam made a small profit, and the route was opened. Left, a Dutch text of 1559 with various coins and their values. A sign of Amsterdam's commercial growth is the weekly list of commodity prices published from 1585. In London this only began 80 years later.

tradesmen, sailors, and laborers, no doubt attracted by opportunities to work and by city wages, which were higher than in the country. The grain trade and its attendant shipping and storage, alone, required many hands. Little is known about the immigrants. With regard to numbers and professions, the city accounts from 1531 contain the names of those who bought civic rights or citizenship. Civic rights gave the possessor marked privileges: the administration was accessible only to them, as was membership in a guild. These rights were hereditary and could be obtained through marriage to a holder, or bought for a rather high fee. Since those who married a holder or a holder's daughter did not have to buy the rights, they do not figure in the accounts. The holding of civic rights, however, was not required for the practice of certain professions.

The growing population of Amsterdam had to be accommodated in the same area as in the 15th century. Any remaining bits of land in the city were used, and building spread outside the walls, in the lastage to the east, and in the west. In the lastage, a kind of shanty town arose; this was the shipbuilding area, and, according to contemporary witnesses, the haunt of all sorts of dubious folk. Officially, it was forbidden to build outside the walls: in case of siege, such houses would have to be demolished and, therefore, they were not built of stone. The danger of fire thus was increased, and it was difficult to oversee these settlements outside the town.

As in the previous period, little is known of the housing of people of more humble means. They lived in small huts, sometimes three or four in a row, in the courtyards of houses owned by the rich, who could rent them separately. A hut consisted of a small room with a fireplace. The poor could probably find space in the cellars of big houses, as well, when the owners did not rent them for other purposes, such as storage. We know more about where the rich lived at that time. The Warmoesstraat and the Damrak, both close to the inner port, were distinguished streets inhabited by powerful merchants; here, business was transacted and the authorities put up famous visitors such as Prince William of Orange and the duke of Alba.

As in all medieval towns, the streets were narrow—at most, 20 feet wide. People lived close together and were in daily contact. In the wealthy quarters, pumps and latrines in backyards had to be shared by two or three houses. To reach the rear lanes where the people lived, many had to use an overpass across their neighbor's yard. By this time, houses had external stone walls, although wooden front gables persisted into the 17th century. On the earliest map of Amsterdam (of 1538), these gables can be located by their pointed shape. Many houses had stepped gables, which meant front gables in stone. During his visit to Amsterdam, Guicciardini noticed that the houses were built on stakes, reporting that the construction of the foundations of a

house cost more than the actual structure itself.

About 1560, even rich Amsterdam merchants led simple lives, although many a house might have a map hanging on the wall, or a painted portrait of the master and his wife. Other paintings portrayed holy subjects or religious scenes. Except for a few silver cups and spoons, and some ornaments, they possessed nothing in gold or silver. Those citizens who were better off owned dishes of tin or earthenware; the rest ate from small wooden plates and used wooden spoons and bowls. The poor would place a piece of rye bread on the table as a plate; they would eat it later, when it had absorbed the fat and moisture from the food.

In the numerous 16th-century portraits that survive today, we can observe that merchants wore dark and heavy clothes, and that the equally gloomy garb of their wives was only slightly embellished by a ring or necklace.

For merchants and higher officials, education was not bad. From the 15th century on, Amsterdam children were sent either to municipal schools or to private ones. Merchants' sons went to the University

of Louvain or even to Orléans. Hardly anybody, however, possessed a large library. A spectacular exception to the staid cultural background of Amsterdam merchants was Pompeius, known as Poppe, or Occo (1482/3–1537), who was the representative of the Fuggers, about 1525. Scholar, humanist, banker, and merchant, he was born in East Friesland, and was trained in Augsburg, where the Fuggers had their headquarters. Perhaps he settled in Amsterdam for the Fuggers, because of the freedom of trade that prevailed there, and the goods (especially copper) that were sent to Antwerp via Amsterdam. Occo had close links with the Danish king Christian II, who had been friendly with a local girl, Duveke, but later married Isabella, sister of Charles V. The dowry had to be paid through Occo, for it was important both to Amsterdam and to the Fuggers that access to the sound should remain in the right hands. Occo's library had more than a thousand books, which was exceptional at that time. He commissioned paintings from such well-known Amsterdam artists as Jacob van Oostsanen, and he kept up his humanist interests, which had begun in Augsburg, and belonged to a small circle of humanists in Amsterdam.

In short, the top layer of Amsterdam society, before 1568, consisted of a small group of important merchants and entrepreneurs. By means of office in the civic administration, some exercised political power in the city. The next strata was a large middle group of tradesmen, small merchants, and "professionals," such as apothecaries and surgeons. Finally, there was a group of porters, servants, day laborers, and sailors, who experienced very lean times in those years when grain was scarce. Nothing is known about the size of these groups.

Of the many changes in the 16th century, one still remains unmentioned: the religious revolution. From the first decades, new and heterodox views caused unrest, especially in Germany, with repercussions in Amsterdam, as well.

Reformation and the struggle for freedom

The 16th century saw great economic and demographic changes. Politically, the Habsburgs became

In the 16th century Amsterdam grew; in 1514 it had 13,500 inhabitants, a smaller population than that of Leyden and half that of Utrecht. Fifty years later it had 30,000 and had become the largest city in the northern Low Countries (Antwerp had 100,000). Wealth and professional skills also grew as is testified by the silver badge of civic postmen bearing a ship and the city's coat of arms, above; above left, the valuable collar of St. Sebastian's guild, a brotherhood of the civic guard (first quarter of the 16th century, Amsterdam Historical Museum). Such collars were worn on public occasions by the victor of the guards' annual shoot.

a world power over whose empire "the sun never set," and the Turkish empire was almost equally powerful. The new religious ideas that appeared shortly after the year 1500 spread rapidly and widely, spurred by the recent invention of movable-type printing.

As we have seen, Amsterdam was part of the county of Holland, and the arrangements between city and county had been definitively settled by 1500. From 1428 on, Holland had been Burgundian, through marriage and the inheritance of the dukes of Burgundy. Henceforth, they became counts of Holland, and tried to forge a single independent empire out of their Dutch provinces, Burgundy, and Franche-Comté. They began to centralize administration over the local bodies. This was pursued even more strongly under the Habsburgs, who became overlords at the end of the century. After a period of opposition, Charles V was able to rule unchallenged in parts of the Netherlands from 1515. Four years later, he succeeded his grandfather Maximilian as German emperor. Shortly after some minor campaigns, particularly over the Duchy of Gelderland,

Left, part of a copper knife with an amorous scene engraved on the handle; a toy horseman in pewter, and a powder flask with relief decoration (Amsterdam Historical Museum). Above, the St. Joris guild's drinking horn (1566, Amsterdam Historical Museum), showing St. George killing the dragon to free the princess, a symbol of the civic guard's guild of that name.

Charles united all 17 Dutch provinces under his rule, for the first time in history. As count of Holland, the emperor visited Amsterdam in 1540, although his attendants greatly feared for his health because of the city's notoriously bad drinking water.

By inheritance on his mother's side, Charles also held the Spanish kingdoms of Aragon and Castile with their colonial empire in the Americas and in India, all under the Habsburg crown. The princes who ruled over so vast an area could not always attend to the details of government. Even in the 15th century, the Burgundians had appointed stadholders—local representatives of the sovereign. The obvious solution for so large an empire was a policy of centralization, a daring idea at that time. Local privileges and traditions were preserved, but new central administrative bodies were established, with a different kind of official in charge, not chosen from the local nobility as had been the custom. Rather, they came from all corners of the empire and had university training.

Modern administrative methods may have been shocking, but the greatest burdens for the citizens were the taxes. Charles waged several wars, particularly against the Turks in the Mediterranean, who were advancing dangerously, and against France. The rich Netherlanders had to furnish much of the money for these campaigns, which were of no concern to them. Moreover, the persecution of heretics—reformers of traditional Catholicism—was, from the start, strongly opposed in the Netherlands. Charles V regarded heretics as threats to the unity of the empire, both in religion and politics.

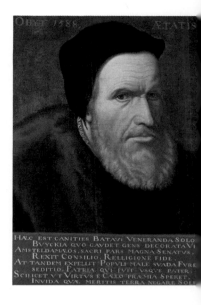

Reform movements

From 1500, criticism of abuses in the Catholic church became increasingly frequent. Trade in indulgences and the loose living of clerics provoked growing opposition. The sacraments and the external splendor of liturgical ceremonies seemed hollow and pompous to people who wanted to concentrate on a precise reading of the biblical text, which they regarded as the true source of knowledge. Among the early "Protestants" there were several groups that had no wish to leave the official church. In 1517, Martin Luther openly nailed his 95 theses on the

door of the castle church in Wittenberg. Charles V reacted quickly with his prohibitive decrees. In Germany, Luther succeeded in winning support even in the highest circles, and, in Holland, the new doctrine gained ground because of the close trade links to Lutheran regions. This strengthened sympathies toward reformers—for example, those in the higher circles of Amsterdam society—about 1530.

Another doctrine with much organized support in Amsterdam, after 1520, was that of the Sacramentarians. Like other Protestants, they regarded the bread and wine of the Eucharist not as the actual flesh and blood of Christ but as symbols. The doctrine of the Anabaptists, related to that of the Sacramentarians, went even further: they found infant baptism inconsistent with the scriptures and held that baptism must be given only to adults. More spectacular were their radical social notions. They believed that the millennium after the second coming of Christ was near. In anticipation, they established a New Jerusalem in the Westphalian city of Münster in 1534. In the new realm, everyone should

be equal and everything should belong to all. Not surprisingly, they won a great deal of support from the lower orders, from officials, and from sailors. Amsterdam, too, had a sizable Anabaptist community.

At first, the municipality acted with moderation, against the wishes of the higher authorities in Brussels, where the Dutch provinces were administered. Some officials with reformist sympathies had no time for the severe decrees of the emperor, and they held to the humanist Christian views, inspired by Erasmus. The mayor, the chief law officer, was at that time a moderate, and Amsterdam became a refuge for Anabaptists expelled from the rest of the country. Münster had been taken without bloodshed, but the group in Amsterdam turned into fanatics trying to establish a New Jerusalem by force. Sailors, women of unspecified trades, tailors, sawyers, and coopers met in garrets to discuss how to create a second Münster in Amsterdam. In February 1535, after a reading of the story of Paradise from the Bible, some Anabaptists ran naked through the

streets, immune to the cold in their exalted state. This incident would leave a deep impression on the townspeople: the men were beheaded in front of the town hall and the women were drowned. The climax occurred in May 1535, when, one evening, the Anabaptists attacked the town hall while the administration, together with some prominent citizens, was holding a large banquet inside. The Dam was festively lit by barrels of pitch, which must have given the attack a somewhat unreal character. At first, the diners did not react: they managed to escape from the building but could not stop some 40 assailants from occupying it. The next day a skirmish broke out on the Dam to recapture the town hall, and the Italian military experience of one of the burgomasters was turned to good account. The occupation was ended forcibly, and new trials and executions followed. On a scaffold before the town hall the guilty men were mutilated and beheaded, and the women were drowned in the Ij or in wine barrels filled with water.

These violent events prevented the city government from continuing to pursue its tolerant policy. In Brussels, harsh measures were demanded and the regent (Mary, the sister of Charles) appointed a new city administration because she mistrusted the old one. This was a highly unusual interference in the city's privileges, although it had happened before in the previous century. The new government proved to be reactionary, and, by 1538, followers of the Reformation were completely barred from the adminis-

"NAVIGIORUM AEDIFICATIO"

Navigiorum aedificatio, the construction of ships, is the title of a series of prints by Sieuwert van der Meulen, some of which are reproduced here (*3, 4, 5, 6, 7*). Not surprisingly, this technical topic was the subject of engravings made for public sale; much of the population of the province of Holland depended on shipbuilding for its livelihood. This tradition dates back to the 14th century. In the following century timber was busily imported from both Germany and Scandinavia. In the 17th century the shipbuilding industry was concentrated in Amsterdam, in the area immediately to the north of the city (Zaanstreek), and in Rotterdam. By now shipbuilding was a heavy industry. It supplied vessels of every type for local and foreign interests: fishing smacks, merchantmen, and warships. There was a brisk demand both because of the growth of maritime trading and because of the gaps created in fleets as a result of naval battles, acts of piracy, and wrecks. Dutch shipbuilding entrepreneurs had no trouble getting credit; there was

1

plenty of labor available; and timber, the principal raw material that accounted for 60 percent of the production costs, was available at low prices because of large-scale purchases. In 1669 an English report stated that ships built in the Dutch republic were costing 40 percent less than English ships. This flourishing activity handsomely filled the pockets not only of naval carpenters and joiners, but also of hundreds of other subsidiary groups: the makers of ropes, sails, masts, blocks, anchors, and fittings. But Dutch supremacy in this field underwent a crisis in the later half of the 18th century. This was due to technical stagnation, protectionism working in favor of the French and English shipbuilding industries, less demand because of the slump in herring fishing and whaling, and fewer sea battles.

At the end of the 15th century the construction yards and refitting docks of Amsterdam were situated for the most part in the area known as the lastage,

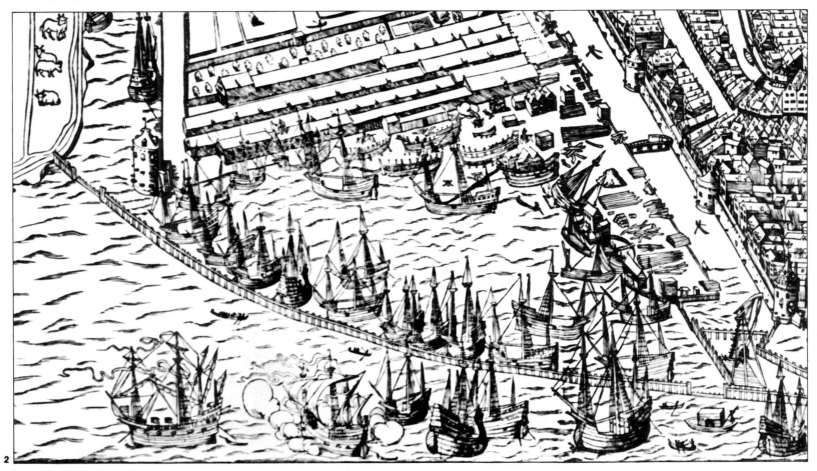

2

outside the city walls (*see 2, from the plan by Cornelius Anthonisz, 1544*), and later on the islands to the east and west of the Ij. In addition to the private shipyards there were also the important docks belonging to the Admiralty and the East India Company, where a thousand people were employed in the 18th century.

But shipbuilding remained a job that was largely rooted in craftsmanship; no two ships were ever the same. The tools used were hand-tools, as is evident, for example, from the shop sign for a block makers' firm (1) showing shipwrights at work. The cost of labor, however, was only 20-25 percent of the overall cost, even though the wages of the carpenters of Amsterdam were higher than those in the rest of the republic and Europe. Construction went ahead under the instruction of the shipowner, or shipping company, and the design was worked out on the basis of the experience of the shipwrights concerned and the technical shipbuilding manuals. The engravings of Sieuwert van der Meulen give us an idea of how they went about their work. First of all, the keel was set out in the shipyard, or on the quay. To this then were fitted the bowpost or stem, the sternpost, and the transom (4). The hull took shape by covering the frame with planking, starting from the bottom, first of all in the "quick work" below the waterline, and then in the topside or "upper works" above (5). When the ship had been decked, work started on the launching (6). This took place in front of the yard, and a successful launch merited a celebration. The fitting-out—in other words the completion and fitting of the masts and rigging—was done with the ship afloat (7).

The upkeep of the hull with the use of "dry-docking" (3) was an important task in the shipyards, especially in the case of vessels sailing to tropical waters, which were subject to rot in the "quick work" below the waterline—even with double planking, tight riveting and nailing, and the protection of the hull itself with resin, whale oil, and sulphur.

tration. Moreover, the well-to-do had been thoroughly frightened: they would not tolerate an enforced sharing of goods. In memory of the Anabaptist defeat, for many years a festive procession accompanied by the ringing of bells paraded through the town in May. The trials of Anabaptists and of other heretics continued until 1552, for Amsterdam, possibly because it was a port, remained a meeting place for fellow believers expelled from other parts of Europe. After the purge of 1538, a group of merchants and entrepreneurs came to power in Amsterdam and maintained their authority until 1578, the end of one of the city's greatest periods of unrest. The Eighty Years' War, or "struggle for freedom" from Habsburg rule, that followed thus had a com-

plex beginning and was greatly influenced along the way by local interests and by power plays.

The onset of the Eighty Years' War in Amsterdam

The Catholic government, after 1538, strictly observed the decrees against heretics. The government felt that Anabaptism had gotten out of hand because the previous administration had been too lax. All seemed well at the start, and the economy developed at a growing pace between 1540 and 1560. However, some progressive merchants excluded from government began to complain. Indeed, it has been argued that this group was richer and more modern in their

trading methods than the merchants who currently sat in the city government. At all events, their exclusion from office must have frustrated their political ambitions. The group's complaints were set out in a petition presented to the regent in Brussels on October 20, 1564. They objected to the family government in Amsterdam, to obstacles impeding trade, and to the slow enforcement of justice. The authors were 70 people who wished to remain anonymous. The burgomasters defended themselves, informing the regent that "sincere and Catholic persons [must sit in the city government] . . . so that the pernicious pestilence of heresy should not gain a hold on the city's administration." Above all, they were afraid of the reformist sympathies of their opponents. The regent ordered an inquiry, the result of which largely justified the complaints of those who had drafted the original petition.

Calvinism

The heresy of which the burgomasters were afraid was no longer just Lutheranism and Anabaptism. About 1560, Calvinism gradually spread north from France and Geneva. This doctrine involved new ideas of church reform and of salvation: the doctrine of predestination was advanced in a more detailed form toward the end of Calvin's life. Except for baptism and the Eucharist, he rejected the celebration of sacraments, and he held that studying the holy scriptures was paramount in reaching a pure version of Christian dogma. In general, Calvinists were moderates, and attached a positive value to work; from the beginning, they were efficiently organized. Unlike the Anabaptists, they came from all levels of society. Membership increased greatly after 1560, especially in the industrial southern Netherlands. As with the Anabaptists, the fact that grain was then in short supply and expensive played its role in the popularity of movement. Everywhere in Flanders thousands gathered outside the towns for the forbidden open-air "hedge-sermons."

Like his father, Philip II was strict with heretics. In 1555, he had succeeded Charles V in the Netherlands, as well as in Sapin and its overseas empire, while the Habsburg lands of Austria were governed

Opposite, 16th-century Italian armor and halberds (Amsterdam Historical Museum). Left, the young Charles V, terracotta by Konrad Meit, about 1520 (Grunthuse Museum, Bruges). He was a Habsburg but his native country, if any, was the Low Countries, where he was born (Ghent, 1500), whose language he spoke, and where he grew up—at Malines and Brussels, with his aunt the Regent Margaret of Austria and among the Flemish nobles he always preferred. His father was Philip the Fair, archduke of Austria; and his mother Juana the Mad, daughter of Ferdinand II of Aragon and Isabella of Castile. After the premature deaths of his parents, at six Charles inherited the Low Countries and Spain. In 1520, after an expensive election, he was crowned emperor at Aachen. Among his many titles was that of count of Holland, and in 1540 he made an official visit to Amsterdam. At the time the city's merchants barely tolerated his endless Mediterranean campaigns against France, the cost of which they often bore. Moreover, the Reformation had divided his subjects. When he abdicated in 1555, he left his son Philip II of Spain the 17 provinces of the Low Countries, 14 of Burgundian heritage and three that he had conquered. Along with northern Italy, the Low Countries were then one of the richest, busiest, most populous, and urbanized parts of Europe; and it was the only area still growing.

by Charles's brother Ferdinand. Philip was a zealous Catholic and regarded heresy as an intolerable injury to the Church. Calvinism, therefore, had to be eradicated. However, religious persecution provoked great abhorrence among the Dutch citizens, as did the constant financial burdens placed on them by the Habsburg ruler. Philip waged many lengthy wars—against France, and, particularly in the Mediterranean, against the Turks. The once prosperous southern Netherlands gradually experienced financial depression. The rapid rise of prices in the 16th century and growing inflation had reduced many to lives of bare subsistence. While merchants and workers in the south became ever more discontented because of Habsburg policy, opposition likewise arose among the nobility: they had economic motives, but above all they resented being excluded from the new administration by officials without roots in the Netherlands.

Iconoclasm

In the spring of 1566, this unrest found an outlet: the nobles sent a petition to the regent in Brussels, asking for mitigation of antiheretic decrees and for more regard for Dutch participation in policy-making administrative bodies. In summer, a wave of violence broke out around Antwerp, Ghent, and Hondschote. Crowds of people smashed statues in churches and overturned altarpieces. On the morning of August 23, some merchants arrived at the Amsterdam stock exchange in Warmoesstraat on their return from Antwerp, bringing with them marble fragments of statues that had been smashed by an angry mob there. The city government was terrified. In the past few months hedge-sermons had been delivered in the environs of Amsterdam, some quite close to the city walls. The burgomasters were afraid that the preachers now might want to enter the town—a move all the more dangerous in view of the thousands that had been seen in attendance at their sermons elsewhere, and in light of the recent famine. The Anabaptist troubles had not yet been forgotten, and, this time, rather more people were involved. When the city government nervously began to empty the two big churches, tension rose

On land and at sea: Left, a musketeer by Jacob de Gheyn, 1607. Below left, a Dutch admiral, School of Pieter Pieterszon (Rijksmuseum). Charles V's splendid inheritance of the 17 provinces did not long remain undivided; 1568 saw the beginning of the northern Low Countries' Eighty Years' War for independence from Spain, overlapping the wider Thirty Years' War; both were ended by the Treaty of Münster in 1648. The peace formalized the de facto political, religious, and military situation: the Reformed northern Seven United Provinces, roughly the present-day Netherlands; and the southern Catholic and Spanish part, or Flanders, roughly modern Belgium. Holland was one among the Seven United Provinces. During the war, they prevailed at sea, while Spain usually won on land when she was able to deploy her invincible infantry. Meanwhile Antwerp, the biggest city in the Low Countries and a world market, was ruined, and Amsterdam rose to be the richest and most dynamic city in the strong republic, which, for a while, became a world power.

and, before the day was out, the Old Church was damaged. A month later, sacred images were destroyed once again, this time in the Minorite monastery, where food stores also were ravaged and the library narrowly escaped destruction. Plundering occurred elsewhere in Holland, too—for example, in The Hague, Leyden, and Alkmaar.

From the Iconoclasm to the Alteration, 1566–1578

About 1566, and again in 1578, when Amsterdam finally had to side with William of Orange in the revolt against Spain, the city witnessed a struggle between different interest groups—as, indeed, happened in other towns in Holland at that time. The Amsterdam councilors were mainly Catholic merchants, a group loyal to the king but even more attached to the city's trade and independence. In any case, they wished to keep the plaintiffs of 1564 out of the administration. There was an opposition group of Reformation sympathizers, among them a small section of grim Calvinists, and also many who had vague Reformist notions but who were opposed to heresy. In addition, there were those who maintained a Christian-humanist position. The opposition was made up of upper-class burghers, a number of whom had signed the original petition, as well as officials and workers. A genuine proletariat did not exist then. Here, too, political motives were combined with religious ones: those burghers excluded from the government wanted more power, as they had in 1564; the lower orders were no doubt motivated by the hard times.

The role of the civic guard

The civic guard, an influential group, was an armed body of citizens. Since the Middle Ages, the guard had had to defend the city and maintain order. In case of attacks—for example, from Gelderland—which were still occurring in the early 16th century, the guard defended the town. Members had to pay for their own outfits, so that they had to be among the richer citizens: harnesses, long bows, short bows, and muskets were not cheap. Normally, the

L. L°. X. ᵗᵒᴮᴬˡ Moscᴏᴇʀᴀ   OQVENDO DEL U. ᴅ Sᴀɴᵗᵈᵒ   ARMAS NON ᴀᴇʀᴠIS OBSTANT LITTERAE.
Figᴠᴇʀᴏᴀ, Aᴠᴅɪᴛᴏʀ ᵈ   Gᴿᴬᴸ. ᴅ ʟᴀ Esqᴰᴿᴬ. ᴅ Cᴀɴ-
TABRIA.

guard confined itself to shooting practice, guarding the gates, and holding banquets, but at times of unrest in the city they could play a significant political role because they were the only organized group of leading citizens outside the government. Among them were Reformist sympathizers who refused to collaborate with the government when hedge-sermons were held. Shortly after the breaking of statues in the churches, the balance seemed at first to tilt in favor of the Reform group, and the government even agreed to assign one of the city's churches to the Protestants. However, the next year the tide turned because of political developments in Brussels. Philip was very angry at the regent's indulgent attitude, and it became increasingly clear that the aristocratic party could not sustain the opposition. Many noble citizens, among them Prince William of Orange, stadholder of Holland, Zeeland, and Utrecht, fled abroad. Although the Reformist opposition group in Amsterdam was now in the majority, it no longer dared exploit its advantage. Moreover, the duke of Alba and his army—summoned from Spain to re-

store order in the Netherlands—were on their way to Brussels, and from him no mercy could be expected. Thus, in 1567, there began an exodus abroad of the richer Reformationists. Many settled in Emden, which became a Calvinist center. The guard was dismissed by the city government for no longer commanding confidence. The burgomasters had to make do with 300 mercenaries. Those who could not flee but nevertheless spoke in favor of the Reformation were condemned to death by Alba's Council of the Inquisition, popularly called the Bloody Council, a special court for heretics. Significantly, the death penalty was inflicted mainly on members of the lower orders, while the more highly placed were punished with exile and the confiscation of their goods.

The difficult period from 1568 to 1578

The loss of capital and merchants in 1567 and 1568 cost the city dearly. Trade languished, the more so since the freebooting fleet of William of Orange,

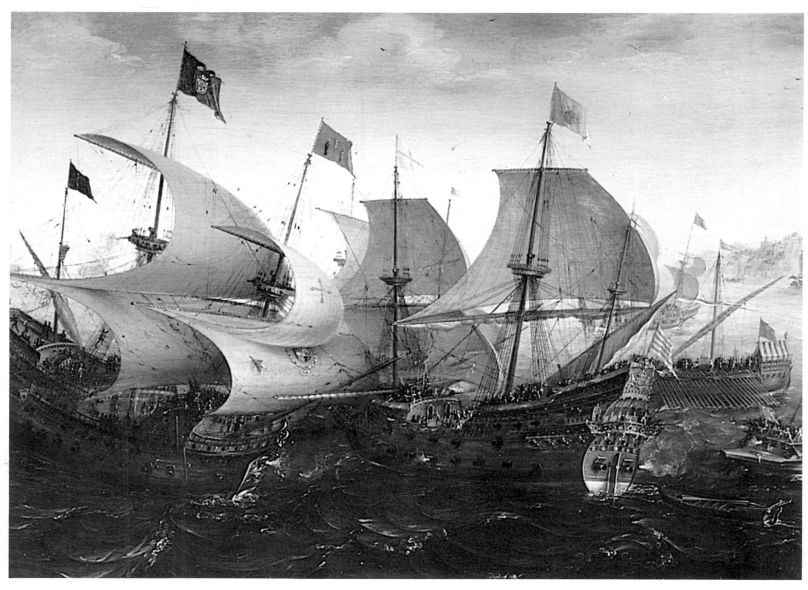

Philip II sent his "Invincible Armada" to the Channel to defeat the Dutch rebels and their ally, the English. The picture above by Aert Anthoniszon (1608) shows the San Martin, *flagship of the duke of Medina Sidonia, attacked by the English* Rainbow *and the Dutch* Gouden Leeuw *(Golden Lion) on August 8, 1588 in the straits of Dover (Rijksmuseum).*

which was called the Sea Beggars, made navigation unsafe. Many merchants who had fled sided with the revolt either by joining the Sea Beggars or by collecting funds for William. Although Den Briel, a small port in South Holland, fell to the Sea Beggars in 1572, and more and more towns sided with the prince and the revolt, Amsterdam remained loyal to the king. During the siege of Haarlem, the Spaniards obtained reinforcements and food supplies through Amsterdam and Alkmaar. Still, Amsterdam persistently refused to admit Spanish troops inside its walls. When, in 1574, Holland and Zeeland joined William's newly founded union and William himself was appointed stadholder, the position of Amsterdam became untenable. The other towns cor-

doned off the city, in order to prevent a Spanish attack from Amsterdam. Many exiles returned from north Germany to Holland at that time. From Hoorn and Enkhuizen they struggled to bring about the surrender of Amsterdam, whose defenses weakened rapidly. The cows kept within the walls for safety seem to have wandered about freely in the many empty merchants' houses. There was hunger because trade was at a standstill, money was scarce, and, for new funds, part of the guilds' silverware had to be melted down into emergency coins.

The distress came to an end in 1578 when Amsterdam finally was forced to side with William of Orange—an event termed the Alteration. From far and wide the exiles returned, often after hard

Top left, an allegory of the war against Spain. In the center, Holland as a girl, on the left Orange fighting Alba, on the right the lion of the States General fending off Alba's successor, Luis Requesens y Zuniga; in front, with the hangman's knot in hand, Don Juan of Austria, captain general of Flanders. Below left, stages of the assassination of William of Orange (1582). Siege of Alkmaar (1573), *drawing by Walter Morgan (All Souls College, Oxford). Attacked by the Spaniards*

years abroad. They could now freely practice their faith, but not yet openly. Catholicism remained the official religion. The mercenaries were paid off and the guard restored. This did not solve the religious question, nor did reformed merchants yet have access to official posts. However, relief was near: some months later the administrators were sent away from the city in small boats and disembarked on the Diemerdijk outside the city's jurisdiction. The takeover was bloodless. The guard, as *de facto* civic representatives, now chose a new council and new burgomasters. An important part of the group—which first made itself known in 1564— now came to power. The four burgomasters were all reformed, but in addition to them the council still

contained Catholics. The guard garnered great political esteem for its activities in 1578; but in 1581 Holland's parliamentary body, called the States, or States General, decreed that only councils could be consulted in political matters. In 1580, the short period of religious freedom had come to an end: Catholic services were officially forbidden.

History had come full circle. Soon, the new civic government again consisted of members of the upper classes, as before. Only now a different group had come to power. There was no political influence from outside the civic government, and Calvinism had replaced Catholicism as the official religion. Amsterdam no longer belonged to the Habsburg Empire but to a still unstable federation of states. As

under Alba's son Frederic, the city held out and earned the motto "Alcmaria Victrix," while the Dutch adopted the hopeful saying "Victory begins at Alkmaar."

THE REPUBLIC
OF THE SEVEN UNITED PROVINCES

The state which we nowadays commonly, but inaccurately, call Holland was the Republic of the Seven United Provinces in the 17th and 18th centuries. It was made up of seven autonomous provinces: Holland, Zeeland, Utrecht, Gelderland, Groningen, Friesland, and Overijssel. Then there were the *Generaliteitslanden,* or lands of the Generality, governed by the central body of the republic, the States General, and the Drente, an allied region but with no vote in the States General. Because of its wealth, Holland was the most influential province. In theory it financed 58 percent of the republic's budget and in practice even more.

In the villages, seigniories, towns, cities, and provinces a variety of legal, administrative, and fiscal rules and regulations were in force, all deriving from the medieval "privileges." The organization of the Republic of the Seven United Provinces was quite complicated when compared with present-day notions of national government. It must also be said that the people living in the republic had the same impression, too. The illustration on these two pages explains some of the basic data: the different sectors in the ellipse represent the seven provinces with their cities and towns, which, in each province, had the right to vote in the respective provincial states; another symbol in each sector indicates the representation of the authorities of the territories outside the urban areas (i.e., the nobility).

In general terms the governments of the seven provinces were remarkably standardized. In each province the highest authority was the assembly of the provincial states. Here sat representatives of the urban bourgeoisie and the nobility—in other words, the representatives of the towns and cities who were "free" in accordance with the communal tradition, and the representatives of the

rural areas who were "enfeoffed" in accordance with the feudal tradition. The relationship between the two factions differed from province to province, and also varied from period to period. In the western maritime section of the republic, for example, the towns and cities were more important than in the eastern part. The assembly of the States of Holland was made up of 18 towns and cities

with the right to vote and just one member of the nobility (the ratio between the city representatives and the nobility in the respective provincial states is indicated very broadly by the numbers in each sector. The first number shows the city representatives, the second the

representatives of the nobility; in the province of Utrecht the third number refers to the clerical representation). Amsterdam was the most influential city in the province of Holland, and in the entire republic as well (in

Friesland
1:4

Holland
18:1

Alkmaar
Amsterdam
Brielle
Delft
Dordrecht
Edam
Enkhuizen
Gorkum
Gouda
Haarlem
Hoorn
Leida
Medemblik
Monnikendam
Purmerend
Rotterdam
Schiedam
Schoonhoven

1

2

3

6:1

Zeeland

the diagram this prominent position is underlined and reference is also made to the four components of its government, which are similar but not identical to those of the other towns and cities; the central bodies of the republic are shown symbolically in the center of the ellipse).

The matters that concerned all the provinces were dealt with by the States General (5), the permanent assembly that sat in The Hague, made up of the representatives of the seven provinces. Deliberations concerning the whole republic had to have unanimous approval, and each province had one vote. A lack of unanimity was not infrequent: when this was the case each provincial representative had to return to his province to consult with his own provincial state, which in turn consulted their cities. The decision-making process was clearly a slow one. Matters dealt with by the States General included foreign policy, supervision of the army and the navy, the granting of commercial monopolies and of political and military powers to trading companies (as, for example, the East India Company), and the government of the Generality. Another central body was the Council of State (3), which was responsible for the formulation of the budget, the organization and financing of the army, the levying of taxes throughout the Union and in the Generality. The Council of State was attended by the stadholder and 12 representatives from the provinces, 3 of whom were from the province of Holland. A third central body, the State Audit Court (4), with two members from each province, was in charge of the management of the funds paid by the provinces for communal matters.

Two other bodies had a central function, too, even though this was not exactly their constitutional appearance: these were the stadholder and the grand pensionary of Holland. The stadholder (1), who was originally the representative in the provinces of the "seigneur" and supreme commander of the army and navy, was in effect appointed separately by each province. Historically five provinces nominated the same person from the House of Orange (the following were stadholders: William I (The Silent), Maurice of Orange, Frederik Henry of Orange, William II, William III, William IV, and William V) and two (Groningen and Friesland) nominated a cousin. The grand pensionary was also an officer of the provincial government. As a legal councilor he had a great deal of influence in the provincial states. In the absence of the stadholder (there were two periods without one: in 1650–1672, after the death of William II, and in 1702–1748, after the death of William III, who was also king of England) the grand pensionary of Holland stepped in to represent the entire republic. This is how de Witt functioned during the first interregnum. The system of government we are describing lasted virtually unchanged until 1795; in reality it was an oligarchic government. The members of the government in cities and provinces alike, on which the system was founded, came from the patrician class. Unlike England and France, for example, the republic never knew the centralized state typical of absolutism, even if there were attempts by stadholders to take a predominant political and military rôle. In the cities government was based on the burgomasters, a council, and a *schout* or sheriff. In the country, fairly large and often highly autonomous groupings were in the hands of members of the nobility, wealthy farmers, and powerful city folk who had bought properties in the country —and the provincial states had an influence on their appointments. The provinces were governed by the provincial states, nominated by the grand pensionary and the stadholder, who could, in many cities, appoint the functionaries of the city government.

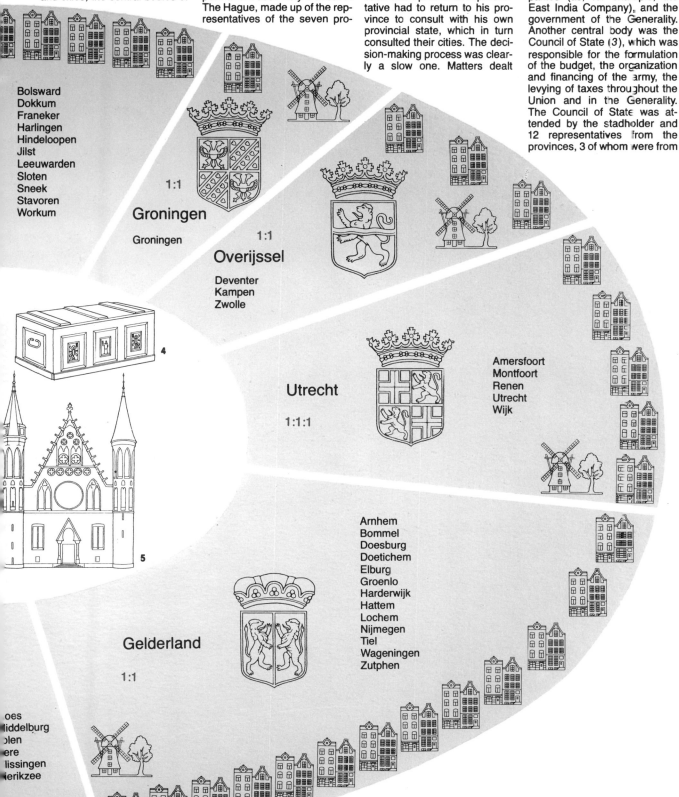

Bolsward
Dokkum
Franeker
Harlingen
Hindeloopen
Jilst
Leeuwarden
Sloten
Sneek
Stavoren
Workum

1:1

Groningen

Groningen

1:1

Overijssel

Deventer
Kampen
Zwolle

1:1:1

Utrecht

Amersfoort
Montfoort
Renen
Utrecht
Wijk

4

5

Arnhem
Bommel
Doesburg
Doetichem
Elburg
Groenlo
Harderwijk
Hattem
Lochem
Nijmegen
Tiel
Wageningen
Zutphen

Gelderland

1:1

oes
iddelburg
olen
ere
lissingen
ierikzee

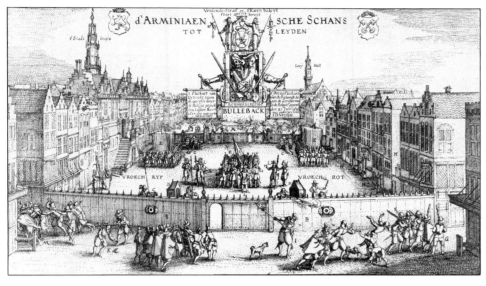

to politics and religion, a new period began after 1580; and the population and economy changed as well.

1590–1600: Amsterdam becomes the world's marketplace

After 1578, the city experienced an amazing surge in trade and industry, based partly on what had gone before and partly on new factors. By 1580, the Baltic trade had resumed on its former scale. When William of Orange as stadholder visited Amsterdam, an allegorical representation of this trade awaited him on the Damrak. Travel on this route was even now not steady, to some extent because of bad harvests. However, merchants could probably cushion fluctuations in supply by turning to other goods that traditionally had come from the Baltic, such as iron, copper, flax, hemp, timber, and potash. There must have been great merchant fleets on regular service to the Baltic. The introduction of the fluit, a new type of swift freighter, was a great advance.

Grain and timber were often sold in areas at war with the Baltic, such as Spain, Portugal, and the southern Netherlands. Philip II resented trading with insurgent provinces, but hunger in Spain was so great that he had no choice, and he especially needed timber, for building ships. Trading with the enemy, particularly in arms—a growing item—was very profitable, but not all Hollanders were in favor of it. The opponents declared that they should rather hurt the enemy by stopping trade with Spain and the southern Netherlands—an area still loyal to Spain. Among Calvinists, trade with Catholic provinces raised problems of conscience. Still, trade continued in spite of freebooters from Dunkirk, and Philip's embargoes.

Amsterdam was fortunate in that, after 1574, Holland lay outside the territory of the Eighty Years' War. The city profited from trading with the enemy, and from the fall of Antwerp and the closure of the Scheld, Antwerp's outlet to the sea: it largely took over Antwerp's role as world market. The northern provinces gained from the vast exodus from Flanders and Brabant and from other southern provinces that had occurred since the mid-16th century. From 1577 to 1589 came the great wave of immigrants, when tens of thousands left their homes. By 1589, Antwerp had been reduced from 100,000 to 49,000 inhabitants. People left both for religious and economic reasons. The plight of Antwerp was so great that people starved to death. Of the new citizens in Amsterdam, 54 percent in the period 1585–89 came from the southern Netherlands, and even by 1600 the figure remained at 40 percent. The arrival of Flemings and Brabanters influenced Amsterdam economically and culturally. Immigrant merchants brought their specialized knowledge and technical skills, as well as capital. Besides, Amsterdam merchants could now profit from the immigrants' contacts with the Mediterranean, among other places. The Flemings, moreover, were skilled in all kinds of trades and luxury industries, such as silk manufacture, sugar refining, diamonds, carpet weaving, gold-tooling of leather, and furniture. All this was quite new, but immigrants joined existing industries, too. Printing and publishing already were established trades, but now the city became internationally famous for them. Publishers and printers, typesetters, and makers of maps and atlases settled in Amsterdam. Many painters came there and found work. The north did not let this influx simply happen, but tried to attract newcomers by offering incentives to people to stay. Citizenship was granted freely, guilds were accessible, and even moving costs were reimbursed and industrial premises offered. The northern "cheese heads" felt awkward

Effigiatio
SYNODI NATIONALIS INCHOATÆ, DORDRECHTI ANNO CIƆ IƆXIX
Jn quo loca tam Delegatorum Illustrice ac prapotentum D.D. Ordinum Generalium Faderatarum Provinciarum, quam exterorum Professorum ac Ministrorum, atq dictarum
Provinciarum, graphice delineata exhibentur.

Boven defen inganck
lyn noch 2 galerie voor
de toe hoorders

among the refined and elegant southerners and mocked their ostentation and refined manners, while still respecting them for their culture. It took a long time for the sharpest contrasts to fade. The 17th-century Amsterdam poet and playwright Bredero, in the *Spanish Brabanter,* describes the conflicts between these opposite groups.

In 1585, Amsterdam merchants still worked with small capital, as the tax registers show, but the arrival of southerners changed this. New investment was sought—for example, in exploring new trading areas. In the north, traffic with Russia via the White Sea was opened up. In the south, Mediterranean traffic greatly increased, with routes to Greece, Turkey, the Levant, and Egypt. Moreover, the first trips in search of an independent sea lane to India turned into spectacular adventures. Amsterdam merchants usually obtained their spices from Lisbon, but since this now meant trading with the enemy, with the help of experienced merchants and mapmakers, the Dutch backed their own first, often dangerous voyages of exploration.

The flourishing Baltic trade, which brought many new goods to the city, trade with the enemy, the fall of Antwerp, the arrival of southern immigrants, and the accumulation of capital contributed to the swift growth of Amsterdam as a world market by 1600. Another factor in this growth was the availability of labor. The population continued to increase after 1580, mainly through immigration from the south, from Germany, and from within the new republic itself. At this stage, many came from North Holland to try their luck in the city. There was ample work in shipping, warehousing, and industry. The close links with the area north of Amsterdam and with West Friesland remained. In fact, it was chiefly northern seamen who traveled to the Baltic for Amsterdam shipowners. Finally, there were technical improvements that arose at the end of the 16th century, such as the development of the fluit. Windmills, which became better adapted to supply power for industry, and the extensive peat cuttings in Friesland and Groningen provided large amounts of cheap energy for industry in town and country alike. About 1600, Holland had become one of the most modern territories in the world.

The Venice of the north

That the young republic of the Seven United Provinces became the first nation of Europe after 1600 astonished contemporaries. What had enabled the Dutch to capture world trade in so short a time baffled everybody. More amazing still was that they should encroach upon the mighty Spanish empire.

In a world ruled by princes and nobles, the republic, with its astute and diligent citizen administrators, was an unusual phenomenon. Within a few decades the Hollanders had established trading posts all over the world. Sovereigns came to Amsterdam to equip their armies and to buy grain for their hungry subjects. Amsterdam capital financed many projects abroad, such as land clearance in France and England. The Dutch merchant and owner of capital acted not from feelings of national interest—a concept unknown then—but mainly for the sake of quick gain and secure investment, although there was some loyalty to the province and still more to the city. What mattered was flexibility, rather than being tied to the general interest. This explains why Amsterdam merchants took part in English, French, and Danish enterprises competing with Hollanders in the India trade, and why in time of war they often sold the enemy guns and ammunition, as well as grain. Soldiers at war with the republic were paid through loans from the Amsterdam capital market.

The flourishing period that lasted until about 1650 was marked by even more economic specialization than in the previous century. On the land, horticulture and forestry expanded and farmers concerned themselves with special crops, such as linseed, which was needed by industry. Whole towns concentrated on making specific industrial products;

Leyden was renowned for cloth and Haarlem for linen. In Amsterdam, many new types of industry arose, and the choice of goods was much more varied than before. At the same time merchants specialized in particular goods. Amsterdam had become a world market, the top of an organized system of local and international markets attracting surpluses from elsewhere.

Nothing essentially new was added to Amsterdam's pattern of trade. The stock exchange, insurance companies, and banking existed in older trading cities, too: Antwerp, Bruges, London, and Venice, for example. However, in Amsterdam these were expanded and perfected. In particular, this was true of freight trade: north-south trade in Europe, the basis of Amsterdam's prosperity, relied on specialized and well-organized merchant fleets. Merchants combined in a new kind of shipping line, in which they could raise large sums quickly to finance an operation. Enough capital was available chiefly because, in merchant families, it passed from father to son: the business had to continue, and when a man died his widow would carry on in his stead. Moreover, merchants were thrifty and preferred to play safe. Money was not thrown away, nor put into risky enterprises. Merchants from Holland adopted more modern trading methods by forming monopolies. To balance unstable supplies with a much steadier demand, different groups joined forces in order to attain a monopoly for a given article, such as Italian silk, copper, and saltpeter. They bought up large quantities in order to store buffer supplies in Amsterdam warehouses; thus, the item could always be supplied on demand.

William Temple, English ambassador to the republic in 1676, was greatly impressed by the neat and orderly way in which the Hollanders conducted their trade. This was due not only to the organization of merchants for large-scale trade, but also to the reliable and high-quality goods achieved through the network of legal protections for the customer. The Waag (or weighbridge), loading and unloading, and transport within the republic were officially controlled by guilds. Until about 1650, the republic developed, unhindered, in many fields. Afterward, stagnation set in, mainly because of protectionist measures by the French and the English.

Because of the enormous growth in the urban population, the city had to expand after 1600. In suburbs beyond the walls, housing threatened to multiply without control. The population was still penned into the medieval space, which created tension and disorder in the residential areas. By about 1542, there were plans for extension eastward. The Italian architect Marco da Verona even prepared a map for it, but the plans came to nothing and the housing shortage worsened. Contemporary estimates put the number of houses and huts outside the walls at about 1,000. An urban commission on a tour of the city in 1565 observed that houses abutting the city walls had fallen in several places and the inhabitants could not pay for raising them so that their apartments were often inundated.

In 1566, renewed proposals for urban expansion were put forward in order to cope with housing conditions. The plan was to push the defenses outward so as to enclose a new strip of ground within the city. However, on the advice of William of Orange, then stadholder of Holland in the name of Philip II, the plan was dropped: it was too dangerous to leave the city temporarily undefended. But things improved after Amsterdam joined the revolt in 1578.

trict of the lastage fell within this extended area, and

Many merchants who earlier had insisted on expansion were now in the city government and warfare had ceased in Holland. Shortly after 1578, the government began a lengthy sifting of plans prepared by the master of fortifications Adriaen Anthoniszon, chief defense adviser to William of Orange and planner of various improvements in

obsolete town defenses in Holland and elsewhere.

Nowhere in the republic was defense adapted to modern war. After much stringpulling between various interested bodies, and at the insistence of William himself, the city government finally adopted Anthoniszon's plan to set up new ramparts outside the western and eastern walls. In contrast with the Italian system, the walls joining the ramparts were made not of stone but of earth. This variant was used throughout the republic. The old shipbuilding district of the lastage fell within this extended area, and became residential. Some years later, in 1591, shipbuilding was shifted to several artificial islands specially created for this purpose in the eastern port. The plans for these islands had been prepared by the burgomaster William Baerdesen; they were characterized by their clear, modern and geometric layout and by the detailed rules for ordering industrial enterprises. On the Singel, the former defense channel west of the city, a new residential area for the wealthy arose. The strip of land from there to the new defense line—later, the Herengracht—was parceled out and built up with houses for artisans and seamen. The subdivision was partly due to speculative operations by a few urban landowners with large holdings.

The "ideal" city

Evidently, expansion of the city was closely linked with military matters. While William of Orange was stadholder, this renewal was undertaken slowly, but under his son Prince Maurice's rule not only the army but also its fortifications in the republic were among the most modern in Europe. Using the theories of Italian military architects and town planners of the 16th century as his point of departure, Simon Stevin, the prince's adviser, known as a mathematician and an expert on fortifications, became the most famous theorist of the new Dutch system. He greatly influenced the new study of engineering, which was offered in Leyden from 1600. Teaching was in Dutch, as opposed to the usual Latin that prevailed in universities. The course included problems of town planning. Engineers and surveyors trained in Leyden were influential in the

design of new towns and fortifications in Sweden—for example, in Kristianstad and Gothenburg.

Applying the ideas for an ideal city, where the links between street, houses, and open spaces were determined by certain rational and mathematical proportions, was not an easy matter in the towns of the republic, particularly where older central areas had to be respected. During the period of rapid expansion, 1580–1680, we find only a few examples where growth could be organized in terms of a single theoretical planning concept. Amsterdam, with its network of canals, was to become an outstanding instance, although the early development of these canals was rather more haphazard than it might appear; indeed, there was no considered plan behind it.

The growth of the city. Above, detail from an allegory of the "fourth extension," by Claes Pieterszon Berchem (1663). Previous page, from top, Nieuwe Vaart, the new canal with the city's latest windmill; the digging of the Herengracht, drawing by A. Blooteling; countryside later absorbed by the city in a drawing by Rembrandt. The extension of Amsterdam was undertaken by prearranged urban decrees, discussed and sometimes debatable, but exemplary in many respects.

THE FACE OF THE CITY: RESIDENTIAL HOUSES

Timber and brick architecture exercised a mutual influence over one another in the western Netherlands. In the Middle Ages brick houses were an exception. Timber cost less and the soft ground was bettter suited to wooden edifices. But timber was also an easy prey to fire: the fires of 1421 and 1452 reduced a considerable part of Amsterdam to ashes. After 1452 the commune made it obligatory to put up stone side walls, although these were not load bearing. The bricks were made along the banks of the major rivers, like the Rhine, and the stone was imported from Belgium or Germany. Because of the increased costs, people often got around the communal building rules and regulations. In 1669 there was a prohibition on the construction of timber façades, and in the course of the 17th century we find the trans-

formation taking place from the timber-built house to the masonry-built house. The timber structure (4) consisted of vertical uprights and beams supporting the floors; these were reinforced by struts. Between the beams there were joists, either resting on top of the beams or dovetailed (6), and the flooring itself was laid on these. In the course of the 16th century the ends of the beams were laid into the side walls, which thus became load bearing. From about 1630 the only load-bearing timber structure was the roof (5).

Initially, houses were quite narrow. The front section was two or three bays or spans across (14–20 feet 1a). The large houses belonging to merchants and businessmen were wider, being built on two par-

1

2

3

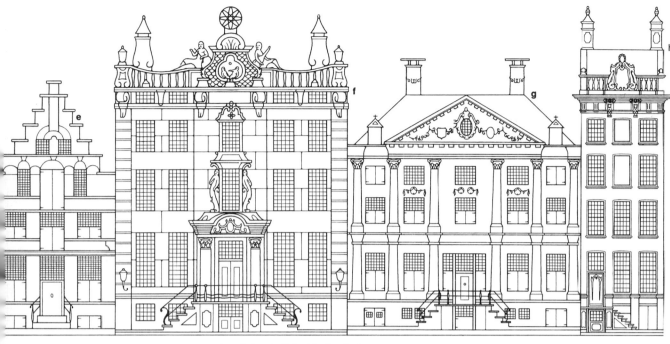

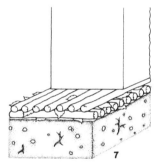

17th century saw the arrival of two new types (*1c,d*), both embellished with volutes, the second one with the side sections emphatically concave. Both these forms also lasted into the 18th century, even if in varied forms imposed by changing tastes. After 1650 the more exclusive houses had large cornices and tympana in the classical style (*1g*), and in the 18th century the cornice also appeared in ordinary houses with different types of balustered and scrolled effects (*1h*).

In the façades of houses we can distinguish between two periods, with the middle of the 17th century as the dividing line. As we have already said, the period from 1400 to 1650 saw the transformation from the timber house to the brick-built house. The backcloth was varied and animated; façades made of timber, timber and stone, or entirely in masonry sported projecting elements, projections with windows set in

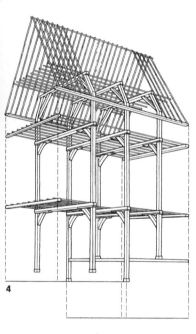

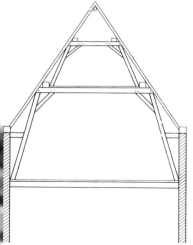

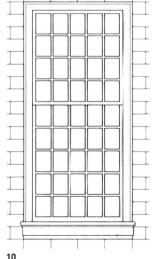

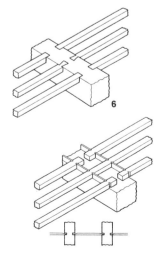

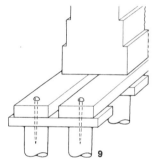

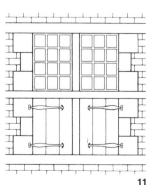

cels of land ("double-fronted houses" *1f*) with the façade five spans across, and the roof parallel with the street. In the 17th and 18th centuries most of the houses were on three floors, with a semibasement for storage or lodging servants, and two attics on two levels. The cost of land tended to make homes tall instead of wide.

The peaty ground posed the problem of adequate foundations, which the light medieval house did not need. After 1400 the house was supported by six-foot walls, for the most part underground and resting on a bed or small tree trunks and branches (*7*). In larger buildings and, in the 15th century, in residential homes as well, the walls were built on stakes driven into the ground and held together by a crisscross grid of beams (*8*). When masonry construction came

into use in the 16th century, because of the greater weight, a system of foundations using double stakes was introduced; these were held together by nailed boards, and after 1630 by crossties between the stakes, with each pair being about 32 inches apart (*9*). The foundation stakes were driven down into the sand, beneath the stratum of peat, to a depth of about 35 feet. With no more than a few modifications this system has lasted into the 20th century.

Until the end of the 17th century the windows were divided into four by a crosspiece, in accordance with medieval practice; they had glass fixed in the upper panes, and wooden shutters in the lower ones (*11*). Light was only admitted through the upper half of the window, and not much of it at that.

Glass was only added behind the wooden shutters at a later date. In the 18th century the sliding window became widespread. This was probably of French origin; it had wooden frames, and was usually five panes of glass across. It could be opened by sliding the two

parts up or down (*10*). The rooms inside were much better lit as a result.

Variety in the urban townscape of the 17th and 18th centuries was provided by the form of the upper part of the façade. The triangular apex, in timber, was the oldest form (*1b*). After 1500, when façades were built in brick, the stepped coping came into use (*1e*). The

them, and other jutting constructions over the semibasement (*2,3*). The timber itself was often painstakingly carved. Brick façades were broken up, with fine decorative effect, by stone structures (*3*). After 1650 the tone changed. The façade no longer had picturesque projecting elements. In fact, the principal urban image was marked by stone stairways, large wooden doors, and French windows.

Amsterdam, city of immigrants

This small-scale expansion was far from adequate to accommodate the growing population, or to meet Amsterdam's needs. About 1570, Amsterdam had approximately 30,000 inhabitants: by 1600, probably about 60,000; about 100,000 in 1620; and some 200,000 in 1660. This was largely due to immigration. Precise numbers are unknown, but marriage registers show how many of the men and women were newcomers and supply us with their places of origin. More brides and bridegrooms emigrated from abroad than from other parts of the republic. In the late 16th century, many came from the southern Netherlands, particularly from Antwerp. From 1600 to 1650, many left the German coast to look for work on ships, in commerce, or as artisans. From 1675 to 1700, they came mainly from Lower Saxony. Many, too, arrived from Scandinavia, and after the revocation of the Edict of Nantes in 1685, many French Huguenots fled north. Among the immigrants South Netherlanders and Iberian Jews were a sizable group. From 1600 to 1650, those from the republic itself were mainly looking for work as seamen.

The city could not avoid expanding; yet uncontrolled building outside the walls had to stop. It is estimated that, by 1609, about 3,000 houses had gone up in this area, although it had long been strictly forbidden to build within 580 feet of the city wall. Moreover, rich citizens insisted on a special residen-

Whenever the city expanded, the walls were demolished and rebuilt farther out, new canals were dug with roads along the banks at least where the upper classes settled, and rows of façades of houses. There was land speculation, and in some parts of the city there were deficient plans or none at all. Right, the Herengracht (about 1660), in a picture by Jan Wijnants (Cleveland Museum of Art), the first townscape with typical tree-lined banks. Below right, the Nieuwezijds Voorburgwal with the flower market and the back of the new town hall (about 1670-75), from a painting by Gerrit Berckheyde. Tower of the herring packers by Abraham Storck. Below, profile of Amsterdam about 1670, drawing by L. Doomer.

tial area reflecting their newly acquired status. Finally, the city spread because it was insufficiently fortified. In 1610, the city government considered the plans of the city carpenter Hendrick Staets, which probably called for a fortified wall around the whole city, but there was no scheme for building up the area between the old town and the new walls. A special study commission of the city government was set up and spent three years considering fortifications and housing. Prince Maurice himself examined the military aspects of Staet's Plans. In March 1613, the council decided to build the fortifications as far out as about one third of the latest canals, to the west of the city. The new area would be built up from the canals, as in earlier expansions, but the new canals were to be arranged in a graded system with a mathematical layout of waterways, quay sides, and building lots, stretching right across existing pastures and ditches. Details of the plan were modified until September 1614, when, for example, there was a proposal not to cut the Keizersgracht, the central canal of the three, but to have a long tree-lined avenue instead. Here, the parceling of land obviously was intended for large-scale houses: the lots were 28 feet wide and 177 feet deep. On the east side of this canal, which was built up after 1585, the houses measured 18 feet by 93 feet. A buyer might even acquire the adjacent lot as well, to build an exceptionally big house. Building regulations were lax enough to lead to an irregular string of houses, large

and small, tall and short, some parallel to the water, some at right angles. Lots could not be subdivided, and noxious or otherwise dangerous workshops were banned; these restrictions later applied to the other canals, as well.

The architectural arrangement of the canal belt was thus shaped by a commission of burghers and not by a prior master plan, mainly because some members of the city government were themselves materially involved, and tried to look after their own interests from within the commission. Burgomaster C. P. Hooft, a good example of an upright, liberal regent, fiercely opposed their plans in council and attacked their greed. The commission's report shows that a certain Jan Huydekoper, a buyer of skins and a tanner, had bought up a great deal of land in the area where the city was to expand and quickly built houses on it, which had long been illegal. He was banking on handsome compensation in case of expropriation by the city.

Many people were displaced by the cutting of canals because this had been a heavily populated suburb. The city government found them a kind of spare site between the canal belt and the fortifications, later called the Jordan. For this part of the expansion a plan did not exist, and the city remained fairly uninvolved. The official surveyor Lucas Sinck started from the existing divisions of fields: ditches were deepened into canals and paths transformed into streets; on unused ground new quarters arose, and existing private buildings were trimmed. Although regulations about noxious trades applied in the Jordan as well, the city barely controlled them there: on the contrary, they used the area to accommodate industries that might be too noisy or smelly for the canal belt—gun and bell foundries, the city's saltpeter store, and various leather tanneries. Besides, for one decade it was still legal to build with timber there, although it had been banned elsewhere because of the danger of fire.

The Jordan evolved into a quarter where all kinds of small traders lived alongside the small canals and

Opposite, the detail from Balthasar Floriszon van Berckenroode's map of the city (1625) shows part of the western extension. The three main canals are, from the left, the Singel, Herengracht, and Keizersgracht. Between the last two we note the division into plots, with houses along the canals and gardens at the back. The last extension completed the half-moon of the canal belts. This happened when population growth slowed and not all plots bought were built on. A section east of the Amstel became a park, the Plantage. In the print below, the central roadway towards the Muiden Gate.

THE SHAPE OF THE CITY: THE SPIDER AND ITS WEB

At the demise of the Republic of the Seven United Provinces in 1795, when the hussars of the French Republic reached the Dam, the city of Amsterdam was shaped like a spider's web with the Dam—the square at the heart of the city—playing the part of the spider sitting virtually in the middle, a hem of military fortifications delimiting the web on three sides, and the whole web then resting on the harbor front on the Ij, which is the site, or at least one of the sites, at the root of the city's wealth and power. Today, at the center of what used to be the double line of piles that delimited the port, there now stands the main railway station.

The city possessed this shape as a result of successive extensions, as is clear from the plan shown below. Amsterdam is a river city. It has sprung up on both banks of the river Amstel, at the spot where the river flows into the Ij, which is, in turn, a tributary of the Zuiderzee. During its glorious history as the leading city in the Netherlands, Amsterdam was, in fact, connected to the North Sea via the Ij and the Zuiderzee.

In the first half of the 13th century, there was a small settlement at the mouth of the Amstel. A document dating back to 1275 refers to *homines manentes apud Aemstelledamme* — "people who are close to Amsterdam." The name "Amsterdam" means "dam on the Amstel." The inhabitants protected themselves from the water with dikes, fortifications, and embankments. From about 1270 there was a dam that regulated the use of the water in the areas lying behind it.

The growth of the settlement on the side to the north of the Ij took place in two basic stages until it acquired the semicircular shape of the city towards the end of the 17th cen-

c. 1350
c. 1380
1425
1487
after 1585
east, after 1593
west, after 1613

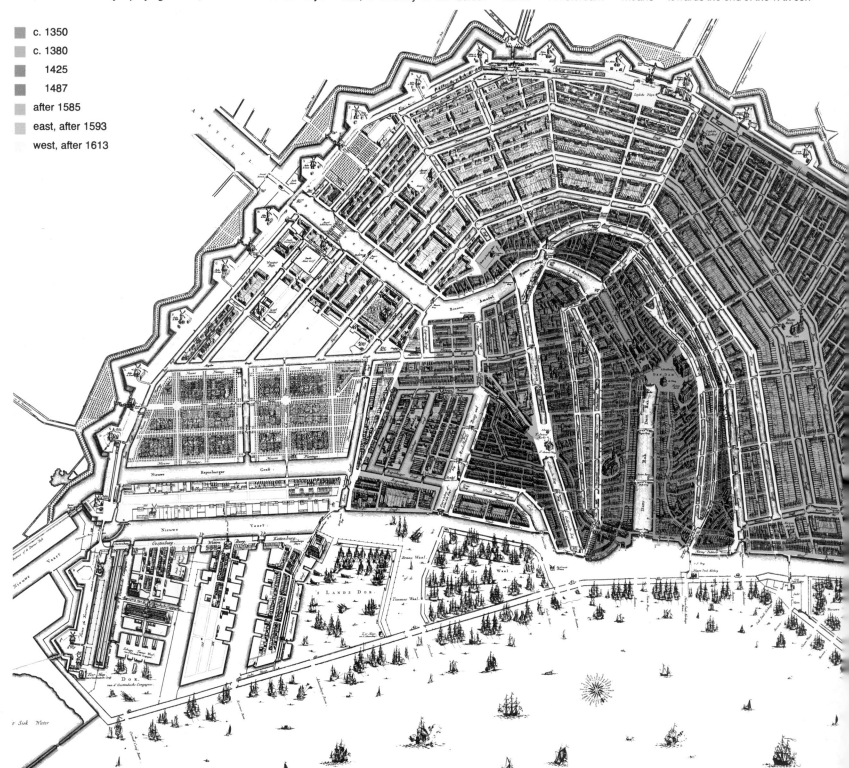

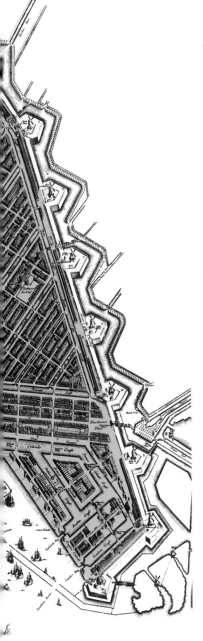

tury. There was a medieval stage, which was at full circle in 1425, and a subsequent stage, which stretched from 1580 up until the 1660s. This expansion was influenced by economic, demographic, and most importantly, military factors. The well-known rings of canals, which are clearly visible in the plan, are part of successive fortified perimeters.

As the city limits gradually spread outward, the canals,

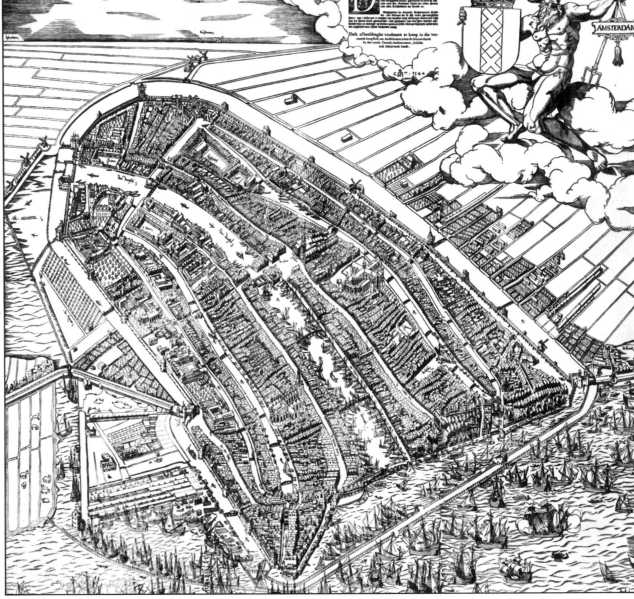

with their originally defensive function as moats, became useful arteries for the movement of traffic. The first canals, as can be seen from the city plan by Cornelis Anthoniszson, in 1544 (*on the right*), ran parallel to the last stretch of the course of the Amstel, which is now covered over. It was as a result of the expansion east and west, that the city assumed its semicircular shape.

As the city expanded, the first measure taken was to move the defense system outward. This was an expensive operation. A new canal had to be dug on the periphery, and new walls had to be put up. Then the land within the new enlarged circle had to be made fit to build on, so the water-logged bed had to be consolidated with earth. Finally, the land had to be parceled out. This was complicated by the fact that despite a ban many

people had built houses outside the fortifications, and these now lay within the extended works. The question debated by the city government in these cases was whether to expropriate these properties. The eagerness for personal gain and the administrators' desire to speculate were among the reasons behind certain measures.

The belt of canals that gave the city its semicircular form was created in the 17th century. In 1613 work started on moving the western defensive ring from north to south. The novel feature of this expansion was that, for the first time, the town-planning project was somewhat divorced from the pre-existing land structure, marked by canals and paths. Instead, it followed a closely defined model with a coherent link-up between canals, embankments, and construction lots. It was soon clear

that the patrician class had earmarked this residential zone for itself, which was obviously different from another new expansion scheme (in Jordan3, where the old and originally agricultural yardstick for land parceling was followed.

By the end of the 17th century Amsterdam was assuming more and more rapidly its spider's-web shape. This was produced by the ever-increasing rings of canals running ike arcs to the Ij where large merchant vessels still anchored to have their merchandise off-loaded onto smaller boats, to be taken to the city center, the Dam. This square is situated by the dam on the Amstel from which it had taken its name. It was one of the few city squares, and it was overlooked by the medieval town hall (and later by the new city hall built by Jacob van Campen). The Stock Exchange

and the fish market were not far off, and in the middle of the square stood the weigh house. If anything important happened in Amsterdam, it happened on the Dam. The spread of the city inland had also meant extending the harbor-front on the Ij. On either side of the mouth of the Amstel there were berths for ships protected by rows of piles, and the shipyards.

tradesmen settled on the avenues; in this respect it was a middle-class district, but in the many streets and blind alleys that soon grew between the houses, and in the rear lanes and back rooms, there lived crowds of poor workmen, sieve makers, pin makers, spinners, and the like.

A final aspect of the expansion in 1603 was the extension of the western port district, needed for the growing trade. More space was required for shipbuilding, warehouses, and several new industries. On artificial islands in this area some merchants built their own domains and housed their workers: men like Jan Bicker and Jacob Rael bought a whole island on which they had warehouses and dwellings built. From his own tall residence Bicker could survey his market gardens, wharves, and his fleet sailing in on the Ij.

The three parts of the city's expansion had thus been planned independently. Only for the first phase, the canal belt, was there a detailed plan, but during the last great period of growth in the 17th century nobody wished to revive the conflict of interest that had occurred within the city government.

In this expansion, the canal belt was extended in a half-moon shape around the city according to a definite plan, both with regard to fortifications and to housing—the latter, as a result of the plans of Cornelis Danckertsz, the city surveyor; Daniel Stalpaert, the city architect; and the engineer Coeck. In 1663, the city began the compulsory purchase of all land. Previous owners were not to have the choice of selling at auction, as in 1613. Moreover, a special building code was established to lay down precisely what architectural rules applied to the new quarter. They became an example for the administrative and technical procedures used in the extension of Utrecht (in 1663–64) and of Haarlem (in 1651).

Just as they had in the older part of the canal belt, mainly rich merchants and entrepreneurs came to live in the new area. From 1664, when the sale of lots began, many bought two lots for a "double house." If he bought additional land on the street or on the canal at the back, a landowner could build a nice coach house or garden pavilion. Thus, on May

Other aspects of 17th-century Amsterdam: below, the city from the west, with bastions, outer ditch, and the Haarlem Gate, in a painting by Hendrik Corneliszon (1566-1640). (Amsterdam Historical Museum)

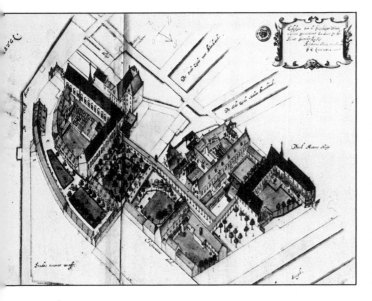

23 and 24, the brothers van Loon each bought two adjoining lots on the Herengracht, where each built a small palace 47 feet wide and 187 feet deep. One pair of lots cost 8,980 guilders, the other, 9,120, and the four lots on the backstreet 1,080 each, for coach houses. The two large houses next to each other, with identical interiors, stood at right angles to the canal and had a splendid outside staircase in the middle. The van Loons were eminent citizens: one was a juror and burgomaster as well as manager of the East India Company; the other was a merchant and official of the Exchange Bank and Loan Office.

On the other side of the canal, the plots were just as wide, but only 157 feet deep. If, as often happened, a man bought the rear lot on the Keizersgracht, he could obtain a plot of land with a depth of over 300 feet.

Contrary to expectation, the last stage of expansion proceeded slowly. After 1670, the population remained at a standstill, so that, in 1682, the region east of the Amstel was no longer used for housing. It was there that the city built the Plantage, a park for walking and for recreation, with lanes and gardens.

The cost of urban expansion was high, particularly since the old fortifications had to be razed and new ramparts and walls of earth put up to replace them. The laying of paths, the digging of canals, and the building of locks that were needed to regulate water supplies were expensive. Moreover, a whole new terrain had to be prepared for building by re-moving existing structures and raising the ground by means of vast quantities of sand brought in by ship from the dunes or from Govi, east of Amsterdam. Thousands of wheelbarrows carried the sand to be used for building onto the land. The city had to expand carefully lest the land remain unsold, with financial disaster the consequence.

Within a century, thousands of houses were built in Amsterdam, largely by unknown carpenters and masons. Master tradesmen mooted the projects, prepared the designs, estimated costs, and supervised building operations. Some also dealt in building materials, for which Amsterdam had special markets: one for mortar, several for timber, one for sand, and one for pantiles and flat tiles. Only the rich could commission known architects and order fashionable houses in Dutch Renaissance or classical style. The city itself commissioned some buildings. The large-scale town hall and many charitable institutions were designed by outstanding architects, and the numerous newly reformed churches were the pride of the city.

A considerable part of the newly developed area was meant for rich citizens. The merchant-rulers lived in the canal belt, in an exclusive residential district. For them, life and work became much more separate than before. The canal belt had grown into an isolated area for a group of people who, through their wealth and changed position, stood apart from the rest of the population. Their beautiful gardens

Above, the fish market, one of the four minor illustrations in a work by Claes Janszon Visscher, inscribed "In eternal memory of the city." Above left, aerial prospect of the St. Pietergasthuis, 1628, by Balthasar Floriszon, the main hospital, one of the various social institutions that are a credit to the mercantile metropolis.

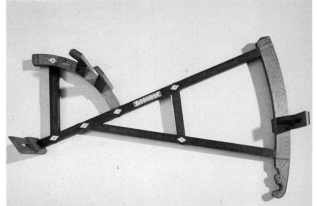

decorated with statues, leafy trees, and shrubs, were worthy of admiration, and the wide quays along the canals, where spacious rows of trees were planted, made this part of the city an agreeable residential area.

The middle classes lived much more modestly in neat, small houses with narrow stairs and windows, where goods could be displayed for sale on the turned-down shutters. Their houses stood in the crossroads of the canal belt, in the Jordan, and in the old city.

Hidden away in the back streets, in backrooms, cellars, or potting sheds, or even in the primitive huts under the arches of the city walls, lived the families of poor workers. Along with bands of vagabonds who did not have a roof over their heads, the poor made up a large part of the population.

The Asian trade

In the 15th and 16th centuries, the center of European trade shifted from the Mediterranean to the Atlantic and the North Sea. Spaniards and Portuguese displaced Venetians, Lisbon was, in turn, outpaced by Antwerp, and when, in 1585, the Spaniards took this city and closed off the Scheldt, it was Amsterdam that became the trading center of Europe. Toward 1600, the Dutch attempted to find the quickest route to India. Up to then, they had secured their Asian goods from Lisbon. King Philip II of Spain and Portugal repeatedly tried to place an embargo on the Hollanders, but his measures were really half-hearted because both parties profited from the trade. In 1591, when Philip tried to exclude the Hollanders from the pepper and spice trade by means of an international syndicate, it was mainly Hamburg that attracted the business, to Amsterdam's displeasure. With supplies from Lisbon declining, the price of pepper rose steeply, and some Amsterdam merchants decided to obtain these products from Asia themselves. In this they were inexperienced, and their geographical knowledge was as yet limited. After three vain attempts at reaching Asia via the Arctic Sea north of Russia, a fleet of four ships left Amsterdam in the spring of 1595 and met with more success. Heavily armed, well equipped, and pro-

Navigational instruments: left, a Dutch compass, about 1700, by Johannes van Keulen. Above left, 16th-century Dutch nautical astrolabe (both from the Amsterdam Dutch Historical Maritime Museum). Top, the Davis quadrant was an improvement on the astrolabe and quadrant because it enabled one to record the height of the sun looking the other way, thus avoiding the glare. Above, measuring distance, a decorative detail in Comitatus Hollandiae Novissima Descriptio, *by B. Florention (1629).*

Celestial (left) and terrestrial globe, by Jodocus Hondius, 1613. Hondius and Mercator (remembered for his projection used in nautical maps), both Flemings, were among the founders of Dutch cartography. The firm of Hondius continued in Amsterdam unchanged until the 17th century. The English, successors of the Dutch mastery of the seas, long called nautical maps "waggoners," after the Dutch cartographer Lucas Janszon Waghenaer, who published Spieghel der Zeevaert *("Mirror of Seafaring") in 1584, a collection of nautical maps for the coasts between Zuiderzee and Cadiz.*

vided with a considerable sum of money, the ships sailed south and, as the Portuguese had done before, rounded the Cape of Good Hope for Asia. One ship was lost and only 87 of a crew of 240 survived the trip, but, while the goods brought back barely covered the cost of the trip, the gain was still great because a direct route to Asia had been found!

The fleet had been financed by several Amsterdam shipowners who had joined forces in a company in order to spread the risk. Until 1601, only 15 north Netherlandish fleets from various companies had sailed to India; 65 ships took part, and 50 returned. For merchants, the disadvantage of successful trips was that pepper and spices dropped in price because of abundant supplies on the European market. In India, sellers profited from competition between Netherlanders, so that prices rose and the profit margin dropped. To solve these problems, long and difficult negotiations between five companies from Holland, one from Zeeland, and the States General led to the formation of a single large company in 1602: the East India Company. Its creation was primarily the work of Johan van Oldenbarnevelt,

grand pensionary of Holland, who represented the States General and sought both a profitable enterprise and a powerful military and economic weapon in the struggle against Spain and Portugal, with whom the republic was still at war.

The East India Company obtained from the States General the trade monopoly east of the Cape of Good Hope, and the right to make treaties in the name of the States General, to build forts, and to raise troops. It became a powerful body, with military, administrative, judicial, and diplomatic functions, a state within the state, for the company was hardly controlled by the States General. It was a kind of limited company, although investors had no voice in its operations and the management was required to account for its activities. In 1602, the company's initial capital was 6.5 million guilders, more than half from Amsterdam. The sums invested varied from 50 guilders to 85,000 and came from all reaches of society, although the large sums were from rich merchants who soon controlled the majority interest through purchase or inheritance. Of the first 1,143 investors, more than one in four were

The great instrument of Holland's colonial wealth was the East India Company founded in 1602. It was governed by the Heren XVII, the 17 administrators connected to the political circles particularly of Amsterdam. In 1644 they declared to the States General that "the places and fortresses conquered in the East Indies must not be considered national conquests but the property of private merchants, who have the right to sell them to whomsoever they wish, be he the king of Spain or some other enemy of the United Provinces." Above, the company's house in a print of 1663. Right, sailors embarking on a ship for Asia, detail from a painting by Jacob Storck, 1663 (private collection).

southern Netherlanders. The original capital was never increased, although the company took up short-term loans.

The company was divided into six "chambers," with seats in cities where pre-existing companies had their head offices: Middelburg, Rotterdam, Delft, Hoorn, Enkhuizen, and Amsterdam. There were 76 (later 60) administrators, of whom 20 were from Amsterdam, 12 from Zeeland, and 7 each from the other cities. Out of this body was chosen the administrative college of 17 (the "Heren XVII"), in which Amsterdam predominated. New managers from Amsterdam were appointed by the burgomasters so that a close link developed between the company and the ruling oligarchy. Each of the company's chambers operated independently, recruiting its own staff, fitting out its ships, and receiving the returning vessels. In the early years, there were no dividends. Only in 1610 did shareholders get a return, but in kind: either pepper, nutmeg, or mace.

In Amsterdam, consortia of merchants with capital were formed, often managers and members of their families, who bought up pepper in vast amounts in order to sell it later at a high price. In the 1620s and 1630s, the same monopolist merchants prevailed—Cornelis and Jacob Bicker, Elias Trip, and Cornelis van Campen,—despite strong protests from shareholders who saw their dividends drop, and small merchants who were unlucky. From 1642 on, imported goods were therefore sold openly by

auction—occasions that were announced throughout Europe in the press and in cargo manifests, so that many foreign merchants attended, as well. Dividends for shareholders were now fixed after a fleet came in, but before auction, since auction prices could be fairly well gauged beforehand.

In the 17th century, the chief Asian imports were pepper and spices, in demand throughout Europe as condiments. At first, the East India Company concentrated on the Indonesian islands, where, in 1619, they set up an office in Batavia (now Jakarta). From the outset, the Hollanders tried to gain monopolies by means of treaties with local sovereigns. The contracts were repeatedly broken because the company was unable to supply the inhabitants with adequate food and clothing by barter, and the destruction of native shipping even led to a shortage of basic necessities. Competition from the people of Makassar and Java, from the English and Spanish, and particularly from the Portuguese made life difficult for the company.

The Hollanders were ruthless toward the natives and regularly engaged in punitive expeditions. In the 1620s, the Banda islanders were either murdered or deported, after which the islands were colonized and the company acquired the monopoly for nutmeg and mace. Forty years later, after bloody wars with producers and even the destruction of clove trees, the company obtained the monopoly for cloves as well, concentrating on trade with Ambonia. However, a pepper monopoly always eluded them.

In addition, the company played a leading role in trade between Asian countries, partly for profit and partly from necessity. European means of exchange —namely, gold and silver—were not nearly valuable enough to pay for the Asian products that the company bought, so it had to resort to other Asian products as payment. It acquired a strong position in the far-flung and age-old trading network of Asia. In India, the company was based in Bengal, where sugar, saltpeter, and silk were obtained, and in Coromandel, the source of cotton goods with which spices were bought in the Moluccas. In northwest India, contacts were more difficult, but Suratte finally became a flourishing post, from which the company developed trade relations with Persia—where

there was competition from the English and the shah held an export monopoly. However, by means of generous bribes, trade here, too, came to be profitable. Persian silk was paid for in silver, partly from the republic and partly from Japan and Arabia.

In Ceylon, the company drove out the Portuguese after tough resistance, thus acquiring the monopoly for cinnamon, as well as nutmeg, pearls, shells, and about 100 elephants a year. The catching and taming of these animals was left to a certain caste of natives. Afterward, the elephants were sold at great profit in Coromandel and in Bengal.

Malacca and Malabar were taken from the Portuguese, and, from 1609 on, the Hollanders had a post in Japan, as well. They were the only Europeans allowed to remain after the others had been driven out. In 1641, they were allowed to settle on the artificial island of Deshima in the harbor of Nagasaki, but only on certain conditions: they could not leave the island without permission, and Christian services were forbidden, as was contact with Japanese citizens, except for prostitutes. Until the 19th century, Deshima was Japan's only window to the West. The Hollanders' main imports were Chinese silk, wool, cotton, skins, pigments, and sugar, while they exported gold, silver, and copper. Through its monopoly, the company made vast profits here. Chinese silk, in turn, was paid for with Japanese copper and silver. In Indochina, the company had varying success. Offices in Siam and Tonkin helped the trade with China and Japan.

About 1680, there were some 20 company offices in Asia. The conquest of these trading posts from natives and European competitors, and their administration and defense proved extremely costly for the company. All establishments were subject to the governor general in Batavia. Formally, he took orders directly from the "Seventeen Masters" at home, but their deliberations were a lengthy affair. After all, it took eight to nine months to travel from Amsterdam to Batavia, and seven months for the journey back. Company officials, therefore, often acted on their own initiative, which led to friction afterward. Many people left the republic for adventure, greed, ambition, or all three, and set out for India. The largest group was made up of seamen and

soldiers, the latter required as a conquering and occupying force. A smaller group consisted of high company officials, domestic servants, preachers, and tradesmen. Recent estimates put the number who left for India, from 1602 to 1700, at 324,000, of whom 113,000 returned, while the rest stayed in Asia—manning ships or offices—and later died there. The proportion who died on board ship was at most 10 percent, except in the early years.

We have the names and often the portraits of the company managers and high officials, but the tens of thousands of seamen are unknown, although, for nearly two centuries, they had sailed to Asia. These men defied storms and shipwreck, fought against pirates and other foes, for little pay and under fierce discipline. Three times a year, the company sent out a fleet. Recruitment of the rough types required for seamen was partly handled by middlemen, called "soul merchants" or "folk holders," who made a handsome profit at their job. They concentrated on unattached people, particularly foreigners, whom they enticed into lodgings, paying for their food and rent, until the company announced with drums and trumpets in every street and byway that one could enlist at East India House. In 1694, a German described how aspiring sailors, egged on by soul merchants dispensing brandy along with their chant, pushed and trampled each other to be first: "As soon as the door was open, hits and blows begin in earnest, for each wants to be first, as if nothing finer

could be had, although it might justly be described as selling oneself into slavery."

For the countless paupers swarming through Amsterdam, service at sea was better than the misery of unemployment at home. Company sailors came from the lowest strata of the population. Heads of poorhouses and orphanages regularly furnished seamen, and, as early as 1614, the governor general complained about their low standards: "There are among them rogues exiled from home, and soldiers who have served with the enemy. Some still have irons on their legs, others have gone insane and when they come here we have to prevent them from getting drunk and molesting and robbing the Chinese." In the 17th century, the company needed even more seamen. From 1602 to 1610, 8,000 had sufficed; between 1630 and 1640, there were 25,000; and from 1670 to 1680, there were some 45,000. Toward 1700, it became increasingly difficult to recruit seamen. Most of them were foreigners: Germans, Scandinavians, and Asians.

Sailors had some privileges, despite their rough existence. Food and shelter on board ship were free, and the company took some trouble to organize adequate provisions. A seaman was allowed to bring back a certain amount of goods from Asia for his own use. In spite of strict controls, smuggling by seamen was rife. This was a drawback for the company because much shipping space was lost and ships were strained by the heavy loads and, con-

The sailor's life: above, instruction in navigation, in a drawing by David Vinckboons, about 1620 (Rijksmuseum). Above left, sailors clewing up sail, from a picture by Willem van de Velde the Elder, 1653 (Amsterdam, Dutch Historical Maritime Musuem). Opposite top, the typical heavily armed East Indiaman with the flags of the company's Amsterdam chamber; glazed tiles, about 1640 (Rijksmuseum). Below, return to Amsterdam of the second Indian convoy, July 1599, from a canvas by Hendrick Vroom (Rijksmuseum). Led by Jacob Cornelis van Neck, it was rather luckier than the first attempt by Cornelis Houtman. The backers made profits of 400 percent.

sequently, were more difficult to maneuver. Hence, the severe controls on this "dirty trade." When a ship was captured, a sailor might get a share of the booty as a windfall, and there were special supplements for dangerous trips, for first sighting land, or for discovering a conspiracy. When a sailor finally reached home and obtained his wages after many formalities, he was easy prey for tavern keepers

and whores as he relaxed from the tensions of life at sea. Paid sailors were called "six-week masters," since, after a lordly life of a few weeks, they were again as indigent as before they signed up. An eyewitness in 1700 tells of the harmless prank of sailors hiring three coaches each: in the first was the sailor's hat, and the count's flag was hoisted; the coachman had to drive fast so that the flag would always fly. In the second coach were the sailor's pipe and tobacco box and, in the third, the sailor himself.

The company abused the poverty of many and brought riches to a few. Besides sailors, soldiers, and clerks, the company employed shipbuilders on its wharves at Kattenburg, and numerous suppliers. Goods from Asia were sold, on the whole, at three times their cost, the profit going to the small group of managers and shareholders.

The composition of the return loads changed during the 17th century. Until about 1650, half the value was pepper, but this was reduced to 11 percent by 1700. In the same period, fine spices dropped from 17 percent to 12 percent. Silk and cotton were the third-largest group of goods; toward 1700, textiles

Above, the Dutch surprise attack on three Portuguese galleons in Goa bay, September 30, 1639, from a painting by Hendrik van Anthonissen. Left, a plate dating from the late 17th century with the monogram VOC (East India Company). Opposite, the company's depot on the Hooghly in Bengal, 1665, from a picture by Hendrik van Schuylenburgh. The company's directors wrote to the States General in 1641: "this honourable company has grown fighting the Portuguese and has secured the monopoly of much maritime trade, and a mean annual profit between seven and ten million guilders is expected, which will go up year after year if the company is allowed to carry on in the same way."

THE EAST INDIA COMPANY

The Dutch East India Company—or the *Verenigde Oostindische Compagnie* (VOC)—was founded in 1602 as an economic and military weapon in the fight against Spain and Portugal, which, at that particular moment, were united under the same crown, and with which the Republic of the Seven Provinces was waging a war for survival. The East India Company came into being as the result of the merger of a certain number of already existing companies, which were in competition with each other. The States General granted the East India Company the trade monopoly with lands lying to the east of the Cape of Good Hope, and in the name of the States General it could sign treaties, build forts, and field troops. Supervision by the States General was always scant, and in the course of the 17th century the company, which was a sort of joint-stock company, grew in stature until it was the most powerful trading organization in the world.

In Asia the power of the company was wielded by the governor general in Batavia (present-day Jakarta, in Indonesia, the state which now embraces what used to be the Dutch East Indies). The governor general, a man usually from the patrician class, was in turn answerable to the East India Company governors back in the republic. During its roughly two hundred years of activity (it was ended in 1799) the company spared no effort, using large numbers of ships, arms, and men to enlarge, consolidate, and retain the commercial monopoly and political power that it won for itself in Asia. In fact, in that period trade with Asia was extremely lucrative. It was by no means exceptional to chalk up a profit of 300 percent on capital invested, and on top of that, the trade with Asia represented only a part of the worldwide commerce of the Seven Provinces. The company imported a huge range of goods from Asia: pepper, which, until 1650, accounted for one half of all imported merchandise, came from Sumatra and the Sunda Isles; from the Moluccan Islands came cloves, nutmeg, and mace (which is the fleshy skin around the nutmeg seed); from Ceylon came cinnamon;

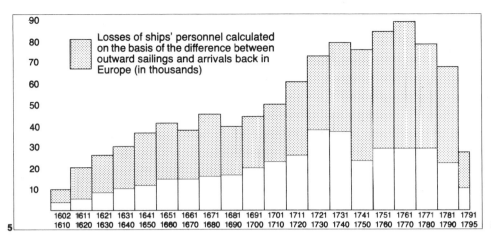

Losses of ships' personnel calculated on the basis of the difference between outward sailings and arrivals back in Europe (in thousands)

90																			
80																			
70																			
60																			
50																			
40																			
30																			
20																			
10																			

| 1602 | 1611 | 1621 | 1631 | 1641 | 1651 | 1661 | 1671 | 1681 | 1691 | 1701 | 1711 | 1721 | 1731 | 1741 | 1751 | 1761 | 1771 | 1781 | 1791 |
| 1610 | 1620 | 1630 | 1640 | 1650 | 1660 | 1670 | 1680 | 1690 | 1700 | 1710 | 1720 | 1730 | 1740 | 1750 | 1760 | 1770 | 1780 | 1790 | 1795 |

5

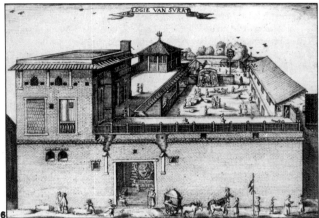

6

from China, Indochina, Persia, and Bengal came silk, both raw and processed; cotton and other textile fibers came from the Coromandel, from Surat, and from Bengal; Arabia and Indochina yielded dyes and medicinal products, precious wood and perfumery essences; saltpeter came from Bengal; and sugar from China, Java, and Bengal. In the 18th century, as the bulk trade in pepper and other spices declined somewhat, their place was taken by increased imports of textile fibers, china, and porcelain from Japan and China, and tea from China. Here are just a few images of the world in which the East India Company operated and traded: the island of Amboina, from the *Travel Journal* of Jacob C. van Neck, 1601 (*4*); the East India Company headquarters in Surat, from *Travels* by Pieter van den Broecke, 1613–1629 (*6*), and the market at Bantam, from the *Account of the First Dutch Voyage to the East Indies*, 1598 (*9*).

Europe had no merchandise to offer in exchange for the goods imported. Its products were either too costly or there was no demand for them. There were, indeed, outlets for woolen fabrics, mercury, cinnabar (which is a mineral of mercury), and African ivory, but in order to offset their imports, the Dutch took an active part in trading in Asia itself, and in particular—in addition to unusual gifts destined for local potentates—to take to Asia, as a means of payment, quantities of gold and silver, either minted or in ingots. Furthermore, the company exported to Asia, for its own use, construction materials such as bricks or lead, weapons, ammunition, fittings, and equipment for its fleet, clothing, food, wine, and beer. The company's squadrons—the basic sailing formation was the squadron, and each one had to be able to defend itself—sailed for Asia three times a year; at Easter, in

September, and in December or January. The route (*1*) was a fixed one, established on the basis of experience gained about the prevailing winds: either through the English Channel or around the British Isles, then out into the Atlantic as far as the Cape Verde Islands, running close to the shores of Brazil, and then eastward towards the Cape of Good Hope (*2*, Table Mountain Bay in 1683, *by Aernout Smit*) where a supply post was set up in 1652; from here they sailed across the southern Indian Ocean almost as far as Australia, and then turned north toward the Sunda Straits and Batavia (*3, shown here in a painting by A. D. Willaerts, 1649*). Some vessels reached Ceylon by way of the Mozambique Channel. The voyage took eight or nine months, outward, but the return journey only took seven because of favorable winds and currents.

The company built its own ships, which, to begin with, weighed about 600 tons and

were less than 135 feet in length. In time the tonnage increased to 1100–1200 tons and the length to 165 feet. There were between 200–300 men on board each vessel: sailors, soldiers for the Asian garrisons, officials, and craftsmen. The crews were mostly foreign. Maritime traffic was quite considerable, as is shown by *tables 7 and 8*, which give, by decade, the movements of ships sailing to and from Asia, and the number of persons sailing in both directions, too. No less

impressive was the loss of human life as a result of accidents, shipwrecks, war, and disease. On the return journey losses ran at between 6–15 percent, with peaks of up to 23 percent in the 18th century. These figures are given in *table 5*; the calculations are based on the differences in numbers between persons sailing to Asia and persons returning home to Europe.

VOC SHIPS SAILING TO AND FROM ASIA					
	to Asia	from Asia		to Asia	from Asia
1602-10	76	44	1701-10	280	193
1611-20	117	50	1711-20	311	245
1621-30	141	71	1721-30	382	319
1631-40	157	75	1731-40	375	311
1641-50	164	93	1741-50	314	234
1651-60	206	103	1751-60	291	244
1661-70	238	127	1761-70	292	233
1671-80	232	133	1771-80	290	244
1681-90	204	141	1781-90	297	228
1691-1700	235	156	1791-95	118	123

7

VOC PERSONNEL SAILING TO AND FROM ASIA					
	to Asia	from Asia		to Asia	from Asia
1602-10	8,000 }	8,000?	1701-10	49,000	22,000
1611-20	20,000? }		1711-20	60,000	26,000
1621-30	25,000	7,000?	1721-30	72,000	38,000
1631-40	29,000	9,000.	1731-40	77,000	37,000
1641-50	36,000	11,000?	1741-50	74,000	23,000
1651-60	41,000	14,000?	1751-60	81,000	31,000
1661-70	37,000	14,000	1761-70	87,000	29,000
1671-80	45,000	15,000	1771-80	77,000	29,000
1681-90	39,000	16,000	1781-90	67,000	22,000
1691-1700	44,000	19,000	1791-95	27,000	9,000

8

9

made up 55 percent in value. Less important, although still profitable, were indigo, saltpeter, tin, copper, and sugar. Most goods were stored at East India House, whose fragrant odor could be detected from afar, because of the vast amount of spices it contained.

Atlantic trade

In the 16th century, trade between Europe, West Africa, America, and the Caribbean was in the hands of the Spaniards and Portuguese. The French and English also took part, but the Dutch participation came relatively late. Dutch merchants established in Amsterdam did, indeed, ship Negro slaves to South

America, and, at the end of the 16th century, they began to make direct contacts with West Africa and the Caribbean. After the Twelve Years' Truce with Spain (1609–21), they redoubled their attempts to chase the Spaniards and Portuguese from the Atlantic. To this end, in 1621 the West India Company was set up; like the East India Company, it could sign treaties, build forts, govern, administer justice, and enlist soldiers. Its trading monopoly covered the region between Africa and the two Americas. The West India Company, in which Amsterdam was dominant, began by acting as sea raiders. Countless Spanish and Portuguese ships were taken, with their booty of sugar, hides, cotton, tobacco, and gold. As a result, by 1630 the West India Company was able

to make serious efforts to dominate the gold and slave trade in West Africa and the production and trade of sugar in Brazil.

The Brazilian adventure, although short-lived, was spectacular. After taking the main Portuguese trading posts on the coast, in 1637 the West India Company appointed John Maurice of Nassau, a distant cousin of the stadholders Maurice and Frederik Henry, as governor and supreme commander of the army and fleet. Under his vigorous guidance, the boundaries of the South Atlantic empire of the West India Company were greatly extended. John Maurice of Nassau conquered the main African slave market São Jorge de Mina, in Guinea, which intensified the slave trade.

The Far East: below left, concert at the depot of Deshima, on a Japanese scroll, about 1690. This was the only contact between Japan and the West during the shogunate of Tokugawa. Below right, the island of Onrust, near Batavia, main depot of the East India Company, painting in the style of A. Storck, 1699 (Amsterdam Historical Museum, on loan from the Rijksmuseum). Bottom, Zeelandia, the fort and Dutch depot on Formosa, 1624.

The Spaniards and Portuguese had long since observed that American Indians were unsuitable for working in cane fields, sugar mills, or gold and silver mines because they could not withstand the ruthless working system and the white man's diseases. Besides, their numbers had greatly diminished through wars against the Europeans and each other. The Portuguese had, therefore, sought the large-scale importation of African Negro slaves, and the Dutch now gained a sizable share in this profitable trade. Under John Maurice, some 10,000 Europeans served in Brazil, among them many French, English, Germans, and southern Dutch. Most of them were in garrisons or in coastal navigation. Nassau was not always successful. The attack

on Bahia, the capital of Portuguese Brazil, backfired, as did an attempt at gaining a foothold in Chile for an attack on Peru. Moreover, the West India Company could not attract Europeans to settle the land. In 1664, the contract with Nassau was not renewed, and, after his return, Portuguese planters who had remained in Dutch territory staged an uprising because they had no outlet for their sugar when the market in Amsterdam stagnated. A long struggle followed, and the Dutch were finally defeated in 1654. So ended the Brazilian episode.

The only territories that the Dutch retained in the South Atlantic were the Antilles and Surinam (independent since 1975) on the Guyana coast. The significance of Nassau lies, above all, in the scientific investigations he ordered. With him went cartographers, naturalists to study plants and animals, and astronomers and geographical observers. His personal physician studied tropical diseases and native remedies. Two painters recorded the Brazilian landscape, and when Nassau returned in 1645, he took back a large collection of Brazilian curios to furnish

The Americas were reserved for the West India Company, which was less successful than the East India firm. From the top, a slave market at Dutch Pernambuco, Brazil, today's Recife (Zacharias Wagner, Dresden, Kupferstichkabinett); cane sugar presses in Brazil, drawing by Frans Post (Brussels, Musée des Beaux Arts).

along the Hudson, Delaware, and Connecticut rivers, was, above all, an enterprise of the Amsterdam contingent of the West India Company. Beaver and otter skins were bought from the Indians and shipped to Amsterdam, partly for the city's furriers and partly for re-export. As in Brazil, the West India Company tried to implement an active policy of settlement by promising the settlers all kinds of advantages. Thus, the company refrained from imposing taxes in New Netherland and allowed people to trade independently. In the 1660s, there were seven to eight thousand Europeans there from Holland, England, France, the southern Netherlands, and Finland, and some Jews and Negroes, as well. The expansion caused occasional friction with the natives. Besides, there was a major political conflict: in 1664, the English, who had earlier settled further south, took New Netherland and rebaptized its main settlement "New York."

The most successful activity of the West India Company was the West African trade. From about 1590, the Hollanders acquired a place in the trading of ivory, pepper, copper, dyewood, and gold, brought to the coast by African middlemen. Trading in slaves was soon added. After the loss of Brazil, this lucrative but inhuman market shifted to the Caribbean, where a great demand for slaves arose when the French and English began to grow sugar cane.

The island of Curaçao, legally under the jurisdiction of Amsterdam, became the central slave market. Between 1626 and 1650, an estimated 175,000 slaves were imported to America, and the number more than doubled over the next 25 years, during which time Hollanders alone brought over more than 75,000. From 1668 to 1672, they imported a yearly average of 4,500 slaves, the losses during the trip running 20 to 25 percent. Dutch trading posts and reinforcements arose on the Ivory Coast, Gold Coast, Slave Coast, and Grain Coast, where the company bought goods and slaves in return for European products such as weapons, copper, iron, and brandy. The West India Company posts were small: besides a few hundred slaves, rarely would there be more than 100 Europeans—merchants and soldiers tormented by heat, disease, and boredom. The turnover of Europeans was high: one in three

his new small classical palace at The Hague (now the Mauritshuir museum). In 1648, the result of these researches was published in *Historia Naturalis Brasilia,* for two centuries the standard work on the people and natural history of Brazil.

North America

Another small area of note in the Atlantic trade was New Netherland, part of today's City of New York. In 1624, the West India Company extended the trading post of New Amsterdam, founded a few years earlier on Manhattan Island, which had been bought from the natives for 60 guilders. New Netherland, with trading posts and small farming settlements

newcomers died within a year. In general, the West India Company did not allow its personnel to bring their wives along. The preachers at Elmina, one of the main slave markets, constantly protested against this rule because of what they saw as the evil consequences. In 1668, one of them described the personnel thus: "Their daily work is whoring and adultery in the fort, almost in everybody's sight, getting drunk daily . . . and constant cursing." As to the

peditions for conquest and garrisons for occupation consumed such vast amounts of capital that the company nearly went bankrupt in 1674. It survived, only to be replaced by a new West India Company, which took over the old company's possessions and part of its debts.

Whaling

The third company of importance to Holland's economy was the Greenland Company, whose job was catching whales. This profitable business was an outgrowth of the Asian trade, because, while looking for a northern passage to India, from 1594 to 1596, the explorers had discovered large schools of whales. After a few unsuccessful independent trips, various shipowners joined forces in the Northern or Greenland Company, although each group operated on its own. The States General gave them exclusive rights to hunt whales and seals between Novaya Zemlya and the Davis Straits. Soon all the main ports in Holland and Zeeland were taking part.

The Northern Company flourished because whales were abundant and the demand for whale products was great. The boiled blubber yielded train oil, which, in turn, was needed for soapmaking and was used for lubrication and lighting. Tanners used it to soften leather, and the wool industry, to prepare wool fiber for spinning. Moreover, shipbuilders used it as an admixture to paint and tar. Whalebone was used for building (for railings and doorways) and for funerary monuments. The pliable bones became picture and mirror frames, knife handles, measuring rods, boxes, fans, umbrellas, corsets, and struts for crinolines.

At first, whales were caught near the coast of Spitsbergen and Jan Mayen island. On Amsterdam island, northwest of Spitsbergen, the Amsterdammers built the first train-oil cookers, and the other members of the company followed. Because of the fierce cold and pack ice in winter, whaling was confined to spring and summer. The animals were hunted from sloops and killed by harpoons. The body was towed to the coast, where the blubber was removed. This was boiled and the resulting train oil was put in barrels. In autumn, the whalers left until

reasons for going to these miserable places, the Amsterdam poet and doctor W. G. van Focquenbroch, second in command at Elmina, had no doubt: gold, he maintained, "is the motive for forgetting the pleasures of life for one year or six, as if one were dead." His years in the tropics were not rewarded: he died in Elmina in 1675.

The West India Company was much less successful than the East India Company. It never succeeded in obtaining a monopoly anywhere, partly because of stiff competition from French and English companies who were often financed by Dutch capital, and partly because of extensive smuggling in which the Dutch, too, took part. Only the slave trade was lucrative for the West India Company. Ex-

Left, Dutch interior at the equator, portrait of Dirck Wilre in Elmina castle, painted by Pieter de Wit, 1669 (Rijksmuseum). Below, colonial consciousness: the people of the world render homage to Amsterdam, seen here as a girl (the "Stedemaagd," personifying the city) seated with her right hand idly resting on the globe and watched by Mercury. Picture by Gérard de Lairesse (1640-1711) (Amsterdam Historical Museum). Opposite above, the courtyard of the West India House in Amsterdam. Below, colonial traces in city architecture: top of façade with statues of negroes and American Indians.

the following season, when they often found their posts destroyed by nature or by competitors. In the winter of 1633–34, two teams remained behind as an experiment, one on Jan Mayen island and the other on Spitsbergen. Only the latter survived, so that the following winter another group of seven men was left on Spitsbergen, but they, too, perished tragically. Their bodies were found in the spring, some in coffins and others in their berths. This was the last entry in their diary: "The four of us still alive are lying in our berths. We should like to eat if someone was still strong enough to light the fire. We cannot move for pain. We pray God with folded hands to release us from this sad world." After this, no further attempts were made at wintering. The victims' grave was rediscovered by a Dutch expedition in 1980.

In 1642, the Northern Company was abolished, and whaling became a free industry. As whales retreated from the coasts around Spitsbergen and Jan Mayen island, hunting had to take place on the high sea. Now the blubber was removed at sea and put in barrels on board ship. From 1670 on, the whales retreated even further north, so that whalers had to

venture into polar waters. This made the enterprise risky, since the ships ran the danger of being crushed by the ice. Sometimes a crew was forced to winter, which usually meant that most of them died of frost, hunger, exhaustion, or scurvy. If their ship became free again, it might drift aimlessly for weeks or months like a ghost ship, with a dead crew.

Whaling provided work for many people: ships' crews, train-oil boilers, and shipbuilders. In the peak years of 1684 and 1721, some 250 ships sailed with about 10,000 men in all. This was work for highly qualified seasonal labor, in which many men from north Germany took part. In later years, the train oil was processed in Holland, in installations that grew up particularly in Zaanstreek, north of Amsterdam. Because of their evil smell, these factories were called "reekies." In Amsterdam the memory of whaling is kept alive by the Greenland warehouses on Keizersgracht 38–44.

European trade

Trade with Asia, Africa, and America strongly appealed to the imagination. Printed stories of travel in strange, faraway countries were very popular in Holland, and the people, animals, and plants of tropical lands were often shown in paintings and prints. So were the ships of the East India Company and the trading posts of both the East and West India Companies. Still, trade outside of Europe was only a small part of Holland's total activity. Shipping in Europe, except for Russia and Mediterranean traffic, was not only older, but also greater and more intensive. This trade was less spectacular and more routine, so that it figures less often in pictures. Dutch freight grew enormously from 1580 to 1600. For a long time, the Dutch fleet was greater than those of England, Scotland, and France combined. In the mid-17th century, Holland had about 1,750 freighters. They were buyers, sellers, middlemen, shippers, and financiers. Directly or indirectly, they formed the link between producer and consumer: directly, when delivering the goods to the buyer; indirectly, when storing the goods in the republic.

The swift development of the Dutch into European sea traders was helped by the fact that ships

development of the special vessel, called the fluit, from about 1595. This was a fast, three-master of large capacity and low draft, which could thus use shallow ports. It had a characteristic round stem fore and aft, a bulging body, and a reduced deck, because tolls through the sound were levied on the basis of deck size. By increasing the volume and decreasing the deck surface, the shippers greatly diminished their dues. The fluit needed only a small crew— from 8 to 22, according to its size—and became the foremost ship, by far, in European sea trade, although it sailed to Asia and America, as well. It was from 93 to 117 feet long and weighed between 150 and 400 tons.

Traditionally, Baltic shipping was the most important aspect of Amsterdam's trade activity, from which much of the city's prosperity resulted. Thus, the cog was often used as the symbol of Amsterdam: it was by means of the cog that medieval trade was conducted in the north. Grain exports from the Baltic were vital for the whole of Europe, but, in addition, there were exports of timber, hides, stockfish, copper, tar, hemp, flax, and saltpeter. These products came mainly from Poland and Prussia, where Danzig, Riga, and Königsberg were the principal ports. The north needed foodstuffs, such as dairy products and North Sea herring; salt and textiles, and luxury goods such as wine, silk, and spices were likewise sent there. Each ship sailing to the Baltic had to pay a toll at the sound. The Danish toll office

The north and the whale. Top, hunting the whale, detail from a canvas by A. van Salm (Amsterdam Historical Museum). Above, remains of Dutch settlement for whale oil extraction on Spitsbergen (17th century). Top right, installation for whale oil extraction by the Amsterdam chamber of the Greenland Company, on Jan Mayen Island; detail from a painting by Cornelis Willemszon de Man, 1639 (Rijksmuseum).

were built more cheaply in Holland, and, besides, capital was obtainable there at lower rates (reputable merchants could readily borrow at 3 to 4½ percent) and there were no competitors. Because of interest troubles, France and England had to impose protectionist measures, between 1650 and 1700, while Spain and Portugal concentrated mainly on trade in the Atlantic and Asia, where, even so, they steadily lost ground; north German ports were no longer able to challenge the republic in an economic struggle. Moreover, the republic was favorably located on the important route from northwest to southeast Europe, and linked to the hinterland by the Maas and the Rhine. Dutch shipping was much enhanced by the

The Baltic, Sweden, Russia. Below, loading timber onto a Dutch ship on the Swedish coast. Right, the port of Archangel, in a painting by Bonaventura Peeters the Elder, 1644 (Greenwich, National Maritime Museum). Bottom, the Sound, key to the Baltic, painting by H. C. Vroom, 1620. The ruling class of Amsterdam was always intent on keeping the Sound open, even if this went against the republic's general policy.

records are extant and give some idea of the huge Baltic trade. From 1600 to 1650, yearly grain exports ranged from 84,000 to 100,000 tons—and, perhaps, even more. Of this, 30 to 40 percent went to Amsterdam and the rest was taken by shippers from Holland or other European countries to ports elsewhere. Between 1580 and 1680, an average 58 percent of the ships that passed through the sound came from ports in Holland, of which three quarters were from Amsterdam. In 1666, it was estimated that about three-quarters of the active capital on the Amsterdam stock exchange was invested in Baltic trade. Profits were, indeed, enormous. Recent estimates put dividends for capital invested in trade along the Danzig-Amsterdam route at 30 to 40 per-

cent, and along the route from Danzig to Spain at 100 percent and even more.

The vast grain exports from the Baltic decreased between 1650 and 1700, partly because wars had destroyed the large grain areas in Poland and Prussia, and partly because importers like Spain and Italy began to grow rice, maize, and buckwheat. The large grain supplies taken to Amsterdam were partly for the city itself, but mostly for re-export. About four fifths of Amsterdam's warehouse space was used for grain. The authorities kept strict records of the amount of grain in the city in order to forestall famine in times of need. They had grain stores built, bought up grain themselves and, if necessary, prohibited its export. When grain prices rose sharply, the

city issued lead tokens to the poor, with which they could buy bread below the fixed price; the city made up the difference to the bakers. When, in 1700, a serious grain shortage developed, the city commissioned its trading agents in Danzig and Elsinore to send back loaded ships at once, and, in addition, the city tried to buy back grain ordered by Spain and Italy.

This well-balanced policy was not merely philanthropic: the burgomasters knew only too well that a food shortage could drive the poor to despair, since bread was the main part of their diet. Joost van den Vondel, the foremost 17th-century Dutch poet, translating a Latin tragedy by his compatriot Hugo de Groot, echoes this view, which de Groot's English

In the Mediterranean the Dutch had to face the Barbary pirates. Bottom right, encounter with Barbary galleys, painted by Jacob G. Loef. Right, model of a fluit, a typical Dutch cargo vessel. Its bridge is not as wide as the bulging body, for the tolls in the Sound went by the surface of the bridge. Below, naval routes from Amsterdam on Europe's coasts.

translator, the poet Francis Goldsmith, put thus (1652): ''From whence great danger to the state still grows/For raging hunger no allegiance knows.''

From Norway, the Hollanders imported vast quantities of timber and stockfish. Timber was needed for building ships and houses. The wharves of the East and West India companies, the admiralty, and private shippers required huge amounts, as well, and when Amsterdam spread out and large new houses rose along the canals, the demand for timber became greater still. A good deal of imported timber was re-exported. Stockfish and dried cod were, likewise, imported on a large scale. Ship's victuals included stockfish almost daily.

From the end of the 16th century, the Hollanders

EUROPEAN TRADE ROUTES FROM AMSTERDAM 1595-1620

traded with Russia, too. The Muscovite trade was in the hands of Amsterdammers, who obtained leather, furs, grain, tallow, and potash from the ports of Archangel and Kola—and even luxury products that had come overland by caravan from Asia, such as Persian silk and Chinese musk and rhubarb. Some Amsterdam vessels traveled directly from Russia to Italy with furs, leather, and great quantities of caviar. Russia took mainly luxury goods readily obtained in Amsterdam's staple market, such as cloth, jewels, ornaments, lace, gold- and silverware, wine, paper, mirrors, ivory, Brazilian timber, and weapons.

For trade with neighboring countries such as north Germany, Denmark, Scotland, England, northeast France, and the southern Netherlands, small ships of 40 to 80 tons were used. From 1600 to 1650, regular services developed, calling at fixed and strictly regulated times in ports like Hamburg, Bremen, Antwerp, London, and Rouen. Grain, timber, linen, and yarn came through Hamburg. Cloth, coal, tobacco, lead, malt, and several varieties of fish were exported from England and Scotland, while linen, herring, cheese, wine, salt, grain, train oil, and timber were sold there. The southern Netherlands received grain, dairy produce, and everyday articles, mainly paid for in silver because the south exported little. France, too, bought dairy products from Holland, herring, cloth, train oil, soap, grain, and timber, in long established ex-

change for large quantities of salt and wine.

For some time, trade with Spain and Portugal had been erratic, because they were at war with the republic. However, these countries were commercially interdependent. As Spain and Portugal concentrated on trade outside of Europe, particularly in Asia and South America, they came to depend on others for European trade, and the Dutch made use of this. In the republic there were discussions on whether "trade with the enemy" was right or not, but economic interests prevailed. From Portugal came salt, tobacco, wine and brazilwood; from Spain, iron, wool, oil, and fruit. In exchange, the Hollanders brought textiles, flax, grain, Russian leather, maritime stores, and even equipment for whole war-

Trade with Europe and the Mediterranean. Left, portrait of Thomas Hees, resident of the States General at Algiers, Tunis, and Tripoli, by Michiel van Musscher, 1787 (Rijksmuseum). Below right, a Dutch ship loading for France. Below left, distribution of grain to the poor, detail from a picture by Hendrik Bloemaert. Shipping grain from the Baltic to southern Europe was a basic feature of Amsterdam's trade; her dominant position in this allowed the civic authorities to ensure that this staple was always available to the city's people.

known north of the Alps, while the Italians were amazed by the realism of Flemish painters. From about 1590, northern Netherlanders, too, developed large-scale traffic with Italy, particularly with Venice. This trade, almost wholly controlled by Amsterdam, arose in part because of regular food shortages in Italy resulting from bad harvests and a growing population. By 1596, there was a Venetian envoy in Amsterdam, and the first Dutch consul in Venice was appointed in 1614. Flourishing Dutch trading houses arose there, and in Amsterdam the small court of Venetia kept alive the memory of the wealth that the merchant Jacob Stoffels had earned in Venice. Italy imported grain, and also textiles, dairy products, fish, and spices; it exported wine,

If commercial navigation on Europe's coasts and across oceans was the mainstay of Amsterdam's economic growth, so was the necessary infrastructure provided by an alert government. Left, the list of commodity prices on the Amsterdam Stock Exchange, June 4, 1674. Below, the Grain Exchange on the Damrak, print by J. Schenk, c. 1725. Right, the Amsterdam Stock Exchange, center of the city's trade toward 1668, in a picture by Job Adriaenszon Berckheyde (Rotterdam, Museum Boymans-van Beuningen).

ships. The Hollanders sailed to Spain and Portugal under a neutral and, therefore, a false flag. From time to time, Spanish ports confiscated Dutch ships, but this could not prevent trade. It flourished particularly during the Twelve Years' Truce, and after the Peace of Münster, in 1648, which finally ended the Eighty Years' War, trade spread unhindered.

For Amsterdam, traffic in the Mediterranean and to Russia and Asia was new in the late 16th century. It had long been the province of the southern Netherlanders, who established themselves in Italy, while Venetians and Genoese came to Bruges and Antwerp. This contact was fruitful not only in commerce, but also in art. Italian art thus became well

fruit, oil, silk, alum, and marble. For building large houses for the gentry, and the new town hall on the Dam, large quantities of marble were required.

With the Levant, too, the Hollanders kept intensive contacts; there, they acquired silk, textiles, angora, and camels' hair for Leyden's textile mills. In North Africa, trade took place mainly from a Dutch base in Leghorn and the Dutch had an active hand in traffic between Mediterranean ports.

"Straits traffic" through the Straits of Gibraltar was not without risk. Until 1648, there was the danger of attack from Spanish and Portuguese enemy ships. In Spanish parts of Italy, too, Dutch ships could be seized. Then there was the longstand-

Finished in 1611 on the model of similar institutions in London and Antwerp, it was not, as now, a place for trading share certificates, but one for dealing in goods (literally "stocks").

ing threat from Barbary pirates in whose service there were, indeed, some Hollanders, with colorful names like Simon the Dancer, Jacob the Whorekeeper, and Thomas the Swindler. Booty was sold in North African towns, and the crews became galley slaves. Sometimes, after difficult diplomatic negotiations, they could be bought free. That is why the Hollanders set up consulates in the main cities of North Africa. To diminish the risk, the States General regulated armament and crew size. Traveling in convoy was usually compulsory in the Mediterranean. From about 1660, French and English traffic there began to exceed that of Holland.

Services to trade

In the 17th century, Amsterdam was Europe's foremost commercial center, having replaced Antwerp in that position. The city, likewise, became Europe's financial center, which meant that goods from all over the world could be obtained there: one could buy grain for a whole town, and rulers could order an entire fleet with crews and equipment, or

start an art collection, or borrow money to wage war or to build palaces. Amsterdammers procured the goods and then stored them.

This huge enterprise was due not only to merchants' initiative, but also to reliable services under official control. The city government spared no effort to make Amsterdam ever more attractive commercially. A merchant who wished to trade in a city had to be sure that services were well organized and reliable. A shipper had to know precisely what were the current prices and where he could store goods, who would quickly lend him money at low interest and where he could profitably deposit his own funds. It helped if he could send off his ship as soon as he bought a complete load of goods, knowing that they were needed elsewhere. This involved using trustworthy agents, hiring sailors, and insuring ships—which the city magistracy did their utmost to provide. These services were not altogether new: they had a long tradition behind them, many of the practices having been in use in Antwerp, but, in the late 16th and early 17th centuries, these measures were extended and perfected. The trend toward

The Ij, the port and city of Amsterdam, engraving by Pieter Bast, 1599. Note the double row of stakes closing the inner port, and the outlet of the Amstel crossed by many bridges. The bigger ships could not enter the port but anchored in the Ij. Loading and unloading involved lighters. The port was the heart of the city's economic life, with all kinds of goods coming from everywhere, and leaving from warehouses to their final destinations. Amsterdam's strength lay in its central position as an international market. In 1665, the London merchant Josiah Child wrote of Amsterdam and the Dutch that "riches and multitude of shipping is the envy of the present and may be the wonder of all future generations: and yet the means whereby they have advanced themselves are sufficiently

municipal protectionism, begun in the 16th century, increased: Amsterdam armed itself against competition not only from abroad but also from other cities of the republic. Some of these services were established in a building, such as the Exchange, the Exchange Bank, and the weighing stations.

The Exchange

This was the place where merchants went to do business. In the Middle Ages, they conferred in hostelries or in the open. Since such methods were too restricted, in 1608 the city decided to install an Exchange building and commissioned the municipal architect Hendrick de Keyser to build it. At the city's expense, he traveled to London to study the Exchange there, and the one he built was, indeed, inspired by those in London and Antwerp. The building, situated on the Dam, was ready in 1611: it was characterized by a rectangular court framed by a colonnade and gallery. The Amstel flowed under it, from the Rokin to the Damrak. Above the gallery there were shops selling luxury articles and curios.

Merchants of all nationalities met in the central court. Near each column a specific article—there were from 400 to 600 of them—was negotiated, according to the weekly Exchange sheets of the 17th century. (The earliest dates from 1585.) These publications were sent all over Europe so that foreigners could form a reliable picture of prices.

The Exchange was a lively and clamorous place where one could meet men of all nationalities. It was subject to strict rules, and trading was limited to fixed times: from 1 to 2 o'clock in the afternoon. Latecomers had to pay a fine to the poor and the orphans of the Alms House. It was forbidden to bring goods to the Exchange, or to sell news sheets there; railing, shouting, hitting, and, particularly, the brandishing of knives or pistols were strictly forbidden, and beggars and children were kept out.

Besides goods, money, too, was traded there. From 1650 on, there was increasing speculation in goods, shares, and public loans. One object of such transactions that has become famous is the tulip. The tulip trade began in Haarlem, but in Amsterdam, too, people speculated on the flowers both in the Ex-

THE EXCHANGE BANK: A FINANCIAL CITADEL

The Amsterdam Exchange Bank (*Amsterdamsche Wisselbank*) was founded in 1609. It was modeled on the Venetian *Banco di Rialto* (1587). Its aim was to facilitate methods of payment, which were complicated to manage and difficult to supervise, and thus hindered the development of trade. In Europe there were a large number of currencies in circulation; their value varied greatly, and they were often made of base alloy. All this made monetary exchanges quite chaotic. In the republic alone there were some 14 cities that had a right to mint coins. Here are some of the coins from those days: a *ducat* from the city of Amsterdam, 1672 (*1*); a *daalder,* a coin worth one and a half florins from the States of Holland,

1683 (*2*); a *duit,* a small divisional coin from the States of Holland, 1702 (*4*). The coins shown in *figure 3,* however, are something of a numismatic oddity: this is a gold coin with no legal rate of exchange, coined in Hamburg (the city is shown in the right-hand picture); the picture on the left shows the coats-of-arm of Hamburg, Nuremberg, Venice, and Amsterdam, four cities where there were exchange banks. When it came to settling payments, merchants had to go to an authorized money changer (*6,* The Money Changer, *by Rembrandt, 1627, Berlin*) for each transaction to have a valuation made of the money in their pockets; then they had to exchange the coins for others that would be accepted in the countries to

which they were going. In addition, they were beholden to private cashiers who, like the money changers, earned a direct profit as a result of the confused monetary situation. The Exchange Bank improved matters by providing money exchange and funding for the public. It was situated in the city hall (*5, a detail of a wooden "bench" in the bank, with cornucopia and coins*) and the administrators were selected from among the patricians by the *vroedschap* or city council. The city authorities required all exchange transactions of one hundred Flemish pounds sterling (600 florins) or more to be deposited for collection at the bank. So merchants had to open accounts. In time even monarchs, cities, and governments had their own accounts at the Amsterdam Exchange Bank. *Table 7* gives a progressive breakdown of the number of account holders at the bank during its entire existence (1609–1820). The peak

occurs in 1721 with more than 2,900 clients. The services offered by the bank included deposits, payments on current account, exchange, and the purchase of precious metals. Money deposited in the bank could not be confiscated by creditors, a protection guaranteed by the city itself. Each new account holder had to pay ten florins to the poor and needy. From 1683 onward it was possible to deposit coins (gold or silver) that were not current or were out of circulation (*negotiepenningen*), and the same went for ingots of precious metals. The countervalue was credited to the depositor, who could then enter into commercial transactions with the credited sum. The receipt of these deposits was negotiable, and a very considerable speculative turnover developed on the basis of these receipts. The value of the receipts deposited rose or fell according to the volume of business abroad, and this dictated the greater or

lesser need for means of payment. Being both practical and speedy payment on current account, which could be arranged by the bank between commercial enterprises throughout

5

1

2

3

4

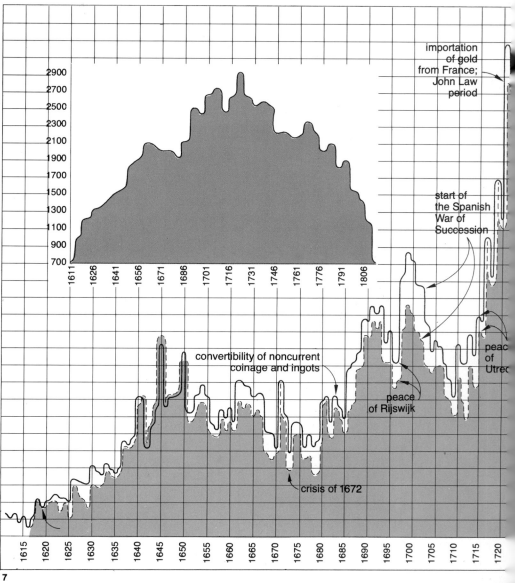

importation of gold from France; John Law period

start of the Spanish War of Succession

convertibility of noncurrent coinage and ingots

peace of Rijswijk

peace of Utrec

crisis of 1672

6

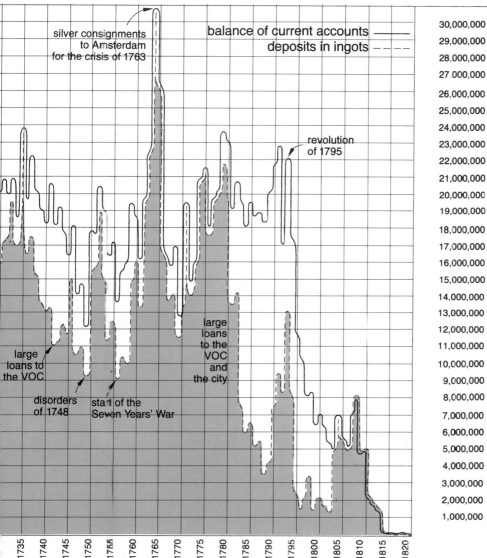

silver consignments to Amsterdam for the crisis of 1763

balance of current accounts ———
deposits in ingots – – –

revolution of 1795

large loans to the VOC and the city

large loans to the VOC

disorders of 1748

start of the Seven Years' War

30,000,000
29,000,000
28,000,000
27,000,000
26,000,000
25,000,000
24,000,000
23,000,000
22,000,000
21,000,000
20,000,000
19,000,000
18,000,000
17,000,000
16,000,000
15,000,000
14,000,000
13,000,000
12,000,000
11,000,000
10,000,000
9,000,000
8,000,000
7,000,000
6,000,000
5,000,000
4,000,000
3,000,000
2,000,000
1,000,000

1735 1740 1745 1750 1755 1760 1765 1770 1775 1780 1785 1790 1795 1800 1805 1810 1815 1820

Europe, was a considerable step forward in exchange procedures.

For the acquisition of precious metals and dated currencies, the bank acted as intermediary or middleman: the metals were sent to one of the mints in the country, which turned them into legal tender.

In theory, the Exchange did not provide one of the fundamental banking services, credit facilities. But in practice within certain limits the holder of a current account could exceed his line of credit, in other words he could deal in sums of money larger than those he had on deposit, and he had to pay—on his "overdraft"—a rate of interest of 3 percent. What is more, the bank would grant short-term credit arrangements both to the city of Amsterdam and to the East India Company. The latter used this credit to fit out its ships and pay salaries. These debts incurred with the bank were settled by the company within a few months with the profits made from their voyages. *Table 7* gives a progressive breakdown, during the period from 1609 to 1820, of two significant figures for the bank: the total amount of third-party credits, or in other words the total figure for current accounts, and the accumulated deposits in ingots. There are several interesting corresponding peaks and low points relating to various significant moments in the history of the republic (*from J. G. van Dillen,* Bronnen tot de Geschiednis der Wisselbanken, *1925*).

So the Exchange Bank was set up to facilitate commerce, even if it did not manage to control the prevalent monetary chaos. It was nevertheless profitable, resulting from the interest paid by clients on their "overdrafts"; from the acquisition and coining of precious metal; from the percentages taken on exchange transactions, which were around 2.5 percent for gold transactions and 2 percent for those in silver; from the sale of precious metals to filigree workers, large numbers of whom were especially active in the 17th century; and from the trade of precious metals, which, incidentally, was officially prohibited.

Amsterdam became the major international center for the trade in precious metals, particularly after the Treaty of Münster, which ended the Eighty Years' War between the Netherlands and Spain, and which was also one of the treaties in the Peace of Westphalia, which put an end to the Thirty Years' War in Europe (1648).

The bank enjoyed a great deal of trust both at home and abroad, and this increased even more when it showed its ability to overcome, with considerable brilliance, moments of

8

crisis like the one in 1672, when there was a rush to withdraw deposits as the invading armies of France approached Amsterdam. This trust, and the secrecy maintained about information relating to the amount of deposits caused quite fantastic rumors to circulate about the precious metal reserves at the bank's disposal. Figures of 300 and even 400 million florins were bandied about. In reality, the highest reserve, which was achieved in 1764, was just 31 millon—a tenth of the rumored figure.

Thanks to the Exchange Bank, Amsterdam was the most important financial center in the world until the 18th century. In this respect a document from the municipal archives of the city is of great interest (*8*): the *Corso di Cambij d'Amsterdam a di 19 aprile 1680* (the Exchange rate in Amsterdam on April 19, 1680). In 1780, at the outbreak of the fourth war with England, the bank loaned large sums of money to the East India Company, to the city of Amsterdam, and to the Province of Holland, in order to build ships, and enlist and equip soldiers. The debts contracted by the East India Company (VOC) were not quickly repaid and clients became suspicious. There was a falling-off of deposits in precious metals, and from then on the fortunes of the bank declined inexorably until its closure in 1820.

Opposite, old merchant warehouses in Amsterdam's Prinseneiland. The beams protruding at the top held the hoists to lift the goods to the various levels. The financial power of the city's dealers allowed vast quantities of goods to be stored and profitably sold when the market was favorable. Right, cranes in the port of Amsterdam, 1665 print. The already cited London merchant Josiah Child saw in the modest interest tax on the dollar the secret of Dutch prosperity, "This in my poor opinion is the causa causans of all the other causes of riches in that people; and if interest of money were with us reduced to the same rate as it is with them, it would in a short time render us rich and considerable in trade as they are now."

Overleaf, the Dam, central square of Amsterdam during the yearly outing of the lepers on the first Monday after Epiphany (1587–1658), picture by Adriaen van Nieulandt (Amsterdam Historical Museum). Left, the old town hall. Center, the Waag with the city's coat of arms; between the two buildings in the second plane, the roof of the New Church. The "outing" of the lepers was forbidden by the burgomasters in 1604.

DE SCHEEPS KRAANEN.
Grües, ou Guindals, pour charger et descharger les Navires.

change and outside. Tulips, imported to Holland after 1650, were at first sold by the piece, and later by weight. The flowers were never at the sale; they were still bulbs in the ground, during the negotiations. From 1634 on, prices began to rise steeply as the whole Dutch population came under the spell of the tulips, which caused exorbitant price levels. When florists and the States of Holland intervened, this "tulipomania" stopped abruptly in 1637.

Grain was traded in a separate building dating from 1617, the Corn Exchange, on the Old Bridge. This, too, was an open space with a surrounding gallery. Against the walls there were boxes in which samples were kept. Grain was examined in the open

hand, preferably in a northern light. The bits that fell on the ground were left for the supervisor. Here, too, the authorities imposed regulations—against grain shippers who obstructed passage with their ships; people who placed their bags on the steps of houses, dirtying them with flour; and children who played on the Exchange grounds, and who would be chased by the attendant and secured in special iron rings until they or their parents had paid a fine.

The Exchange Bank

In the Middle Ages and for a long time after, the circulation of money was chaotic and quite confusing.

THE NEW CITY HALL
AN ELEGANT SEAT OF POWER

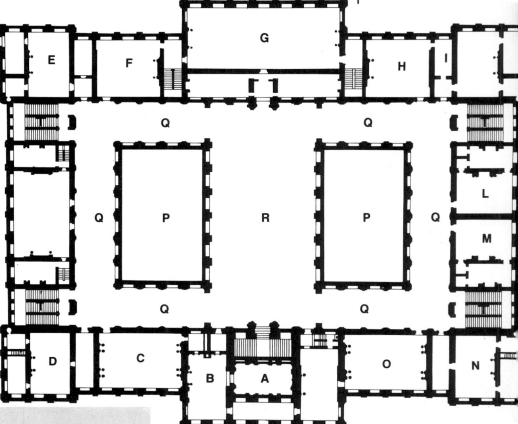

On January 20, 1648, workmen sank the first of the 13,656 piles that would consolidate the site on which the new *Stadhuis* or city hall was to be built, in Amsterdam. The old medieval town hall was about to collapse from old age, and in any case by now it was too small to house all the offices and government functionaries and the city administration. The designer of the new building was the painter and architect Jacob van Campen (1595–1657), an artist whose work was influenced by Italian classicism. In 1665, 17 years after the first pile had been driven home, the building was opened with due solemnity, but the second floor was still incomplete. It took seven more years to complete the roof. The decoration of the building was not finished until 1705 and 100 years after that Louis Bonaparte and then the Orange dynasty turned it into a royal palace.

It sported a hitherto unseen grandeur, with two porticoed courtyards around which were offices and conference rooms (1). The enormous central atrium, the *Burgerzaal,* was impressively lavish.

The city hall was the seat of power, the driving force behind the city government. Here were to be found the burgomasters, the sheriff, the aldermen, the council, the whole bureaucracy, as well as the Exchange Bank with all the legendary wealth it contained. It towered over the Dam, the heart of the city, and was the proud symbol of the wealth and power of Amsterdam. Sculptures, paintings, and other decorative elements carried a didactic significance. By references to classical mythology and the Bible, they reminded onlookers of the

Plan of the first floor

A	*Vierschaar, or Hall of Justice*	I	*Hall of the Sheriff*
B-C	*Hall of the Burgomasters*	L	*Chamber of Bankruptcy*
D	*Treasury*	M	*Chamber of Insurance*
E	*Treasury Extraordinary*	N	*Office for Orphans*
F	*Hall of the Commissaries for Minor Matters*	O	*Council Chamber*
		P	*Courtyards*
G-H	*Hall of the Aldermen*	Q	*Galleries*
		R	*Burgerzaal*

supremacy of Amsterdam on land and at sea, its prosperity, its wise government, and the harmony in which its citizens lived.

Most of the sculptures are by Artus Quellinus and Rombout Verhulst. There are two tympana on the façade. The one facing the square represents the oceans, paying homage to Amsterdam, which is represented by a girl, the *Stedemaagd.* At the three angles there are three bronze sculptures: Peace (as we have already mentioned, construction started in 1648, the year of the Peace of Münster, which ended the Eighty Years' War and marked the international recognition of the republic of the Seven United Provinces), Prudence, and Justice. The other tympanum, facing the canal (2), depicts the four continents, which are offering up their treasures to the city, a pointed representation of the

4 fruits of navigation and trading. At the top of the triangle stands Atlas, carrying the world on his shoulders, with Moderation and Vigilance on either side of him. On the cupola there is a shimmering pennant in the shape of a ship, the *kogge*, the instrument of the first voyages that paved the way for the fortunes lying ahead. The allegorical magniloquence is carried on inside. In particular there are richly decorative marble sculptures in the Burgerzaal, in the porticoes, and in the *Vierschaar*, the hall of justice, where not infrequently death sentences were pronounced (*3, the doors to the Vierschaar*). There are festoons and garlands of plants, fruit, flowers, and shells. The entrances to the various offices are heralded by statues alluding to their function — a subtle way of guiding the visitor through the bureaucratic labyrinth. Thus, Venus surveys the marriage hall, and Justice the

Chamber of the Aldermen, the judicial college. There is also a *Desolate Boedelkamer*, the chamber of bankruptcy. Here we find Icarus, in bas-relief, falling during his foolhardy flight (*4*) and more folkloric motifs of emptied coffers, broken padlocks, poisonous plants, and loathsome rats crawling about. In the council chamber or *Vroedschap* (*5, a meeting in the Vroedschap in 1774*) and in the hall of the burgomasters the marble friezes refer to the good and just government, with appropriate references to biblical episodes and ancient Roman history. The paintings produced for the city hall by Ferdinand Bol, Govert Flinck, Jan Lievens, and Jacob Jordaans also touched on biblical and classical Roman sources, to urge the men of the government toward integrity and a sober life-style (or praise them for such qualities). In the atmosphere of latter-day human-

ism the burgomasters were fond of comparing themselves to the consuls of Rome, just as it was also common to trace parallels between the revolt of the Batavi against the Romans and the insurrection of the northern provinces of the Netherlands against the Spanish. For the city hall Rembrandt painted *The Oath of Claudius Civilis* (he was the leader of the revolt of the Batavi), which is now in the national museum in Stockholm. The work had been commissioned along with seven others to decorate a large gallery in the building. Documents tell us that it was almost immediately returned to the artist to be repainted. Perhaps the intense artistry of the great master did not correspond to the didactic taste for allegory of the commissioners. This is not the only instance of misunderstanding between artists and government. Govert Flinck, who, shortly before his death, man-

aged to finish his *Solomon Invoking Wisdom,* which is appropriately hung in the hall of the *Vroedschap,* was then more popular than Rembrandt. His praises are sung in more than 20 poems by Joost van den Vondel, the Dutch national poet.

The majestic construction of the city hall appealed to contemporary citizens. Some of them brazenly regarded it as the "eighth wonder of the world." It certainly commanded the respect befitting power.

In effect the hall of justice, the Vierschaar, is in the prominent position; death sentences were carried out on a scaffold in front of the building; cells and torture and flagellation chambers also took up quite a lot of room. And they were all embellished with unmistakably pointed decorations (*6*).

Each year, cities, provinces, and states issued all kinds of coins that wound up all over the world. For any cash transaction, merchants first had their money valued or exchanged into the agreed currency. To put some order into this chaos, in 1609 the city of Amsterdam established the Exchange Bank in the town hall. It never achieved genuine monetary reform, but it did manage to facilitate payments: one could safely deposit money there, open an account, transfer money to another account, and have foreign money valued and obtain locally accepted currency instead.

The Weighing Offices

For goods sold by weight a reliable balance was

essential. In 1556, a new weighing building, the Waag, located in the center of the Dam, was inaugurated. This Renaissance-style building dominated the Dam for nearly two-and-a-half centuries. On its roof were two weather vanes, a reference to the city's prosperous maritime trade: one representing Neptune, god of the sea; the other, Fortuna, goddess of good fortune. Both are now in the Amsterdam historical museum. Inside the main door and the six side doors of the Waag hung large weighing scales, and within the building were two smaller ones. The building was always surrounded by a crowd of porters, carriers, and carters bringing goods in and out.

When the Waag could no longer do all the work, St. Anthony's Gate, now within the walls and no longer an actual gate, was transformed into a weighing office. This occurred in 1617–18, during the city's period of sudden expansion. Here the heavy goods were weighed, such as anchors and cannon. Beside it there was a high post for hoisting these articles. They were then dropped from a great height onto a heavy iron block, with a thunderous din: if they survived the test undamaged they received the city's stamp. In 1618, a third weighing office was opened, for which another gate—the Regulating Gate—was transformed; there, dairy products were weighed.

Aside from these services provided by the building there were many others for helping trade. To take goods to ships one had to use certain guilds of lighters. Members of the corn-lighters' guild unloaded grain ships. Large articles were hoisted from ships by means of pulleys in the masts or by the city's

Above, decorative frieze in Amsterdam's new town hall, showing the adoration of the golden calf. Bottom, the city's great seal, 1654. Opposite, documents concerning the civic treasury, stored on the wall of an office, detail from a picture by Cornelis Brisé, 1656 (Amsterdam Historical Museum).

Reijsen ghelt

Procesen

Fabrijck Campt

Ordinaris wedden

quitantien van Grooten Excijs

Coninge
Erven

cranes. There were two of these, owned by two social institutions, St. Peter's hostelry and the new Huiszitten house. Once goods had been brought onto the quayside, members of the transport guilds took charge of expediting them. Thus, there were weighing carriers and, more specialized carriers for beer, peat, and corn.

The city authorities controlled storage and transport firms, ensured that the regular transport services for goods and passengers to and from the city ran on time, and regulated weights and measures, as well as postal services. After the Peace of Münster in 1648, postal routes and deliveries on horseback developed considerably. Postal trips to and from Hamburg and England became Amsterdam's monopoly, so that trade information was available there earlier than in other cities. Another means of communication was the newspaper, which gradually evolved from regularly issued merchants' letters and printed bulletins were full of sensational reports about fires, comets, wars, and the like. The oldest-known newspaper printed in Amsterdam is the *Courante uyt Italien, Duytsland & C* (News from Italy, Germany, etc.), of

June 14, 1618. Two years later, Amsterdam was the only city in Europe with two newspapers, and, by 1700, it had four. The authorities did make certain demands, such as repressing reports that might help competitors or insult foreign heads of state.

The city, likewise, supervised brokers. These middlemen between buyer and seller or merchant and shipper were long mistrusted as unreliable, self-seeking, and responsible for driving up prices. In the 16th century, they obtained more elbow room although they were not allowed to look for clients directly: they had to wait until buyers or sellers came to them. Here, too, trade contributed to the needy: 0.5 percent of receipts obtained through a broker went to the almoners' orphanage. Brokers gained recognition when they formed a guild. Their house on the Nieuwe Zijds Voorburgwal still bears the inscription: "Freedom is not for sale at any price."

A service branch of industry that was well thought of in Holland was insurance. Freight traffic involved countless risks: a ship could capsize in a storm or shatter on the rocks, fall into pirates' hands, or be taken by enemy ships. Throughout most of the

From left, cornice of Tuchthuis (House of Correction) reproducing instruments of torture, employed to obtain confessions, without which punishment could not be applied. The blood band, which judges wore on their shoulders over their black gowns when pronouncing capital sentences. Detail of the stark benches in the Vierschaar, the law court in the new town hall. Justice was administered by the college of jurymen (schepenen); the growth of the city with its more complex relationships through commerce determined the development of specialized bodies for various types of civil cases.

17th century, the republic was at war with Spain, England, Sweden, or France. The enemy was constantly on the lookout for ships from Holland; in the channel, the sound, the Straits of Gibraltar, and important byways rightly called "the strangling points of the Hollandish body," ships were particularly vulnerable. The risk was traditionally spread by distributing ownership of cargo and ship among several people. Like other service branches, maritime insurance developed quickly toward 1600. The Amsterdam Chamber of Assurance dates from 1598. Here, policies were registered and disputes resolved. Insurance business itself could be settled in the Exchange.

In Amsterdam, tariffs were so attractive that foreigners often insured themselves there. The English did even when they were at war with the republic. The premiums always depended on the nature of the trip in question and the risk at the time. In peacetime, they varied between 3 and 5 percent. In 1615, a trip from Bergen in Norway to Holland or Zeeland was insured for 2.5 percent; for the much more dangerous journey from Malaga to Holland or Zeeland the rate was 6 percent. In wartime premiums might rise to 15 percent. Clearly, the Amsterdam authorities took close interest—down to the details—in providing reliable services to trade. This is not surprising, considering that the city officials were themselves merchants. In practice, things sometimes went awry. In spite of strict controls, rules were broken and bunglers were able to thrive in various areas of economic life.

The plains of Holland

"The ground of the province of Holland," reports William Temple in 1676, "is generally as flat as the sea when calm and looks as if after a long struggle between land and sea it had finally been divided between them. What is remarkable are the many canals which lead not only to each village but to each farm on the plains." That this struck Temple is not surprising: the network of both natural and manmade inland waterways that crisscrossed Holland in the 17th century was unique in Europe. It was the physical counterpart of the close link between the towns, and between town and plain. In the mid-18th century, Amsterdam alone had 800 shipping services to 180 different destinations in the republic.

A good example of the link between rural industry and the city was the extensive industrial area in the Zaanstreek, the flat and windy terrain north of Amsterdam. By 1630, it counted 53 sawmills, 45 oil presses, 19 flour mills, 5 paper mills, and 4 hemp mills. A century later, the wings of 600 windmills turned for industry. This area was suitable for receiving raw materials and producing finished goods because of the nearby Amsterdam market. Shipbuilding, paper, and, in the 18th century, train-oil production were important trades. The grinding of hundreds of blades must have been a piercing, almost frightening noise, not to mention the stench of train oil, which even reached Amsterdam if the wind blew in a certain direction. In the 17th century, fishing was the main livelihood of many in the plains villages. The foremost industry was herring—which were caught off the shores of England and Scotland—providing work for thousands. Modern estimates put the herring fleet at 500 Dutch boats, of which some 200 were from North Holland. The sailors came from all types of hamlets, such as De Rijp. The chief harbor was Enkhuizen. The operation was financed mainly by the cities: the plains people were unable to bear the risk involved in using rather small boats. Fishing involved a further link between town and plains: to preserve herring a great deal of salt was needed—some 46½ tons a year for the whole of Holland's catch. Amsterdam imported the salt from France, Spain, or the Cape Verde islands, and exported the herring to France and the German hinterland.

To satisfy the urban demand for fruit and vegetables, horticulture was developed throughout Holland. Around Leyden there were some 238 hectares of market gardens. Growers cultivated the common, rougher varieties of vegetable like cabbage, beets, and carrots, as well as the more refined spinach, lettuce, artichokes, and cucumbers. Amsterdam had extensive fruit and vegetable markets to which goods were taken by special barges and where shopkeepers and householders could buy. Tree nurseries in South Holland supplied the urban canals and gardens with

special trees and shrubs. Revolutionary developments occurred in the growing of bulbs. Until 1650, agricultural prices rose. This was a good reason for urban merchants to invest large amounts in the reclamation of land. Part of the newly won terrain could be devoted to growing special crops needed for industry, such as the seeds of cabbages or beets used for lighting and for soap making. Part of the land was used for cattle breeding: the region north of Amsterdam was internationally famous for this. There, Danish bullocks were fattened on the loamy soil. Amsterdam was noted for exporting cattle: in 1667–68, some 8,788 bullocks arrived there. The fattening of cattle was largely the occupation of city people, and supplied the city's meat. Butter and cheese had always been typical exports from Holland, and Edam, even then, was one of the best-known varieties of cheese.

The economy of the plains was strongly tied to that of the city and largely determined by it. Where possible, the city tried to call the tune by enforcing such restrictive and discriminatory measures as confining dirty or dangerous trades to the outskirts. Amsterdam had six powder factories outside the walls and at least 80 cotton-pressing shops. This did not interfere with the citizens' attraction to the quiet of the countryside: near the towns, there were many small gardens and outhouses along the seemingly endless paths and lanes. The well-to-do built pleasure grounds along the rivers, in the dunes, or on the reclaimed land. This occurred along with capital investment in land. The sustained contact between city and plain and the considerable prosperity of some farmers brought urban culture into country homes. The more well-to-do owned paintings, mirrors, china, books, and clocks.

City administration

As before, administrators came from a small, exclusive group of burghers, most of whom were merchants. C. P. Hooft—one of those exiled after 1568, and several times burgomaster between 1588 and 1610—found this a good thing, as attested by this statement in his memoirs: ''The aristocratic form of government is the safest and most appropriate form

Above, the standard bearer, portrait of Loef Vredericx, who attained office in Amsterdam in 1626, painted by Thomas de Keyser in the same year (The Hague Mauritshuis). Opposite below, the courtyard of the Tuchthuis, by H. Schouten (Amsterdam Parish Archive), and above, the company of Captain Hooghkamer, by Jacob Lyon (Amsterdam

Historical Museum), one of the main group portraits of the civic guard that transmit the features of Amsterdam citizens. The guard consisted of men who could pay for their arms and equipment, an expression of a middle citizenry outside the governing oligarchy and a potential political force. In certain critical situations it did indeed act as such.

of government." He adds that, nevertheless, rulers must always take the burghers into account and not imagine themselves so powerful that they might "impose anything on them." The rulers must be guided by a sense of duty, moderation, and unselfishness. Such ideals were shown in word and image in the administrative quarters of the new town hall. The patriciate, or group of families from which the city government was chosen, regarded themselves as best able to fulfill the tasks of leadership. That other classes had no influence on government is borne out by this 17th-century view: "Then the community shall take over the city administration and aim to run everything in its own way." During the 17th and 18th centuries, the form of administration remained unchanged and, in spite of a few minor uprisings, untouched.

At the top of the administrative pyramid stood the four burgomasters. Their power was unlimited: as masters of mighty Amsterdam, their authority extended beyond the walls and the province of Holland, and, indeed, beyond the republic. They controlled everything that was going on within the city, like spiders in a web. While they were not answerable to anybody, they could appoint other people to positions for which many thereby felt obliged to them. First, the burgomasters, at the suggestion of the council, chose the jurymen and the mayor—positions that earlier were officially filled by the count. Next, there was an enormous list of offices and commissions, from the highest to the lowliest: treasurers for the city's finances, commissioners of the Exchange Bank, wardens of orphanages, tax assessors, directors of charities, heads of guilds, Reformed preachers, teachers, and even the market cobbler. The burgomasters themselves decided what they might seek the council's advice on. Much happened outside this body, but for new imposts and major decisions such as urban extensions, they did need approval from these representatives of the richest citizens. In general, the council was docile: conflicts between it and the burgomasters hardly occurred.

The number of offices had increased greatly since medieval times. This is not surprising, for the city had become larger and more complex. Besides the

bench of jurors, there were now five lower courts. Church marriages of non-Reformed people were invalid and had to be performed before the College for Marital Matters. In 1584, the College of Treasurers was split into ordinary and extraordinary members. The latter organized the collection of certain taxes, while the former levied excise rates on houses in the city, and personal taxes on citizens. Moreover, they paid out the salaries of officials.

A college of accountants supervised the officials. All the colleges were housed in the medieval town hall, which had now become much too small, unsuitable for the administration of so big and mighty a city. In 1639, the administration bought some 60 properties around the old building and demolished them in order to build a new town hall. The foundation stone was laid in 1648, and, in the summer of 1655, a festive procession of the mayor, burgomasters, jurors, former burgomasters, and other important officials crossed the Dam, in order to occupy their new offices, although the second story was not yet finished. After a stirring meeting in the burgomasters' room, where Burgomaster de Graeff made a suitable if incomprehensible speech, everybody went to his own office. In the afternoon, the meeting was followed by a banquet.

The patriciate

The patriciate, which, for centuries, provided members of the city administration, consisted mainly of merchants and families of entrepreneurs. However exclusive the circle eventually became, it was not a closed oligarchy. After 1573, the administration was open to all kinds of new people. A good example of this is Jacob Poppe, son of a simple German office employee. His father had worked his way up in Amsterdam to become a rich merchant, and the son started as an officer in the civic guard and attained the post of burgomaster, the highest in the city. When he died in 1624, he was said to have been the richest man in Amsterdam. Patrician families shared among themselves the many city positions; favors granted were honored by favors received. Presiding burgomasters were not salaried, but, by their right to appoint, they could fill all sorts of posts with friends

Festive occasions in the life of the city were official visits of famous people. Opposite above, fireworks on the Amstel in April 1689 for the coronation of William III and Mary Stuart. Below, the entry of Maria de Medici on her visit (1638), engraving by S. Savry. Top, Czar Peter the Great visits the port (1697), painting by Abraham Storck. Bottom, alongside the Ouderzijds Herenlogement, built on the city's commission by Philip Vingbooms in 1647 to house important visitors, who previously used the Prinsenhof, originally a convent of St. Cecilia on the site later occupied by the new town hall. Panel by Gerrit Adriaenszon Berckheyde (Rijksmuseum).

and relations, for which they received considerable sums. They took care that the right man got the right job.

A youngster of patrician birth could begin his career at 20. With ability and the right connections, by 40 he could become a burgomaster, which, in turn, could lead to important posts outside the city: delegate to the States of Holland or the States General, or ambassador to foreign courts. After that, he could always return to the city as a burgomaster. The highest rungs of this ladder were not easy to climb. Before elections, there was much jostling and bargaining for votes, tipsy promises at the banqueting table sometimes leading to awkward situations.

Between 1625 and 1650, the patriciate became more exclusive, and during the first period without a stadholder (1650–72) some 70 percent of the city administration came from the old patriciate. The same situation prevailed during the second interregnum (1702–47). A stadholder in the republic limited patrician power. The most blatant example was the political strife between the few families and individuals who were competing for the position of

"magnificat," the term used for the leading burgomaster and his family. From 1627 to 1650, it was occupied by Andries Bicker and his relatives. As the city's leader, he headed the rural parliamentary faction, which repeatedly obstructed the plans of the stadholder, Frederick Henry. The grand pensionary of Holland, Johan de Witt, who largely determined the country's policies from 1650 to 1672, had married a niece of the leader of Amsterdam, Cornelis de Graeff, and so secured the city's support. Once the potentates of Amsterdam were in the saddle they often opposed the stadholders, while other families used the central power to attain administrative seats. Still, having reached their goal, they would put the city's interests first.

As in previous centuries, it could happen that the central authorities opposed the city's power, or purged the city administration of undesirable elements. Yet, after a while, the new administrators would again begin to turn against the stadholder. The law was challenged in 1618, when Prince Maurice appointed some new council members and burgomasters to force the city to follow his plans. Similar opposition occurred in 1650 and 1672, by William II and William III, respectively.

"Mercatores sapientes" as administrators

Throughout the 17th and 18th centuries, Amsterdam's political climate was determined by a mode of government that might be called libertarian. It had occurred during the previous two centuries and was rooted in the typically Dutch moderation that characterized their religion and philosophy, distaste for fanaticism, and the humanist ideas of men like Erasmus of Rotterdam. The ethics of the city's ruler were intensely practical and marked by moderation, even in religious matters. Compared with rulers elsewhere, those of Amsterdam and other cities in Holland were noticeably sober and unpretentious and, for the period, humane in their ways of governing. Indeed, even in cases of minor uprisings, the administration remained rather detached.

The administrators were men of considerable culture. At banquets they would recite Latin verses of their own, and Burgomaster de Graeff is said to have

Left, Johan van Oldenbarnevelt, one of the great statesmen of Holland. Below, Coenraad van Beuningen, by Caspar Netscher. Patrician, burgomaster, skilled diplomat, patron of the arts, interesting member of Amsterdam's ruling

class, he spoke for the council when in 1683 the stadholder had gone to the city in person to ask for more troops: "even the presence of a prince of Orange cannot stop the free deliberations of the Council." Right above, mausoleum of Admiral de Ruyter, by R. Verhulst, in the New Church. He died at Syracuse (Sicily) in 1676 from wounds received in the sea fight at Stromboli, lost to the French. Right bottom, a commemorative print in which William III is surrounded by previous stadholders, William I and Maurice on the left, Frederik Henry and William II on the right, to mark his entry in the city on August 12, 1672.

known not only French and German but Greek, Hebrew, Chaldean, and Syriac, as well. Some burgomasters did valuable scientific work—for example, Nicholas Witsen, who wrote a book on shipbuilding; Johannes Hudde, who did mathematical research; and Nicolas Tulp, the well-known medical man. Toward 1700, the shipbuilder Witsen and the mathematician Hudde held all the administrative strings, but they were exceptional men. In the main, the leaders of Amsterdam continued to be merchants and businessmen, whose practices, such as supporting piracy, equipping enemy fleets, conniving at tax evasion, and betraying commercial secrets we should now find odd. As long as these activities remained within proper limits they were acceptable, but scandals like land speculation by certain officials during periods of urban expansion went too far, even for their contemporaries.

Although the patricians' lifestyle long remained quite simple, the 17th century saw a widening gap between administrators and the rest of the population. By means of family trees, titles, colorful escutcheons, country homes, and pavilions on the city canals, the rulers tried to give form to their status. Still, they did not try to emulate the nobility, because they were nothing if not proud of their burgher origins. "Did not your grandfather sell vegetables or run a small chandler's shop?" candidates for the post of burgomaster would tease each other. Toward the lower orders the patriciate formed a powerful front. The many acid pamphlets distributed by the poorer classes and even their uprisings could not break the power of the patriciate, and this was regarded as proper: being the richest, most honorable and distinguished, were they not also the cleverest? In retrospect, it seems that the 17th century administration fulfilled its task responsibly, given the criteria of that period.

Jurisdiction: mayor and jurors

Civil and criminal justice was in the hands of nine jurors. From 1560 on, the seven new jurors and the four burgomasters chose a president and vice-president from the retiring college. The jurors' bench exercised its jurisdiction along with the

WILHEM HENRICK PRINS VAN ORANJE EN VAN NASSOV ETC.
STADT-HOVDER CAPITEYN ADMIRAEL GENERAEL DER VEREENIGHDE NEDERLANDEN.

GEDENCK-TEECKEN HOEDANICH ZYN HOOGHEYT DE H. PRINS VAN ORANJE EN NASSOV ETC ALS STADT-HOVDER

mayor, who formally remained the highest official. In practice, his power was subordinate to that of the burgomasters. The mayor was head of the police and had to make sure that regulations about urban and rural imposts were being observed. Together with

the burgomasters and the jurors, he organized the city's quality controls. In contrast to the jurors, who served for one year, the mayor served for three or more, but without salary: he was given half of all civil and criminal fines, and the moneys that the more well-to-do paid to avoid prosecution.

Under the mayor were five assistants who each supervised a part of the city, at a fixed salary of one third of all criminal fines. A marine mayor did the same in the port, overseeing proper conduct in the buying and selling of ships and in the hiring of crews. Mayor and assistants had the help of servants, or "catchers," who carried out investigations, arrested people, and who could confiscate

goods, carts, sledges, and carriages. The marine mayor's servants could remove a ship's rudder and store it at the town hall if the vessel was forbidden to leave the palisade.

Soon after 1578, the jurors' bench could no longer cope with the volume of civil cases. Moreover, the expansion of trade required better organization of jurisdiction. The swift and reliable conduct of cases was essential, as life had become more fast paced.

A number of lower jurors' benches, with special duties, took over parts of the work. Insurance matters came under the jurisdiction of the Chamber of Assurance, and maritime litigation, except for insurance, under the Chamber for Maritime Matters. Bankruptcies were dealt with by the Chamber of Desolate Possessions. Other civil cases, among them those involving more than 600 guilders, came directly before the jurors' bench. On fixed weekdays, the jurors would hold sessions for special cases; for example, cases involving inheritance were dealt with on Tuesdays. Those whose litigation had already been brought before a lower court could register an appeal to go before the jurors. If this still failed to be satisfactory, one could go to the Court of Holland at The Hague. In civil cases, where, at times, huge sums were involved, many resorted to these possibilities for appeal.

As the population grew, so did crime. The number of petty thefts involving silver buckles, walking sticks with silver tops, or even handkerchiefs was legion. Such minor cases first came before the Commission for Small Matters; the rest came directly before the jurors.

In the Confession Books, where evidence was recorded, we find an army of petty thieves, purse snatchers, beggars, quarrelsome drunkards, prostitutes, and brawlers. Nobody could be condemned without making a confession. Large property crimes, such as the case of Rutgert Vlieck, accountant of the Exchange Bank, who had lightened the bank's coffers by 300,000 guilders, were exceptional. The penalties seem to have been rather harsh. They varied from small fines to the pillory—when a sign explaining his crime was hung around the culprit's neck—whipping, branding, exile, prison, and capital punishment, the last reserved for manslaugh-

Left, a beaker with engraved map of the siege and conquest of Breda by stadholder Frederik Henry, on July 23, 1637 (Rotterdam, Museum Boymans-van Beuningen). Opposite, banquet of the civic guard to celebrate the Peace of Münster in 1648, by Bartholomaeus van der Helst (Rijksmuseum). Opposite below, Allegory of Justice, by Quellinus (The Hague, Rijksvoorlichtingdienst). Breda, in North Brabant, was occupied several times by rebels and Spaniards, and besieged in 1577, 1581, 1590, 1624, and 1637. The surrender of Ambrosio Spinola's Spaniards on June 5, 1625, after a ten-month siege, was painted by Velasquez. The Dutch commemorative beaker is dated 1648, when the Eighty Years' War came to an end.

ter or murder and for major crimes involving property. A recidivist, too, might end up with the death penalty. Garotting, hanging, beheading, and breaking a criminal on the wheel on a scaffold in front of the town hall were all meant to serve as a deterrent to the onlooking crowd. Two or three times a year there were public executions of some 40 prisoners, and the populace flocked to the Dam. Even schools were closed. At a special ceremony in the courtroom at the town hall, which required the approval of the burgomasters, the mayor declared the condemned ''children of death.'' The mayor and jurors were dressed in black gowns with straight satin collars; over the left shoulder was a blood-colored sash with the city's coat of arms.

The prisons

Often a person received more than one punishment, such as branding and prison. Amsterdam was the first European city with a house of correction. In 1596, a reformatory was opened where young beggars, instead of being punished, could learn a trade in order to re-enter society. The idea was mooted by the humanist Coornhert. Another idea of his for fighting the rise of begging and stealing was to assign criminals work on the dikes, building fortifications, and the like: toward 1600, laborers with iron collars and chained feet were put to use to further the urban expansion. There was little else in the way of

temantel wrote that if merchants, shopkeepers, or others were subjected to a house search, the shame would exceed the transgression. On the other hand, a Reformed preacher was indicted in 1636 for complaining that one who had no money or influence had to die, while a person from a good family could buy time and obtain a pardon.

In the Confession Books we find mainly non-citizens, members of the lower orders. This was partly due to the fact that, at the end of the 14th century, Duke Albrecht of Bavaria had done away with arrests. Citizens merely had to appear before the court when called and could present written documents in their defense, but non-citizens could be in-

The "English wars" were about trade. The first (1652-54) arose from the Navigation Act, which harmed Dutch maritime trade. The second (1665-67) was due to

reeducation. The Rasphuis, as the house of correction was called, developed into a regular prison, as did the Spinning House. These prisons were the first of their kind in Europe, as was the notion of sentencing a person to prison instead of cutting off an ear or garotting him. After 1654, beggars, who officially had been banned since 1595, could be picked up without trial and sent to the workhouse to process hemp and mend nets. This applied to men and women alike, although the latter went to the Spinning House.

Many people in the 17th century did not find the lack of equality abnormal. In 1660, the juror Bon-

carcerated for interrogation and had no right to legal assistance. Torture was a common method for extracting confessions. Those with money could agree on a compensation sum with the mayor, after which he would refrain from prosecuting them. The only solution for an authority that could not cope with the problem of over-population was severe punishment. Countless people could not escape the vicious circle of poverty, punishment, and the return to poverty—such as Trijntje van Marienholt, who in 1709, at the age of 74, was released from the Spinning House. She had come to Amsterdam as a young girl and could not immediately find work. To eat, she had to

English envy and rivalry of Dutch sea-based prosperity. The republic had much to lose and England much to gain. In these maritime wars the Dutch fought valiantly with varying success. Top left, commemorative medal of the Four Days' Battle (1666), by Wouter Müller. Top right, medal by Christoffel Adolfszon for the Peace of Breda, 1667, ending the second war. Center, the final stage of the battle of Scheveningen, by van de

Velde the Elder (London, National Maritime Museum). Between August 7 and 10, 1653, off Scheveningen, 115 English ships under Admiral George Monck met 110

steal—for which she had been whipped 33 times, sent to the Spinning House 16 times, and branded several times.

The civic company: the new guard

In 1580, William of Orange had established, in addition to the old guard of six companies, 11 new civic companies, with officers and men from 11 areas of the town. Every citizen between the ages of 18 and 60 who could pay for his equipment had to serve. Thus, in practice, these companies comprised an organization of rich burghers and the middle classes. The old guard, which had confined itself primarily to

the Spaniards: the year before, a lot was cast for those who would have to go. Several times the guard manned the city walls to protect Amsterdam—as in 1650, when William II was preparing his coup. Inside the city, the guard ensured peace and order around the clock. After 1681, they were on duty only at night. At half past nine in the evening, the guard shut the gates and deposited the keys in the town hall, in a chest that only the presiding burgomaster and the duty officer could unlock. In case of riots the guard went into action, but they were specifically forbidden to use live ammunition against the people, except in extreme emergency. The administration used the guard for nonmilitary purposes as well—

Dutch ships under Admiral Maarten Tromp, who died in the battle. Stranded on the coast and under gunfire from the English at sea, the Dutch lost 20 ships and 7,000 men.

the rich burghers, rapidly dissolved into the new civic companies. Reminders of the old guard were their depots, which, from the late 17th century, the administration had taken to using for festivities and banquets. The depot commanders were kept on, and regularly practiced with their companies on the shooting grounds. Every year, the guards held a splendid banquet in the depots until about 1650, when they had to be demolished; in 1672, the functions of the depot commanders ceased.

The task of the civic companies was similar to that of the old guard. In 1633, a group of 200 men went to Zwolle to help defend the country against

for example, for the 1630 and 1698 census, for collections, payment of taxes, and the like. These matters were conducted regionally. A more festive character prevailed during the parades on the Dam and when escorts were needed for famous visitors to the city.

As the city expanded so did the guards; in 1680, there were 60. Each area had a company, under a captain assisted by a lieutenant and three sergeants. The ensign was traditionally young and single. On guard documents he usually appears smartly dressed, with an enormous flag. The companies were united into five regiments, each of which had a color. In paintings of the guards, their sashes denoted the regiment to which they belonged. Civic companies are estimated to have had about 10,000 active members.

A war council consisting of captains, and of two colonels directly chosen by the burgomasters, led the civic companies. Although this council formally chose the higher officers from the immediate area, the burgomasters, too, had some say in the selection. During the 17th century, it became more and more common for friends and relatives of the administrators to obtain these posts and for higher officers no longer to live in the area. In 1672 and in 1748, the citizenry tried to stem the influence of the administration by demanding that the guards appoint their officers themselves and the war council have administrators among its members. However, the administration could not allow itself to give in to the potential political danger of such organized power. This was obvious when the guard kept out of small disturbances because it favored the insurgents. Still, the citizens never succeeded in opposing the administration for long.

The policy of the republic

How the republic of the Seven United Provinces was administered was not always clear even to its contemporaries. It was a federation formed in the late 16th century in the fight against King Philip II of Spain. Each province remained independent—retaining its administrative, judicial, and fiscal privileges set down in the Middle Ages—and was administered by representatives of the burghers and the nobles. In Holland and Zeeland, it was the towns that predominated, but in the east the nobles were more influential.

The provinces had a judicial adviser, the grand pensionary, and the one for Holland often became so influential that he acted as minister of foreign affairs for the whole republic. Another important office was that of stadholder. In theory, each province could appoint one but, in practice, they wound up being descendants of William of Orange or of his brother John of Nassau. In 1747, the office became hereditary. The stadholder could influence the choice of certain city officials. In wartime he was supreme

The First English War occurred in Cromwell's time; the second, during the reign of Charles II, ended much more favorably for the Dutch. The English sailed under Admiral George Monck, the Dutch under de Ruyter, who was later to sail up the Medway, capturing and towing away the King Charles, the most glorious feat in Dutch naval history. Below right, an episode in the four-day battle in the Channel (June 1-4, 1666), in a picture by van de Velde the Younger. The ship is Prince Rupert's Royal James, partly unmasted by Dutch gunfire on the fourth day of the battle. A large part of the naval effort fell to the Amsterdam admiralty, for whom Ferdinand Bol (1616-80) painted the allegory (top right) with mythological elements (Neptune, Mercury, Victory). From the first war onward, the republic's foreign policy had been guided by the grand pensionary of Holland, Johan de Witt. In 1672, at the end of the first period without a stadholder, William III was nominated, de Witt retired, and on August 20 was assassinated with his brother, Cornelis. Left, their corpses hung from a post, in a canvas by Jan de Baen.

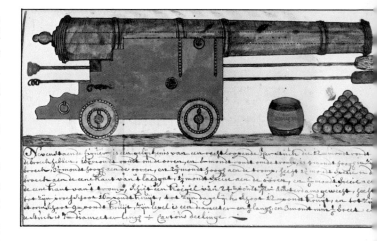

Below, gun factory of Hendrick Trip (1607-66) at Julitabroeck in Sweden. The Trip family had large interests in Swedish copper and became linked through marriage with the de Geer family, merchants powerful in grain, iron, salt, wine, and banking. Together, the Trip and de Geer families promoted the Swedish economy. There were many instances of Amsterdam finance and enterprise working abroad. Panel by Allart van Everdingen (Rijksmuseum). Below right, naval gun of the East India Company's Amsterdam chamber, made by G. Kosterus, 1615. Top right, gun, powder, and shot, technical drawing by Daniel Galschut, about 1700.

commander of the army and the fleet in his province, and, from 1625, in the whole republic. Both grand pensionary and stadholder could become very powerful, which often caused serious internal conflict. Stadholders tended to pursue centralized policies, and, therefore, to try to capture political and administrative power, and they behaved like princes. By contrast, the grand pensionary advocated independence and freedom for his province and its towns. Twice the republic went through a long period without a stadholder, and it was then that city rulers were able to pursue independent policies.

Matters concerning all of the provinces were settled in the States General, a permanent council of provincial delegates in The Hague: they dealt with the republic's foreign policy, declared war and concluded peace, sent out ambassadors and envoys, and received foreign diplomats; moreover, they supervised the army, the fleet, and the East and West India companies. Since provincial delegates were tied to a fixed mandate and often had to return to their province for consultation, decision making in the States

General was slow and laborious. Holland, by far the richest province, paid some 58 percent of the taxes imposed by the States General and thereby enjoyed a powerful position. In turn, Amsterdam was the most influential city, and, therefore, could often set her stamp on the republic's policy. The States General, the States of Holland, and other federal bodies were domiciled in The Hague. Since the embassies of foreign governments were based in The Hague, it was a center of Dutch and, indeed, of European diplomacy. As a city it was much more modern than Amsterdam, less caught up in trade and practical affairs, but all the more refined and fashionable for that.

Members of urban and provincial administrations and of the States General came from the upper orders of society and regarded themselves as the only people qualified to look after the country's welfare. They formed a kind of administrative aristocracy, referred to as such by the rest of the community, from whom they were totally removed: the stadholders made the laws in the republic, even if the lower classes regarded the princes of Orange as princes of the Netherlands, and, in contracts with inland rulers, the East India Company called Maurice and Frederik Henry "kings of Holland" for simplicity's sake.

At no administrative level did the republic have a vast bureaucracy, thus occupying remarkably little space in the old town halls. One reason for this was that many official tasks were carried out by lawyers as a sideline, the grand pensionary being the extreme example of this practice.

The fleet

How unperspicuously the republic was organized is evident from the way in which the fleet was run. There was no Dutch fleet as such, but five independent admiralties in the coastal provinces with one fleet each: in Holland, they were located, alternately, in Amsterdam, Rotterdam, Hoorn, and Enkhuizen; in Zeeland, in Middelburg; in Friesland, in Dokkum and, after 1645, in Harlingen. The admiralties had arisen toward 1600, when the naval forces consisted of exiles and privateers with escort vessels for sea

Example of industrial activity. Top, sawmills outside the walls, drawing by Philip Koninck (Amsterdam Historical Museum). One of the elements favoring industrial growth was cheap energy from the wind-driven mills. Left, linen workshop, typical of the refining of imported raw materials, etching by Claes Janszon Visscher. Below, fire in an Amsterdam soap factory, drawing by Jan van der Heyden (Amsterdam Historical Museum). Below left, two workers sawing a trunk lengthwise, drawing by Hendrik Avercamp (Sotheby Parke Bernet).

THE GOVERNMENT OF THE CITY & THE CAREER OF THE PATRICIAN

In the 17th and 18th centuries the wealth and prosperity of Amsterdam made it the most powerful city in the province of Holland, and because of its economic weight it was often influential in determining the political direction of the republic. The real power of its administration thus extended well beyond the city limits. Amsterdam was also a largely autonomous city with regard to the central government, and this was a common characteristic of the other cities of the Seven Provinces. The tradition of autonomy dates back to the Middle Ages and was founded on the "privileges" granted to the seigneur who wielded his own sovereignty in accordance with the feudal organization. Because of this, it was in effect a state within a state.

The government of the city, or its administration, was in the hands of four burgomasters (1, Glorification of the Burgomasters of Amsterdam, *17th century, detail*). Originally, the appointment of the burgomasters was a prerogative of the seigneur, but from the 15th century onward they were elected by a complex system (3). A college made up of the outgoing burgomasters and the aldermen, as well as those who had in the past held these posts, elected three burgomasters. In a second stage, the three newly elected burgomasters coopted

the fourth burgomaster, choosing one of the four outgoing men. These elections were held on an annual basis and the system described above, which was instrumental to the power then wielded by the burgomasters, only took place in Amsterdam.

The burgomasters were in command of the civil guard and the troops stationed in the city. They also exercised great influence in the appointment of the city functionaries, the administrators in charge of the welfare of orphans and of vacant succession, charitable institutions, and the captains of the companies of the civil guard. The person responsible for the judicial sector was the *schout* who was a representative of the seigneur (2)—formerly an executive and then no more than a formal representative. The schout was the chief of police, the public prosecutor (like an attorney general), and president of the tribunal of aldermen. He was appointed by the burgomasters, whereas in other cities in Holland this was the prerogative of the provincial states. In his judicial function the schout was assisted by a college of nine aldermen (*schepenen*). The aldermen were chosen annually by the stadholder from a "list of 14" presented to the stadholder by the vroedschap, or city council. When the post of stadholder was unfilled (as in

1

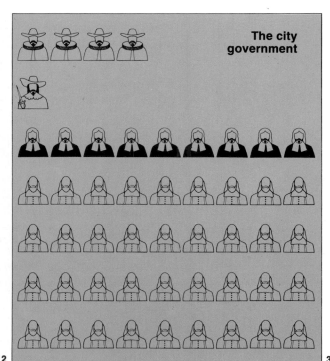

The city government

2

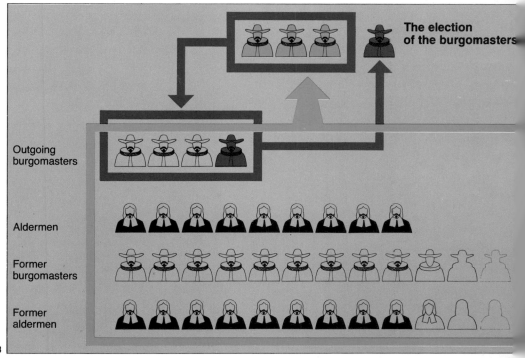

The election of the burgomasters

Outgoing burgomasters

Aldermen

Former burgomasters

Former aldermen

3

the periods 1650–1672 and 1702–1748) the aldermen were chosen by the burgomasters. The burgomasters, the college of aldermen, and the vroedschap all carried out the legislative duties of the city. As the fourth body of government (2), the vroedschap was the direct backup to the power of the burgomasters. It was a college of 36 members, "men both rich and wise," whose task was to "counsel" the burgomasters. This college had been institutionalized from the first half of the 15th century, and although its counsel was not regarded as binding, because it was the expression of the upper middle classes in the city, it is not hard to imagine its influence in the government of the city. A seat in the vroedschap was for life, and vacant posts were filled by co-opting. The members of the colleges that constituted the city government belonged to a small group of rich merchant or land-owning families, generally closely inter-related. These families made up a patrician class, but this was not a completely closed élite. It was not impossible to gain access to it, either by marriage, or by being co-opted into the vroedschap. In the period from 1578 to 1650 and from 1748 onward the patrician circle was fairly permeable. This is shown in table 4, which, for the various periods of the history of the city, shows composition by percentage and on the basis of the "origins" of the members of the vroedschap. In the lower band we can see the percentage of members coming from the patrician class in other cities, or who have entered the upper echelons of Amsterdam; the upper band shows the percentage of members whose entry into the patrician class was assured by virtue of their having a seat in the vroedschap. The social origin of the patrician class in Amsterdam was originally entrepreneurial: members of the bourgeoisie (i.e. burghers), dealers, merchants, and shipowners. Subsequently, as is also the case in other city oligarchies, various changes took place: business was replaced by private income as a source of wealth and power. Table 5 charts this transformation. It gives for the ruling class those elements that enjoyed incomes from capital as compared with the entrepreneurial basis of the previous class. In fact, we can see the increase in the percentage of those who "had no occupation," in other words, those who had private incomes and those who were owners of country properties—an indication of a situation and mentality of the rentier.

During the two centuries of the republic, the son of a family belonging to the patrician class was in some sense predestined to wield power both within and beyond the city. Before the young man there opened up a cursus honorum in which he could give some proof of his talents. A promising young man would start off in the city offices at the bottom of the ladder. If he carried out his allotted tasks satisfactorily in due course he would rise to the post of burgomaster, which, in turn, would lead to appointments on a national, and even an international-

al, level. In this respect a good example is given by the merchant Andries Bicker, from a patrician family, who lived from 1586 to 1652 (6). In 1614, at the age of 28, he started out as a commissary for minor matters. Two years later, and on three separate occasions thereafter, he became an alderman; from 1617 to 1620 he was the commissioner for matrimonial affairs; in 1621 he was commissioner for pawnbroking; the year after he took a seat in the vroedschap. Further still, he became a commissioner at the Exchange Bank, and a burgomaster—for the first time at the age of 41, and thereafter nine more times. On two occasions he was the treasurer. He was also ambassador in Sweden, Brandenburg, and Poland, and four times counselor of the Admiralty of Amsterdam. In 1640 he became director of the East India Company. He once again joined the government of the provincial States of Holland and for three years he was a member of the States General. He died at the age of 76.

Social origins of the members of city council

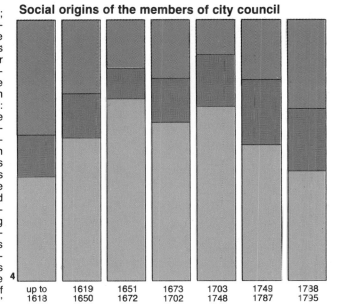

4

| up to 1618 | 1619 1650 | 1651 1672 | 1673 1702 | 1703 1748 | 1749 1787 | 1738 1795 |

From business to private income

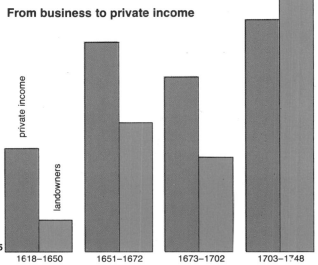

5

| 1618–1650 | 1651–1672 | 1673–1702 | 1703–1748 |

(y-axis: private income / landowners)

	1614	1615	1616	1617	1618	1619	1620	1621	1622	1623	1624	1625	1626	1627	1628	1629	1630	1631	1632	1633	1634	1635	1636	1637	1638	1639	1640	1641	1642	1643	1644	1645	1646	1647	1648	1649	1650	1651	1652
Member of the States General																																	•	•	•				
Ambassador in Sweden																																•							
Member of the States of Holland																									•	•													
Director of the East India Company																											•	•	•	•	•	•	•	•	•	•	•	•	•
Counselor at the Admiralty of Amsterdam																								•	•	•												•	
Ambassador in Sweden, Brandenburg, and Poland																							•																
Treasurer Ordinary																						•																•	
Burgomaster														•		•		•		•	•		•			•	•		•					•				•	
Commissioner of the Exchange Bank												•																											
Member of the Council									•	•	•	•	•	•	•	•	•	•	•	•	•	•	•	•	•	•	•	•	•	•	•	•	•	•	•	•	•	•	•
Commissioner of Pawnbroking											•		•																										
Commissioner for Matrimonial Affairs				•	•	•	•																																
Alderman			•						•	•		•																											
Commissioner for Minor Matters	•	•																																					

6

convoys from the cities, and heavily armed merchant ships.

Among the admiralties' tasks was the escorting of merchantmen on dangerous routes, in exchange for convoy fees. They regulated and collected entrance and exit fees on ships—not without some fraud—distributed booty from conquered enemy ships, and had certain juridical-duties. The moneys raised paid for the fleets. In wartime, the States General imposed a special fleet tax, but, since the inland provinces preferred to give their money to the army, the payment of this tax was usually late and irregular, so that the naval personnel often had a long wait before receiving their salaries.

In wartime, the stadholder became chief admiral. The cities, provinces, and the stadholder had much influence in the appointment of high-ranking officers, and more than once engaged incompetent protégés. Ordinary sailors were taken on by the captains. Orders from admiralty to fleet commanders were not always very clear and there was much rivalry between the admiralties. The fleets were not constantly maintained at full strength. When war

threatened, merchantmen were rapidly converted into warships and crews had to be assembled at top speed. During the First English War, even beggars were pressed into service as sailors. That in spite of such defects the Dutch fleet, in the 17th century, was often superior to any European navy is due to the tactical skill of a number of admirals like de Ruyter and Tromp, to the quality of the ships, and sometimes to a weak enemy.

Until the mid-17th century, warships were regarded as floating fortresses: sailors rammed enemy ships and jumped on board to fight the enemy crew until one party gave up. Guns played a secondary role. Fire ships were much in use: small vessels loaded with combustible material were steered toward the enemy and set afire at the last moment, while the crew tried to return to base on a small sloop. In time, guns became more popular, giving rise to cannon duels. Imitating the English, after 1650 the Dutch went over to the tactics of the line. Ships sailed one behind the other alongside the enemy and bombarded him with cannon fire. A weak spot in warships was the ornate but unprotected stern. It was, therefore, important to meet the enemy at right angles from behind and then unleash a full broadside so that the cannon balls might travel the whole length of their targets. The largest Dutch warships had some 100 cannon, on three or four decks. The English had heavier but less maneuverable ships. The East and West India companies supplied their own armaments and were able to fight off weaker enemies on their own. Both companies did great damage to the naval powers of Spain and Portugal.

The army

When the duke of Alba entered the Netherlands in 1567, he commanded an army of 10,000 men. During the revolt, the Spanish troops grew to 85,000. Against Alba's hardened men, the insurgent provinces could field only miserable small detachments of mercenaries supported by irregularly operating Sea Beggars and by citizens in the towns.

When Prince Maurice became stadholder in 1585, he began to organize sound military forces. With his

rapier and a musket that extended to, at most, 330 feet. Loading was so slow that, at best they could fire one shot every two minutes. The range of the cavalry's pistols was only about 15 feet. Even the heaviest guns of the artillery had a range of little more than two miles.

Alba's conquests had shown that an army had to be properly organized and that towns had to modernize their fortifications. Sieges outnumbered set battles. The thick medieval walls could not withstand the ever-bigger guns. New plans were, therefore, made for defense—ideas first developed in Italy and further worked out in the Netherlands. The mathematician Simon Stevin, military adviser to Maurice, published a manual *Stercktebouwinghe*, in 1594, on the theory of building fortifications specially adapted to Dutch geographical conditions. Six years later, a course for military engineers was started in Leyden.

Throughout the republic, the profile of cities changed toward 1600. The old, high stone walls and the solid corner towers were replaced by low earth walls reinforced at regular intervals by five-cornered bastions with guns on top. Outside the walls was a moat with small defensive islands. Beyond these lay a system of trenches (with or without water). Besiegers tried to cut off the city as thoroughly as possible and had to complete a whole set of measures to roll up the defenses. Amsterdam, too, was protected by earth walls and bastions. Moreover, the whole of Holland could take shelter behind the Waterline—a system of rivers and tracts of land that could be put under water in time of war, thus forbidding passage to the enemy. The line ran from Muiden via Utrecht to Gorkum and was strengthened by forts at the weakest points. From the sea, no enemy could reach Amsterdam. The Zuiderzee was difficult to navigate and formed another excellent barrier. Until the end of the 18th century, Amsterdam was never besieged by a foreign army.

Politics from 1609 to 1702

The war between Spain and the Netherlands dragged on with varying fortunes. In 1609, a Twelve Years' Truce was concluded. During that time, the republic

nephew, the Friesian stadholder William Louis, he studied Roman treatises on war and reconstructed ancient battles by means of small lead soldiers in order to gain strategic insight. The two men established a standing army trained under rigorous discipline, introduced armed exercises (then new and even subject to some ridicule), and standardized the soldiers' equipment. Maurice taught his men to move with speed in order to achieve maximum surprise. His numerous military successes induced many foreign officers to follow his methods, which were promulgated by a book published in 1607, *The Handling of Weapons, Rifles, Musquets and Spears*, a manual richly illustrated by Jacob de Gheyn; it was immediately translated into English and German.

During these years, the state army had grown to some 60,000 Dutch, Germans, French, English, Scots, and Swiss. Even in the highest ranks, a large part remained foreigners. Ordinary soldiers usually came from the lowest social orders. The core of the army was the infantry, consisting mainly of pikemen and musketeers. The former were armed with rapiers and pikes some 17 to 20 feet long. Musketeers had a

experienced further economic development, but also serious political and religious strife. The main figures in these conflicts were the Stadholder Maurice and the "land advocate" (as the grand pensionary used to be called) of Holland, John van Oldenbarnevelt. Maurice, the ambitious general, had been opposed to the truce and wished to fight, win fame, and beat the Spaniards before they could regroup; Amsterdam and Zeeland were, likewise, against the truce, because they could no longer hunt rich Spanish merchantmen. However, van Oldenbarnevelt served the province of Holland, which was groaning under the heavy burdens of war and desperately needed a breathing space.

Religious conflicts were intricately mixed up with this political and economic antagonism. The latent religious quarrel between orthodox anti-Catholics and the more liberal Calvinists in the republic now came into the open. For political reasons, Maurice sided with the orthodox; they won, and their doctrine prevailed at the Synod of Dordrecht (1618–19) where, among other things, it was decided that only members of the Reformed Church could hold public office. In the years after the truce, the economic and political power of Amsterdam became fully developed. Through its influence in the States General,

the city largely determined policy both at home and abroad. Wherever trouble threatened in Europe, Amsterdam at once became involved in deciding which side should be supported. Indeed, the siege of a port or the blockade of a sea route could cause trade to stagnate.

The growing political struggle became apparent while Frederik Henry was stadholder; he succeeded his half-brother Maurice, who had died in 1625. At first relations with Amsterdam were good, but

WINDMILLS

Everyone thinks of Holland as the land of windmills, as indeed it is. In the 19th century there were some nine thousand windmills in existence, and today there are still about one thousand. But the windmill was not, in fact, a Dutch invention. The first windmills, designed for grinding grain—dating from the 13th century in Holland—were no different from those scattered throughout northern Europe. The major Dutch innovation was to apply this ancient instrument to the task of reclamation and drainage.

Essentially, the windmill is a motor that makes use of natural energy and transforms it into movement. The movement can then be applied to a variety of machines and activities—grinding grain, pressing oil, fulling or milling wool, sawing timber, producing dyes by machining tropical woods, and manufacturing paper. The typical, but not sole use made in Holland of the windmill was pumping water. In this instance the motor drives a wheel that dips into

water and raises it up to a height equal to the radius of the wheel. In practice the gain in height was about five feet. By using a series of windmills, each successive windmill would raise the water to a level above that reached by the previous one. Thus land once covered with water was rendered fit for tilling. This procedure was followed until the same task was carried on by steam-powered water scoops.

The illustrations on these pages, taken from a famous Dutch treatise (*Groot Volkomen Moolenboek,* by Leendert van Natrus and Jocob Polly, both builders of windmills, and Cornelis van Vuuren, Amsterdam, 1734) give some idea of the excellent engineering and versatility of these machines.

The oldest type of windmill, first used for grinding grain, was adapted to drawing water. It consists of a pyramidal structure of beams supporting a parallelepiped, also of wood (2), which supports the blades. The upper part with blades rotates

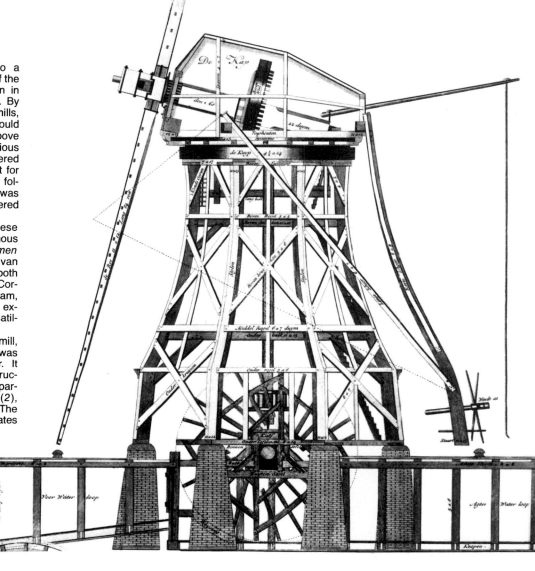

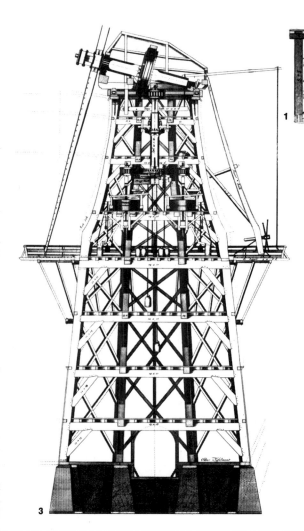

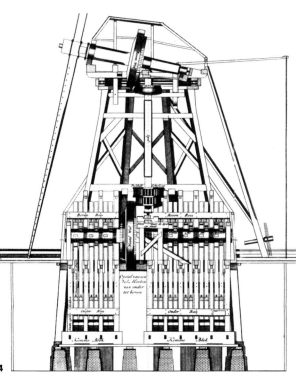

on the lower fixed part in such a way that the blades can be set in the perfect position, head-on to the wind. The windmill is oriented by means of a winch or windlass, which can be seen in the illustration at the lower end of the access ladder, situated opposite the blades. On the ground, all around the windmill, there is a series of solid stakes or pickets. To these are fixed the cords on which the winch pulls to make the required change of position. The axle for the blades supports a toothed iron flywheel, which transmits the movement to the vertical axle situated in the hollow blade holding the two parts together —the fixed part and the movable part of the windmill. At the lower end of this axle another pair of gears transmits the movement to the axle of the waterwheel. The four blades are made up of wooden slats or trelliswork, over which canvas "sails" are stretched. This wind motor has an optimum speed of rotation — too high a speed might cause serious damage. If

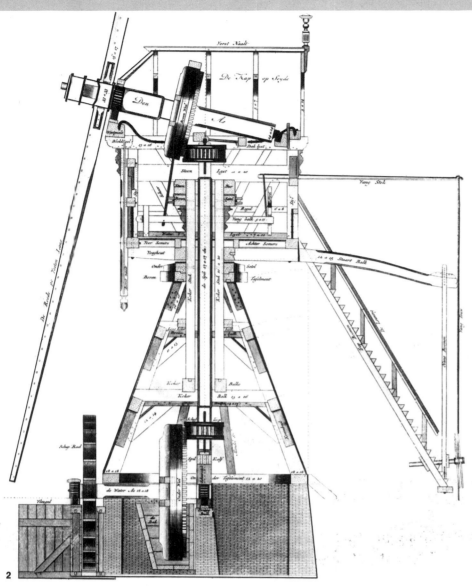

2

the wind is too strong, the sail area must be reduced, exactly as in a sailing ship at sea.

The first application of the windmill to drawing water is documented in Holland in the year 1414. The type of windmill described above was rather fragile. Its replacement, the octagonal mill (1), represented a considerable technological innovation. Here only the upper part rotates. This rests not on a hollow blade, but on the terminal section of a solid tower with a wooden framework.

The sides of the tower are covered with reeds. The construction is thus lighter than that of a brick tower, which was a great advantage on the soft ground of the Netherlands. The other illustrations show various industrial applications of the same kind of tower-based mill. The classic mill for grinding grain, for example (3), in which the movement of the blade axle is transmitted to two millstones, is visible in the upper part of the tower just above the balcony structure.

The tower is quite high. As we know, the countryside in this part of the world is extremely flat. Mills were thus positioned on even the slightest rise or mound in the landscape, but also it was often necessary to make the tower very tall so that the blades could be set in a position in which the wind would catch them without being interfered with by other constructions. In this example, about half way up the tower, note the balcony from where the upper part of the structure with the blades was rotated by means of the rear axle and the winch. Other examples are the fulling mill (an operation involving the felting of wool), which worked by means of a shaft with horizontal cams, a series of presses (4); the sawmill (5), where a circular saw was run off the mill in the long lower building to cut tree trunks; and the oil-pressing mill (6) where, once again, a camshaft drove a series of presses (the pressed blocks of residual vegetable matter—the secondary product of the process—were used as cattle feed).

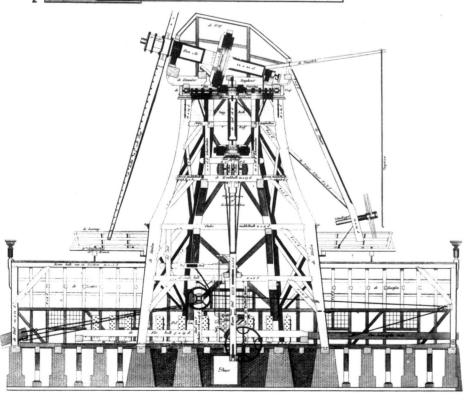

5

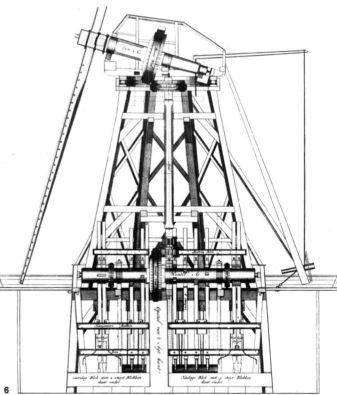

6

they began to cool in the 1630s. Frederik Henry, the conqueror of cities, had monarchical ambitions; he surrounded himself with an elaborate court, had luxurious palaces built, and acquired a place among European princes by the marriage of his son William II to the daughter of the English king. All this, together with Frederik Henry's growing influence in the States General, did not please Amsterdam. A conflict broke out when the stadholder made a move to centralize the control of the fleet: Amsterdam, unwilling to give up its admiralty, violently resisted and won.

Another incident occurred when the Danish king raised the tolls through the sound, which led to the Swedish-Danish War of 1644. According to treaty, the republic owed allegiance to Sweden, but Frederik Henry refused assistance because he wished to preserve his forces for conquering Antwerp. He found Amsterdam radically opposed to his plans: the city was intent on keeping the sound free and had no wish that Antwerp be taken, since that would mean economic renewal for its former rival. After a stormy tug-of-war, a compromise was reached: a

If the heads of all levels endeavored to immortalize themselves in group portraits, the anonymous crowd of small artisans, "the trades," lives in Dutch genre painting, which is more attentive than any other type of picture to daily life, although at times it is mannered. Top left, a cobbler, by Mathijs Naiveu. Above, a smithy, by Cornelis Beelt (Rotterdam, Maritime Museum "Prins Hendrik"). Left, a peculiar but vital profession in a city with bulging grain stores: a rat catcher, statuette by Albert Vinckenbrinck (Rijksmuseum). Opposite, a woman ironing, by Jacob Duck (Utrecht, Central Museum).

Dutch fleet went north to ensure that the sound remained open, and a campaign was waged in the south without managing to take Antwerp.

Frederik Henry's military successes, the French victories over Spain in a war that had been dragging on for years, and an uprising in Spain itself had caused a general financial crisis in that country that gradually made Spain favor peace. In 1648, the Treaty of Westphalia ended the Thirty Years' War: the Spanish Habsburgs lost their hegemony in Europe, while, for the republic, it was a resounding success. The king of Spain dropped all claims to the Seven Provinces and recognized the United Netherlands as free and sovereign. The southern Netherlands remained under Spanish rule, the Scheldt remained closed, and Spain agreed not to sail to territories conquered by the East and West India companies. Frederik Henry did not live to see the peace celebrations, having died the previous year. His son William II looked like he might become an equally tough stadholder, who would continue centralizing policy. This meant immediate conflict with Amsterdam. In 1650, he nearly took the city by force, but his troops lost their way and a postal messenger from Hamburg reported this fact in the city in the middle

of the night. The adventure fizzled out, and some months later William II died of chicken-pox at the age of 24—eight days later his son was born— which meant that the Dutch provinces, except for Groningen and Friesland, were without a stadholder for the time being, a situation that lasted for 22 years.

During this interregnum, one man dominated the political life of the republic: Johan de Witt, grand pensionary of Holland, an exceptionally gifted statesman, upright and intelligent, who was able to maintain his position for 19 years, not least because of his close family links with the ruling patriciate of Amsterdam. He advocated provincial freedom and kept the aspirations of the House of Orange in check. In foreign affairs he became involved in the growing jealousy between England and France: both countries were irritated by the republic's commercial power and took protectionist measures. Moreover, the French king Louis XIV tried to push his borders east and north. The republic was at war with England three times in two decades. In 1651, the English parliament passed the Navigation Act, which, among other things, decreed that certain goods from Europe could be imported only on English ships or

on vessels from the country of origin. Goods for England from outside Europe had to be carried on English ships. Since the Europen freight trade was largely in Dutch hands, war inevitably followed.

Economic motives were at the root of these wars, and dictated their limitations. In 1665, when the English tried to involve the Swedes in the Second Dutch War, the Swedish chancellor said that it was an excellent idea to humiliate the Hollanders, but that it was neither in Sweden's nor in England's interest to ruin the republic. Mutual trading links were too closely knit. At the Peace of Breda two years later it was decided that both countries should keep their conquests abroad: England kept New York and the Dutch, Surinam. Moreover, goods traveling on the Scheldt or the Rhine were to be exempt from the Navigation Act.

In 1672, the first interregnum came to a dramatic end. In this disastrous year, England, France, and the archbishops of Cologne and Münster declared war against the republic, which was nearly overwhelmed. The French, under Louis XIV himself, crossed the Rhine with 120,000 men and took Utrecht. The troops of Münster and Cologne occupied the eastern part of the country. The republic was

taken by surprise and, the army having become disorganized, it could not react at once. Johan de Witt was blamed for this sudden disaster; he had underestimated the French danger, let the army decay, and always limited the power of William III. De Witt and his brother Cornelis were foully murdered by a gang of Orange supporters at The Hague, near the spot where 50 years before the other grand pensionary, Johan van Oldenbarnevelt had been beheaded.

Orange support had lately begun to surface and William III attempted to increase his influence. Had not Louis XIV become king for life at age five, had not his father-in-law, Charles II, been declared king of Scotland at 18, and his uncle, elector of Brandenburg at 20? Why then should he not become stadholder at 22? In February, even before the French invaded, William became commander-in-chief of the army, and in July he was appointed stadholder. He brought the army to full strength and retired behind the Waterline. The French occupied Naarden, barely 12 miles from Amsterdam, but, because of the Waterline, could not advance. The city built additional fortifications, set up 200 cannon, increased the guard, and hired more soldiers. Conditions became alarming when a severe frost caused the rivers to freeze over, in December. This was the flaw in the effectiveness of the Waterline and of all the moats in Holland. The French crossed the rivers with 1,000 men and massacred two small towns, but they had to beat a hasty retreat when the thaw set in.

Meanwhile, an English fleet had been defeated, and this prevented any attempts at landing. Auxiliaries of the Austrian emperor—always ready to attack the French—and of the elector of Brandenburg threatened the French from east and south. Some Dutch victories followed by land and sea. The last and decisive sea battle, when, according to an eyewitness, "the whole sea stood in fire and flame," could be observed by the Hollanders from the dunes. When the English king could raise no more money from parliament, he made peace with the republic in 1674, and Cologne and Münster followed in the same year; four more years elapsed, however, before the French gave up and returned all the land they had occupied. The Netherlands once more had a powerful stadholder, William III, married to the daughter of the English king. In 1688, at the request of leading Protestant circles in England, William crossed the channel and deposed his Catholic father-in-law, James II. Parliament declared William and his wife, Mary, King and Queen of England. Until his death in 1702, the stadholder-king played a leading role in European politics. He always managed to contain the expansionist ambitions of the French "Sun King" and to establish a European balance of power.

In the 17th century, the republic had grown from a small but lively rebellious country to a politically and economically powerful state of the first rank. In the last quarter of the century this power was already waning, and, in the 18th century, strong and centralized states like England, France, and Austria were to determine the fate of Europe.

Arts and crafts

In 1700, the great variety of work being done in Amsterdam was astonishing: along the harbor, in the packing sheds, and at the Waag on the Dam, porters were toiling with all kinds of goods from abroad. Others, in small boats, brought the merchandise

across the water to its destination. The small shops of the inner city, at the crossroads of the great canal belts and in the Jordan, were bulging with consumer goods, from luxuries to the simplest articles. Those who liked the finer things could admire splendid damasks, brocades, or silks, fashionable hats and gloves, and ribbons of silver and gold wire. Gourmets were catered to by shops selling delicacies like oysters and rare fish and bakers at street corners offering all sorts of bread for sale; there also was no shortage of good French and German wines. Furniture, clocks, watches, gilded-leather hangings, car-

The many occupations that made Amsterdam varied and prosperous are shown in the reliefs on buildings; they also served as address plates. Signs of professional pride and the appreciation of skill, they are surprising and touching streaks in the townscape. Some are obvious (the fishing, spinning, butchering, sailing, writing); the relief at center right is a buoy and the fantastic panther at top right perhaps refers to the proprietor's name, while the inscription on the one below says "the three East India sailors."

132

pets, and paintings abounded. In short, whatever a wealthy inhabitant of Amsterdam might want to decorate his house was made or sold in that city. Citizens had long been used to the foreign accents by which many shopkeepers betrayed their origins.

In general it was quieter along the main canals. A woman selling vegetables might trundle past with her cart, or a man selling bread with loaves on a sledge, might go from door to door. The peace of the rich inhabitants was not disturbed by the noise, stench, or dirt produced by some trades, since they were explicitly prohibited from the more prosperous neighborhoods and confined to less exclusive areas outside the walls. The peculiarly biting smell of tarring and caulking on the wharves, the stench of copper and bronze foundries, of cotton boiling mills, and of factories making printers' ink, the pollution of the water by tanneries and dye works—all were a great nuisance. Trades that were too dangerous, such as the making of gun powder, or that needed space, like the 60 sawmills, were situated outside of the city. In corridors and backrooms in town, men and women, often without much light, worked from

dawn to dusk. These craftsmen made such things as pins, pencils, bodices, sieves, boot-laces, shuttles, and scissors.

Throughout the city was an army of street vendors trying to interest passers-by in their wares. Depending on the season, bridges were occupied by salesmen with baskets of strawberries or apples. The aroma of roasted chestnuts mingled with that of fresh fish or cheese. Brooms, chairs, wooden spoons, and earthenware, secondhand clothes, shoes, and hats also could be bought in the streets.

Most of these activities were regulated by city laws and conducted in an orderly way. The rules stipulated who might sell what and when, what quality the goods must be, the length of working hours, level of wages and prices, and the numbers of journeymen, and the city administration supervised their enforcement. The administration also tried to attract new activities and technical skills that were lacking. This stimulated not only industry but trade, as well. Many foreign specialists could start to work in Amsterdam because they were given free accommodations, workshops, or exemption from certain regulations. They contributed to the growing specialization and diversification of industry.

The rise of internal trade from the late 16th century on was due partly to the growing population (mentioned earlier) and partly to the higher purchasing power of the population. Foreign markets remained open until about 1650; thereafter, France and England began to take protective measures to stimulate production at home. This affected the republic's industries and, therefore, the welfare of Amsterdam. Foreign countries negated the advantage that the republic had gained through efficiency and sensible mechanization. Paying higher wages than foreign employers began to cost the Dutch even more heavily. For an industry like textiles, which employed expensive labor, this was ultimately fatal.

Skilled immigrants

It is remarkable how many foreigners took part in the city's economic life. Some groups concentrated

on those skills in which they were already specialized. The first wave of immigrants consisted mainly of Flemings and Walloons; we saw earlier how they introduced certain luxury industries into Amsterdam, such as the making of silk, carpets, and gilded leather. At the same time, a group of Jewish merchants and businessmen from Portugal arrived in Amsterdam, some from Antwerp, others straight from the Iberian peninsula. Through their previous trading links with India and South America, they had access to the raw materials for the silk, diamond cutting, and tobacco industries which were founded largely by them. A second wave of immigrants that left its mark on Amsterdam's industrial life were the French Huguenots, who, in 1685, had to leave their country for religious reasons. They gave a boost to the textile industry and a number of lesser trades, such as printing and publishing. Not as visible but still important in numbers were the immigrants from the German Empire—impoverished by the Thirty

Years' War—and from Poland, among them many, mostly poor Jews. The Germans often found work in their former trades—for example, in lead foundries.

The city did not greet this flood of newcomers passively. As early as 1597, it had signed an agreement with an Italian glassblower, Anthony Obissi of Venice, who was allowed to move to Amsterdam to make crystal glass; this was a new industry for the city, and, in exchange, he had to build his own furnace and set up the workshop. Some years later, the administration decided to spend 120,000 guilders on buying raw silk, so that Manuel Rodrigues de Vega, a Portuguese merchant, could establish the silk industry. Another Portuguese obtained the right to run two silk mills in a house where he could live rent free, provided that he taught others to weave silk. In the same period, the south Netherlander Hans le Maire received a workshop and an advance of 2,000 guilders to produce gilded-leather hangings.

Similar measures were taken after the arrival

Plans of the city in mid-16th and early 18th century on pages 66 and 67, show how much building went on in Amsterdam at the peak of its prosperity and population growth. The architecture of Holland in that period was influenced by the modes and decorations of Italian and European styles, but it remained true to itself in its human scale. Above, drawing for a row of façades, by Philip Vingboons, 17th century. Far left, frontispiece of Architectura Moderna *by* Hendrick de Keyser, 1631; *and left, section and plan of a three-story house, about 1670 (both from Amsterdam Parish Archive).*

Detail of a house in Kloveniersburgwal with sea animals flanking the pediment. Right, the

Bartolotti House, the most famous planned by de Keyser and built for Bartolotti, who rose from

beer brewer to banker. A fine example of houses the rich built on land reached by urban expansion.

of the French. An example involving excessive amounts of capital is that of Pierre Baille, a silk weaver who, several times, received sums of 10,000 to 40,000 guilders to set up a plant with some 60 looms. A French hatter was allowed to employ far more journeymen than was customary in that trade. French hatters, gilders, silk and brocade weavers, and ribbon and lace makers were exempt from the fee for citizenship, and often received an initial small amount of capital and free accommodations, on the condition that they would revitalize the stagnating textile industry. Sometimes an argument was advanced to create new jobs. In 1613, the administration voted in favor of establishing a new glass industry, provided that 50 unemployed people could be put to work again.

The interrelationship of trade and industry

From medieval times, certain industries in Amsterdam had grown together with trade. Soap boiling, oil works, cloth making, and shipbuilding were important even then. In the 17th century, with the increase in trade, there developed a number of finishing industries where raw materials or half-made goods underwent further refinement.

An important finishing trade was the refining of sugar. Raw sugar, mainly imported from the West Indies by the West India Company, was transformed into various sugar products. One of these was the syrup still popular in Holland today and, even then, confined to the internal market. In 1603, there were three sugar refineries in the city; in 1650, 60; and, in 1771, 110. They were highly important: about 1650, the refiners accounted for a quarter of the taxes on goods weighed in the city. From early on, the Jews played a role in this industry, and, in 1632, the administration rejected a gentile attempt to displace them from it; the city apparently was primarily concerned with keeping this industry flourishing.

The tobacco industry was another important example of a finishing industry. Shortly after 1611, tobacco first reached Holland from America. The climax came between 1700 and 1725, when Amsterdam was one of the largest tobacco-working centers in Europe. One reason for this was the cheap to-

bacco available from the eastern part of the republic. On the initiative of Amsterdam merchants with capital, the inland growing of tobacco had begun during the 17th century. Virginia tobacco imported from America was much more expensive. Now, this finer variety could be mixed with the home-grown kind. At first, many rich Portuguese-Jewish traders were involved, but, about 1700, an estimated 3,000 people earned their living in this industry. Most of them worked in the 35 big tobacco-rolling shops, where women and children, too, were employed. Some of these workshops had up to 100 workers. Moreover, Amsterdam then had tobacco-cutting shops and 40 stalk presses where the tobacco was pressed into flat leaves for the cutting.

Diamonds

Diamonds are another enterprise that has survived in Amsterdam. Unlike sugar and tobacco, which were refined in factories, diamonds were a domestic industry. Dealers supplied raw diamonds to be worked

at home. Jewish merchants played an important role in this field throughout the 17th and 18th centuries. Portuguese contacts with India were the first source of diamonds. The poorer Portuguese and, above all, German and Polish Jews worked for relatively low wages. This provoked increasing envy from gentile craftsmen who, in 1748, sent a petition to the city administration in which they asked for a stop to further Jewish immigrant workers, prohibition of Sunday work, and an examination for craftsmen already employed. The Christians complained that they were not like the Jews who, "following their inborn ways can earn their crust by buying shoes, cleaning materials, combs, spectacles or old clothes," and would, therefore, have to go abroad to earn their bread. However, the administration did not agree, because the Jews had always succeeded in making Amsterdam's diamond industry prosperous. An estimated 600 Jewish families earned their living in the diamond business in 1750. Amsterdam diamond merchants acquired worldwide fame with their products and managed to extend their work to jewelry, in general. The ornaments worn by members of the French court were often bought in Amsterdam.

Textiles and shipbuilding

These were important activities in the 17th century. We already have seen how the administration tried to maintain the more refined textile mills by seeking official help in preserving employment there, although with rather indifferent results. The quality of cloth-cutting (the finishing of cloth woven and dyed elsewhere) of woolen and silk materials was particularly famous.

Shipbuilding and, particularly, ship repair offered employment to many. Some 1,000 people were working on the East India Company's wharf and almost as many on the Admiralty's separate one. Medium-sized concerns employed about 75 men. Toward 1650, the industry did well. Raw materials like timber, pitch, and tar were quite cheap on the Amsterdam staple market. Demand at home and abroad was considerable. Besides ships for trade, war, and fishing, many smaller boats were needed to take peat, vegetables, dairy products, and other goods from the plains into the city.

Trades

In addition to the finishing industries, there were many highly specialized trades in the city. Usually a master worked with several journeymen, as in the Middle Ages. The workplace and shop were in the master's house, and some journeymen and apprentices lived there, as well. In some trades, specialization had started earlier and continued—for example, furniture making, which, in 1600, included mirrored wardrobes, Spanish chairs, ebony work, spinning wheels, and trunks. Tin foundries also were further broken down into those that made lids, spoons, or jugs.

Within a trade there were great differences in prosperity and activity: some masters traded in the raw materials of their craft, either in person or under a head journeyman. Although attempts were made to preserve equality among the members of the guilds,

this was not always achieved, in practice. Besides, the administration tried to attract foreign labor and, therefore, ignored certain limiting regulations.

After the resolution of 1578, the guilds lost their religious character. They became associations of fellow professionals that looked after their members' interests and acquired from the administration the right to demand membership. Thus, the guilds had some standing with regard to public law. The city kept an iron grip on the guilds through the appointment of their leaders, confirmation of their quality stamps, and the fixing of wages and prices.

In general, the city left the guilds to organize themselves internally and tried wherever possible to agree to protective measures against competition from home or abroad, unless this was too harmful to the interests of wholesale trade and industry or to the consumer. The butchers' petition against competition from the plains was allowed for a trial period of one year because the city wished to be sure that there would be sufficient supplies of meat for the citizens. Biscuit makers and bakers had their way, with the

Dutch painting is a high point in the history of art. Rembrandt, though not born in Amsterdam, lived and worked there. At the root of the different genres were the different kinds of public and private "consumers." Left, Self-portrait with His Wife *(about 1530), by Jacob Corneliszon van Oostzanen (1470–1533) (Toledo Museum of Art). Right, elegantly painted paintbox attributed to Antonie Janszon van Cross, (1606–62) (Rijksmuseum). Opposite, the painter's studio, by Adriaen van Ostade (Rijksmuseum).*

consequence that those from Wormer and Jisp, where there was a flourishing trade in ship's biscuits, had to leave the Amsterdam market to their colleagues there. By means of quality control on all kinds of merchandise, the city wished to protect the good name of its products and, indirectly, the consumers' interests. On foodstuffs, the control was very strict, lest disease be spread. As a rule, only masters—and, therefore, citizens—were members of the guilds. The one exception, ship's carpenters—journeymen could join, as well—was due to the fact that, in shipbuilding, the head journeyman often managed the wharf while the moneylender remained in the background, so that the journeyman's

position was about the same as that of a master. Women were members of some guilds: for example, peat carriers and fishsellers. Jews could join only the guilds of brokers, booksellers, and surgeons. Membership in a guild gave a craftsman some measure of security: he could expect regular work and, when sick or old, he received a small sum from the guild's benevolent fund, as might members' widows.

Training took place in the master's house. After working for some years as an apprentice, often in return for board and lodging, a youngster attained the status of journeyman, without a test. After further years of work he could submit a masterpiece and, in principle, could then start as a master himself. In practice, this was not so easy: the new candidate had to buy himself into the guild and, if a noncitizen, pay his citizenship fee, which, by 1650, was the considerable sum of 50 guilders. Marrying a master's daughter or widow was often more advantageous.

During the 17th century, more and more specialists lived as journeymen—on the whole, apparently without much dissatisfaction—perhaps because of the high level of wages in Amsterdam. We know that cloth cutters several times succeeded in forcing up wages. Among the hatmakers' and builders' journeymen, too, there was some unrest—a situation that prevailed among men who worked in groups and, therefore, had more opportunities to plot with one another. The initial recriminations sometimes had a familiar ring: the masters accused the builders' journeymen of being drunk, lazy, and excessively addicted to tobacco, besides refusing to do heavy work outside the city because their families were in town. In return, the men reproached the masters for working with foreign labor willing to do heavy tasks at lower wages, the difference usually finding its way into the masters' pockets. In the case of strikes, the city intervened with force and tried to restore order by mediation.

The number of guild members was not limited. A census shows that in 1688 the tailors had the largest membership, 881 men. The cobblers had 658; gold and silversmiths, 334; fruit merchants, 364; and loaders and carriers, who handled goods to and from ships, 770. Certain guilds, however, were tied to a

fixed number of members and the city's hold on them was much greater because it had to appoint the membership. The groups concerned were the brokers, men who measured and taxed corn, beer carriers, peat carriers, and porters at the weighing stations. These guilds were essential for the smooth running of the wholesale trade. Weighing porters numbered 283 in 1766. Of these, some 150 were organized in teams of six to eight, who worked together for a fee. The teams were distinguished by the color of their hats: blue, red, yellow, green, etcetera. They specialized in certain goods, or worked for a given group of merchants. The work of the Scottish and Zeeland teams was involved in trade with those areas. They ensured the weighing, customs declaration, and packing or storing of the goods. For the city, the essential part was the customs. The special position of these guilds is evident from the fact that, in times of unrest, the city provided them with arms. The 366 peat carriers had to help in case of fire, as did the weighing porters. Such members were exempt from duty in the guard. In the 18th century

no further guilds were formed, perhaps because the city was less in favor of compulsory membership.

As in the wholesale trade, large industries such as the finishing workshops existed outside the guild organization. However, this did not mean that they were unorganized and unregulated. Here, too, the city took great care to control the quality of goods. Moreover, entrepreneurs felt that they should form some kind of association—like the cloth cutters, who met regularly even at the national level—in order to adopt joint measures. The brewers kept in touch within each province. The soap makers formed a society, and the linen merchants, a college of chiefs; silk dyers, too, were organized. However, sugar refining, tobacco, and diamonds remained quite independent.

Architecture: building in the city

A 17th-century visitor approaching Amsterdam from the Zuiderzee would come upon a forest of masts.

Coming from the landside, one saw a typical profile of a Holland city: walls with windmills on top, and behind them, many church roofs and slender towers between the domes of the town hall and the Lutheran New Church. Once in the city, there were no more windmills, but an astonishing variety of gabled buildings and, suddenly, along a canal, the vista of a church tower reflected in the water.

In the 16th century, a new Renaissance style of building began to reach the northern Netherlands. This first became visible in the temporary triumphal arches erected for festive processions, and, more permanently, in the old Gothic houses decorated with "modern" Renaissance motifs. Renaissance architectural theories found a firm footing in the Netherlands as a result of the influence of Italian architects who came to work there and of the illustrated Italian architectural textbooks available in translation.

From the end of the 16th century on, new houses were erected, with gables of red brick alternating with layers of light natural stone. Decorations took the form of masks, scrolls, and garlands. It was a lively architecture in which stepped gables, shutters, and doors, mainly painted red, created a highly cheerful aspect. The first big building in this style in Amsterdam was the Waag, made of massive blocks of stone. In the same period, about 1565, the Old Church was given a new spire with modern features. The dials, set in a classical portal instead of a Gothic frame, were merged organically into the spire, while obelisks replaced the medieval pinnacles, two of them supporting balusters. This tower, for 50 years the city's highest, became the prototype for many others both in Amsterdam and elsewhere.

In the 17th century, Amsterdam was overtaken by a building boom: government buildings, churches, synagogues, orphanages, and almshouses sprang up everywhere, as well as thousands of houses along the canals. The builders were practical men, master carpenters or masons, who drew plans and estimated costs, and were closely involved in the actual building work. However excellent their designs, their names are mostly lost to us. Not so with another type of builder, the architect—then, a new term. An architect was a learned man, trained in theory and

Andrew Marvell, in his **Character of Holland,** *wrote that "Hence Amsterdam, Turk, Christian, Pagan, Jew,/ Staple of sects and mint of schism grew:/That bank of conscience, where not one so strange/Opinion but finds credit and exchange" (1653). Left, a bookshop, in a drawing by Salomon de Bray (Rijksmuseum). Below, the splendid leather binding of* **Entrée de la Reyne,** *the famous visit of Maria de Medici, by Caspar Barlaeus. Right, a graphic chart of atlas production in 17th-century Amsterdam.*

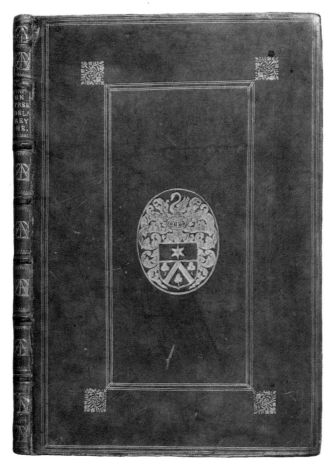

Amsterdam was a cultured city. Because of its tolerance and freedom from censorship, in the 17th century no country published as much as the republic.

Production of atlases in the 17th century

■ Hondius-Janssonius
■ Blaeu

(each rectangle indicates one volume in each edition)

1606
Gerardi Mercatoris Atlas
(Latin; 144 maps)

1619
Gerardi Mercatoris Atlas
(French; 150 maps)

1630
Gerardi Mercatoris Atlas
(Latin; 164 maps)

Atlantis Appendix

1631
Appendix Theatri A. Ortelli et Atlantis G. Mercatoris

1635
Theatrum Orbis Terrarum
(Latin, French, Dutch, German)

1636
Mercatoris Atlas
(English; Dutch and German in 1638, with title *Novus Atlas*)

1638
Novus Atlas
(Latin, French; German in 1642, Dutch in 1645)

1640
Theatrum Orbis Terrarum
(Latin, French; Dutch and German in 1642)

1645
Theatrum Orbis Terrarum
(Latin, French, German; Dutch in 1646)

1646
Novus Atlas
(Latin, French; Dutch and German in 1647, Spanish in 1653)

1650
Novus Atlas
(Latin, French, Dutch, German; Spanish in 1666)

1654
Theatrum Orbis Terrarum
(Latin, French, Dutch, German)

1655
Theatrum Orbis Terrarum
(Latin, French, Dutch, German)

165?
Novus Atlas
(Latin, French, Dutch)

1658
Atlas Major
(Latin; Dutch with title *Nieuwen Atlas*, German with title *Novus Atlas Absolutissimus*)

1662
Atlas Major
(Latin; French in 1663 in 12 volumes, Dutch in 1664 in 9 volumes, Spanish in 1672 in 10 volumes)

building practice, and often with an artistic background. Some of them are well known: Hendrick de Keyser, the sculptor and city architect; and Jacob van Campen, the painter and architect who designed Antwerp's town hall. De Keyser designed the first church built specifically for Protestants: the Southern Church, whose foundation stone was laid in 1603. Seventeen years later, his Western Church was begun. The 283-foot-high tower, tallest in the town, is surmounted by the imperial crown. This, more than any other, is the structure that has become the symbol of Amsterdam. The active de Keyser also designed the Stock Exchange and perhaps the Northern Church and some of the gates, and he added new spires to several towers in the old city walls. His most famous dwelling was the luxurious Bartolotti House on the Herengracht, designed for a beer brewer who had worked his way up to banker. The publication of de Keyser's work in book form was handled by a younger contemporary, the painter and architect Salomon de Bray.

In 1624, four years after de Keyser's death, a house was built on the Keizersgracht, opposite the Western Church—a building that was to become a forerunner of a whole new style: classicism. The clients were the Coyman brothers, rich merchants originally from Antwerp who wanted something "modern." In Jacob van Campen they found the right architect.

Classicism, flourishing in Italy, had been inspired by Roman architecture and became famous in the Netherlands mainly through the architectural treatises of Scamozzi. It is strongly based on theory and directed at an ideal harmony between parts, and between parts and whole. Typical of the style are the strict design of gables, the use of pilasters, and the triangular gable crown. Decorations such as garlands, capitals, and statues are not excessive. Dutch classicism has a kind of severe integrity. The peak of this style is the Amsterdam town hall, but another example is the Trippenhuis along the Bowmen's Bastion moat (Kloveniersburgwal), an imposing building with the air of a palace, built by Justus Vingboons for the brothers Trip, important industrialists, traders, and makers of arms. In the gable are

Of the three medals, the top one is of the booksellers' and printers' guild; the center one commemorates the Hortus Medicus, *the botanical garden where exotic plants brought back from commercial expeditions overseas were planted and served in the practical preparations of physicians and pharmacists. The third concerns the* Athenaeum Illustre, *a college for upper-middle-class education, founded in 1632 when the Latin school proved insufficient for access to Leyden University.*

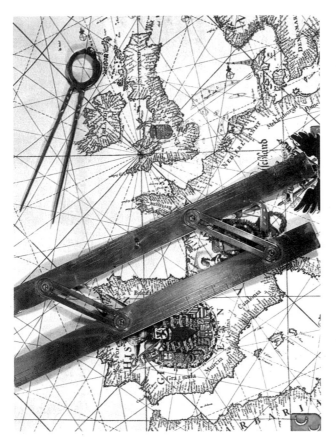

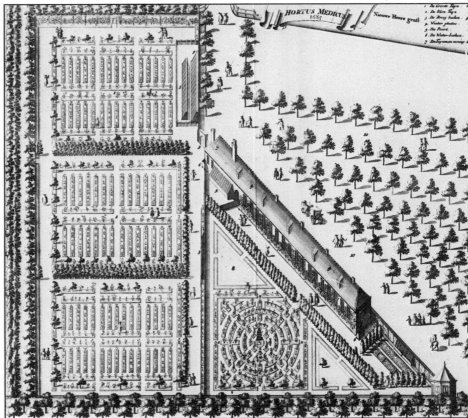

two cannon, and, on the roof, two chimneys shaped like mortars.

Two other architects deserve mention: Daniel Stalpaert and Adriaen Dortsman. The former designed the Admiralty Arsenal, a huge building on the Kattenburg (an artificial island), which was raised in barely nine months in 1656, and the equally imposing East India Company warehouse nearby. His colleague Dortsman built houses along the canals, as well as fortifications; he also designed the Lutheran New Church, the one-and-only domed church in Amsterdam.

The overall urban look of Amsterdam gradually changed during the 17th century. Because of lack of space and the high cost of land, houses grew taller. Besides step gables, neck- and bell-shaped ones increasingly appeared. Toward 1800, the horizontal ledge gable became fashionable, often decorated with a sculptured top. Houses were often modernized simply by adapting the gable to a new style, while the structure remained unchanged. Stone gradually replaced timber in gables. Brick gables were mostly red, and stone ones were painted yel-

low. Until the 17th century, doors were mainly red, but later ochre or brown was used. The arrangement of windows, likewise, changed: after 1650, small leaded frames gave way to big windows.

Most people were housed in far from pleasant quarters. The poorest lived in rear alleys, backrooms, and the cellars of tiny houses, close to each other. These unhealthy quarters were primitively built and often in timber, so that they easily burned and few survived.

TRANSPORT
ON INLAND WATERS

It is clear that at a time when there were few roads, and very few indeed that were fit for traffic, transportation by water was comparatively fast and convenient. Because of its geography, Holland was at a considerable advantage in this area. Countless waterways crisscrossed the flat landscape. The inland lakes were navigable, and two large rivers, the Rhine and the Maas, flowed out into the North Sea through Dutch territory. These inland waters were used by boats, mainly in a north-south direction during the Middle Ages, but it was not until around the 1580s that traffic on the inland waters became customary. In addition to its large number of waterways and lakes, another special feature of Holland was its human geography, which was not unlike that of Flanders or the Po Valley in Italy. It was a country of towns and cities. As early as 1514 half the total population of the country was living in towns, whose influence on the countryside was evident: food and fuel came into the towns from the country. The towns and cities were the marketplace for the products of the surrounding countryside, and these were mainly dairy products.

There was also brisk trading between towns. In about 1580 conditions led to increased inland waterway traffic. The predominance of towns in the settled areas, and the absence of any strong central authority naturally permitted the towns and cities to develop this type of transport. In the 17th century Holland had a well-organized waterway network for carrying goods and people that was unique in Europe. It is worth noting the three types of shipping: vessels used for transporting goods, "scheduled" vessels, and haulage vessels. Freight vessels provided the towns and cities with victuals and fuel. Boats laden with vegetables and fruit, with peat, milk, and various other products arrived in Amsterdam three times a week, on market days. In the 17th century the city allocated fixed moorings to the various vessels. In addition it dealt with the checking and distribution of the merchandise.

After 1580 the various cities came to an agreement between them for regulating and organizing the transport of goods and people, with a system of fixed connections using sail-driven vessels, and these were "scheduled" journeys (3, the vessel that plied between Amsterdam and Deventer). Each shipping line was granted a fixed number of boatmen by the city. But although they were appointed by the city, they provided their services on their own. They often owned their own boat and used one or two "ship's boys." The profits often went into a common fund from which all the boatmen drew equal pay for their services. This got around the problem of a boatman carrying only a few goods earning less than one fortunate enough to be fully laden. In other words, the system was an embryonically cooperative one. The landing stages were set up by the city, the merchandise was subject to controls, and various rules and regulations governed the purchase of the goods. These boats, with their spritsails and movable lateral keels, plied rivers and lakes.

The haulage boat came into being in about 1630 because of the need to transport people. It was a long narrow vessel, fitted with a mast and a long deckhouse where the passengers sat on benches (2, a haulage boat moored alongside a quay on the Amstel in Amsterdam, in a drawing by Jacob Cats). From the top of the mast a cable attached the boat to a horse, which then pulled it from the towpath, in the charge of an attendant. This type of boat—in effect a barge—could be towed along the banks of the existing waterways, but the best and most efficient way of using them was along the towpaths beside straight canals.

In Holland and in the northern part of the republic, 411 miles of canals and towpaths were constructed to this end in two phases (1630–1647 and 1656–1665), by 30 towns and cities (1, the Haarlemmervaert—the Haarlem canal—in the latter half of the 18th century). This involved a major organizational and entrepreneurial effort. The required capital was amassed by the various cities by issuing shares. The land needed to build the system was bought and the excavations and earthworks were put to tender in various lots and to various operators. For a canal of this type, some 10 miles in length, it took 1,540 laborers working for six months to complete the job, and the cost was about 180,000 florins. Once the

1

2

5

job was done, shipping services could start. The boats left from the two terminals on fixed timetables. The investment —no small sum for those days —was partly paid off by the profits made from selling tickets, but these profits also had to be used to pay the boatmen and their crews, and so the cities also levied transit dues. Use of the canals was free to anyone who paid these fees. Tolls also had to be paid by people wanting to walk along the towpaths. The importance of the horse-drawn barge was that it made available to the public a swift and safe means of transport. It cruised along at 4 mph, as opposed to the less than 3 mph of the sailboat, and

could sail in all seasons, regardless of the weather. The boats on night duty along certain routes were famous (4, the night boat to Utrecht, in a drawing by J. Greenwood, 1759). The times of sailing were closely adhered to, as were arrival times at the other end, because of the steady pace of the specially trained horses. The upper middle classes had their own vessels, but everyone else used these haulage boats. During the 18th century the one line from Haarlem to Amsterdam annually carried 250,000 people. These vessels were a means of mass communication (6, the varying dimensions of the boats used by different lines). Poor people traveled

free of charge—a stipulation made by the city in order to keep beggars away.

But it was not all smooth sailing. Some routes involved moving from one canal to another one on a different level, in places where the conflicting interests of two cities had hindered the provision of a basin or lock. When this happened there was an *overtoom* or staging point, by means of which the boat could be dropped or hoisted from one canal to another. It was towed by hand or with winches using wooden rollers (5, an engraving by Nooms), while the passengers waited on the bank. To begin with, Amsterdam did not have a predominant position in the sys-

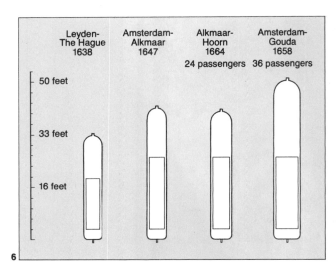

Leyden-The Hague 1638	Amsterdam-Alkmaar 1647	Alkmaar-Hoorn 1664 24 passengers	Amsterdam-Gouda 1658 36 passengers

50 feet

33 feet

16 feet

6

Aspects of city life and setting during the great centuries of Amsterdam. Above, a fair: the storyteller on his ladder, the crowd around the stage with players, the sellers of specialties with *their trestle, and a curious boy. Painting by Cornelis Bellekin (The Hague, Bredius Museum). Below, the great meat market, in a drawing by Pieter van den Berge (18th century, Amsterdam Parish* *Archive). Opposite, the delightful garden of van Loon House on the Herengracht.*

Painting

Both inventories and foreign travelers' records confirm that, in the 17th century, most Dutch houses displayed pictures. "All endeavoured to adorn their houses with paintings, particularly the rooms on the street side," the English traveler Mundy wrote about his visit to Amsterdam in 1640, adding that the baker and butcher—and even blacksmiths and cobblers—had pictures in their shops. This confirms what we see in paintings of interiors, of the period, which often show pictures hanging on the wall.

It would be wrong to think that all and sundry owned the masterpieces now in our museums. Many painters worked in the Netherlands, and paintings were made as on a production line: they were cheap and much in demand. The cost depended mainly on the amount of time and the materials required. A small routine landscape might have cost one or two guilders, but the work of a valued painter could have run to several hundred. The poorer one was, the

fewer pictures one owned, and the lower would be their quality.

Unlike neighboring countries, in the Netherlands a painter depended primarily on the burghers. Nobility and court were less important clients, and, toward 1600, the Catholic Church ceased to commission artists. Reformed churches were austere and opposed to representational art. Only the organ wings were generally covered with paintings. From the 14th and 15th centuries on, painters had worked in Amsterdam, but all that remains from that period are the vault decorations in the Old Church. The earliest extant paintings are 16th-century altarpieces; portraits of a merchant, his wife, and his household; and depictions of members of the guard.

Toward 1600, profound changes occurred in the life of a painter: he not only had to exist independently of commissions for altarpieces or other church decorations, but he also had to cope with an influx of refugee colleagues from the southern Netherlands. These Flemings, with their greater experience and professionalism, exerted a deep influence on painting in the north.

The Dutch painter, by origin, was a craftsman first and foremost, and he earned his crust by paint and brush, as a carpenter does by wood and mallet. A member of the guild of St. Luke, he painted houses, shop signs, glasses, banners, decorative arches for the triumphal entries of princes, and pictures on commission or for the open market. Often he made woodcuts, copper engravings, and etchings. In the 17th century, a division arose between the "rough" painters—those who decorated the doors, shutters, and woodwork of houses—and the "fine" painters, who made paintings. Among the latter, specialists developed in the different genres, such as portraits, seascapes, church interiors, and still lifes. Within each genre there were further specialists: some landscape painters concentrated exclusively on forests or winter scenes, and, among still-life painters, there were experts skilled in portraying sober images of food-laden tables, flowers, or scenes with hunting trophies. Painters, moreover, differed in status. Some had plenty of orders and were esteemed in high circles. At the same time, there was an army of busy painters producing endless series of small

landscapes or seascapes as a kind of mass production, their names and works soon to be forgotten.

Dutch painting is often praised for its so-called realism and truth to nature. This is rather misleading because painters worked only partly from nature. They made preliminary studies in pen or chalk on paper or drew inspiration from prints and sample books, which provided the elements for composing a picture. Even seemingly realistic landscapes are never spontaneous copies of nature. The painter did, indeed, make open-air sketches of tiny landscapes, houses, trees, small bridges, and human figures, which he later incorporated into his pictures in the studio. Although the result always seemed realistic, the composition was actually carefully built-up of

single elements that, individually, were true to nature. A telling example of this "studio" realism are the still lifes of flowers in which varieties that never could have blossomed at the same time are portrayed together.

In another respect, too, the term "realism" is not quite appropriate. Behind the seemingly realistic interiors, still lifes, and the like, there lies a deeper symbolism that was more apparent to contemporaries than to us. Netherlanders were fond of hidden allusions and ambiguities, which occurred in their everyday language as well as in painting and literature. Often a picture would contain a moralizing message, pointing to the transience of life and to death. This is obvious whenever a picture is inscribed "memento mori" or "the end achieves the work." A skull, a snuffed-out candle, or an hourglass were recognizable symbols of death and the passage of time. However, it became more difficult to grasp the veiled symbolism of an ace of hearts in the hand of a woman, perhaps a warning against amorous flattery. A lute in the hands of a woman may point to harmonious love between her and her husband, while a bell-ringing boy tells us that humans are as vulnerable as soap bubbles.

The various painting genres were valued differently. Still lifes and landscapes stood in low esteem, while historical pieces, now regarded as rather un-Dutch, were greatly prized. A historical piece might represent a biblical scene, an event from antiquity, or from national history. Here a painter could show that he had mastered all the lower genres, for such pieces always contained portraits, figures, landscapes, architecture, and still lifes. The historical painting, more than the other genres, was linked with international traditions.

It was mainly public bodies and private citizens of the highest social layers who ordered such pieces, and in a few cases, the stadholder. Often such paintings glorified and admonished. They were hung in public halls whose function was closely linked to the subject depicted. Thus a Judgment of Solomon often appeared in courtrooms to remind judges of their task. High points of Dutch historical painting are still found in the town hall of Amsterdam. They encouraged burgomasters—who liked to compare

AN AGE-OLD PROBLEM: RECYCLING THE WATER

Amsterdam is a city with an important waterfront. It is situated on a branch of the Zuiderzee called the Ij, and its shape is determined by the river Amstel (after which the city is named) and by the various rings of canals, dug at various times for the purposes of defense, and subsequently essential for the transportation system. The landscape painting by Jacob van Ruisdael (*4*) shows the city (in about 1675–1680) seen from the banks of the Amstel, with the fortifications and the windmills sitting atop them. Originally the water flowing through Amsterdam was clean and fresh. People fished in the in-land waters, and the water itself was used for cooking and making beer. But in the 17th century, as one burgomaster lamented, the canals looked like rubbish dumps. By widening the communications between the Zuiderzee and the North Sea, near Texel island, the tides made their influence felt more markedly in the Ij, and the fresh water of Amsterdam started to be mixed with salt water. The population increase, from the 16th century onward, increased the pollution. The canals became the dumping grounds for waste from latrines, brick factories, dye factories, and for the garbage from the markets. As

1

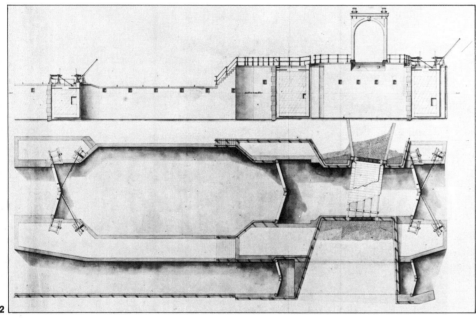

2

3

boats and ships sailed along the canals, they stirred up the water and shifted the canal bed, consequently causing a most unpleasant stench. Wells had to be dug to supply drinking water; rain water had to be collected, too, or water had to be brought into the city by boat from outside.

The authorities tried to protect the city from pollution by posting prohibitions against discharging waste, by dredging the canals, and by recycling the water. All these measures were partially effective, but none of them really solved the problem.

The oldest prohibition against discharging waste dates back to 1413. Latrines had to be discharged onto boats, and the waste taken outside the city. But this and other later rulings were not respected. Dredging the canals, which did have some positive effect, did not get at the root of the problem. The recycling of the water was never done carefully enough. It was an ingenious method, but it had its drawbacks. It was not until the introduction of water scoops driven by steam in the 19th century that a really decisive technological advance was achieved.

The city canal system was separated from the waters of the Ij by locks. The painting by Meindert Hobbema (1660–1661) shows one such lock, the *Haarlemmersluis* (*1*). Another lock, the *Eenhoorn Sluys*, or Unicorn Lock, can be seen in an engraving by Reinier Nooms, who was also known by the name of Zeeman (*3; plate no. 2 shows a related 18th-century lock construction plan*). When the high tide flowed into the Ij, the locks and

4

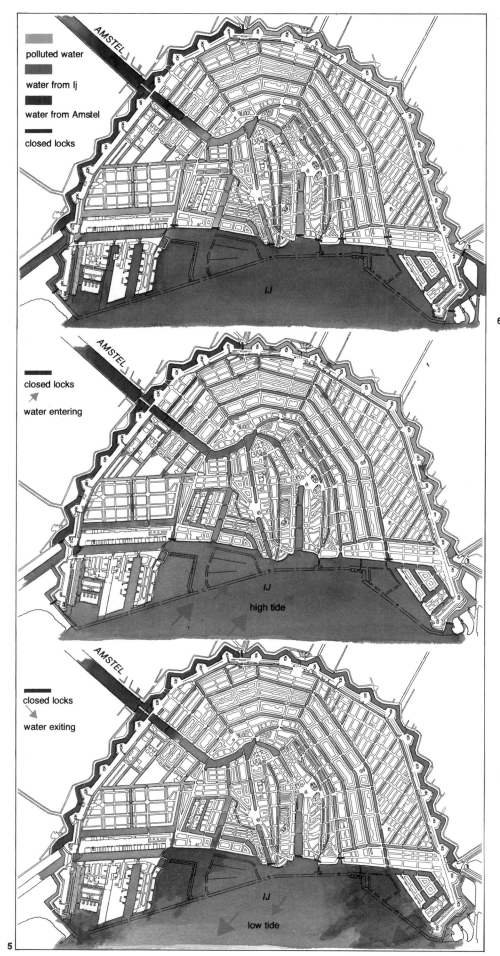

polluted water

water from Ij

water from Amstel

closed locks

---

closed locks

water entering

---

closed locks

water exiting

AMSTEL

IJ

high tide

low tide

5

6

sluices were opened and the clean water poured into the city canal system until it reached the Amstel. The technical difficulty lay in the need to keep the water level constant throughout the city. The buildings of the city were built on pile foundations and too great a variation in the water level might well accelerate the process of rot. In addition, too high a water level flooded basements, which was often where merchandise was stored; too low a level increased the smell from the canals. The city was divided up into four districts, each one with its own water gauge and depth scale, and the influx of clean water and the outflow of dirty water were regulated separately by each district. The system was complicated and faulty, and the need grew for more locks, which increased in number as the city grew in size. They also seriously hindered traffic within the city. It was further necessary for the districts to be in agreement with the farmers in the surrounding countryside, where the excess water had to be leveled off. The lock keepers were often negligent, sometimes letting too much water through. And there was also the problem of the water in the Amstel becoming too low. In both cases the water flowed too fast. Then in 1673 locks were constructed on the Amstel (6, an engraving by P. Schenk, ca. 1710). By doing this, all the inland waters in Amsterdam could now be controlled, as could the movement of water from the Ij and the Amstel. Later, the four districts became one, and this greatly facilitated the circulation of vessels along the inland waterways.

In the 18th century the recycling of the water in the city was finally achieved, as shown in the three plans on the left (5). Twice every 24 hours, at high tide, one or more of the locks on the Ij were opened at the right moment. The clean water coming from the Ij circulated through the canals. At low tide this water, which had cleaned the waterways, was once again discharged into the Ij at different points so as to prevent the following tide from pushing back into the city the dirty water that had just been removed. The system never worked perfectly, and there were countless proposals and experiments to improve it. For example, when the tide in the Ij was not very full because of winds blowing in from the south, the flow of clean water was insufficient. When, on the other hand, the level of the Ij did not drop enough with the low tide, it was difficult to discharge the water from the city into it. In these instances the windmills were not even capable of drawing up a sufficient quantity of water in the inland network to be discharged into the Ij. This problem was not properly solved until the 19th century.

themselves with Roman consuls—to moderation, virtue, and just and wise administration. For the burgomasters' room Govert Flinck painted the scene of Marcus Curius Dentatus refusing gifts from the Samites, to underline that burgomasters should not be bought. In the jurymen's room, where the highest court sat, hangs Ferdinand Bol's *Moses with the Tables of the Law,* to keep alive the memory of the Ten Commandments.

Amsterdam was an artistic melting pot; countless painters from other towns in Holland came to live there and many genres and styles were practiced in the city. Thus, there is no typical Amsterdam school of painting. A genre for which there were many orders was the group portrait. Directors of orphanages, hospitals, reformatories, presidents of guilds and inspectors used to have themselves painted together. Many such paintings survive, some still in their original place. Directors are portrayed in their assembly rooms, a round table on which there lay paper, pens, cashbooks, and coins to underline their administrative function. A shy orphan symbolizes the object of the association, and in the background there is a bare-headed employee to contrast with the director. Older than this type are the guards' pictures, the earliest extant example dating from 1529. Guards met at their depots, buildings with a yard in back, where they held their shooting practice. The various companies had themselves painted regularly and the pictures were hung in the depots. The individuals represented paid according to the amount of space they occupied in the picture. Since many such pictures survive, their development is easily traced.

Because there were many people to be shown, the painter was confronted with a compositional problem. In the earliest guards pieces we see one or two rows of heads or busts next to each other without careful arrangement. In order to achieve the links, painters began to show the guards grouped around a table, which gradually produced a lively effect: the heads received more individual features, and the carriage of the figures was more natural. Guards pieces became ever bigger, up to almost 23 feet across. The picture was made even more vivid by alternating sitting and standing figures, lively gestures, and variation in the very colorful attire. We see a varied but always carefully considered mixture of banners, pikes, and halberds, sashes and plumed hats; light is reflected on armor, on the metal mountings of muskets; and the wine sparkles in the beakers. The effervescent splendor of such group portraits reached a climax in the works of the Haarlem painter Frans Hals and in Rembrandt's *Night Watch*.

Goldsmiths and silversmiths

Another guild of superb artisans was that of gold- and silversmiths. This craft flourished particularly in Amsterdam and The Hague. There were many commissions, not so much from nobles, church, or court, but from civic administrative offices, guilds, guards, and individual burghers. The authorities usually ordered pictures on the occasion of splendid events or as memorials for military victories. Medals and cups were given to meritorious burghers.

The guilds, too, bought beakers, often of great size. Moreover, they owned silver funeral plaques on which the tools of the guild or members at work were represented. When they buried a guild brother, these plaques were attached to black drapings round the coffin. Two precious 16th-century drinking horns belonging to Amsterdam guard companies still exist; they are symbols of fraternity between guards. We also have two guards' chains, which the winner of the yearly competitive shoot could wear round his neck.

Burghers owned silver utensils, such as goblets, dishes and jugs, saltcellars, candle sticks, cutlery, and beaker screws (a foot in gold or silver in which a wine glass could be fixed by small clamps). Their beauty and value can be seen in splendid still lifes. We must remember, of course, that their glow can contain a hint of the transience of all earthly things and a call to moderation. Beside large and valuable pieces, there was a wealth of smaller silverwork, such as cutlery, small boxes for snuff, tobacco, or perfume, sewing kits, book covers, bag handles, clasps, buttons, tops for walking sticks, and delicate toys. Silver was attractive, and silver utensils were useful, but above all this precious metal was a good investment. Gold and silver objects were taxed first according to weight, then according to artistic value.

Diversions on ice, by Hendrick Avercamp (Amsterdam City Museum). The cold northern winters transform the Dutch landscape when the waters freeze over in canals, ponds, and lakes. In the past there were many more lakes than now, for example, see the chart on page 16. Many of these were gradually turned into polders and dried out. Frost did indeed contribute to the ending of the oligarchic system of rulers in Amsterdam, when in 1795 the French were able to cross the frozen rivers and reach the city.

These metals could always be melted down, and much of it was for emergency coinage in times of war.

The grand master of Amsterdam's guild of gold- and silversmiths was Johannes Lutma the Elder, friend of the great artists of his time. Rembrandt made an etching of him as an old man. Lutma designed, among other things, the copper railing in the choir of the New Church, gold and silver medals, and a splendid jug and dish for the inauguration of the new town hall.

Books and maps

In the 17th century no country produced so many varied books as did the republic, doubtless because of the climate of tolerance that prevailed in the Netherlands. Neither state nor church exercised a paralyzing censorship; everything could be printed. Only once did the authorities intervene, after strong pressure from right-thinking Protestant preachers. When the Walloon parish once complained to the administration about a disliked author, burgomaster Hudde, who was not inclined to intervene, replied laconically: "We live in a free country. He has written against you, well now, you write against him." A second favorable factor was the influx of highly trained experts who had fled from the southern Netherlands around 1600. It was, in part, their skills

and money that raised typography, illustration, printing, and binding to so high a standard. The smooth adaptation of guild regulations helped as well, enabling entrepreneurs in the book trade to operate freely. Book printing was indeed cheap here. Authors' fees hardly mattered, and because there was little protection for writers, there was a lot of reprinting. Paper was the costliest element in bookmaking and in Amsterdam a huge international paper trade developed.

All kinds of books were published: bibles, theological tracts, and hymn books made up the bulk. Moreover, there were scientific books and books that were banned elsewhere. Controversial matter from authors like Galileo, Descartes, Bayle, or Hobbes could be freely printed. Exotic typography was no obstacle: there were books in Hebrew, Armenian, Arabic, and Greek. Among ordinary burghers literacy was very high in the republic and a whole flood of small books appeared primarily for them, such as almanacs, forecasts, puzzles, moralizing tracts, song books, and collections of symbols. A special and much sought-after genre was the travelers' tale. The Dutch were immensely interested in overseas events, and they devoured descriptions of distant lands, their people, flora and fauna, and accounts of adventurous trips full of shipwrecks and lost wanderings. Hundreds of such books appeared, most of them in Amsterdam.

Maps

Cartography developed very rapidly due to the great demand for information about distant countries and the practical need for reliable maps for sailors. By the 16th century there existed a tradition of map drawing for the military and for the control of waterways. Toward 1600 this was enhanced by the skills and money of cartographers, copper engravers, printers, and publishers from the southern Netherlands.

In the 17th century, Amsterdam supplied the whole of Europe with maps. These were made by a number of fiercely competing firms, among which Hondius, Janssonius and Blaeu were the biggest. They tended to take over each other's maps with small changes and vied with each other in the field of atlases, the ever more comprehensive editions of maps and descriptions of lands, seas, cities, and the stars. The climax of this race was the French edition of Blaeu's 12-volume *Atlas Major* in 1663, which appeared in Dutch, Latin, and Spanish. The firm of Blaeu was official mapmaker to the East India Company. As soon as a company fleet arrived, the captain had to hand in his logbooks and maps to the office so that the mapmakers could amend the old maps with the latest information. The company took great care that such trade secrets should not fall into competitors' hands, and cartographers were pledged to secrecy. After 1700 the French and eventually the English as well became formidable cartographic rivals to the Dutch. However, the Amsterdam firm of Van Keulen & Son maintained a strong monopoly in quality atlases and maps in the 17th century.

Maps were not only informative, but also decorative. They were brilliantly designed and carefully colored by hand. Along the borders were views of towns, coats of arms, portraits, allegorical pictures, and animals. As geographic knowledge became more accurate, the decorative aspect receded. More and more unknown regions could be filled in, reducing the space available for illustrations. Printed atlases and terrestrial and celestial globes were often presented to visiting foreign rulers as gifts. The higher the ruler, the larger the atlas and the luxury of its binding, in parchment, morocco leather, velvet,

or gold cloth. Some collectors amplified their own atlases with additional maps, topographical drawings, historical prints, and portraits, so that in the end they consisted of dozens of volumes.

The ordinary burgher, too, had an eye for beautiful maps. Many pictures of Dutch interiors show not only paintings on the walls but maps as well. Visual material obviously attracted the Dutch. Besides paintings and maps, prints were also in great demand. These were mass produced and were sold loose. Since certain loose prints were actually book illustrations, one could have a volume bound either with or without illustrations. The demand for prints of current events was enormous: representations and maps with explanations of land and sea battles, sieges, entries of rulers, portraits, and caricatures. The artistic standards of Dutch landscape engravings with their woods, fields, and villages with small figures walking, fishing, or skating are universally known. Landscapes especially flourished around 1600, probably because people valued and extolled the Dutch countryside, as is also evident in literature. Their own land, conquered from the Spaniards, was something to be proud of and sing about: Arcadia no longer lay in Greece but was within immediate grasp.

Science

Until the end of the 19th century Amsterdam had no university. Its practical citizens were not inclined to set up an institution for difficult theoretical studies. Moreover, the University of Leyden, founded in 1575, was strongly opposed to a rival in Holland, even when Amsterdam planned to establish an *Athenaeum Illustre* in 1632. The aim of this body was to be a bridge between the Latin school and the university. At the Latin school the syllabus included Latin and Greek, theology, logic, ethics, ancient history, mythology, and calligraphy. Amsterdam had two of these, but its young candidates for university were ill prepared and immature.

When the Athenaeum was opened, two university professors made sonorous speeches: Vossius, the historian and writer of textbooks, and Barlaeus, the poet and philosopher. Barlaeus emphasized in his

Above, dike repairs, drawing by Roelant Roghman. All technical needs in the fight against and the control of water and inland drainage created a body of knowledge that led to investment abroad.

speech *Mercator Sapiens,* the valuable counterweight that science provided for the merchant's life and the need for a trading city to look after the intellectual development of its citizens. The Athenaeum flourished for some decades, after which its standards declined. Even in the 16th century, under the influence of Erasmus, education had a humanistic character. In Amsterdam this was reinforced after the Alteration of 1578 when most Catholic teachers disappeared and the vacuum in the Latin schools was filled by men from the southern Netherlands. One of them, Petrus Montanus, with his fellow refugee and brother-in-law, Jodocus Hondius, kept an edition of Ptolemy's *On Geography,* with illustrations by Gerard Mercator. Nine years later Montanus published a Dutch edition of a Latin description of Amsterdam. Both editions are typical of a new scientific outlook directed both to classical authors and personal research.

A rich source for study in Amsterdam was the city library, established in 1578 in the New Church at the burgomasters' initiative. Contemporary experts like the librarian of Leyden praised this library—which was open to everyone—for its diverse holdings. Most of the 765 titles available there in 1612 (in 1,400 volumes) were on theological topics, but there were also the handbooks, dictionaries, and texts required for studying law, medicine, history, mathematics, and languages.

Amsterdam was not a genuinely scientific city, but one form of practical teaching and research was an exception, namely anatomy. In the mid-17th century there were some 250 surgeons and 50 physicians. The former were practical men who dealt with wounds, fractures, sprains, and blood-letting. The physicians had a theoretical and practical university education behind them. They made diagnoses, treated the sick, and were able to operate. To en-

Right, Amsterdam houses after a fire. Opposite below left, firemen fighting a blaze, drawing and illustration in the Brandspuitenboek ("book of fire engines"), both by Jan van der Heyden (1137–1712), painter, inventor (of the fire pump), and head of the fire brigade. In this department Amsterdam was quite modern, as she was in other ways, too. For example, the first carriages appeared about 1610, and by 1615 traffic problems led to the introduction of one-way streets, while in 1634 private vehicles were banned from the urban belt. To light the city, in 1595 the authorities ordered that every 12 houses must light a lantern at night, and in 1597 a body of lantern lighters was formed. In 1669, Jan van der Heyden presented to the council a scheme for oil lamps for outside use and was appointed inspector of public lamps, which by 1697 numbered 133; by 1689 there were at least 2,380. They were lit simultaneously and were filled with oil measured according to season, as the nights varied in length. Toward 1700, the city had stations for hiring carriages, somewhat like taxi ranks today, for travelers and merchants, and a hundred inns.

hance instruction in surgery, there was an annual dissection of an executed criminal, which greatly increased anatomical knowledge. This occurred in winter because corpses did not decay so fast and the stench was more bearable. The public could attend these dissections for a fee, and laymen came from far and wide. The anatomy lecturer was appointed for life, and it was he who performed the dissection. This figure is often portrayed in paintings with a group of important surgeons around the body. One of them, Nicolas Tulp, was the first in Amsterdam to assemble a pharmacopeia, an official handbook for preparing and applying drugs, compulsory for pharmacists, surgeons, and physicians. Tulp decided to publish this book after a serious outbreak of the plague in 1635.

A later colleague, Fredrik Ruysch, developed a special technique for preparing bodies and organs. His collections of specimens and skeletons attracted international attention, and after his death it was sold to Csar Peter the Great of Russia. Surgeons and pharmacists, moreover, received practical instruction in the *Hortus Medicus,* the rich botanical garden, which was regularly supplied with plants and seeds brought back by sailors.

Schooling

As early as 1560, Guicciardini remarked on the Dutch people's ability to read and write. Traditionally, education was largely in the hands of the Catholic Church. When the Reformed Church became the most important in the northern Netherlands, education was deliberately aimed at the masses. Everybody had to learn to read and write, especially the former. The church particularly wanted everyone to read the Bible. Moreover, one had to know the Heidelberg Catechism and the new psalms, the more so since in 1580 there were only a few Dutch Calvinists. The Synod of Dordrecht in 1618 at first favored free education for the poor and decreed that schoolmasters must belong to the Reformed Church. Besides ensuring the spread of Calvinist doctrine, education aimed at producing useful members of society. In 1623 the administration of Holland declared that "schools are like plant nurser-

ies in which the young must have godliness and respect for the authorities established by the law inculcated in them."

Preachers and provincial as well as civic authorities jointly ensured that these aims were observed in the schools, which were regularly inspected, usually by members of the church council or by representatives from the city administration. The church had the strongest hold on primary schools, frequented by boys and girls from the lower social groups. Schools were relatively inexpensive. Classes began at eight in the morning and ended at half past four, with a midday break. Classes were held in the evening, too: children who were in training with a master during the day could go to school at night.

Classes were held in one large room, mostly at the teacher's home. Sixty to a hundred children between ages 5 and 12 sat on loose benches and trestles. On a high stool in their midst the schoolmaster towered above the crowd and ordered each to come to him in turn to be heard. Older children helped the small ones with spelling and everybody worked separately at his own pace. School was not compulsory,

had to pass a test. Teachers sometimes advertised in newspapers, as in this piece from *De Amsterdamsche Donderdagsche Courant* (Thursday Courier of Amsterdam) of September 29, 1689: "Master Pieter, schoolmaster at Amsterdam, will teach reading or writing to all people between twenty and fifty years who have previously missed out."

In about 1750 free teaching for the poor was introduced. At Amsterdam there were then eight schools for the poor, run partly by the city and partly by the diaconate. There had been earlier attempts at Amsterdam to teach the poor. For example, around 1680 the city sent girls from families on the welfare rolls to work in the Silkwinding House, provided that they would also receive some education there —little came of it. Boys from better backgrounds could go to the Latin school, which was not open to girls. The school decree of 1625 fixed the syllabus and textbooks, and organized it into four or six classes for the whole country. Although religion was included, the classics were stressed. The Latin school was typically Renaissance and humanist in

however, and parents often kept children at home, sometimes for weeks. Reading matter was the same everywhere: children learned to read from an ABC, the so-called *Haneboek* (book of the cockerel, after the picture on the cover). After that, a child might try the *Trap der Jeugd* (ladder of youth) in which sets of increasingly harder words and finally little rhymes appeared, such as "God will not lightly punish us, but there's no doubting when he does."

Learning to read was time consuming because there was no proper teaching method. For a change children could practice on texts from the Ten Commandments and on questions from the Heidelberg Catechism. At the age of eight a child could begin to study writing. About this age boys often became apprenticed to a master. Moreover, learning to write entailed greater school fees so that many parents either could not or would not pay. Therefore there were some who could read but not write. Some learned arithmetic as well, but that meant a considerable increase in fees.

There was no special training for schoolmasters, although one who wished to exercise this profession

style. It led to a higher school, such as the Athenaeum in Amsterdam or the university.

A more practical line was taken especially by the French schools, which became increasingly popular in the 18th century. They were for children from better families who wished to follow a commercial

career. Here the pupils were taught French, perhaps English, bookkeeping, and arithmetic. There were all kinds of small private schools, among them those for Catholics: here teaching had to be more or less secret. Catholic education was badly served and did not improve until the 19th century. In better circles patrician children received much of their education at home. Many French tutors and governesses found work in this way, especially in the 18th century.

This mass effort in education was successful in many ways, despite the often crammed and stuffy classrooms and the low quality of the teachers. From 1650 the number of literates grew rapidly, and by 1800 the republic was among the most literate countries in Europe, along with Scandinavia, Scotland, and Prussia.

Pedagogic theories, and games

In the 17th century, children were educated at school, at home, or at their master's in a way intended to keep them dependent and obedient. At school this might mean severe punishments. Children were often made to stand for hours in class with a notice round their neck, received a rap over the knuckles with the cane or a thorough caning, or had to sit on a cushion made of pins. Still, master Dirck Adriaenszon Valcooch, in an 1591 instruction pamphlet for schoolmasters, advised them "not to hit so hard as to draw blood or break limbs." Jacob Cats, grand pensionary of Holland and the best-loved Dutch moralist poet of the early 17th century, regarded too much tenderness as unreasonable. He argued that "it is good for children to cry a little, for when somebody sheds tears, the damp brain is rid of its bad vapors." Only in the course of the 18th century, under the impact of the ideas of the English philosopher John Locke, did people begin to see that children must be educated at their own pace and with themes that they could understand. Children began to be regarded as children and were no longer treated as little adults. Particularly after 1750, children's books and verses appeared, in which authors tried to follow the child's own development: he had to be educated to be a good citizen, with Christianity a dominant element.

In contrast to the dull recital of letters and religious texts, there were many small games that children played, especially out of doors. The kind of game changed with the seasons. Marbles was something for winter, like skating and sledging. Kites were flown in autumn, and at slaughtering time boys would blow up pig's bladders for ball games, and throw cattle bones at targets. Even then children played avidly with tops, hoops, knuckles, skipping ropes, swings, or at shopkeeping and imitating their mother, as contemporary pictures testify. In toy shops well-to-do parents could buy small drums, playing balls, dolls, marbles, and diabolos, and perhaps "centsprenten," cheap and simple woodcuts with popular strip cartoons for children at a cent a piece.

Music

In Catholic services, music, particularly for the organ, was very important. Calvinists, however, held music to be a distraction from the essentials of the service, namely the reading of the scriptures and the sermon. In 1618 the Synod of Dordrecht accordingly barred organ music from the service. Some would indeed have liked to demolish the organs, but the towns prevented that, recognizing that music before and after the service was an important diversion, perhaps keeping people from drinking shops or worse. From 1580, Amsterdam had as city organist the composer Jan Pieterszon Sweelinck whose recitals at the Old Church were internationally famous. Besides these free recitals, there were fixed times at which one could hear many carillons in the towers of churches and town halls. After 1660 this was refined by the brothers Hemony from Lorraine who had, at the administration's request, settled in Amsterdam, receiving free lodging and a foundry at their disposal, where, incidentally, they also cast guns. They were the first to tune bells accurately.

The playing of the city carillonists was virtually drowned out by the street noises. The true street music was provided by the many strolling musicians and reciters of songs. The latter in particular were a thorn in the administration's side, no doubt because of the political texts of their songs, which they dis-

The Slippers, a canvas attributed to Samuel van Hoogstraten, about 1660 (Paris, Louvre). As early as 1549, the Spaniards were impressed by the neatness of Dutch houses. Concerning cleanliness, Huizinga writes: "The fact that it is so distinct north of the Ij is partly due to economic reasons. Cheese was made in the peasants' houses and because the slightest speck of dirt could spoil the work of weeks, everybody automatically understood that strictest hygiene was essential throughout the region.... Perhaps, though, the need to see everything well cleaned and washed has deeper roots in the people's character. The Dutch have always attached great importance to the simplest objects and understood the value of everyday things. It was in harmony with their deepest devotions to consider and appreciate everything as gifts from God, and this made them see all things as beautiful and urged them to preserve things whole and keep them new by polishing, sweeping, and mending, which became for them a true passion."

tributed as pamphlets or "flying leaves" to the crowd of listeners. Sometimes they sang about dramatic events that were illustrated on a large canvas behind them. Surrounding shopkeepers constantly complained about this nuisance. During the day, street musicians would enliven the scene with their drums, shawms, trumpets, bagpipes, viols, and barrel organs. They could not play at night, and landlords could throw them out if they entered without

Above, Clothing the Orphans, *by Cornelis Holsteyn, from the decorations in the directors' room in the Orphanage, 1656 (Amsterdam Historical Museum).*

invitation. Sometimes the performance of better-trained musicians would strike the passer-by: here a few more permanent professionals played a serenade in a house on request. These recognized musicians played at weddings and parties, too, and gave lessons to children from better circles.

There were many music halls in which the public could listen and dance. At times guests had to contribute a small piece on instruments lying ready for

this purpose. All kinds of music halls existed, from places for serious music to disguised brothels. Many people gathered there at night: sailors, soldiers, travelers, and the general populace—Amsterdam had the exciting nightlife of a seaport.

The well-to-do played the harpsichord, viola da gamba, flute, or violin. There was no shortage of sheet music: until the 19th century Amsterdam's music publishers were world famous.

The street scene

Beside musicians, all sorts of other entertainers could be seen in the streets: jugglers, bear tamers, puppeteers, street poets and story tellers, acrobats, and clowns always attracted a group of curious onlookers. A highlight were the fairs held on the occasion of the annual markets. At these everybody, from outside the city as well, could sell anything. They were free markets where the strict guild rules were waived for three weeks, except those regulating foodstuffs. Throughout the city there were stands with toys, herbs, glassware, earthenware and porcelain, linen, clothes, shoes, haberdashery, copper and tinware, and all sorts of frying and cooking stands offered snacks. The high point was always a visit to the butter market, where a dense crowd shuffled around between shows by acrobats, magicians, clowns, and animal tamers. Around the year 1750 there were some 700 stands. No wonder that at such periods the transport barges were overcrowded.

On January 3, 1638, shortly after the Athenaeum had been established, Amsterdam's first theater opened, with a play by the poet Joost van den Vondel. It was a tragedy about the fall of Amsterdam in the time of Count Gysbrecht van Aemstel around 1300. This play is still performed every January. The *Schouwburg* (theater) evolved thanks to the initiative of a group of eminent people of intellect and artistic sense; they followed the Amsterdam rhetoric rooms, which went back to the 16th century, and formed an association for poetry, plays, recitation, and music. Their outlook was formed by the Renaissance and focused on the classics. The tragedies of Vondel, the more popular comedies by Gerbrand Adriaenszon Bredero, and the refined plays by the writer Pieter

Corneliszon Hooft, son of the burgomaster, set the tone in the Schouwburg for the first 50 years. Painters, too, belonged to this circle of Amsterdam intellectuals. The members of *De Eglentier* (eglantine) and *De Amsterdamsche Kamer* (Amsterdam chamber), as these clubs were called, consciously tried to improve the Dutch language. The Athenaeum had sprung from the same endeavors.

After 1670 the Schouwburg was dominated by French and Italian influence. In general, plays, music, and ballets were not very good. The presence of Vivaldi, who conducted for the centenary in 1739, and the visit of the child prodigy Mozart in 1766 were exceptions in an otherwise mediocre repertory. Foreigners complained about the shouting during performances and the throwing of bottles, glasses, nut shells, and cups in the hall. The Schouwburg had its permanent players both for stage and the 12-man orchestra. Performances were on Monday, Tuesday, and Thursday—on other days there were sermons. The show began late in the afternoon and might last for five hours. Foreign groups, particularly French, Flemish, and Italian companies, which were popular, could not play at the Schouwburg; they had to appear in wooden sheds outside the walls or in smaller halls on the edge of the city. The strong concert season and the theater bore the stamp of Amsterdam's burgher society. A court or a church, which elsewhere were patrons of the arts, did not exist here. The title of the play given by the administration for the visit of the elector of Brandenburg in 1666 speaks volumes: *Robert Leverwurst* cannot have been terribly uplifting.

Food

If music and the theater were not of a particularly high standard, as foreign contemporaries confirm, the same is true of eating and drinking habits. The 17th-century Dutchman has been described as immoderate, in spite of all the church's encouragement to strict and quiet behavior, or perhaps because of it. From a book of manners (1683) we learn how people behaved in better circles, or rather how they did not behave: "When eating, keep your mouth shut and do not smack; above all cut the food into small pieces so that the cheeks are not bulging like an ape's because the morsels are too big. Also, do not spit food onto the plate or lick the tableware. At table you should keep your hat on but take if off when passing dishes. If this happens several times in a row, do not remove the hat, in order not to confuse and upset the others.''

In the late 17th century there was a move toward refinement, which under foreign influence became

more pervasive in the 18th century. Besides, the Dutch had begun to notice that their manners compared unfavorably with those of the foreigners who now lived in the city in large numbers. Amsterdam families who could afford it at all, from small merchants and officials up, had three or four meals a day in the 17th and 18th centuries: an early breakfast of bread, cheese, and sometimes butter, usually with beer or water, or, in the 18th century, tea; the main

Distributing Bread to the Poor, 1627, by Werner van den Valckert (Amsterdam Historical Museum).

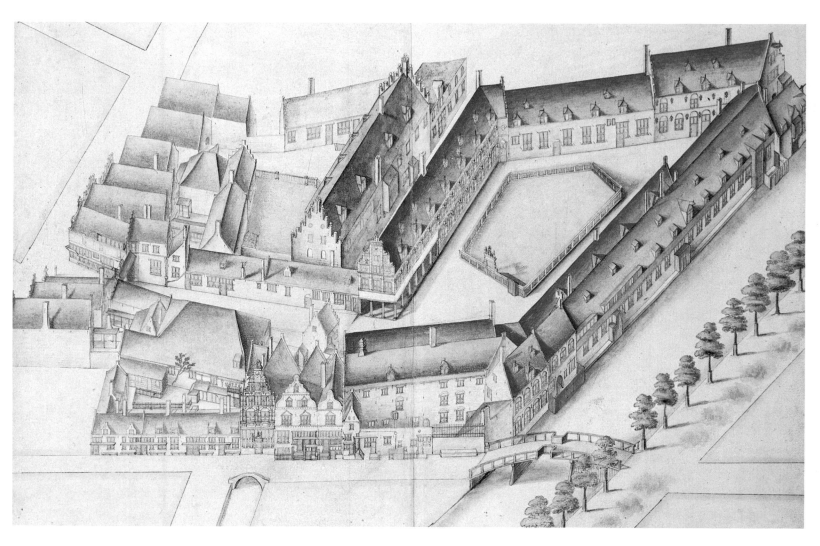

The civic orphanage of Amsterdam. Above, aerial view, 1631, by B. F. van Berckenroode; right, the boys' courtyard; below, orphans' uniforms in a frieze with the city's coat of arms on the cut edge of a register. Opposite, the directors' room. Formerly a convent transformed into an orphanage in 1578, now the Amsterdam Historical Museum.

meal in the middle of the day consisted of soup followed by meat or fish, salad, vegetables or fruit, and a dessert such as rice pudding or pancake; at four in the afternoon a snack of bread and cheese, with beer as at midday, and in the evening leftovers from the main meal filled out with bread, cheese, and butter. However, many had to make do with much less. Working people, according to an Amsterdam physician of the period, ate rye bread, which was often hard and of poor quality, chickpeas with dripping and raisins, stews made with turnips, salted meat, bacon, pickled cod, and salt herrings. Peas, beans, gruel, buttermilk pap, bread and cheese, and rarely meat or fish, were the fare in the city's social institutions. Many Amsterdammers did not have enough to eat. However, the republic did not experience famines as, for example, did contemporary France.

This was an exception in Europe at the time and shows how high a standard of living existed in Dutch society. The city authorities certainly helped to forestall famine by storing supplies to feed the poor.

The very wealthy citizens could avail themselves of ample choice of finer foods: oysters, caviar, delicate fish such as carp and pike, birds, often caught by the master of the house when hunting, and vegetables from their own gardens. An assortment of confectionery and pastries adorned their tables, on which polished tin dishes and plates, knives with decorated handles, painted porcelain vessels, and brown-gray jugs formed a colorful sight. For beer they used green glass rummers, while Rhine wine or red wine, the rich man's drink, glowed in high fluted glasses. Forks were not yet in use for eating.

In the 18th century a table was set with more order and symmetry. Everybody had his own eating utensils, including a fork, his own glass and plate, earthenware or porcelain. Sets came from China, or, later in the century, from England or Delft.

Above, the poor registering for aid, relief by Albert Vinckenbrinck. In 1611 there were 2,511 assisted families. By 1673, there were 5,860, according to Jan Wagenaar, the city's historian.

Disasters

In August 1656, some 180 barrels of pitch at various places in the city burned for several days on end. They served as a precaution against the plague, which in that year claimed 16,727 victims, about one ninth of the population. The stench in the West Church cemetery, which was too small for the many dead, was appalling. The theater was shut, the administration issued a ban on imports of plums, spinach, and cucumbers, which were thought to be the cause of the infection. A century later, the historian Jan Wagenaar wrote that the disease noticeably caused deaths among "common folk," concluding that it might be because of their scanty or unhealthy food. We now know that the plague was introduced by fleas from rats, which were to be found mainly in the densely populated poorer quarters of the city.

Earlier outbreaks had occurred in 1601–2, 1617, 1624, and 1635–6. During the last one, in 1663–4, the death toll was 9,572 in the first year and about 24,000 in the second. According to the city's historian, Caspar Commelin, mortality was such that many eminent people fled from the city to their country houses. The plague was then raging throughout Europe, and in London in 1665 between one sixth and one quarter of the population died. After the 17th century, the plague never returned to Amsterdam in epidemic proportions.

Fire

House fires were a common event, especially in the poorer quarters where the authorities tacitly allowed wooden buildings, and where the more fire-prone workshops stood. Until 1657 the members of the city's fire service, namely people who belonged to the guilds of Waag porters, beer porters, and peat porters, had to fight fires with water-filled leather buckets: in two long rows full buckets from the canal went from hand to hand to the burning house. In 1672, the city had 12,600 buckets stored at fixed points in the various quarters.

After 1657 the administration reinforced the existing system in the 60 quarters by setting up fire pumps bought in Germany. These were rather heavy

and had the further disadvantage of producing a variable jet. About 1680, the well-known painter and inventor Jan van der Heyden overcame these problems by producing a jet that came through hoses from a suction pump, which drew its water straight from the canal, also by hoses. The jet ends could be carried to the fire from several sides and the flames quickly tackled. Bucket chains were unnecessary. Van der Heyden, then supervisor of the 2,380 street lanterns, which he had significantly improved as well, set down the advantages of his system in a brilliant book with text and pictures, listing the points for and against the old and new system. The hose jet, an example of one among many 17th-century Dutch inventions, was adopted throughout Europe.

Helping those in need

During the period of the Seven United Provinces Amsterdam had an elaborate system of what we would now call social assistance for the disadvantaged—orphans, widows, the poor, and the elderly. Many foreign visitors have left their impressions of these programs and have shown their surprise and admiration at seeing the city so well ahead of the rest of Europe.

The city had benevolent bodies linked with the various churches, both Dutch Reformed, other Protestants, and Catholics, too, expressing a spirit of Christian charity. In addition there were civic institutions supervised by the city and its officers or promoted in a spirit of public service. These sprang from a collective sense of charitable duty or from political calculation. Indeed, the city at that time pursued a deliberate policy of increasing the population by immigration, which provided additional hands for the development of trade, navigation, and manufacture, but which in turn led to immense poverty beyond the control of economic measures alone. Here lay a potential source of danger to the established social order and to the ruling position of the patriciate.

Freedom of belief

Until far into the 17th century, the republic was unique among European nations in that it was the

only country where freedom of belief was assured. Nowhere in 17th-century Dutch pamphlet literature is this principle ever discussed theoretically: freedom of belief was a matter of daily practice. Although there was no official freedom to hold religious services, in fact, through the system of restrained tolerance, the different religions could worship as they chose. There was no religious compulsion, torture, or corporal punishment, still common elsewhere. Freedom of religious practice had been the great ideal of William of Orange, who wanted to see Protestants and Catholics living side by side in peace. In the treaty that the seven pro-

vinces concluded with each other at the Union of Utrecht in 1579, it was provided that "each person shall remain free in his religion and nobody shall be arrested or questioned because of his religion." Everybody could freely decide what religious ideas he wished to profess. Only two years later the Reformed Church succeeded in officially forbidding Roman Catholics to hold their services. The property of the Catholic Church fell to the authorities and largely came to be used by the Reformed Church. Still, Catholics were not persecuted. Certain Protestants, such as Lutherans and Baptists, were not officially tolerated either. The Dutch Reformed Church managed to acquire official status in the republic, with the largest financial and material subvention, and in theory all government posts had to be filled by its members. Nevertheless, it never became a genuine state church.

The Dutch Reformed Church

In about 1579 only a small portion of the population was Calvinist, or Reformed as they were called. Their position was strongest in the provinces of Holland and Zeeland, where in their grim religious zeal they had been the backbone of the revolt. Owing to their excellent organization they succeeded in spreading their influence. Their numbers were doubtless greatly strengthened through the influx of Calvinists from the southern Netherlands around 1600. Besides looking after the poor, they took as their foremost tasks the establishment of a proper education for future preachers in the republic itself. Among other things, William of Orange founded the University of Leyden in 1575. Other colleges and universities soon followed, and educating Reformed clerics was a vital part of their program.

During the Truce (1609–21) in the Eighty Years' War, a fierce controversy broke out among professors at Leyden about whether man could influence his lot, either here or in the life to come. The theologian Gomarus argued that only God decides whether a person is predestined for salvation or damnation. Members of the opposite camp, under the theologian Arminius, held that through leading a good life man can positively influence his fate. Linked with this

theological quarrel was the question of the relations between state and church, which had been unsettled since the republic's birth. The pastors desired at the least to be free from state authority and would have liked the power to force the state to silence dissenters. City rulers, and authorities in general, put the state above the church. The Gomarists or "dirty beggars" and the Arminians or "baboons" fought each other in a stream of pamphlets, in thundering sermons from the pulpit, and in street discussions. Because of the mixture of theological and political aspects, Prince Maurice's choice of a party was crucial; in 1618 he openly sided with the orthodox and, therefore, indirectly with those who wished to enhance the power of the church.

At the request of the States General, a national synod met at Dordrecht in 1618, at which a number of outstanding foreign theologians and professors were asked to adjudge the conflict. The orthodox, or Gomarists, won and the Arminians were expelled from the church, officially condemned, and considerably restricted for many years. The orthodox were recognized as having the only true doctrine. The synod was also historically important for having decided to translate the Bible from Hebrew and Greek into Dutch. After years of intense labor by eminent theologians and orientalists, the work appeared in print in 1637. The language of the *States Bible* deeply influenced the Dutch language.

After 1618, when Prince Maurice had opposed the city administration of Amsterdam, orthodox pastors there acquired great power for a time. This meant a short period of religious intolerance, which ended about 1630. As elsewhere in the republic, the orthodox could not retain power for long because their severe and dogmatic line did not fit the Christian and humanist outlook that inspired many rulers. Moreover, the authorities, particularly in Amsterdam, above all wanted peace and quiet in order to create the right climate for a flourishing economy: intolerance would frighten off many who now poured into the republic. Besides, the Reformed Church did not acquire the power that some preachers still openly continued to demand throughout the century. The authorities were stronger than the Church: everywhere they had the ultimate power to appoint pastors because the city treasury paid clerical salaries, the churches were city property, and organists and carillonists were engaged by the city.

In rapid succession, four new churches were built in Amsterdam. The first was the South Church, in 1611. They differed from their Catholic precursors by their sober interiors, whitewashed walls, the absence of paintings and statues, and the central position of the pulpit. The Reformed clergy also obtained the use of the previous two parish churches of the city, the Old Church and the New Church, which were now emptied of their Catholic décor.

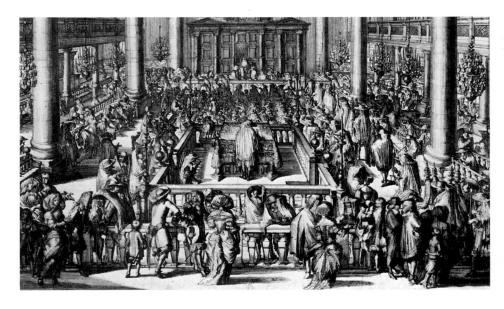

Pieter de la Court, industrialist and writer on economics in Leyden in the 17th century, observed that "freedom or tolerance in matters of serving or worshipping God is a powerful means for preserving many inhabitants of Holland and for inducing foreigners to live among us." Whatever were the motives behind this, historians think that the republic was the least intolerant country in Europe for two centuries. In the print (right), the secret Catholic churches of Amsterdam. Huizinga writes that the system regulating religious life could be called neither complete liberty nor tolerance on principle. It was a practice that, by closing one eye, made the life of sects as bearable as possible. Officially, Catholic services were forbidden, but anyone could find out where the secret churches were.

Protestants, Catholics, Jews

The Reformed Church greatly influenced daily life: its members were politically advantaged because they enjoyed official preference for office and could manipulate the well-organized care for the poor. Its handsome churches symbolized its supremacy. Nonetheless, there were several other Protestant churches that could more or less officially function as well. In spite of strict prohibitions, a freedom of religious belief and practice continued to exist. Although the authorities went on issuing severe decrees through pressure from certain orthodox pastors, they hardly, if ever, enforced them and explicitly refused to prosecute or impose heavy punishments. As a result, other churches and sects could function in the republic. Particularly in Amsterdam, where so many immigrants went for economic and religious reasons, many confessions were represented.

Walloon and English Presbyterians, as foreign branches of the Reformed Church, had a privileged status, and the city soon gave them church buildings. There were other Protestant sects who were regarded as dissenters, foremost among them the Remonstrants, the group who had been condemned as Arminians at the Synod of Dordrecht. They had many sympathizers in broad circles of the upper classes, and after 1630 they could follow their creed undisturbed.

The Lutheran doctrine, too, was at first forbidden but after 1630 could likewise freely go its way. In 1632, Lutherans received the city's approval for building a large church, followed by another in 1671, the New Cupola Church. However, the authorities remained intolerant of baptist groups, among them the Mennonites. They, too, could function more freely in the course of the 17th century, but their social views continued to provoke hostile reaction: for example, they refused to bear arms and were therefore exempt from serving in the civic militia of Amsterdam. Nevertheless, they were free to hold their services in "hidden churches."

Those who had remained Catholic constituted a problem for the authorities. At first, the Catholics were more numerous than all Protestants put together: in about 1760, the historian Wagenaar put them at about one fifth of the population. The Heidelberg Catechism (1536), the creed of the Reformed, severely condemned the Catholic service. When in 1581 the holding of Catholic services was officially forbidden, Catholics were forced to meet secretly in private houses and to give secret help to their poor. Because of renewed missionary zeal, Catholicism did not decline during the 17th and 18th centuries, and even grew.

Gradually the meetings in "hidden churches" could take place somewhat more openly. Behind simple house fronts on the street side there were often large church halls with rich altars and chapels. Many Catholics belonged to the wealthy classes. Some rulers were related to Catholics. This, and the size of their group, caused the authorities to leave them practically undisturbed in their affairs. There were indeed some concealed tensions between Reformed Protestants and Catholics. In the eyes of their opponents, the Catholics were too quick to sympathize with the enemy, first the Spaniards and later the French. Events abroad, such as the mass murders during the Thirty Years' War, the cruel per-

175

secution of the Waldensians in Piedmont, and the slaughter of Huguenots in France, caused anti-Catholic suspicion to flare up in the republic. In return, the Catholics nursed a deep grievance against the Reformed sect and the authorities because of the large sums they were forced to pay the mayor and his servants in order not to be molested during their services. For example, in 1617 the Jesuit father Ryser of the Holland mission wrote about the situation in Amsterdam: "Not long ago we had to pay 15,000 guilders to escape the chicaneries of the mayor and to extricate the priests who were almost treated as if arrested." In other fields, too, such as education, the Catholics felt like second-class citizens.

In addition to the "second-rank" churches and groups, there were all kinds of smaller sects in the city, such as Collegiates, Labadists, Quakers, and Brownists. The last two had fled from England to the republic. In 1656 the city authorities punished one of their leaders with branding and the pillory. A year later the church council observed with displeasure that there were several Quaker meetings in the city. The authorities refused to take any countermeasures. Equally tolerant was the stance of the Amsterdam authorities toward the pastor Balthasar Bekker at the end of the 17th century. Influenced by ideas of the French philosopher René Descartes, who had lived in Amsterdam in 1634, certain Dutch theological circles developed a more rationalist line in the course of the century. Reason and common sense were given an important part in judging the Bible and life in general. Bekker followed this line: he strongly condemned the beliefs in witches, comets, miracles, and magicians. When his book *The Bewitched World* appeared, it provoked a strong reaction among Reformed pastors, and in the end he was dismissed from his office. Still, the city administration, where he had some sympathizers, refused to prosecute and even paid him his salary for life.

At the end of the 18th century the Jews formed about 10 percent of the city's population. They occupied a place apart because they were a separate religious community and kept to themselves socially. There was no ghetto, but the Jews in the republic did live close together. In Amsterdam a Jewish quarter developed in the eastern part of the city. At first the position of the poor German Jews was not comfortable, but during the 17th century both the Iberian Jews, who were generally well off, and the poorer German and Polish Jews could freely follow their beliefs. In 1642 the stadholder Frederik Henry made an official visit to the synagogue of the Iberian Jews. The others, too, could establish their synagogues. However, in economic matters, Jews enjoyed less toleration than in religion: only a few guilds accepted them as members, so that their professional avenues were limited. More than once, gentiles tried to expel their Jewish colleagues from an occupation. But on the whole, the Amsterdam administration protected the Jews.

The Jewish philosopher Spinoza, who until 1656 lived and worked in Amsterdam, was much criticized both by Jews and gentiles. Because he approached the text of the Bible scientifically, taking it to be the work of men, the pastors more than once tried to have his writings banned. Soon after his protector, the grand pensionary Johan de Witt, had been murdered, the city administration issued a prohibition against Spinoza.

In general, the authorities wished to act only where certain basic principles of Christian belief were involved. This was the case with the Socinians from Poland, who had put the Holy Trinity in doubt. The same approach was applied to the banning of books. Thus a remarkably tolerant climate developed in the republic, certainly by the standards of that time. The various religious groups took root in Dutch society, and this influences Dutch social life even today.

René Descartes (above, portrait by Jan Lievens) came to Holland in 1628 at 34 and lived there till 1649 except for short trips to France. His main work, Discourse on Method, *was published at Leyden in 1637. Benedict (Baruch) Spinoza (top, from a print) was born in Amsterdam's Sephardic community, which expelled him in 1656 for his views. In addition to his* Commentary on Descartes' Principles of Philosophy, *during his lifetime he published only the* Tractatus Theologico-Politicus *(1670), which made him many enemies. Left, interior of the Nieuwzijds Chapel of Amsterdam, about 1655, painted by E. de Witte (Utrecht, Catharijneconvent).*

The republic in the 18th century

Politics, the republic in decline

In 1702 the king-stadholder William III died in London. He was childless, so for a second time the republic entered a long period without a stadholder. Shortly before, he had set up a Grand Alliance against the French, with England, Austria, Prussia, and the republic. From 1702 to 1713, the alliance engaged in the War of the Spanish Succession to decide whether Philip of Anjou, grandson of Louis XIV, would succeed to the Spanish throne.

The republic took part by land and sea, at great financial cost, but the land battles took place outside its territory. The war went badly for Louis XIV and ended in the Peace of Utrecht, which decreed that Philip could become king of Spain but would be barred from the French throne; the southern Netherlands passed to the Austrians, and the Dutch were allowed to maintain a few garrisons there to ward off future French aggression.

At Utrecht it became clear that the republic had had its international role. During the negotiations a French diplomat put it thus: "Here there are negotiations by you, about you and without you." Other European states were to be the leaders in world politics: first, England, the winner in Spain, then France, who fought constantly with England over colonies in Asia and America and who would involve the whole of Europe in a series of revolutionary wars toward the end of the century. In central Europe, the powerful Austrian empire fought against aggression from the Turks in the south and the Prussians in the north. Prussia, a young agrarian state where officers and civil servants ruled, acquired territory at the expense of Austria and Poland. Finally, Russia acquired western features and became a world power. These states, all with monarchical, absolutist governments, rational administrations, and economies under strong national direction, formed varying alliances with each other, thus maintaining a balance of power in the 18th century.

The republic lacked most of the modern characteristics of these countries, and her clumsy structure now showed its drawbacks. The whole federal system simply made an absolutist monarchy impossible. A Louis XIV, Frederick the Great, Catherine the Great, or Maria Theresa would have been unthinkable in the Netherlands. There was no national economic policy, and Dutch military readiness was minimal. The wars of William III and the War of the Spanish Succession had emptied the coffers of the union and the provinces, particularly Holland, and the republic could afford no more wars: it had to steer carefully between the great powers and try to pursue a neutral policy.

Since no stadholder was appointed except in Friesland, active policy fell back into the hands of the cities, without any counterbalance. For almost 50 years the rulers freely appointed their own relatives to all sorts of posts and sold offices to the highest bidder. The long-subdued anger at this system exploded, as in the "year of disaster," 1672, after a French invasion. When France and Austria were at war in 1747, a French army had invaded the Austrian Netherlands. When the French tried to take parts of the republic as well, the resulting panic called for a strong leader. William IV, a scion of the Friesian Nassau branch of the House of Orange, and stad-

TOURIST DELIGHTS

The journals of visitors to Amsterdam (men of learning, diplomats, clerics, well-off lay-abouts—invariably people from the upper classes) recorded essentially similar impressions, usually of admiration. This limited "tourist industry" had its statutory visiting places. The city hall, which some considered the "eighth wonder of the world," finely represented the wealth of the city and the power of its denizens. Although peo-

ple would have preferred a solemn monumental portal instead of the seven small existing doors that symbolized the Seven Provinces, they did appreciate their defensive usefulness in the event of upheavals. The Stock Exchange was another tourist attraction and a place where interesting encounters could be made (*1*), like the East India Company headquarters, scented with the spices warehoused there by the company. Business matters seemed to pervade the whole city like a fever. There was

very large numbers of private collections (*3, the collection of Jacob de Wilde*), collections of paintings, prints, objets d'art, natural and exotic oddities, in accordance with baroque taste.

There were pleasant surprises to be had from the cordial nature of the inhabitants and from the order that reigned over the city. The shady trees along the canals, the well-kept cobbles, the pavements swept clean every day, the sparkling windows, always washed clean, and the shining door handles. There were no beg-

compared well with similar institutions elsewhere. In the Rasphuis the convicts, half-naked, would rasp Brazilian wood for the dye industry. Loafers would be whipped. The religious and, as a rule, the intellectual tolerance of the city was famous. It was quite an experience to visit, in one and the same city, churches belonging to the Dutch Reform confession (*Calvinist, 6*), the Lutheran and Presbyterian faiths, and then the synagogues. Bookshops sold books—in every language —which could not be published

business chatter in the commercial institutions, in the streets, in homes, and in cafés. In fact, the inhabitants of Amsterdam seemed to have just one thing on their mind: money. Or almost one; the people of Amsterdam tended to avoid cultural conversation and did not conceal their boredom with it. The theater (*2, the theater on the Keizersgracht*) did not fill them with enthusiasm. It was possible, however, to visit the

gars to blemish the streets. Social welfare was efficient and institutions could even be visited (*4, the old people's hospice on the Amstel*). At the Dolhuis, which was the lunatic asylum (*5*), visitors could watch food being distributed to the inmates, who were brought down into the courtyard for this "ceremony." The Rasphuis and the Spinhuis, the men and women's prisons, were certainly not salubrious places, but they

outside the Seven Provinces.

Finally, there was no shortage of excursions for the foreigner. Trips to inns outside the city walls, visits to collections of live animals—precursors of our modern zoos—dance halls, or the "red light district" (*7, Tony's tavern, c. 1780*) for which the city was famous as early as the 17th century.

holder of Friesland, Groningen, and Gelderland, seemed the right man, and the other provinces, too, now appointed him as stadholder. Married to a daughter of the English king, William received English support and considerable power. For a start, the posts of stadholder and of captain and admiral general were declared hereditary.

The burghers, the class immediately below the rulers, who had been systematically excluded from governmental influence, saw in William a way to limit the rulers' powers and perhaps to acquire some political role themselves. William confirmed their expectation: he could put an end to the rulers' nepotism and the hated system of tax farming, which actually brought in most excise. Tax farmers hired an excise for a certain period in which they had to win back the fee. Any surplus was their own. The farmers, often working with spies to prevent smuggling and fraud, were thoroughly detested, and there had been risings against their malpractices in the 17th and 18th centuries. After unrest in the cities of Holland, William did introduce some reforms, but in

essence nothing changed. William IV was no William III. He was well intentioned but weak and irresolute. He died in 1751 when his son, William V, was still under age. Now the burghers could expect nothing more from the House of Orange, their movement lost strength, and by the 1780s new events were to grip the republic. Up until then, internal policy debate in the republic mainly concerned expanding the army and the navy. Holland, and particularly Amsterdam, always favored the navy; the stadholders and inland provinces preferred the army. As a result of this dragged-out conflict, the republic's defenses were badly neglected.

Trade

In the 18th century French imports and exports increased five fold, and those of England three fold. Trading in Hamburg, Norway, Sweden, Prussia, and Russia expanded, but in the republic it remained static; other centers were catching up.

There had indeed been some changes in Holland's

Dutch international trade and continued riches from the colonies. Left, a view of Smyrna with the reception by the Turks of the Dutch consul Daniel Jan, baron of Hochepied, a Turkish painting from about 1730 (Rijksmuseum). Opposite above right, Dutchmen at dinner in their depot on Deshima island at Nagasaki in Japan, in a Japanese painting. Below, the governor of Ceylon gives audience to the yearly embassy of the king of Kandy, 1772, by Carel Frederick Reiner. The valuable box below left was given to Stadholder William IV by the West India Company in 1749 (Rijksmuseum). Mythology adapts itself to colonial themes: beside the inevitable Mercury there are a negro man and woman. The monogram GWC on the coat of arms stands for Geoctrooieerde West-Indische Compagnie (Chartered West Indies Company). When William III died in 1702, the second interregnum began. The War of the Spanish Succession (1702–13) weighed heavily on the republic's finances, and at the Peace of Utrecht (1713) it was clear that its international role had expired. When the republic was drawn into the Austrian War of Succession and was partly invaded by the French, a stadholder was reinstated in William IV. The office was declared hereditary to the House of Orange, but the question arose only once, with William V, the last stadholder.

trade. First, European freight made less and less use of Amsterdam as a staging point. Other countries built their own fleets, thereby becoming less dependent on Holland's freighters, and cargo traveled directly from producer to consumer. Moreover, the Hollanders increasingly tended to take part in this direct traffic. Next, there was a trend in Dutch trade toward concentration on nearby areas such as France and England and, of course, the German hinterland. The republic continued to profit from its favorable position on the route from the Baltic to the Mediterranean, and between England and Germany. An exception to this contraction was the trade with Dutch colonies in Asia and South America, which increased due to the growing demand for coffee, tea, rice, cotton, and sugar. In addition, trade within the republic became even more highly concentrated on Amsterdam and to a lesser degree on Rotterdam. Amsterdam became a stronger center from which a network of trade relations stretched out. The more or less dominant position of Amsterdam's staple market vanished, because Hamburg and London took

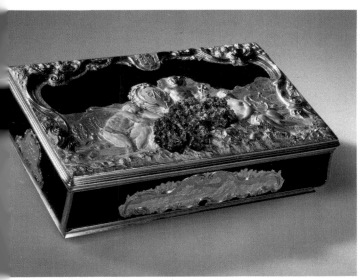

over parts of it. Finally, in the 18th century there was a marked shift from active to passive trade. Hollanders no longer appeared primarily as busy traders and freighters, but rather as financial supporters: the merchants became bankers. Through the economic expansion in the 17th century, enormous capital had accumulated in the Netherlands. Since between 1700

and 1750 building land was cheap, investment in new land was not profitable; and since the great supply of capital lowered interest from 5 to 6 percent in 1650 to 2½ to 3 percent by 1800, it became attractive to invest abroad. Foreign enterprises, particularly the English South Sea Company, princes, government, and even the Bank of England borrowed extensively in the republic.

An example of a banking house with international connections was the firm of Deutz in Amsterdam. They loaned huge sums to the Austrian emperor in return for the income from imperial tolls and the surety of certain properties such as the Styrian quicksilver mines and Hungarian copper mines. Clearly this involved risk. For example, when the Prussians took Silesia from the Austrians in 1740, at one stroke income from that area ceased, whereupon Deutz broke relations with Austria and the house declined. About 1790 it was estimated that some 1,500 million guilders was invested abroad.

Amsterdam continued to flourish as the financial center of Europe. The good name of the Exchange Bank, the abundance of capital, the low rate of interest, and a monetary reform in 1694, reducing the number of cities entitled to mint coins from 14 to 8, ensured this position. Insurance also developed, and around 1700 a new method of financing arose, whereby a banker gave a merchant a letter of exchange without immediate cover in goods. The merchant could draw cash on the letter of exchange and buy goods. This was a short-term credit on trust, not without risk but a modest rate of ½ or ⅓ percent. Such letters were even transferable. Foreign merchants drew vast profits from Dutch capital without having to use Dutch vessels or ports.

There was an active market for bills of exchange and letters of credit: the abundance of capital seemed to promise splendid times ahead for eccentric entrepreneurs who sold shares in companies they had created often with impossible aims. Rich and poor alike would speculate on the shares, especially in coffee at Amsterdam, but many of them collapsed and bankruptcies followed. Such crises undermined confidence in credit, caused business to stagnate, and led to unemployment. Dealers in shares were insulted in poems, caricatures, and plays and sometimes received real blows. During one of these affairs, in 1720, unemployed laborers came to the Dam with a puppet representing a shareholder, caused merchants' wigs and hair to fly, and attacked the coffeehouse Quincampoix in Kalver street, a typical meeting place for "sellers of wind." The authorities put an end to the uproar and managed to

stop the trade in shares, which had gotten out of hand, just as they had stopped the tulipomania of the 17th century. The "trade in wind" made some very rich, meant bankruptcy for many, but had little influence on trade as a whole.

Industry

In contrast to trade, industry flourished, though it varied according to place, period, and product. During the preceding centuries, it had been able to develop because of cheap energy from peat and wind, cheap labor, a developed network of waterways, and

Amsterdam merchants did not lose their money-making skills in the 18th century. The Stock Exchange and the East India Company remained two of its sound pillars as in the 17th century. Left, a plan of the ground floor of the Stock Exchange, with legends where specialist dealers gathered. Center right, the heads of the East India Company assembled for the visit of Stadholder William V (S. Fokke, 1771). However, merchants now worked in a different setting: world trade had grown and the one-time near-monopoly position of the Dutch had now vanished through competition from new European powers: Holland was being surpassed. Below right, the envoy of the States General received by Louis XV as a child, July 24, 1719 (canvas by Louis Michel Dumesnil). These were the years of speculative fever provoked by John Law and his bank. Top right, Dutch print of the rue de Quincampoix in Paris, site of John Law's bank, 1716–21, and the wild dealing in shares that went on there. Share dealings in companies with absurd objects raged in Amsterdam, too. In a rising in 1720, unemployed workers invaded a café in Kalverstreet, which, not by accident, was called Quincampoix, and wigs and hair were flying among the speculators assembled there.

a steady supply of raw materials and half-finished goods. Moreover, since there was little competition from abroad, Holland had a very strong export position.

During the 18th century, these advantages were lost. Other countries with their own raw materials encouraged industries of their own by adopting new techniques of production, improving their infrastructure, granting export premiums and erecting barriers to foreign imports. Foreign entrepreneurs could not only use Dutch capital but Dutch know-how as well. Specialists left the republic, and with their industrial secrets went to England, Spain, France, Russia, or the Austrian Netherlands, while foreigners came to the republic to perfect themselves in industrial techniques only to take tools and machines back to their own countries. Since foreign products had become both better and cheaper, Dutch exports receded greatly. Cities that had specialized in one product found this particularly disastrous; for example, the linen industry in Leyden and Haarlem declined and so did the manufacture of earthenware and pipes in Gouda and Delft. Salt and soap in various towns also experienced a decline.

By contrast, textiles on the plains where wages were lower, and sugar refineries (Amsterdam was the store for West Indies sugar) and oil works survived well. Some industries prospered: paint, tobacco, diamond cutting, distilleries, and until about 1760, cotton printing. The great demand for distilled liquor (85 percent for export abroad) was linked with a changing pattern of consumption. Coffee, tea, and gin were well liked, whereas beer fell from favor. Shipbuilding on the Zaan had a splendid run but collapsed after 1745. In Amsterdam, where repair was important, that industry continued. The Zaanstreek with its hundreds of mills remained an industrial area, only the number of sawmills declined.

Farming and fishing

In the 18th century roughly half the Dutch nation worked on the land, but farming, like trade, began to stagnate after 1650. This was because the population of Europe had stopped growing, and this reduced demand and lowered prices for grain and dairy

products. Moreover, various countries introduced protectionist measures. For example, England excluded Irish butter, which now came to the continent and depressed prices.

The War of the Spanish Succession had caused Dutch taxes to rise, and farmers in the coastal provinces had to face a new enemy as well: the insect called a borer. On the water side, Dutch dikes had two rows of vertical timber planks with seaweed or reeds in between. From 1731 dikes, locks, and even ships were ravaged by borers, which ate through and thus damaged the wood. Dikes were weakened and inundations occurred. A new system of building dikes was developed. On the water side a stone slope was built, requiring large amounts of imported stone from Norway and north Germany. Farmers, among others, had to bear the taxes for this. It was indeed a profitable investment because after 1750 there were fewer floods, and maintenance costs went down.

A second natural enemy of Dutch farmers was

less easily tackled, namely cattle plague. Three epidemics occurred in the 18th century, with a rough loss of 70 percent of the herds each time. Meat and dairy production tumbled, and although the farmer received more, he was bound to go into debt to replace his cattle. There was no systematic slaughter of infected beasts because there was no central authority that could have enforced it. Only in the 1770s did Dutch farmers attempt vaccination. During such an epidemic, the towns tightened controls on meat imports. In 1713, Amsterdam prohibited the sale of infected meat because this might produce "a very harmful and dangerous disease." Transgressors were fined 300 guilders, and 600 if the offense was repeated. Those who could not pay were to be "put on show with the useless meat tied round their neck." After 1750, things improved for farmers in some regions. The population increased as did the price of grain, and the Dutch began to grow potatoes, whose harvest steadily increased.

In so typically Dutch an occupation as fishing, activity declined. In 1768, the periodical *De Koopman* (The Merchant) commented on the chance nature of fishing, calling it "a sort of lottery rather than a steady and orderly commerce." The number of herring boats from Holland declined from 500 in 1630 to 219 in 1763. Here, too, protective measures by neighboring countries took their toll. Bans on imported Dutch herring were imposed in France, the Austrian Netherlands, Prussia, and Denmark and there was strong Swedish competition in the Baltic. Moreover herring was simply being eaten less. Not only fishermen, but herring packers and salesmen, shipbuilders and transport workers on the wharves lost their jobs. Whaling, which is not, strictly speaking, fishing, but rather a hunt, was also declining because of English competition and the falling numbers of whales. Still, a fleet set out every year because the system of share shipping reduced the risk.

Unemployment

The rise in unemployment caused by the decline of industry and fishing was generally disturbing. The gap between rich and poor widened. In many cities the population fell noticeably, and the poor who re-

Scenes of Dutch navigation in the 18th century. Left, sketch from a log book showing "keel hauling," a punishment for serious misdeeds: the victim was dragged by rope from one side of the ship to the other under the hull with its sharp incrustations of mollusks. Opposite, detail of a East India Company ship in a Japanese painting (Amsterdam, Dutch Historical Maritime Museum). Dutch navigation continued to be considerable, but many countries had their own merchant fleets and Amsterdam was no longer a transshipment center.

mained behind became an increasing burden. Amsterdam, Rotterdam, The Hague, and Schiedam were the only cities whose population increased in the 18th century. Everywhere else it went steadily down. Formerly prosperous textile towns like Haarlem and Leyden lost almost half and one third respectively. A very strong drift away occurred in smaller northern towns of Holland, above the Ij, where trade and fishing ceased and cities died. Many of the poor moved to the plains, where they tried to make a living by begging. Sometimes they formed armed gangs, consisting of unemployed farm laborers, discharged soldiers, small traders, and officials; they would go on plundering expeditions at night. The authorities repeatedly had to act against this. In 1725 and again in 1760 the States of Holland decreed that when the bells rang, burghers had to assemble armed in order to scour the countryside for beggars and vagabonds. Those who were caught were severely punished. Roaming gypsies were systematically persecuted and in the end expelled or eradicated.

The population seems to have suffered poverty quietly. A few riots occurred against high prices of food and heavy indirect taxes. Women played a leading part in this, as they did in France and England. There was not much violence, nor were there large-scale hunger riots. The city authorities were always alert to store enough grain in times of lean harvests so that the worst needs could be met. People revenged themselves against the hated tax farmer by pulling his clothes off, thereby humiliating, rather than harming him. Their houses were plundered, but according to certain codes of conduct: furniture was smashed to pieces, houseware thrown out of the windows, food and drink were consumed, but there was hardly any stealing, and the Bible was spared. In general the authorities tried to quell riots; there were no mass arrests, but the instigators, if captured, were executed.

Attempts at improvement

Observing the 18th century from a distance, one wonders if the decline of so many aspects of economic life could not have been foreseen and if no

The mills of the Zaanstreek, in a picture of 1756. An important industrial zone just north of Amsterdam, the Zaanstreek had about a hundred windmills to supply motive power to various industries. Shipbuilding once flourished there but declined after 1750; the area nevertheless remained industrially active. The two charts on the left illustrate the role of windmills in the Noorderkwartier, the region north of Amsterdam.

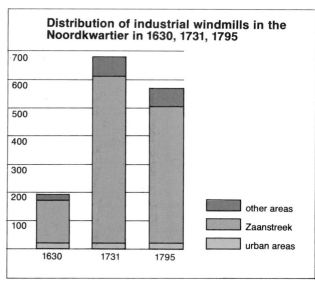

Distribution of industrial windmills in the Noordkwartier in 1630, 1731, 1795

- other areas
- Zaanstreek
- urban areas

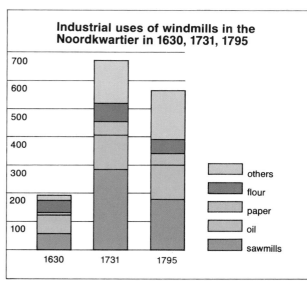

Industrial uses of windmills in the Noordkwartier in 1630, 1731, 1795

- others
- flour
- paper
- oil
- sawmills

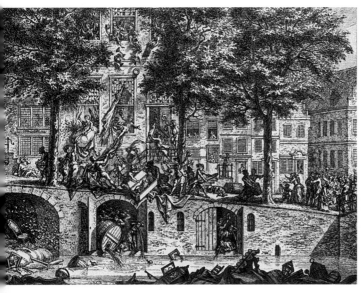

Government remained in the hands of the small patrician class. These were mainly quiet years, except for disturbances that were economic rather than political. Left, the sack of tax farmer A. M. Aerssen's house on June 25, 1748. Below left, the four burgomasters, powerful heads of city government, in a drawing by D. Bas (Amsterdam Parish Archive).

Above, the coats of arms of those who had been commissioners of city finance from 1702 to 1725 (Amsterdam Historical Museum). Top, a political caricature: the cripple on the cart who works as a dog catcher alludes to the republic facing tasks of international politics beyond its powers.

measures could have been taken to stop the decay. As to the first question, the answer must be yes. The ailing state of industry and fishing was obvious and people doubtless criticized the "inactive and sluggish" ruler who invested his money in his magnificent country home or in foreign loans instead of in his own country's economy. Moreover, there was criticism of the army of foreigners, particularly Germans, who came to live in the republic or to do seasonal work making hay, cutting peat, or going whaling. Foreign workers accepted lower wages and put up with poor housing, since it was still better than what they earned at home. To take strong revitalizing measures, the taxation system had to be reformed, roads and canals improved, and countless internal tolls abolished; and this required a strong central administration, which the republic lacked. Each city tried first to protect its own economy, to find the surest and most profitable investments in money or goods, whether agricultural or industrial, domestic or foreign.

While in England the Industrial Revolution led to stormy social and economic developments, its beginnings were less dramatic in the Netherlands. Entrepreneurs were understandably reticent about investing in new machines because "the smaller sales of factories allowed but a weak prospect for the expected returns," according to J. van Heukelom in a discussion of industry in 1779. The low sales, he adds, "forces a producer so often deceived in his

best forecasts, to confine himself to everyday products." Industrial renewal makes sense only when there is prospect of greater sales, which was not the case abroad because products were better and cheaper there, nor at home, because demand remained low. The population hardly grew and wages remained steady while prices rose, a vicious circle that no producer could escape. There was no national economic plan whatever. There were, however, initiatives from private circles of burghers to help provide work for the poor, partly for economic and partly for charitable reasons. Workhouses were built in Dutch towns where there was weaving and spinning; it relieved the benevolent funds and taught the poor a trade. Because of inefficient conduct and the low quality of their output, these institutions remained unsuccessful, for all their good intentions. Besides, this was, at best, a tampering with symptoms.

Only once a clear plan for recovery was advanced, invented by some eminent merchants from Amsterdam and Rotterdam. This so-called "Proposition of 1751" suggested that Dutch ports should become free. With some exceptions to protect farming and industry, there should be no fees for imports, exports, or transit goods. Debate went on for two decades, which led to nothing but "peat baskets with arguments," according to a Dordrecht merchant. The stadholder put the plan before the States General, but nothing came of it. The admiralties,

who depended on the taxes to be abolished, were opposed. They demanded compensation, to be raised from all provinces. As a central figure William IV might have been able to implement the plan, but he died in 1751. A slight economic upturn made execution less urgent.

Occasional official measures, to meet requests from industrial circles, were indeed taken, in the form of granting premiums and tax exemptions, the 3 to 4 percent export premiums for herring in 1750, for example. In 1775 the States of Holland granted a premium of 500 guilders to each working herring boat. Moreover, the directors of church and other institutions were asked to offer herring as often as possible.

Certain imported products were taxed to protect home industries. The problem was that it harmed the Amsterdam staple market, which always gained by bringing in and taking out as much as possible as cheaply as possible. An embargo on foreign industrial products often did not succeed for fear of reprisals by the country concerned. For example, in 1774 sailing canvas weavers in Holland asked the States of their province to compel Dutch ships and windmills to use Dutch canvas. However, the States feared Russian countermeasures, control was difficult, and the cost of millers and shipbuilders would rise if they could no longer use good and cheap Russian canvas. An example of an embargo on the export of raw materials is the repeated ban by the

Far left, print showing the terrible effects of the **paalworm** *(woodworm), a mollusk probably from the West Indies, which ate away at the wooden stakes in sea dikes. Above, Kattenburgerplein of Amsterdam, in the flooding of November 15, 1775, a print by N. van der Meer. Opposite, a drawbridge on Hoogte Kadijk, Eastern Islands, Amsterdam. The invasion of the paalworm led to new ways of dam building. Instead of replacing the two rows of wooden stakes filled with spoil, stone was used, which was imported from Norway and northern Germany. The required investments did, however, yield the benefit of fewer floodings and lower maintenance costs.*

Amsterdam 1702-1780

States General on the export of old fishing nets, ropes, and rags, required for inland paper mills. To support Dutch industry, the States of Holland in 1703 decided that their troops must be clad in material woven in Holland. William IV declared that he, his court, and his family would set the example. This kind of measure may have had some minor effect, but usually too late. The waste of divided effort through protection by the States and the conflicting interests of the various branches of industry doomed any plan for revival. No wonder that attempts at reconstruction went not much beyond encouraging consumption of more herring and the reuse of old fishnets.

The population of Amsterdam in the 18th century varied between 200,000 and 220,000, about one tenth of the republic. After London and Paris it was the biggest city in Europe. Just as in the 17th century, Amsterdam was the dominant city in Holland and therefore in the Netherlands as a whole. Immigration from inland and abroad continued, which shows that Amsterdam still had work to offer. Many came from the German empire, particularly from Lower Saxony, among them many women seeking domestic employment. Because of the growing prosperity of the well-to-do, the demand for servants

Businesses large and small, as well as new trades: "Business is business," as the Dutch say. Above, a sale of pictures in the New Market, in a picture by I. Ouwater, 1783 (Amsterdam Historical Museum, on loan from the Rijksmuseum). Opposite top right, wigmaker's shop, by Cornelis Troost. Center right, a merchant's office, 1794. Below left, smoke from a glass workshop; below right, effects of explosion in a gunpowder factory, engraving, 1758.

had risen greatly. A special immigrant group were the Jews from Poland, Russia, and central Europe. They settled mainly in the eastern quarter, though they were not compelled to: in their area there were also gentiles. In 1700, the proportion of Jews in Amsterdam was 3 percent, and in 1800 three times as many.

In 1742 and 1747 a once-only tax was raised to meet the high cost of war. The data for this are extant and provide a picture of income and capital. One of these taxes concerned people earning more than 600 guilders a year, a sum adequate for a very decent style of life. A bare third of the population was involved, most of whom were not earning very much more than that: shopkeepers, independent craftsmen such as carpenters and tailors, free professionals such as lawyers and surgeons. A very small group of very rich people consisted of merchants, city administrators who pocketed the yield of all sorts of functions, and financially independent individuals. About 11 percent of the population earned between 300 and 600 guilders a year; these were the skilled workers, simple craftsmen, and small independents. More than half the population had less than 300 guilders a year, among them unskilled workers, small shopkeepers, some craftsmen, servants, laundresses, and seamstresses. Part of the population had no regular income at all—the beggars, street singers, and rat catchers, who lived hand to mouth and often had to fall back on assistance.

After 1755 poverty increased, as witnessed by the number of foundlings, which between 1700 and 1800 rose from 30 to 500 a year. The number of patients admitted in the Internal and External hospices rose from 500 a year in 1785 to 800 a year in 1796. This was not because of an epidemic but because of poverty and the consequent loss of strength. Rye was the people's staple food, and as its price rose, so did the number of patients.

This rising poverty was due to a number of causes. First, there was high unemployment. As we saw, the character of trade was changing. Merchants changed from labor-intensive trade in goods to finance, which did not require loaders, unloaders, porters, weighers, and sailors—but only a few clerks and messenger boys. The decline of whole branches of industry, of fishing, and the attendant shipbuilding swelled the ranks of the unemployed.

For those who remained at work, wages remained at the same level. These were indeed high compared with those of neighboring countries, but the cost of living went up: heavy excise on goods and services, and the high level of wages itself, put enormous pressure on prices. The tax burden in the republic and particularly in Holland was extremely high. Provincial and civic excise were heaviest on necessities, above all grain, meat, and peat. The republic was an expensive country in which to live. Since food and bread in particular had to be bought, less was left for other necessities, which in turn lowered

Left to right: peat cutter, grain porter, and peat carrier—three wooden statuettes of occupations, 18th century (Rijksmuseum). Many workers were organized into guilds that were supervised by the authorities. They tried to mitigate economic differences, but also to watch over the city's general interests, although these tended to be those of the mercantile, financial, and entrepreneurial patriciate. The carriers of grain and peat and porters at the Waag were controlled even more strictly because orderly conduct of wholesale trade was involved.

the sales of finished goods, which through foreign protection had recently become more dependent on the internal market.

Several times the despair about the stranglehold of high living costs exploded: in the 1740s, when food prices rose steeply throughout Europe because of bad harvests, there were riots in the towns of Holland. In Amsterdam it was over the prices of bread, buckwheat flour, vegetables, and apples. In 1740 and 1757 there were winter riots because of the high price of drinking water, which was brought in boats from outside the city. With frost, the boats could hardly reach the city with icebreakers, so that water was scarce and expensive. In 1744 the city suppressed a cotton printers' strike for higher wages— one of the rare cases of a preindustrial strike in the republic.

Protest against the rules

A more serious riot occurred in 1747; it ended the second period without a stadholder. Another riot in 1748 was also politically motivated. For the first

time, there were protests against the form of the city's government, even if fairly vague ones. Some burghers who were systematically kept out of office became disturbed about the rulers' customary behavior. Since there was no stadholder, the rulers had a free hand in appointing all sorts of officials. There were some 3200 civic offices to be distributed. The small ruling group decided who among them should determine each appointment. It is not surprising that friends and relatives were given preference, and ability was secondary. The circle of rulers who distributed positions became smaller and smaller with the aim of keeping newcomers out of office. Moreover, the rulers formed rival factions among themselves. Sometimes ruling families collaborated for years in running the administration, such as the Corvers, Trips, Hoofts, and Pancrases. Often children were appointed. Burgomaster John Corver gave his grandsons of 6, 10, and 12 the postmasterships of the offices in Antwerp, Cologne, and Hamburg respectively. These children did not have to concern themselves with collecting the moneys from these postal services: a substitute employed on a low wage did the work. Their half-brother became captain of a company of soldiers in Amsterdam at the age of nine. Without doing anything, he received 600 guilders a year. Adults, too, had proxies. Jacob Bicker Raye, author of a spirited diary, followed his brother as chief auctioneer of the Great Fish Market but had someone do it for him at 400 guilders a year, while he himself pocketed 2½ percent of sales, which came to at least 500 guilders a month and sometimes twice that. Nor was it unusual for proxies to employ proxies in turn; sometimes offices even remained unfilled, but the rulers still took the money.

Everybody knew that this went on, but there was little protest. "Things were allowed to drift," in the words of Cornelis Schrijver, a high-ranking officer of the Amsterdam Admiralty. "Today to please this gentleman and tomorrow another, and so one dirty hand washes another but neither becomes clean." We must, of course, remember that the office of burgomaster or juryman was poorly remunerated, if at all, and that handing out petty offices was regarded as normal. Sometimes rulers who went too far were sued.

Silver figurine representing a peasant woman, an 18th-century toy (Amsterdam Historical Museum) certainly for rich children, but reflecting the fact that at the time half the population of Holland was agricultural, a lower percentage than in most of Europe. The flourishing Dutch agriculture was, however, affected by stagnation in its exports because Europe's population ceased growing —thus, grain and milk prices fell—and also because importing countries became protectionist.

In 1747 William IV was appointed stadholder of all provinces and the Orangist Amsterdammers celebrated the event with flag waving and illuminations in the evening, the houses being lit with small candles and lanterns. In September some burghers handed a petition to the burgomasters asking for various reforms. They wanted the office of stadholder to become hereditary in the female line as well, and guards to choose their own officers. In November there was a riot in which the town hall was attacked and some burgomasters beat a hasty retreat. A group of burghers climbed inside, opened the windows, waved their hats to the crowd and showed the cushions on which the rulers used to sit. As a symbol of justice they produced an owl. Such mockery of the rulers was unthinkable and the guards cleared the building. After this riot Holland and then the other provinces declared the office of stadholder hereditary in both lines and some of the burghers' grievances were met. The States of Holland decided that civic offices must be carried out by the person appointed and not by proxies. The burgomasters, after fighting tooth and nail, relinquished the lucrative

right to appoint postmasters, which henceforth was a provincial matter.

Tax farmers' riots, 1748

In June 1748 opposition flared up again. From Groningen and Friesland a plundering riot against tax farmers crossed into Holland, and from June 24 to 28 Amsterdam was in an uproar. The trouble began after a minor incident in the butter market in which a guard suddenly opened fire; there were several dead and wounded. A contemporary report that there was a "shameless slut" who "several times raised her skirt, smacking her bare behind saying 'that's for you.'" The guards were provoked and shot the "female in her bare fundament"; she later died. The people left the place for the Keizersgracht where they began plundering the house of a tax farmer, the first of a long series of such events. Nothing was spared: furniture, bedding, porcelain, books, cutlery, wardrobes, mirrors, and a harpsichord— everything was smashed and thrown outside where large heaps formed in the canals. The mud dredgers took days to remove the debris. It was not a case of rapacity, but sheer love of destruction. Money boxes, too, were emptied into the canals, and jewels, watches, gold, and silverwork were smashed and flung into the water. An art lover who was an eye witness reported with horror how a whole cabinet of paintings was cut to shreds, among them a canvas by Melchior de Hondecoeler, "as beautiful as any to be seen," and a painting by Weenix. About one of the plunderers, whom his cronies called "Burgomaster," the writer was so incensed that he "would fain have seen him torn to pieces" because "with his great and fearful claws he smashed a handsome piece by Flip Wouerman on a banister knob."

The destructive rage was boundless: groups formed themselves and, with a list of addresses, worked through the tax farmers' houses. The guard, unwilling to protect them, remained aloof. When, on the morning of June 25, drumrolls could be heard here and there to alert the guard, only plunderers appeared and threw the drums into the water. The burgomasters were powerless and announced that they had taken cognizance of the burghers' wishes and had conveyed them to the States of Holland and the prince to institute inquiries as to how their wishes could be met. This did not restore peace and the plundering continued; it now included houses not belonging to tax farmers. This time the guards reacted and cleared the streets. Some rioters were killed and others arrested. After four days order was restored, but dozens of houses had been ruined and emptied. On the fifth day two ringleaders were hanged from the Waag on the Dam: a fish buyer from Nieuwendijk and the "Burgomaster" who had so busily smashed pictures. The crowded Dam was barred by the guard with fixed bayonets. After the execution some shots were fired causing mass panic. Dozens were trampled underfoot, others were pushed into the water of the Damrak and drowned. Under the impact of fearsome reports from Amsterdam the States of Holland had meanwhile decided to abolish tax farming at once. Henceforth salaried provincial officials would do the collecting. In Amsterdam, new demands of a strongly political character were now put forward. The burghers wanted further reductions in the power of ruling families and a transfer of postal income from the rulers to the prince. Moreover, they demanded free elections of guards' officers, which was important because the guard was the only source of power at the burghers' disposal.

Amsterdam and William IV

To realize these civic demands, all hope centered on the stadholder. On his side William IV was indeed inclined to restrain the burgomasters' financial and political power. A more or less organized civic movement arose. From various quarters representatives were chosen and assembled in the Kloveniersdoelen, a tavern and auction room where the guard formerly met. There were two currents in this "Doelist" movement, the radical and moderate. The moderates were in constant touch with the stadholder and conveyed their demands to the burgomasters. The pressure of the stadholder backed by the burghers drove the burgomasters and council to declare angrily that they would resign. Since the dismissal of civic rulers was a right of the stadholder,

William was asked to come to the city. With a great suite preceded by a banner proclaiming "Orange and Freedom," William arrived on September 2. A crowd of a thousand welcomed him with high hopes. William actually proceeded to dismiss the burgomasters and council, though not bitterly. To the departing burgomaster Corver, a widely respected man, he complained about the fatal circumstances and even expressed regret at having to take the necessary steps. Corver replied that he understood, and Henry Fagel, the clerk of the States General who was present at the town hall for the events, wrote in his diary: "Both had tears in their eyes and they embraced in the most pleasant manner." William appointed four new burgomasters, but from the old

Control of weights and measures protected consumers and the good name of traders. The Amsterdam Historical Museum has an interesting collection of instruments, such as the balance (left) with silver weights in an ebony box showing the city's coat of arms and the oil and wine measure in copper (above). Top right, comparative table of measures of length, engraved by Adam Ateitz, 1769, on a copper plate: it shows the measures of Amsterdam, the Low Countries, Venice, Genoa, France, Spain, Portugal, England, Sweden, and Danzig.

ruling families, while for the council he chose political newcomers.

In sum, the prince had done little, as the Doelists soon saw. In the dead of night some radicals among them invaded the stadholder's room in the Oudezijds Heerenlogement in order to present their demands, but to no effect: William was tired of having to act for the burghers and shortly afterward left the city. Not much was achieved, but 1747 and 1748 were important years because they saw the first inroads on the seemingly unimpeachable position of the rulers. The Doelist movement declined and even fell into discredit. When their leader Daniel Raap died in 1754, there were disorders at his funeral. The crowd even demanded his body. Only under the protection of the guard could he be buried in the Old Church, under cover of darkness.

The burghers had lost confidence in the House of Orange and even suspected it, and it was the rulers who prevailed. Another ruling group had come into the town hall and could still distribute office, if only in secret. Thus there was no genuine renewal of the ruling elite, although some new burghers came in and were promoted to offices that would have remained inaccessible to them without William IV. The current plans for economic reform played a role in William's careful appointments. By closer links between trade and administration a revival would have been possible. Indeed, Amsterdam merchants asked the prince before he had changed the law whether he would look after trading interests. He promised he would, "to the last breath of my life," and 12 of the new councilors did indeed come from merchant families who had never before been in the council. Among the burgomasters the commercial element was likewise strengthened: of the 37 burgomasters chosen from 1752 to 1795, 13 had never been in trade or business but were linked to trade through close family ties with the others. Of the 24 burgomasters chosen between 1718 and 1748, only two had been merchants.

Until 1780, when the Fourth English War broke out, the republic went through a relatively prosperous and peaceful phase. In the 1780s this calm was to be disturbed again; 1748 was just a mild foretaste.

Daily life: Amsterdam dwellings

On a cold winter's day in 1672, burgomaster Nicholas Tulp stood in his front house in the Keizersgracht to wait for his guests. For 50 years he had been a councilor, and to celebrate this event he was giving a dinner, as Hans Bontemantel relates. At about two

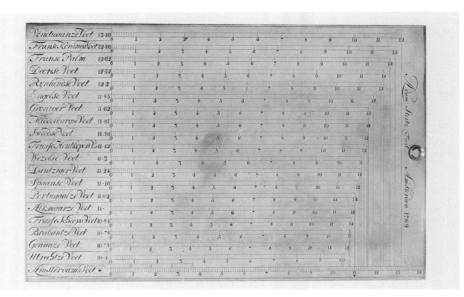

Right, grain measure. Below, from the left, an Amsterdam five-pound weight, a measure for lime and coal, and wine measure with the city's coat of arms. Bottom, copper ruler marked 1773 (Amsterdam Historical Museum).

199

The villa on the canal, the towed barge picturesquely decorated and reflected in the water (top, in an engraving by J.C. or R. Pellettier); and people conversing on the terrace of the Stadlader, a place of recreation, in front of the festive and animated pleasure boats (above, in an engraving by Adriaan Aartman). These pictures reflect the more relaxed tone of the wealthy of Amsterdam's society in the 18th century.

"front-house" style the large high rooms were entered directly from the street and extended the full width of the house; now they had shrunk to a much smaller parlor, with an adjacent sideroom, useful for those who liked the streetside. The front house had led to a narrow corridor running along the inner room, a small courtyard and the main parlor, or the reception room. Painters often chose the front house and connection with the hall as their subject. The next floor with bedrooms followed more or less the same plan. Above it were one and sometimes two attics used by the housewife for ironing and drying and for storing peat and goods for sale. Below the main story, there was a semibasement with a kitchen where the family usually ate, servant quarters, and food stores.

The rooms in a so-called "single house" were along one side of the corridor. In the "double-house," which became fashionable after the large town extensions, the rooms were arranged symmetrically on both sides of the corridor. Since the double-house was considerably more spacious, a separate staircase would develop alongside the corridor after 1650.

Behind the house there was often a garden, which in the canal belt could be quite deep. The toilets usually stood against the backwall of the house, accessible both from house and garden. In the garden there might be small pavilions, garden houses, or sheds for coaches and stables. Except for some extensions, this arrangement of a merchant's house belongs to a development that prevailed throughout the 18th century.

In 1700, a rich patrician's house had some special rooms for music, art, receptions, and childbirth. This applied only to a thin top layer of society. Average people lived in single houses simply divided and with smaller rooms. A large group, estimated at 18,740 families in 1748, lived in rear dwellings (built on the rear courtyards of street houses), in cellars or basements of larger houses. In comparison, 22,821 families lived in proper houses. However primitive conditions were for these poor, at least they had a roof over their heads, in contrast with the homeless, of whom Amsterdam must have had a fair number.

o'clock, his colleagues arrived with their servants. After a first welcome by the burgomaster, his son showed the visitors to the inner room and to the "beautiful room," the salon further back in the house. When all were present, the banquet began in a specially erected wooden lodge in the garden. After the second course, guests warmed themselves by the fire in the parlor, where tobacco and pipes were laid out in small dishes on a table. Returning to the lodge the guests helped themselves amply from dishes of fine sweetmeats and confectionery. At about eleven, the guests left.

The arrangement of Tulp's house was the usual one for a merchant's dwelling. In the medieval

Furniture and fittings in the 17th century

Furnishings, especially in the wealthy houses, changed considerably with time. Until 1670, a typical Dutch manner prevailed. Rooms were dark and had little furniture. In wealthier homes there were red or yellow glazed tiles on the floor or larger stone tiles in white, blue, or black. On the upper floors and in simpler houses, the floor was of large wooden planks, sometimes with attractive floral patterns. The plastered walls were whitewashed. Corridor, kitchen, and front houses were lined with white or decorated blue tiles. In the living rooms of the well-to-do the wooden paneling reached about two thirds

up the wall. The panels were set in artistically carved frames with a protruding top ledge on which were placed copper candlesticks, tin dishes, jugs, and ornamental plates in earthenware or Chinese and Japanese porcelain. A very few could afford wall carpets. Many had maps and paintings on their walls. A suffused light filtered through the light green of yellowish lead-framed glass windows and was the more mysterious when the high cross-barred windows had the lower parts covered by shutters. Sometimes the light was reflected in a copper chandelier hanging from the heavy oak beam, or it shone on a curious dessiccated fish or other exotic object brought back from foreign travels and hung in the

Hendrik Pothoven's Family in an Interior, 1774, was one of many pictures in which 17th-century burghers have fixed their serious, reliable, and comfortable style of life. A recent essay on 17th-century Amsterdam culture speaks of the "development of the first autonomous bourgeois culture in modern times"; in the 18th century it seems that people wished to enjoy its fruits with moderate pleasure.

room. The ceiling consisted of beams, resting on sculptured supports. The timber was usually undecorated, although some beams had painted floral motifs, particularly a tulip design.

Within this fixed pattern the furnishing remained subdued. The cupboard was the main item. There were cupboards for various things: linen, clothes, art objects, food, or eating utensils. At first most cupboards were in oak or walnut, decorated with an inlay of small pieces of rosewood and ash. After 1650 cupboards were made of more exotic woods such as ebony. The heavy table, like the cupboard, rested on spherical feet, against the wall near the window, the main source of light (later in the middle of the room as well); it was the center of domestic life. Here people drank beer or wine together, made music, or played cards. Often an Eastern carpet was spread on the table. In the kitchen, collapsible tables were more practical. Chairs were hardly comfortable: they were high, covered with Spanish leather or more simply with matting. After 1650 velvet or plush-covered chairs became available. The bed was at first in the living rooms, as a separate piece, bedstead, or wall-bed. Later the fourposter with its fabric sides and top stood in separate bedrooms, but bedsteads remained in use in various parts of the house.

After 1675, interiors began to boast more luxurious features: among other things many exotic kinds of wood and a great variety of furniture came into use, gilded leather hangings on the walls of the rich, marble tiles on the floors of rooms and corridors, covered with large Eastern carpets or Spanish mats to ward off the cold, and the first use of stucco appeared in corridors and staircases and on ceilings. New kinds of wood and new materials, such as lacquer from the Far East, were used in furniture. By means of intarsia techniques, furniture makers applied decorative motifs in walnut, rosewood, and mahogany to grooves in hardwood. Marquetry used the same woods applied in walnut or ebony layers of veneer that were glued on oak panel. The beams in the ceiling were now covered with square wooden panels decorated with paintings. The wooden paneling and the chimney niche were painted blue or blue-green. There were special small porcelain corners or nooks where large pyramidal shelves, some-

times with mirrors, displayed the family's chinaware and silver.

Interiors in the 18th century

After 1675, French influence increased sharply, in part because of the refugee architect and interior decorator Daniel Marot. Rooms were now decorated so that doors, windows, chimneys, and ceilings were treated as a strictly symmetric whole. At first, the natural wood was painted blue or green, but from 1730 lighter colors prevailed. The walls were often covered with Utrecht velour, a velvet with motifs stamped on by wooden rollers and steam. Wooden beam ceilings went out of fashion and disappeared from the main rooms of richer houses. Stucco enclosed large central areas, and artists like Gerard de Lairesse and Jacob de Wit decorated them with illusionistic ceiling paintings. More sculpture figured in the decoration, which was to be seen in corridors, staircases, and on chimney mantels in every patrician house. Above doors and chimneys, too, there were painted representations in grisaille, white-gray, or beige, imitating reliefs in marble, stucco, or wood.

The new larger sliding windows with their lighter glass admitted much light into these refined interiors. Heavy curtains framed the windows, and mirrors between windows and in the chimney made the rooms look bigger. The high 17th-century chimneys

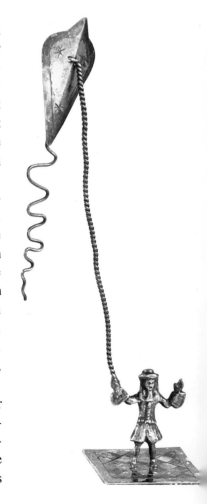

were replaced by much lower mantels that caused less trouble with smoke.

Typical of the period was the use of cabinets for storage. The heavy 17th-century cupboards were moved to more remote parts of the house. A cabinet consisted of a top case with two doors and a lower part with several drawers. Cabinets were made for all sorts of purposes, among them storing porcelain and precious articles. Desk cabinets began to appear. Other new French furniture included commodes and secretaires. Various smaller and easily shiftable pieces, such as occasional tables and playing and sewing tables reflected the changing social customs.

About 1750 it looked as if, under the influence of the rococo style, patrician interiors had been designed in one fell swoop. Stucco ornaments linked corridors and staircases. Decorated frames of doors, chimneys, windows, and banisters echoed this movement. Concave and convex curves masked sharp corners. The colors of woodwork were now sea green, pink, or off-white, livened by gilding. In the midst of all this there were light and quite low pieces, many Chinese or Japanese tea tables and screens, cases with porcelain, silver, books, and works of art. The walls were covered with cloth and were therefore less suitable than they had been for hanging paintings.

After 1775 the republic, too, adopted the simpler and stricter neoclassic Louis XIV styles. Form and ornament were inspired by ancient Greece and Rome. Amsterdammers were quick to arrange their houses in the newest fashion. Volutes and playful curves disappeared in favor of straight lines and a much simpler and stricter ornament. The walls sometimes bore large wall paintings, on which Dutch, Italian, and fantasy landscapes were represented. The Amsterdam painter Jurriaan Andriessen excelled in this genre.

The domestic styles outlined above occurred in the less luxurious houses of the middle class as well. They had no gilded leather or precious woods, and wooden floors and ceilings long remained in use, as did white walls. Woodwork received a bit of color, following the fashions of the time. About 1750 and after, these houses received special "burgher furniture," which imitated that of the patricians.

Running a house

It was quite a task to run a patrician house, or even a well-to-do middle class one. In Holland, the mistress of a house was deservedly famous for extreme cleanliness. Many anecdotes survive about her sometimes excessive fear of small splashes and spots. For example, this story is told: a traveler, who had an appointment with the master, had rung the bell and the servant girl opened the door; it had been raining, and the girl, without greeting the stranger, looked aghast at his dirty shoes. Still without speaking, she grabbed him under his arms and carried him, much to his surprise, to a bench in the corridor, where she began to take off his shoes. Only after he had been

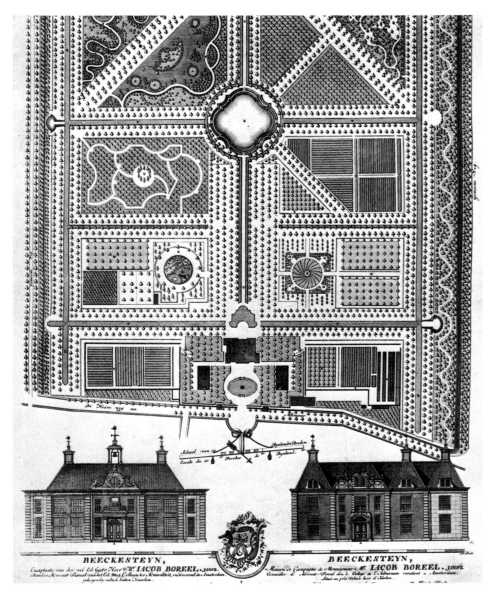

BEECKESTEYN,
Lustplaats van den wel Ed. Gestr. Heer en M.r IACOB BOREEL, Jun.r.
Raad en Advocaat Fiscaal van het Ed. Mog. Collegie ter Admiraliteit, residerende in Amsterdam;
gelegen by oosten buiten Haarlem.

BEECKESTEYN,
Maison de Campagne de Monseigneur M.r IACOB BOREEL, Jun.r.
Conseiller & Avocat Fiscal dans le Collège de l'Amirauté résident à Amsterdam.
Située au près d'Haarlem vers le Nord-Est.

The mania of country holidays. Left, leaving for the country, the month of May, in a series of prints illustrating the months, by Cornelis Troost. Above, the country house and park of Jacob Boreel, councilor and fiscal advocate of the Admiralty College of Amsterdam, 1772.

put into a pair of slippers was he allowed to proceed!

Merely looking after the linen and clothes was a lot of work. The washing was done by a girl at the pump in the basement or in a public wash house. Some had their clothes washed outside, giving them to the small washing boats that traveled from Amsterdam to, say, Beverwijk, north of Haarlem, where there were great laundries. This would happen every six months, which meant quite a store of linen. In well-to-do circles an inventory of 100 tablecloths, 500 napkins, 40 bed sheets, 100 pillowcases, and 50 towels was not unusual. These and the many handkerchiefs, scarves, caps, cuffs, shirts, and collars meant a fair amount of starching and ironing. Then there were silver and copper to be cleaned, tin to be scoured, and wood to be polished. Floors were cleaned with broom and soap. Windows and other outside parts were also regularly cleaned. Nor could the outer stairs and the street in front of the house be neglected.

There was naturally a great demand for domestic and kitchen help in the 18th century. French cooks increasingly ruled the kitchen. Ladies of standing no longer brought up their children themselves, so that wet nurses, children's maids, governesses, and tutors were needed to look after the youngsters. From a tax register of 1748 we learn that Amsterdammers with a yearly income of at least 600 guilders (about one third of the population) usually had at least one servant. Some had two or three, and a few four or five. At 14 to 15 years of age a working-class girl went into service with a well-to-do family, which was not necessarily a hardship: she was often fed and lodged and probably well treated. Foreigners were amazed that in the absence of the master Dutch ladies and their children would eat with the servant girls.

If a girl remained single, she could rise to head of the household, a very responsible job. From contemporary farces we know that minor quarrels between servant and mistress occurred much as they do now: the mistress would bark at the girls who, in turn, would all too often vie with the mistress by dressing conspicuously. Servants and other employees received high tips from guests. They took this for granted, but the mistresses often felt that this

204

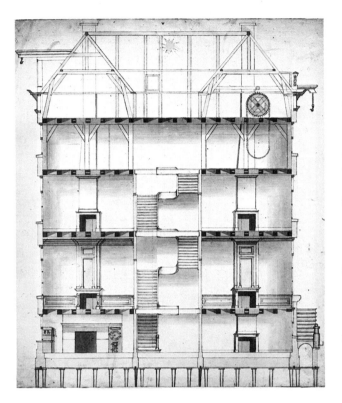

habit tended to get out of hand. At all events, Amsterdam servants were far from shy. In 1765 the administration had taken measures to improve the canal water by means of better circulation. At once 33,000 cleaning women sent a petition to the town hall opposing the plan. There were 20,000 houses in the city, they said, that had to be rubbed down four times a year because of the stench and emanations from the canals: without the stench, once a year would prove enough, which would mean three days less work at 12 five-cent pieces a day or a total of 36,000 guilders of income. Moreover, they would lose two or three days extra scouring of copper, tin, and silver, which also affected income. Besides, dealers in brushes, clogs, and even members of the painters and glaziers guilds, who used to replace windows broken during cleaning, might be displaced.

Country retreats and gardens

As early as the 16th century, Amsterdammers who could afford it looked for life in the open air. Some bought a large farm where they built a separate house for themselves, a so-called gentleman's lodge.

Tones of refined elegance and a certain taste for ostentation mark the 18th-century family portraits of Amsterdam burghers who liked to show themselves against their decorative interiors in fashionable dress and engaged in their favorite pastimes. Above right, Jeronimus Tonneman listening to his son playing the flute. Carel Mander's Schilderboek, *with legible title, figures here on purpose: it is a theoretical and graphical treatise on painting and particularly on Dutch painters, in imitation of Vasari. Canvas by Cornelis Troost (Dublin, National Gallery of Ireland). Left, Chinese tea service decorated in Holland (Amsterdam Historical Museum).*

Others bought genuine castles, for example, in the dunes. Closer to town there were small rural cottages or simply gardens with small garden sheds.

The drift to the country intensified in the 17th century, partly for reasons of status, partly because land was a good investment. The possession of a manor and the title and privileges that went with it offered prestige. Various regions were fashionable: along rivers such as the Amstel and the Vecht, in the newly won polders, such as the Beemster and the Purmer, and on the sand pits in the dunes. In the vicinity of the city, for example in the Watergraafsmeer, country houses were erected as well. In the 18th century these places became veritable pleasure gardens, where the tired citizen could recover in the peace and quiet of nature. In May, the whole family— father, mother, children, and domestic staff—left the hot and often smelly city by private yacht or coaches. The lady of the house, the children, and staff remained in the country all summer, going for excursions on horseback in the neighborhood, visiting friends and relations or nearby pleasure gardens. The master enjoyed hunting with friends, a pastime

that boys from well-off homes learned to practice from an early age.

Walking in gardens carefully laid out after the latest fashion, or in the somewhat wilder parks, always filled the owner with pride. The couple liked to boast about their baroque French garden with its straight hedges and lanes, many ponds and fountains, flower beds and lawns, and pretty garden pavilions. Gardens in the dunes had the advantage of more hilly terrain, so that some belvederes could be arranged; this was an important element when the English style of landscape became popular after 1750. In the kitchen gardens the owners grew ordinary fruit and vegetables, as well as some rather exotic plants brought home from Asia or America. Thus a respected lady of Amsterdam grew pineapples around 1700, and an East India Company administrator had in his country garden the first coffee plant and banana tree in the republic. Of course in the Dutch climate one had to use small hot-houses, but that was no problem: many practical guides on this could be bought. Even exotic birds and wild animals could be admired in aviaries and cages.

Peacocks and turkeys wandered about freely.

Other country places lay within a stone's throw of the city and could be admired by simpler folk who on Sundays or after work in summer liked to rest in small boats or walk out of town. There were many taverns and tea gardens where one could enjoy a pipe and a good glass while talking and contemplating the meadows where "you see the cows through tender clover tread / with udders swelled, till farm wives bring relief, / who with such care await the milking hour / and sing a happy song in the morning light." The city dweller saw rural life through rose-colored glasses but still was glad to go back to his beloved city. In winter he could read in well-illustrated books descriptions of each splendid country place, separately by region.

Water

In the gardens of country places there were often grottoes and fountains. On a much smaller scale there were simple waterworks, as in the gardens behind town houses on the canals. For their constant scouring and scrubbing, servants needed buckets of water usually taken from the canals. But drinking water was a different problem altogether: Amsterdam struggled with this as early as the 16th century. More and more people came to live in the city, so that water pollution grew swiftly. Moreover, after 1550 the Zuiderzee silted up rapidly and so, therefore, did the Ij. The administration tried to improve things, for example, by forbidding rubbish from being thrown into the canals, but without much success. Besides canal water, Amsterdammers started using rainwater from butts and underground reservoirs, although this was none too clean and often poisoned by lead from gutters. Groundwater pumped from fountains was poor as well. The dreadful plagues of the 17th century underlined the need for good drinking water.

Shortly after 1660 the city's beer brewers, for whom water was essential, joined forces to bring fresh water by boat from the Gein, a small stream near Amsterdam. Later they fetched water mainly from the Vecht, a river in nearby Utrecht. The boats left early each morning, drawn by a horse, and re-

turned towards dusk. In winter one could use ice: some brewers had an icebreaker built jointly, which by periodic shuttle trips kept the main channel open. In normal winters this required about eight horses, but if it was exceptionally cold, 20 or 30 might have to be used. Around the icebreaker were men armed with axes to break up the ice, which always attracted hundreds of spectators. No wonder, because the supply of drinking water was vital. During some very harsh winters the icebreaker could not pass, and even if it could, the cost of bringing water became so high that the poor could no longer afford fresh water. Jacob Bicker Raye relates how in 1740, 1757, and 1763 the poor in despair melted frozen canal water for drinking, which made them seriously ill.

Only in 1784 did the city take over the running of

the icebreaker from the brewers. Moreover, the supply of drinking water now came into the hands of professionals, who were given boats by the city and had to observe city hygiene regulations. Sellers of drinking water were united in the Fresh Water Society. Before entering the city, water from the large water boats had to be transferred to much smaller boats with a pump on top. Here people could fetch water in buckets. During this period, many more or less daring plans for improving water supplies came to nothing, mainly because of the high cost or technical obstacles. Plans for aqueducts, systems of pipes, reservoirs, and large civic fountains in the city's squares remained dreams on paper. At the end of the 18th century the city finally implemented the plan for building drinking water reservoirs at several points in town.

Stimulants

In the 17th century water and beer were the main beverages of the people of Amsterdam. Trade with the Far East and America brought new products to the European market and greatly influenced social life. Since Amsterdam was a world market, it was soon fairly easy, at least for the privileged, to buy new items like tea, coffee, and tobacco. After strong clerical opposition to the use of tobacco, and hot debates between physicians about the pros and cons of tea and coffee, the custom became ever more widespread and after 1750 was completely accepted in broad reaches of society.

Tea

Around 1610, small amounts of tea were first introduced into the republic. When in 1667 the East India Company more or less by accident brought a large load to the Amsterdam market, the demand for it was huge. At first tea, recommended by some physicians for its medical virtues, remained confined to the circles of humanist intellectuals such as Pieter Corneliszon Hooft and the professor Barlaeus. High-sounding Greek and Latin hymns of praise appeared about this exotic curiosity. In the Botanical Garden an example of the tea plant could be admired. Tea

drinking became increasingly popular after 1680. Ladies from well-to-do circles visited each other for a cup of tea. One vied with the other by producing even nicer China cups, silver teapots and tea caddies, handsome, inlaid Japanese lacquer tables, and the most splendid confectionery. The rich even arranged special tearooms for these social gatherings, or if there was no space for this, the ladies sat in the front house on the street side. Once arrived, the party sat around the tea table on which stood teapots, various sorts of tea, small cups and dishes, candy and biscuits, small sugar balls and other confectionery. The ceremony began by the hostess preparing samples of various sorts of tea, which the guests tried one by one. Their qualities were discussed at length, and after due consideration, a unanimous choice was decided. The lady of the house then quickly made a large pot of the chosen sort, of which the ladies proceeded to drink many cups each. All this moisture tended to produce excess internal gases, which from time to time were released with emphasis, with an apologetic "by your leave" as the victim briefly rose from her chair. Nobody was offended by what to us seem dubious manners, on the contrary, this was part of the performance. After a while the servant girl removed the tea things and the moment had arrived for a little drink. In a very rich house this might be Rhine wine, but mostly it was brandy with sugar and raisins. Somewhat light headed, the party dissolved at the end of the afternoon.

After 1750, when tea prices dropped, the habit spread to the wives of craftsmen. They, too, had their teatime, usually around four o'clock. For breakfast, tea now replaced beer. Indeed, the habit became universal: at breakfast, teatime at home, but also in the gradually developing public tea gardens, everyone drank tea. There were even street vendors for tea with milk. Tea pavilions in the country places developed into designs of remarkable architectural imagination, with the Chinese pagoda style becoming conspicuous after 1750.

One of the more significant social aspects of the mania for tea was that for the first time ladies from higher circles had an excuse for leaving the house and meeting other women. Up until then they had led isolated lives at home. "The household went to rack and ruin, for when a man came home from his office he found no wife and went to the tavern." Thus we read in satirical pieces and pamphlets of the period, emphasizing the funnier side of the new fashion. Of course, the men went to a hostelry or wineshop on other occasions anyway, and there were more than enough of these in the 17th century. Here you could smoke a pipe and enjoy a glass of beer. The landlord mostly sold tobacco as well, or one could buy leaves in a tobacco shop marked by a sign on which a smoking farmer or sailor was pictured. While passing a pipe, the men could play dice and drink their beer. Women from the lower orders often came here, too, and it was regarded as normal that they smoked as well.

In the course of the 17th century tobacco plugs came into fashion. After chewing, it was usual to spit into a special dish, the cuspidor. It was a fearful mistake to spit the plug on the ground as foreigners occasionally did.

Coffee

For gentlemen coffee was common by 1700. Amsterdam then had special coffeehouses, where in the beginning you could not get wine or beer, although liqueurs were available. Pipes stood ready in rows. Long Gouda pipes and coffee drinking were inseparable in the 18th century. About half past ten, when

The love of beautiful objects: in Amsterdam you could buy the best, whether imported or made locally. Opposite, an elegant Louis XV piece by Andries Bouger, late 18th century, decorated with gilded bronze and floral inlays, in the French style fashionable among Dutch burghers. Above, a valuable watch made by Jacob Hasius in Amsterdam. Right, a porcelain plate with family coat-of-arms. Such ceramics were made in China for rich clients in Amsterdam (all from the Amsterdam Historical Museum).

the coffeehouses opened, well-to-do burghers drifted in. When the coffee was ordered, one read the papers at length and soon the company engaged in hot debate over current political and economic projects. Much of the notorious ''wind'' trade in shares took place in coffeehouses, the French one in Kalverstraat being particularly famous.

There were no genuine literary coffeehouses, which in London offered a high standard of conversation. On the contrary, a scoffer about 1730 described the talk as a concatenation of ''amusing jokes and quaint ideas.'' Many young men just out of bed went to a coffeehouse, according to another ironic author: ''Here he reasons about everything, walks up and down and meddles in every conversation.''

Art in the 18th century

After 1675 European life came under strong French influence. The grandeur and refinement emanating from the sun king's court was echoed in countless princely palaces throughout Europe, and the bourgeoisie likewise looked to Versailles. French baroque influenced both architecture and interiors. People dressed in the Paris fashion and behaved according to French books on etiquette. French literature and drama set the tone, and the whole of cultured Europe spoke and wrote French. In spite of the political antagonism between France and the republic, French culture took a hold in the Netherlands, too, especially with a wave of Huguenot refugees containing many trained craftsmen that came after the revocation of the Edict of Nantes. One of them, Daniel Marot, especially inspired Dutch architecture and interior decoration. The classicism of Holland with its strict forms came to an end towards 1700. Marot introduced a more playful building style in which decorative curves and sculptured ornaments of acanthus leaves and shell motifs broke through the geometric rigor. This is evident in Marot's palaces for William III in England and the Netherlands, in buildings for the States General, and in burghers' houses in The Hague and Amsterdam.

More than in architectural exteriors, baroque and, later, the more refined rococo showed in interiors.

Here Marot's influence was great, for he published prints with models of furniture, paneling, chimneys, and stucco ceilings. This became visible in the handsome town houses and in the country houses along the Amstel and Vecht and in the strip along the dunes. The curved line predominates. Scrolled work often decorated with gold leaf surrounded the legs of chairs and tables, mirror frames, cupboards, and chimney mantels. Ceilings were carefully stuccoed and painted. Dutch baroque, originating from Catholic inspiration, was never so exuberant as in churches, monasteries, palaces, and libraries in France, Spain, Italy, southern Germany, Austria, and the southern Netherlands. From the 1760s, architecture and interior design became formally much stricter, a result of a new turn toward classical architecture and 17th century classicism. Scrolls slowly disappeared in favor of quiet and lighter lines of neoclassical style. A noteworthy creation after 1775 is the building of the Felix Meritis society by Jacob Otten Husly. The stately edifice with a front of four engaged columns running the height of two floors, and decorations symbolizing various arts, was inaugurated in 1788. For years, the Felix Meritis building and its drawing studio, concert hall, space for scientific experiments, museum of scientific instruments, and rooftop observatory, was the cultural center of Amsterdam.

During these years, the city architect was Abraham van der Hart. Besides burghers' houses he

THE PORT OF AMSTERDAM

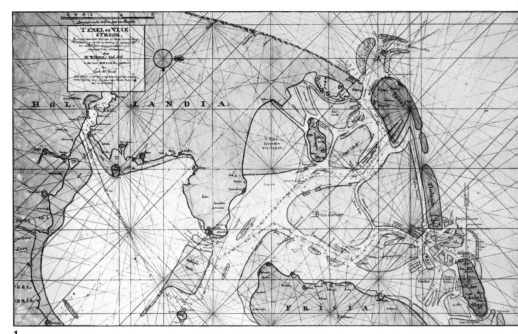

1

The most important ports of the republic of the Seven United Provinces were situated on the estuaries of the Maas and the Scheldt, and along the shores of the Zuiderzee. Although these ports knew periods of great prosperity, their poor accessibility was infamous. From the point of view of actual navigation, they had major drawbacks: they were situated behind series of sandbanks, and other shallows were created by the materials brought down by the rivers or, in the Zuiderzee itself, by the ebb and flow of the tides. In order to reach these ports, it was always necessary to proceed with great caution, and to ensure the assistance of expert pilots who knew the pattern of currents and shallows. Then there was the problem of ice, and there were the prevailing westerly and southwesterly winds, which could severely hamper ships trying to leave.

The problems grew worse in the 17th century because of the increased draught of vessels and the progressive silting-up of the ports. So it is not surprising that a great deal of care and attention was paid by the city and provincial authorities to the upkeep of the port and to improving and increasing accessibility to it. Pilot services were organized, the depth of the shallows was checked at regular intervals, and buoys and beacons were laid. Lighthouses, and stone or wooden markers to help with the business of alignment also made navigation easier.

It should be remembered that in the period with which we are dealing, access to Amsterdam by sea was via the Zuiderzee; Amsterdam harbor was entered from the east along the Ij (3). Nowadays access is from the west through a canal that links the North Sea with the Ij (4). In the period we are talking about, therefore, in order to reach Amsterdam from the North Sea, it was necessary to navigate the treacherous waters of the Zuiderzee, treacherous because of the shoals and banks, and because of the short, violent waves often found there. In 1672 the English ambassador to the republic observed that sailing along the shores of Texel island and across the Zuiderzee was more hazardous than sailing from England to the ports of Spain, even though that route meant having to tackle the fearsome waters of the Bay of Biscay. It is worth having a look at the nautical chart of Izaak de Graaf of 1712 (1) with the routes from the North Sea to Amsterdam (north is on the right-hand side). Ships headed for Amsterdam would enter by the Marsdiep or further to the northeast by the Vlie. Part of their cargo would be offloaded on Texel island and then put aboard smaller craft so as to reduce the draught. And on Texel island the Admiralty also made sure that the proper dues and taxes had been paid on im-

5

6

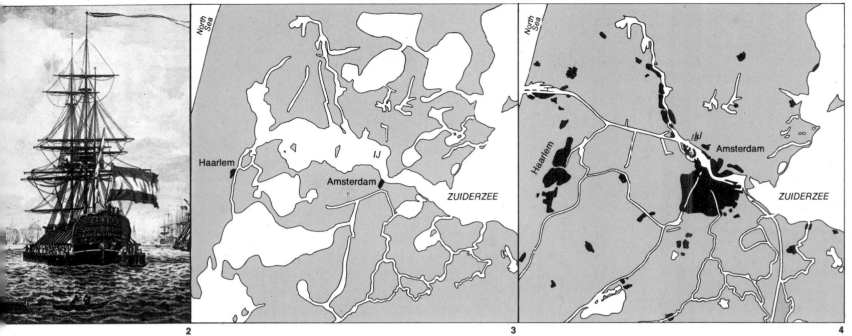

2   3   4

ports and exports, as well as the levies for the upkeep of auxiliary services (beacons, buoys, lighthouses, etc.) for shipping.

In 1699 three lighthouses were built along the coast of the Zuiderzee, and their upkeep was financed by an annual tax on shipping. Special tokens made of lead depicting three lighthouses (5) were used to indicate that payment had been received. Again at Texel island ships leaving port took on supplies of fresh water and sometimes had to wait there for weeks for the right wind before they could sail. From the Marsdiep or the Vlie ships approaching port would sail cautiously southward. At the mouth of the Ij they would then have to negotiate that much-feared obstacle called the Pampus. These were hazardous shallows and ships with a deep draught were unable to go beyond this point. The practice then was to attach various tanks filled with water to the hull beneath the waterline. As these tanks were emptied by means of pumps, this helped to lift the ship up in the water and enable it to sail over the shoals and shallows. At the end of the 17th century the system reached perfection, with specially fashioned tanks that could be fitted to the sides of the ships (*these were called "camels"; 2, in an engraving by M. Sallieth, 1780*). Thus raised, the ships were moored on the far side of the Pampus. The port itself was reached via the Ij (*6, an engraving from the early 17th century*). From as early as the 14th century the port was protected by a double series of piles. Behind these were the *walen* or basins, which, in turn, were marked out on all sides by piles. The mud that was shifted by the tides came to rest against these even rows of piles. In this way, the piles not only offered protection from enemy attacks, but also dampened the waves coming in off the sea and helped prevent the port from becoming silted up.

The port, incidentally, had to be periodically dredged to keep it in efficient working order. In the 16th century these dredges were worked by manually operated winches. By the middle of the 17th century animals were used instead: horses harnessed to the shafts of a winch would drive the dredging machine (*7, a harbor dredger in a drawing by Reinier Nooms, also known as Zeeman, 17th century; 8, the cross-sectional drawing of a horse-powered dredger from the* Groot Volkomen Moolenboek *by L. van Natrus, J. Polly, and C. van Vuuren, 1734*). The four or five city dredging machines used in the port removed about 260,000 cubic yards of mud each year. The port authorities allocated a mooring inside the piles to all ships arriving at Amsterdam. Or, if the vessel was very large, it would have to anchor outside the basins. The cargo was transferred to special lighters or barges by dockers and lightermen, using hoists fixed to the mast, or small movable derricks and cranes. For heavier freight, like millstones or pieces of artillery, the city crane was used.

Once the cargo had found its way onto the quayside, the various transporters got busy. They were organized as corporations, and it was they who sorted out the various merchandise and sent it on its way by boat along the canals, or by wagon or cart, or on someone's back, until it reached the weighing station or the warehouse. The harbor traffic was the city's lifeline.

7

designed utilitarian buildings, such as the home for Catholic orphan girls on the Spui. This so-called maidenhouse, which at the rulers' request was built from 1784 to 1787, "without any splendor or decoration, but strong and solid," had room for 350 to 400 orphans and staff together. Some years earlier in Roeter street, van der Hart built his greatest edifice, the New Workhouse, where up to 800 people found refuge, in two categories: male and female voluntary and compulsory workers. Van der Hart aimed at designing a big rational complex with due care for proper sanitation and an efficient arrangement for the directors. After the town hall, this was the largest building in the city and became internationally famous. The courts of St. Petersburg and Vienna asked for descriptions, and in Hanover a workhouse was built on the Amsterdam model.

In painting, too, there was French influence, above all owing to Gérard de Lairesse (1640–1711), who spread French academic theories of art, themselves based on Italian prototypes. In 1648 the Académie Royale des Beaux Arts was founded in Paris, for practical and theoretical courses in art. According to the theory, art was governed by fixed rules. Choice of subject, composition, and use of color, all were subject to rules; nothing could be left to chance. Spontaneous and individual expression were banned.

The style here imported into architecture, painting, and sculpture had an ideological motive: art had to proclaim the power and glory of Louis XIV, or of other princes, cities, and civic institutions. When Lairesse came to Amsterdam in 1667 or 1668, he found a tradition of painting historical subjects on commission from the town hall, charitable institutions, and patricians. This he was able to combine with his own French theories. At the same time he had contacts with the men of letters and actors who belonged to the association "Nil Volentibus Arduum," and who practiced their classical views in their fields. Painting and poetry were seen as coequal sisters: painting is silent poetry, poetry is vocal painting.

Lairesse spread his views by means of lectures later collected in *Foundations of the Art of Drawing* (1701) and *Painting Book* (1707), often reprinted

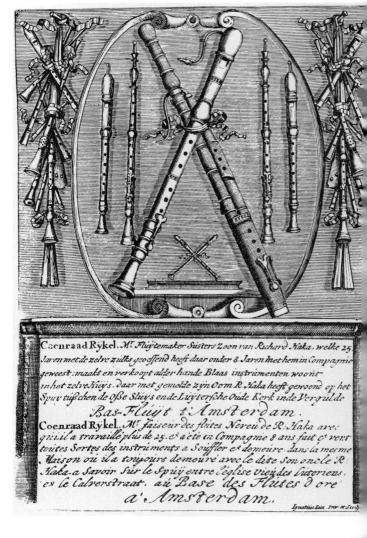

Right, a "visiting card," the advertising leaflet of flute maker Coenraad Rijkel. In Dutch and French, it states "Flute maker, nephew of R. Haka with whom he has worked for over 25 years . . . makes and sells all sorts of wind instruments and lives in the same house where his uncle has always lived." Below, reunion of a music society, print by Langendijk, 1799.

and translated into French, German, and English. He emphasized the "infallible rules of art." A painting had to be instructive in content and inspire moral thoughts and deeds. One had to choose an exalted subject, preferably biblical or mythological. The characters must be represented clearly and with idealized features. There were rules for the expression and gestures that belonged to a particular state of feeling. He describes in detail how a peasant spoons his soup and how a lady of rank would do it. The artist works not from nature or everyday reality; instead, he creates, with textbook in hand, a new reality. Neither everyday life, close to the basic subjects of landscape or still-life, in which 17th-century Dutch painters excelled, nor the mysterious chiaroscuro of a man like Rembrandt could have impressed Lairesse. He himself strictly obeyed these rules. For

William III, the Amsterdam merchant houses, and the Leprosy House, he carried out paintings on walls and ceilings. These last are imaginative expansions of space characteristic of the baroque as a whole. High in the air we see figures floating about, representing Science, Charity, or Reason. Gods and goddesses in flowing garments hover between the clouds surrounded by tumbling putti.

In order to master this technique, a thorough knowledge of perspective was essential. The painter had to take into account the height of the ceiling, the incidence of light, and the ideal place for observing the painted clouds. Extensive sketches always preceded the final execution. Lairesse stressed the art of drawing, which he saw as the basis of painting. By technical skill in drawing the human figure, one was able to make blueprints of a painting. Following

Above, the theater in Leyden Square, drawing by Hermannus Petrus Schouten. After the theater on Keizersgracht burned down in 1772, the new one shown here was built of wood in the carriage yard of the Leyden Gate and inaugurated on September 17, 1774. A box cost 18 guilders, a place in the stalls, one guilder and four stuivers, and entrance, six stuivers.

French cities and inspired by Lairesse's ideas, people set up drawing academies in the republic during the 17th and particularly the 18th centuries. Amateurs and professionals could practice their drawing here. In Amsterdam this could be done in the Felix Meritis society and in the more distinguished City Drawing Academy where Lairesse's theories were the subject of lectures.

Lairesse had very few Dutch successors. He was unique in trying to introduce an international style, but the results were not brilliant, perhaps because of the ideological character of his art: in the republic there was no need for such propaganda. There was no clergy or nobility to be glorified; town halls and other administrative buildings already had their 17th-century historical pieces and "exalted subjects," which not everybody could understand, and which probably had little appeal to the sober taste of Dutch burghers. The only potentate who wished to show his power through painting and architecture was the stadholder and his court, by whom Marot and Lairesse were occasionally retained. However, when in 1702 the stadholder died, this, too, was at an end. Burghers in the cities made do with less exuberant works, though still clearly under French

influence. Here we must mention Jacob de Wit of Amsterdam, a Catholic who had long lived in Antwerp where he had studied the baroque styles of the southern Netherlands under Rubens and van Dyck among others. He obtained commissions from Catholic churches in the republic. He also created countless paintings on walls and ceilings for merchants' town and country houses and a large biblical scene for the town hall in Amsterdam. The portion still in place measures 18 by 40 feet. It represents an Old Testament episode (Numbers 11) in which Moses, inspired by God, chooses 70 wise elders who, led by the holy spirit, would assume part of his own task. The picture was meant for the council chamber. Just as Govert Flinck's *Solomon's Prayer for Wisdom,* which was already hanging, it had a direct link with the function of this hall, suggesting roughly that God's blessing rests on the 36 councilors as on the 70 elders. De Wit, too, was a master in adapting optical tricks. Just as Lairesse before him, he painted vertiginous sky gods, clouds, and little angels. A specialty of de Wit was grisaille putti, which at a distance looked like stucco reliefs. Punning on his name, people called them "little wits."

Eighteenth-century Dutch painting was influ-

enced only partly by France. In general, the old traditions continued, though without reaching 17th-century standards. Many painters concentrated on interior decoration. Education for painting still took place in a master's studio and then in factories for wall hangings. In well-to-do circles it was no longer fashionable to cover walls with gilded leather, instead they employed hangings showing paintings of Italian Arcadian landscapes. Later in the century, Dutch landscapes were preferred.

The tradition of portraiture continued, but the lively pieces that had been made in the previous century were replaced by stiffly posed and overdressed individuals, set pieces against a bourgeois background, as if behind these bewigged and wealthy faces every emotion had been stifled. The formality of 18th-century life is reflected in painting. An Amsterdam painter far above his contemporaries was Cornelis Troost (1696–1750) who painted portraits but also many spiritual genre pieces in which he showed his love for theatrical scenes. He came from an actors' family and had himself been on the stage for some years. The pieces that inspired him were not markedly weighty or of much psychological

depth. Often they were of French inspiration and formed a mild reflection of the original: pieces full of secret trysts, disguises, mistaken identity, and unexpected returns of a spouse. With his witty brush he railed at his compatriots who tried so hard to imitate French elegance. He showed how Dutch burghers time and again gave themselves away by boorish behavior. Moreover, he parodied the exalted theories of Lairesse, and his irony obviously pleased the public, for after his death his watercolors and paintings were reproduced in countless prints.

The genre of floral still lifes retained a high standard in Amsterdam, through Rachel Ruysch, daughter of the anatomist and botanist Fredrik Ruysch, and through Jan van Huysum, both producing brilliant examples, fresh in color and highly valued even then. In the genre of townscapes there were also small masterpieces. Both Jan ten Compe and his younger fellow citizen Izaak Ouwater were able painters of clear and detailed, but not in the least frigid, city views.

The love of Holland's landscape and of cities and villages shows in drawings and prints even more than in paintings. Few areas in the world have been so completely sketched as the 18th-century Netherlands. Countless draughtsmen traveled all over the country with pencil and sketchbook in order to fix the landscape in innumerable drawings: the plains with castles, cows, windmills, and steeples in the distance; the long canals with, here and there, a barrier or a tea pavilion and a slowly passing canal boat; the immobile hamlets dozing in the summer heat, occasionally disturbed by a rattling cart or by a company of marching soldiers. We obtain an impression of country houses along the Amstel, the Vecht, and in the dunes, with their regular gardens where nature is pressed into a corset, straight hedges and decoratively clipped trees alternate with ponds and flower beds. We have views of the castles in the eastern part of the country and wooded landscapes where the artist sometimes represents himself withdrawn into the shadow of the road.

As against 17th-century draughtsmen and painters, who constructed a landscape with the help of sketches partly based on imagination and partly on widely separate places, topographical draughtsmen of the 18th century worked from nature. The rather idyllic picture that they gave could not have been far from reality. There was indeed much unemployment in the country, floods and cattle plague, and the ravages of the woodworm, but in general the republic was no worse off and there was no devastation through war. Draughtsmen worked out their sketches in the studio, partly for collectors and partly for publishers. Just as in the 17th century the interest in books about distant lands had been overwhelming, so in the 18th century books with prints of the homeland became immensely popular. There were countless publications that glorified the Netherlands in text and printed pictures. Titles such as *Glorious Netherlands, Holland Arcadia,* and *The Triumphant Vecht* speak for themselves. It is as if the waning influence of the republic in the political and economic sphere was reflected in this kind of art: the time of great expansion was past and the Netherlands withdrew to its own terrain.

After 1775 both drawing and painting took a renewed interest in nature. This was strongly influenced by 17th-century landscape art, which under the influence of classical theories had long been regarded as realistic. Along with a general romantic reassessment of wild nature throughout Europe, this development was linked with the rise of factories for printed hangings. Countless painters trained in landscape on wall coverings were thus thrown out of work. Because of the new trend they could find new work by producing landscape paintings. Professional graphic artists in the republic had plenty of work. Along with topographic prints there was much demand for illustrations for Bibles, historical works and novels, and loose topical prints of sensational events such as floods, explosions, and riots.

Like The Hague, Amsterdam was a paradise for art collectors. They could not only visit many collections there, but also buy at the numerous auctions. Until Paris took over after 1775, Amsterdam was the European center for the art trade. Many princes had their agents buy the most expensive pieces from the important collections being auctioned. Their status demanded that they keep an art gallery in their palaces, and around this time it became customary to open the galleries to the public. In many cases

these princely purchases formed the nucleus of national or civic collections in France, England, Italy, Scandinavia, and the Netherlands. Remaining collections assembled by stadholders are now in places like the former palace of John Maurice of Nassau and the rebuilt picture hall of stadholder William V, both in The Hague and at the Rijksmuseum in Amsterdam.

Top, the artist's house, drawing by Jacob Cats (Amsterdam Parish Archive). Above, a lesson at the drawing academy, which in 1764 was at the Leyden Gate, engraving by Reinier Vinkeles.

The Enlightenment and the rise of an educated middle class

The current of thought called the Enlightenment marked European intellectual life in the 18th century. Central to it were experience and reason, which were regarded as the instruments for discovering truth. If hitherto murky superstition, rigid dogmatism, unproven tradition, and borrowed authority had kept the world in darkness for centuries, now rationally acquired knowledge would bring light. Just as in the 17th century the natural sciences had attained great results with a new method based on reason and experience, so in the 18th century enlightened thinkers tried this in other fields as well, such as politics, economics, jurisprudence, education, and religion.

Optimism was dominant: in principle, the world was knowable and man good. Society had made him bad, but if, so the argument ran, education was made perfect, then man and society must become so, too. Ideas about new forms of society took various shapes, from moderate to radical. Freedom and equality of man, extended franchise, basic laws guaranteeing human rights, and even sovereignty of the people were main topics in political discussions.

The Enlightenment questioned the unlimited power of emperors and kings, censorship, religious intolerance, and alleged civic immaturity. These ideas came exclusively from the middle class at pains to emancipate itself, so that the call for greater influence for the people was limited: the burghers did indeed wish to displace the nobles above them or at least have an equal share with them, but they were hardly prepared to grant freedom to the lower orders.

In the Declaration of Independence of 1776, by which the North Americans broke away from the United Kingdom, freedom and equality for all citizens was fixed as the first principal of a state. Thirteen years later the French Revolution broke out and in the chaotic period of wars, conquests, and coups that followed, the old certainties of Europe were shaken to their foundations. Only after 1815, when Napoleon was finally beaten, could balance be restored: Europe had shed a number of feudal structures, the bourgeoisie had become the leading class in politics, but kings returned and the lowest social classes remained for the present a silent and amorphous mass.

Left, library of Hermannus de Witt, print by Reinier Vinkeles, 1763. Below, picture sale in the presence of a crowd in the courtyard of the Oudezijds Herenlogement. The collection, belonging to the Leyden burgomaster Jan van der Mark, was sold on August 25, 1773. Print by Simon Fokke.

The Dutch Enlightenment

Ideas advanced in the republic during the Enlightenment cannot be called revolutionary. Older views were attacked, but not as venomously as in England and France, except in political pamphlets of the 1780s. There are several reasons for the moderate character of the Dutch Enlightenment. First of all, one Enlightenment principal was traditional here: a climate of tolerance, which, for many reasons, was nothing new in the republic. The Dutch were used to foreigners, and had seen them come to the republic as refugees: Flemings in the 16th century, French Huguenots in the 17th, and Jews from Spain, Portugal, and Eastern Europe. From 1500 to 1800, a flood of people had entered the republic in search of work. The Dutch traded with foreigners, on the Stock Exchange or abroad. As sailors they had traveled to distant lands and come to know the customs and habits of their inhabitants. And if Dutchmen had not been abroad themselves, they could find out these things from the abundant literature on travel. The Dutch had a developed cultural relativism: as long as they were not affected, they did not mind other customs and religious views.

The republic differed from its neighbors not only in tolerance, but also in the absence of state repression. The people did not live under an absolutist regime, as did the French and the Prussians, and church control of everyday life was moderate. Literary censorship could occur only after the event and rarely came from the authorities. Usually, after repeated requests from aggrieved pastors, a book might be forbidden or an author prosecuted, but even then only locally, sometimes provincially, and hardly ever for the whole republic. In the case of Rousseau's *Emile,* the States of Holland, under pressure from high-minded preachers who found the book "highly impious, scandalous, annoying and profane," revoked its privilege. The same year, his *Social Contract* was banned and so, in 1765, was a translation of Voltaire's treatise on tolerance. These were exceptions, however, and in any case, three further Dutch editions of Voltaire's book appeared within a few years.

The republic was not a source for new Enlightenment ideas but rather a conveyer and disseminator of them, especially abroad. Because of the great tolerance and the enterprise of book printers, everything forbidden abroad could be published here. Without the Dutch, Enlightenment thought could not have been spread as it was. Voltaire, who visited the republic seven times and had some of his work published there, observed that the Dutch traded in books as in textiles and were concerned more with their value as goods than with their content. Just as in the 17th century, everything printable was printed in Amsterdam, the center of the European book trade. Several new genres were added, such as semiscientific journals, children's books, and novels.

Christian inspiration

The Dutch Enlightenment was markedly Christian. Nothing resembled atheism or even deism. Thinkers, mostly from liberal Protestant circles, stood for the new research based on trusting one's own understanding and experience, but this did not lead to secular philosophy as often happened abroad. On the

DVM TERITVR COS   LITERATIS VSVI
ET LITERIS   PROSIT BONIS

contrary, the many scientific discoveries did not lead to a godless, materialistic view but were used as a proof of God's existence. Such physico-theological thinking was first theoretically underpinned by the doctor and burgomaster Bernard Nieuwentyd. In 1715 he published his *Right Use of World Views,* in which he admitted two kinds of truth: one attained through understanding, the other through divine revelation. There was no opposition between scientific and biblical truths, but rather a reconciliation. Between 1715 and 1759 the book had seven reprints and was translated into French, German, and English.

The synthesis between reason and revelation had indeed been attempted before. In the 17th century Jan Swammerdam, the son of an Amsterdam apothecary, and founder of entomology, in a letter accompanying a sketch of a louse, wrote: "I present to your Highness the almighty finger of God in the anatomy of a louse, wherein you will find miracle upon miracle and the wisdom of God stored and clearly displayed for inspection in one small point."

Swammerdam was a thorough empiricist, who took nothing for granted from older writers or from "our rickety ideas." He started from observation of what he could see, directly or through the microscopes he had built. Some 60 years after his death, in 1736, the famous Leyden doctor Herman Boerhaave published Swammerdam's literary remains, the results of years of detailed embryological and anatomic research. He called the book *Bible of Nature,* reminding us once more of the strong link between science and theology.

The thirst for knowledge, the urge for research and the beginning of private scientific collections were widespread among burghers and rulers alike. In the same year that the *Bible of Nature* appeared, the scientist Petrus van Musschenbrook, inventor of the Leyden jar, wrote: "Never were there more amateurs of natural science in the United Netherlands than at the present time: for not only does this science flourish with the most learned, but also with many eminent merchants and people of all ranks and condition, who through reading the excellent world views of the wise and god-fearing master Nieuwentyd first became aware of the great powers of observation and learning that our Almighty Maker has created in us." Among the burghers science became a kind of mania. The instrument maker Fahrenheit from Danzig, famous for his thermometers and barometers, lived in Amsterdam from 1718 to 1729 and gave courses on chemistry and physics. Even the man in the street was curious, although his theoretical insight must have remained limited. The diarist Jacob Bicker Raye tells how in 1745 thousands of Amsterdammers crowded together for a demonstration with an electric machine as a kind of fairground attraction. Bicker Raye had himself electrified: holding the machine with one hand, he could set fire with the other to a spoonful of brandy. When another took his place he seemed to be able to draw sparks from Bicker Raye "across two pairs of stockings without burning them or causing me any pain." The Swedish astronomer Bengt Ferrner, visiting the city in 1759, referred to the "Thursday Evening Society" in which merchants and eminent bankers attended a course on mathematics and physics. Moreover, he admired the observatory of the mer-

Opposite, neoclassical façade of the society Felix Meritis, *built by Jacob Otten Husly on Keizersgracht, 1786–88. Left, laying the foundation stone of the building, in a print by Karel Lodewijk Hansen. The society was in tune with the cultural atmosphere of contemporary Europe, the world of Hume, Voltaire, and Rousseau.*

chant van de Wal outside the Leyden gate.

Besides natural science, burghers like the Amsterdammers Lambert ten Kate (1674–1731), Jan Wagenaar (1709–73) and Hermanus Noordkerk (1702–71) also studied the humanities. Ten Kate, a rich grain merchant, was the founder of historical linguistics and scientific etymology. He was the first to base linguistic research on sounds instead of letters, which enabled him to point to comparative regularities. In 1723 he published his magnum opus, *Introduction to the Knowledge of the Elevated Dutch Language,* which included the first Dutch grammar and a dictionary of 20,000 Dutch words with an equal number of foreign ones. Ten Kate was a Baptist, as was Jan Wagenaar, who came from the lower bourgeoisie and combined application, tolerant piety, and love for art and science. In 1758, after having written several books on history, he received the honorable task of compiling a new history of Amsterdam, for which he was given the exceptional privilege of access to the archives. His book on Amsterdam, its birth, growth, and history, the first vol-

ume of which appeared two years later, remains an admirable and readable, though not impartial, standard work.

It is no accident that Wagenaar was commissioned when he was. Like the burgomasters he was against the stadholder and, like the rulers, opposed to the uprisings that had shaken society to its foundations in the 1740s. In short, to the burgomasters he was an ideal historian. Moreover, his friend Noordkerk had lately published four heavy folios containing all the city's laws from the beginning, a colossal work for the use of the administration, the historian, and the burghers. Noordkerk, a child of the Enlightenment, was an unselfish and impartial lawyer who had become famous for, among other things, defending the 80-year-old John van der Velde. This publisher had been condemned to exile for publishing a paper containing a mixture of ideas from Descartes and Spinoza. Neither the Amsterdam Church council nor the magistrate had felt it necessary to forbid the book, but since theologians at Leyden had called it blasphemous, a case had been brought in which Noordkerk had van der Velde acquitted on appeal.

A scientific demonstration in the physics hall of Felix Meritis, *in a drawing by Jacques Kuyper. For many years, the society, which linked an interest in science with the features of a socially exclusive club, was the center of Amsterdam's cultural life. It had a concert hall, drawing studios, scientific cabinets, a collection of scientific instruments, and on the roof an astronomical observatory; the more active members had cut a slot in the ceiling of the concert hall, where they could perform experiments on free fall from a height of 125 feet.*

FELIX MERITIS.

COSTUME: SOMETHING OF SPAIN, AND SOMETHING OF FRANCE

The remarkable family portrait above (*1*) was painted by Dirck Santvoort, probably in 1634. They are the well-to-do Dirck Bas family. He was a merchant, sometime ambassador, and burgomaster of Amsterdam on

several occasions. He is portrayed seated beside his second wife Grietje Snoeck, with their five sons and daughters on either side, including their daughter Machteld, who is with her husband, Abraham de Vischer, likewise a merchant and one of the administrators of the East India Company, and one of their small children (Abraham and Machteld are the first two figures on the left). One of the most interesting features of the painting is that one can see, between the two generations of parents and children, a marked change in the type of clothing worn. This change came about precisely in this period. The clothes worn by the elderly are relatively simple and austere. The clothes of the younger people are more elaborate, more refined, and more elegant. Both the parents in the painting are wearing the so-called "millstone" collar, which had come into use at the beginning of the century. White, stiff, heavily pleated, with a wire support holding it up, it is the focal point of their apparel. The younger people, on the other hand, are all wearing the flat lace collar. Note the high-waisted dress of Lysbeth Bas

(on the extreme right). The position of the waist in women's clothes underwent periodic shifts. Between 1620 and 1640 it moved upwards, but a generation later it moved back down again. Likewise, in the austere gentlemen painted by Cornelis van der Voort in 1618 (*5*, The Regents of the Old People's Hospice, *detail*), with their strikingly tall headwear, we can see different types of millstone collars, which were in the process of development in this period. The young people in the polder painted by H. Avercamp are figures of more or less the same generation as the Bas parents, as is evident from the style of the collars; it is also clear that the dress of the day was much less austere for people not of the ruling class.

Dutch costume was generally originally influenced by con-temporary Spanish dress (*the Dutch gentleman depicted by Cesare Vecellio, 2, shows the type of clothing worn in the later years of the 16th century*). It subsequently underwent various French influences—France and Spain were the two predominant cultural forces in Europe at that time. One or two of the details are somewhat curious: in the latter half of the 16th century the male doublet

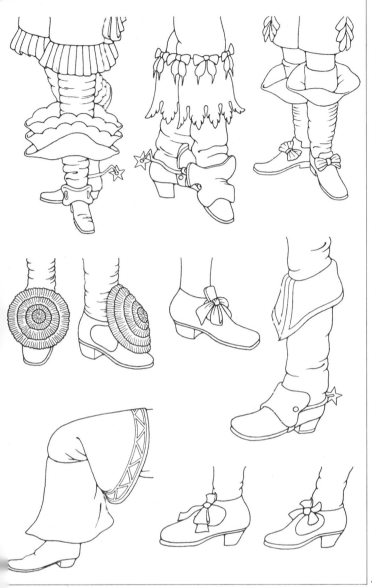

or waistcoat was stiffened with whalebones or cardboard ribbing to give it the "puffed" appearance at the chest; small slits made it possible to have a glimpse of the colorful lining inside; trousers were puffed, too, and silk or satin stockings were worn on the legs. Around 1630 trousers were large and held up by tapes around the waist, which were passed through slits in the jacket and then tied in handsome bows. Later on trousers were supported by hooks and lacing inside the jacket, which had become somewhat longer, but there were still bows, now sewn on the outside of the jacket. After the mid-17th century sweeping cloaks and plumed hats became very much the fashion; the jacket grew shorter, revealing the shirt beneath, and the trousers were combined with a short, wide kiltlike skirt, with the broad leg pieces showing beneath. In female attire influenced by Spanish models the skirt first fell stiffly over the felt or horsehair undergarment, but then padding was placed around the waist, which made the skirt jut out conspicuously just below the waist, before falling straight to the ankles. Later in the century various "curled" pieces had the effect of raising the skirt a little and giving a glimpse of the colored petticoat beneath.

The various sartorial accessories showed great variety and great imagination and were often simply bizarre. We can get some idea from looking at the footwear: the various examples shown in *plate 4* were in vogue over a 30-year period in the 17th century: high

boots with various types of flaps, crotchet effects, bows, and frills; open, light shoes were worn, invariably with quite a high heel.

The details given thus far refer mainly to the clothes worn by the upper classes. Changes in the attire of the lower classes came about much more gradually and were sometimes virtually imperceptible. It was more important to have clothes that

lasted than to feel fashionable in what one wore. The drawings of a fisherman and his wife (6) and a "peasant and his woman" (7) are by Coronelli and show dress dating back to the late 18th century. The world depicted is one of dignified simplicity. The last illustration (8) shows a fishmonger from Amsterdam: by now we have reached the beginning of the 19th century.

His book on the privileges of Amsterdam appeared between 1748 and 1755. In his own words, in it were recorded all "pillars on which the structure of civic society rests."

Journals

Although Dutch scientists and amateurs gained noteworthy scientific results in the 18th century, the Dutch Enlightenment as a current was broad rather than deep. Ideas on education, morality, science, and politics reached the learned amateur mainly through popular scientific publications and societies for art and science.

One mark of the optimistic and moralistic mentality in the 18th-century Netherlands were the cultural journals. These were popularizing weekly or biweekly periodicals that brought science from the university or library to the houses of burghers. Journalists wrote essays, dreams, satires, fables, all but fictitious letters and dialogues. Between 1718 and 1800 there were more than 70 Dutch journals, 25 translated ones, and 10 in foreign languages. They reflected the Dutch Enlightenment spirit: Christian in inspiration, moderate, and encouraging virtue.

That this reasonable outlook had its limits and that toleration could clash with moderate Christianity became obvious in the 1730s. An awareness that the republic's political and economic role had declined was a recurrent topic in the journals. Often the authors pointed this out in the decay of customs. Justus van Effen, the promoter of the first journal and himself editor of the *Hollandsche Spectator* and member of the Royal Society of London, put it this way: "The simplicity and ability of the older generation has disappeared in the younger." The influence of French ways, in particular, was responsible, he held. When in the early 1730s woodworm undermined Dutch dikes and a wave of proceedings against homosexuals swept the country, the otherwise moderate van Effen saw causal links in this. The woodworm infestation, too, he and many pastors regarded as a hint from God, a punishment for such "provocative horror." He must have been satisfied: between 60 and 85 people were murdered with ghastly cruelty for being homosexuals, and

Example of 17th-century publishing in Amsterdam. Left, flyleaf of Lambert ten Kate's Introduction to High Dutch, *(Amsterdam 1723), containing the first Dutch historical grammar. Below, frontispiece of a city atlas by Cornelis Ploos van Amstel, with drawings by Jan Stolker, 1777. It contains most of the city's public buildings, sacred and profane. Opposite, flyleaf of Watergraefs or Diemer-Meer, "the delights of the Watergraefs or Diemer-Meer near the city of Amsterdam, shown in pleasing views of its places of amusement, fields, gardens, fountains, fish ponds, lawns, lanes, passages, bridges, hostelries, accurately drawn from reality by Daniel Stopendael and written by Matthaeus Brouerius van Niedek, doctor of law" (Amsterdam, 1725).*

some hundred more had to flee. Later in the century several more such mass prosecutions occurred. Like the eradication of the gypsies, these events sounded a harsh dissonance in the otherwise calm Dutch atmosphere.

Societies

The Dutch burgher interested in art or science and feeling obliged by his status to be able to talk about them, not only awaited the latest number of his journal but could also join a literary, mathematical, scientific, or even medical society in his city. The names of these societies typify the mentality that led to their founding. For example, one could join "Diligence is the Nurse of Science," "For Instructive Diversion," or the more expensive "Servantis Civibus" and "Conamur Tenues Grandia." Here people discussed the latest discoveries, held lectures and practiced *physique amusante* by making tests with electrifying machines, vacuum pumps, or Leyden flasks. They started collections and answered competitions in which handsome honorific medals could be won. We can rightly speak of a rise of "philosophical" societies. Thus between 1748 and 1808 52 well-organized societies were established, 32 of them in the province of Holland. Most of them were modeled on the *Hollandsche Maatschapij der Wetenschapen* (Holland Society of the Sciences), established in Haarlem in 1752. In the same town, the first Netherlands Museum was opened. In 1778 the rich silk and linen weaver Pieter Teyler had died there, and by his will a theological society and one for art and science were set up. In 1780 a museum building was started whose core was to be Teyler's rich collections of art and natural history.

Besides the recreative interest in science, which was partly a matter of fashion, there were some societies with social concerns, of strictly charitable, educative, or utilitarian aims. An example is the "Society for Saving the Shipwrecked" (Amsterdam, 1767) and the "Groningen Institute for the Deaf and Dumb" of 1790. In the field of popular education there was the important *Maatschapij tot Nut van't Algemeen* (Society for the Utility of the Community) of 1784. Its aim was to bring knowledge to the poor, since knowledge always led to insight and insight to virtue. The society was to take the undeveloped and "reform him into a glad Christian, a patriotic citizen, a happy family man and a useful member of society." In short, the lower orders had to be taught bourgeois values. What was

new in this society, whose head office was fixed in Amsterdam in 1787, was its decentralized setup. Everywhere in the country branches arose to organize lectures, schools for the poor, and libraries; and to publish pamphlets, popular scientific works, and

abuse of drink, and the inadequacy of benevolent funds led to further efforts to revive the economy. In 1777 a subdivision of the Society for the Sciences, the Economics Branch, was established. Set up throughout the country, like the Society for the Utility of the Community, the branch through its members tried to reach solutions to social problems, and in the spirit of the time this was done through competitions. In the 1780s the authorities and private individuals in Amsterdam founded the Naval College in order to raise the standards of naval officers.

"Felix Meritis"

The best-known Amsterdam society was *Felix Meritis* (Happy Through Merit), which consisted of five divisions: commerce, physics, drawing, literature, music—each with its own room. There was an observatory on the roof and a collection of scientific instruments; the keen members had even built an opening in the ceiling of the concert hall to allow falling experiments from a height of 127 feet. Between 1777 and 1795 membership rose from 40 to 400, all Christians from well-to-do circles. Women could not become members, and in his inaugural

Below, the pleasant urban villa Frankendael and, left, a page from the logbook of the ship of that name (1778) recording with a marginal sketch the sighting of a whale. Jan Gildenmeester Janszon, owner of villa and ship, had another house on Herengracht, with a rich art gallery, right, in a panel by Adriaen de Lelie, 1794–95.

textbooks while looking after the training of teachers. In its optimism, the society was a typical Enlightenment body. Poverty and ignorance were not regarded as inevitable and incorrigible, but as something caused by circumstances and capable of being remedied and even prevented. The republic's educational ideas came not so much from France or Rousseau, who was published in Holland but hardly read, but rather from England and Germany. In 1698, five years after its publication, there appeared a Dutch translation of *Some Thoughts Concerning Education* by John Locke, who had lived some years in the republic.

The same constructive spirit is found in the earlier-mentioned rather unsuccessful efforts to set up factories where the poor could spin, weave, and knit. Here, too, the idea was that the poor could become independent through education and work. The increasing unemployment and impoverishment, the

speech for the new building in 1788, J. H. van Swinden explained why: a woman who was more interested in "an important scientific discovery than in the smiles and tenderness of her babies or the teeming noise of small children jumping or running round her always trying to attract her attention with imploring eyes and outstretched arms.... is neither a praiseworthy girl nor an exemplary woman, nor a true mother." Van Swinden must have known, for he was professor of philosophy, mathematics, and astronomy at the Athenaeum Illustre!

The drawing section attracted many art-minded amateurs who practiced from prints, plaster casts, and models. Drawing, like reading and writing, belonged to a proper education. In the academy or society of which one was a member, one listened to lectures and discussed art. Time and again members admired each others' collections, consisting of prints and drawings often on plates bound into large volumes, paintings, or sculptures.

Even in the 16th century the arrangement of an art cabinet had been a habit of European princes, scholars, and rich merchants. This might have been for reasons of status and investment as much as love

of art. Such collections usually consisted of natural and artificial objects. The former included stuffed animals, plants, stones, shells, and whatever was curious in nature; the latter concerned both archeological and ethnic topics, and sculptures, coins, drawings, prints, and paintings. In the 17th and 18th centuries specialization began, but the true collector tried to make his collection as comprehensive as possible. Rich Holland burghers did not have an art gallery, like princes. Usually there were one or two rooms—art cabinets—set aside for art. Gerrit Braamcamp, merchant in wine and timber, had spread throughout his house some 300 paintings; 900 art objects in glass, porcelain, gold, silver, and lacquer work; and 82 statues. This sort of private museum, and certainly Braamcamp's, were internationally famous and a must for art lovers who visited the city.

The forming of political opinions

Felix Meritis was strictly nonpolitical. In other societies there might be political discussions or talks. Informally, burghers could express their political views in the coffeehouses, where they talked about the latest national or foreign developments, or expounded their notions about the future while smoking and drinking coffee; and here they perused the latest journals and newspapers. Dutch newspapers, with news from home and abroad, commercial reports, and advertisements, were avidly read, even

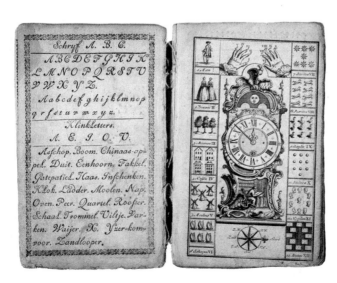

in foreign countries in translation. Often they discussed Dutch political news as it took place: journalists could readily obtain news of secret debates or commissions of the States General. The clumsy administrative structure made it necessary to send a copy of each decision or proposal to each province and from there to the towns, so that secrecy was impossible; too many clerks and copyists were involved. The consequent leaks regularly embarrassed rulers and envoys. The newspaper reader derived great amusement from this. When in 1721 an Amsterdam paper printed various secret letters from state envoys, an angry François Fagel, chancellor of the States General, wrote to his ambassador in France, Cornelis Hop: "What is easier than to force such a journalist to reveal from whom he received such letters, and with that lead one could disentangle the skein. I do not know from what principle people are so lax in this." The case is the more interesting since a relative of van Hop, the Amsterdam burgomaster Aegidius van den Bempden, shared in the profit from the paper concerned, so that he was suspected of having supplied such letters to the editor in order to improve circulation and so his profit. The authorities were, in fact, powerless against such "dirt," as Fagel called it. Indeed, he knew how matters stood and commented that "the trouble lies in the form of government."

The American War of Independence

In the 1770s the politically interested citizen avidly discussed the American War of Independence. After the American settlers had declared themselves free from England in 1776, a spate of books and pamphlets about that distant country appeared. Two years after the Declaration of Independence, France was the first nation to recognize the young American republic. War between England and France was inevitable. True to tradition, the republic tried to remain neutral. Although they could not, therefore, openly support America, the Dutch had an extensive contraband trade with the insurgents. Via St. Eustace, a rocky island in the Caribbean, they supplied the Americans with spare weapons, gun powder, ammunition, and hard liquor. This trade was a thorn

Above, an ice bowl in painted china (Amsterdam Historical Museum). Left, a new primer, Amsterdam 1759. The level of literacy in the republic, great even after 1550, was among the highest in Europe by 1800.

in the side of the English. Their agents informed the burgomasters what ships from Amsterdam were leaving for America but could get no satisfaction. When in 1776 the fort on St. Eustace fired a salute to an American ship, the English protested strongly, and they were furious when three years later an American pirate captain was welcomed like a hero in Amsterdam. In spite of an embargo extorted by the English, contraband increased. A pound of powder of 8½ stuiver was worth 46 stuiver on St. Eustace. Dutch gun powder mills could not keep up with the demand.

Amsterdam merchants hoped for an American victory because the new country might become an enormous market for their products. However, as usual, they first waited to see the outcome. The role of Amsterdam's burgomasters was ambivalent. They had a local banker, Jean de Neufville, sign a secret draft treaty with an American envoy, William Lee, who was trying to gather European support for the rebels. For two years the treaty remained secret. In 1779 another envoy sailed to Europe with a copy of the treaty, but his ship was stopped by the English, and when the envoy threw the box with the compromising documents into the sea, the English fished it back. The British government inflated the incident: how could a city in a neutral country enter such a treaty with rebels? They asked for satisfaction

Family of Jeronimo de Bosch, in a canvas by Tibout Regters, 1754 (Amsterdam Historical Museum).

and punishment of the Amsterdam burgomasters. The States General met these demands only in part, and this gave the English a long-sought pretext for declaring war on the republic in order to take St. Eustace and prevent the Dutch from joining the alliance of armed neutrality that Catherine of Russia was in the process of organizing among European states as a counterweight to the English. War was in the air. Insurance for freight to St. Eustace rose 20 or 25 percent. On December 20, 1780 the United Kingdom declared war—the fourth between the two countries.

The Dutch fleet was in deplorable condition. For years there had been talk of extending the fleet and army, without any positive results. Harbors were silted up, coastal batteries neglected. An indecisive naval skirmish in the North Sea was triumphantly glorified in the republic, while the English easily blockaded the Dutch coast. In the first months they intercepted many Dutch ships whose captains were unaware of the war. Trade, shipping, and fishing were badly hit. The English took several Dutch col-

onies, beginning with the hated St. Eustace. The war also prevented the Dutch from joining the Grand Alliance.

During this war, but not before American victory was in sight, the United States was recognized, first by Friesland and then by the other provinces and the States General. Amsterdam bankers, among them a number of young ones with strong interests in the new country, now agreed to offer loans. America became an example for the enlightened burghers in the decayed republic. But in the end it was England and not the republic that was to win the American market.

The Fourth English War came at the end of a period of relative peace and prosperity that had begun in 1748. Underlying tensions built up during this quiet period began to break, for economic and political reasons. There had been a shift in prosperity: the top layer of very rich merchants and bankers had shrunk, and poverty in the lowest orders had grown apace. In between, there was an undeveloped middle class suffering the consequences of eco-

Left, inaugural meeting of the Nut, *a society for the public weal, on August 10, 1790, in the Old Lutheran Church of Amsterdam. The society aimed to "promote education and moral culture for the lower orders." Engraving by J. de Wit.*

nomic recession but politically too immature to take countermeasures. Since 1748 this class no longer expected help from the stadholder, and they disliked his policies, which favored England, their rival in trade. The rulers would lend support so long as they, too, were opposed to the stadholder. However, when the burghers were granted reforms that affected the rulers' power, too, support ceased. In the end the burghers had to rely on themselves to gain political influence, and in the 1780s their political activity ended in a civil war.

Patriots and Orangists, 1780-1787

Early in the morning of September 26, 1781, the inhabitants of Amsterdam and other important cities in the republic found a strange little booklet in their streets. It was anonymous and entitled *To the People of the Netherlands*. It gave a survey of Dutch history in which the people's origins were traced back to the Friesians and Batavians. Through the centuries, it argued, the people had been enslaved by kings and stadholders. Moreover, the book contained a direct attack on Stadholder William V. The prince, born of an English mother and surrounded by English friends, was accused of faint-hearted behavior toward England and was held responsible for the country's ruin. The author demanded election by the burghers of "a moderate number of good, pious and virtuous men" who, along with the rulers, were to carry out the burghers' wishes. Finally, the author called out: "Arm yourselves and choose those who are to command you and, like the people of America, where not a drop of blood was spilt before the English attacked, go about everything with calm and modesty."

This long-winded, document, to our minds, caused great upheaval and was banned by the authorities, although in Amsterdam it was banned without enthusiasm since the burgomasters were not especially offended by attacks on the stadholder. The same year there were several reprints, and translations appeared in France, England, and Germany. Only in the 19th century was the author discovered: John Derk, Baron van der Capellen tot de Poll, an eccentric nobleman from Overijssel with revolutionary

tendencies. This pamphlet sharpened the opposition between the Orangists and the Patriots. Who were these groups that waged a small civil war in the republic during the 1780s? First, we must observe that the two factions were not parties in the modern sense, instead, they were groups of people with similar ideas or interests but without a clear ideology inspiring their union.

Patriots

On one side were the Patriots, a collective name for two political tendencies that shared a desire to limit the stadholder's power, or even to abolish the office. The "democrats" came from the wealthier middle class and were a new element in Dutch politics that arose between 1781 and 1787: men from the free professions, intellectuals, lawyers, doctors, liberal preachers. Among the "aristocrats" were rulers mainly from Holland's cities who were traditionally against the stadholder. For some years these two strands shared their antistadholder stance.

Orangists

The Patriots clashed with the followers of William V. These prostadholder Orangists formed a mixed group of people from various classes. There were rulers and officials who owed their office to the stadholder, military men from the state army of which the stadholder was commander-in-chief, orthodox Calvinists, Protestant farmers from Holland, and ship's carpenters from Amsterdam who were traditionally in favor of the House of Orange.

At first the quarrel between Patriots and Orangists took place in the form of political discussions in coffeehouses, societies and universities, and even through sermons. Blows were exchanged only in pamphlets and newspapers. Both sides aimed to establish their legitimacy by appealing to history. The aristocratic Patriots fervently employed the term "freedom"—a term that for them recalled the time of Oldenbarnevelt and Johan de Witt, strong representatives of Holland's patrician rulers. Moreover, the term "people" meant something different then: for the democrats, "freedom for the people" meant

freedom and administrative influence for the citizen, and they tried to prove that this had existed in the past. Enlightened political ideas were probably not especially important among the Patriots, although they closely followed the American War of Independence and its ideology.

The Orangists, for their part, emphasized the link between God, people, fatherland, and the House of Orange. They offered the House of Orange as protectors of the common people against the arbitrary city rulers. The Orangist side was able to raise vast popular support, as were the Patriots. In Amsterdam the poor who were arrested during riots as Patriots or as Orangists came from the same social groups and districts. There was no strong Orange ideology: what united these men was their dependence on the prince, who offered no leadership and remained largely a symbol.

The parties exchanged caricatures and satirical poems. The Patriots' symbol was the spitz (keeshond), named after one of their leaders, Cornelis ("kees") de Gyselaar, and they were represented as timid little dogs blindly marching behind French revolutionary illusions. In return, the stadholder was shown as an unpleasant drunkard. In the Patriot volume of poems, *The Merry Little Kees,* we read "The fifth of Williams is a swine, the ally of a mob, quite sodden in Burgundian wine, the head of all that rob."

Plaques with portraits of William V and his wife, Wilhelmina of Prussia. Orangists wore various badges and signs during the political struggle with the Patriots during the republic's final years.

Silver medal struck in 1782, commemorating the recognition of the United States by the States General.

From paper war to military action

The paper war that raged in the 1760s and 1770s was reflected in the symbols sported by the two sides: Patriots had silver pins and corkscrews, pipe rods and tobacco, and perfume boxes with a spitz represented on them. They wore black buttons. The Orangists had orange cockades and orange ribbons with catch phrases like ''Vivat Oranje'' or ''Oranje Boven'' (roughly, three cheers for Orange up), and representations of an orange tree, the Orange coat of arms, and because of William's wife (a Prussian princess), the Prussian eagle. Moreover, they carried silver hangings with the somewhat round faces of the stadholder and his wife. The earthenware makers of Delft did a good business with small plates carrying both portraits. Like the term ''freedom,'' the perennial freedom symbol, a hat on a long stick, was used by both sides. These partisan symbols seem innocent enough, but they were provocative and wearing them sometimes led to arrests.

Paper and pipe rods were peaceful manifestations of political preference, but the struggle hardened when the Patriots took to raising freedom companies and societies for military exercises. The burghers began to arm themselves, as van der Capellen tot de Poll had suggested. Everywhere in the country they formed small armies with proud names like ''Pro Patria Libertate.'' They practiced with the arquebus and paraded in colorful uniforms and listened to tales that were as heroic as they were long-winded.

The Patriot movement acquired national features, which was unusual in the republic. In June 1785 freedom companies from the whole country joined in an act of union, swearing to defend the basic republican laws to the death, to root out all administrative abuses, and to establish the rights of citizens. This, too, shows that the patriots demanded reconstruction of a society with an influential citizenry, a condition that had never actually existed. The institution of the stadholder was retained, for the union was really directed against the rulers: it rejected ''independent family rule.'' The democrats and aristocrats now parted, so that there were three elements: the democrats, the Orangists, and the rulers. Some former Patriot rulers now themselves inclined toward the stadholder's camp.

The attacks on William V, who was good natured but a feckless administrator, became crueler. He was blamed for the harmful consequences of the Fourth English War, which had been ended with a mild peace in 1784. His power was diminished and the cities of Holland deprived him of the right to order appointments, so that in 1784 he had to dismiss his influential adviser, the duke of Brunswick. The States of Holland even prohibited the wearing of Orange and the singing of Orange songs and relieved William of his function as commander of The Hague, where he was no longer welcome; he then settled in Gelderland.

After the war, England tried to regain her influence in the republic by means of the Orangist movement, which it did everything to strengthen in order to restore William's prestige. In this task the English envoy armed with secret service funds worked hard. Orange societies and Orange free companies were set up as a counterweight to Patriot organizations. A network of Orangist correspon-

British sacking of the Dutch island of St. Eustace in the Lesser Antilles, in 1781, in a drawing by Cornelius Brouwer. This happened during the Fourth English War (1780–84), which was fatal for the republic's maritime and colonial trade.

dents and publishers developed.

With the Orangists mobilizing and the Patriots becoming more openly aggressive, tension grew between 1784 and 1787. Under pressure from Patriot free companies, some cities admitted Patriots into their government. It was unheard of in the republic for burghers to oppose the law. In February 1787 a crowd surrounded the town hall in order to force the council to make a certain decision. In April a college of burgher delegates was elected by Patriot societies, sergeants of the guard, and members of the free companies. With a list of signatures, this committee could count on support from some 15,000 Amsterdammers.

On April 21 the guards and the free companies barred the Dam, after which a petition was handed in at the town hall asking for the resignation of nine council members. This was granted, and they were replaced by Patriots. On July 5, two burgomasters were dismissed under pressure, and Patriots were appointed instead from the ruler class (no ordinary citizen could as yet occupy the burgomaster's seat); the act was nonetheless revolutionary.

Escalation

These local actions and the power of the free companies, which in May in Utrecht even ousted a detachment of the stadholder's troops, were becoming intolerable to William. On May 27 he issued a declaration in which he claimed all rights for himself and ordered all Patriots to leave their administrative posts, thus taking the side of the ruling families. This was the spark to explode the powder keg: the following day Amsterdam Patriots stormed an Orangist coffeehouse and expelled the guests. The Orangist ship's carpenters or *Bijltjes* (little axes) were alerted and in their turn freed the coffeehouse. A day later the Orangist coffeehouse "s'Lands Welvaren" (The Country's Welfare) was plundered, with the guard intervening much too late. As in 1747 and 1748, the guard was not neutral, its actions were politically colored.

The day after, plundering was widespread and people were molested. The Bijltjes transformed Kattenburg island, the center of Amsterdam shipbuilding, into an enclave by raising the bridge and mounting guns. With rafts, the guard, helped by a free company, attacked and, after a night of fighting, managed to lower the bridge. There followed large-scale plundering of Orangist houses on Kattenburg and the guard again was slow to intervene.

In the summer of 1787 the republic saw a stalemate. Three provinces were Patriot (Holland, Groningen, Overijsel) and three Orangist (Zeeland, Gelderland, Friesland), with Utrecht divided. First, the stadholder had to be restored to an honorable position in The Hague. Since William was not allowed to go there, his wife decided to go in his stead. However, a free company stopped her coach halfway and she had to turn back. Although there were Orangist actions in the country, the coup had failed.

It now looked as if the Patriots must win, but England exploited the incident of the intercepted coach and involved Prussia in her plans. Wilhelmina was the sister of the Prussian king, so the incident was taken to be an insult to him. Indeed, Prussia lodged a request for satisfaction with the States of Holland, who had approved of the interception. The answer was negative and the situation became tense. In Amsterdam the guard openly took sides. In July, 15 traveling boats with guardsmen left the city in the direction of Utrecht, led by an enthusiastic crowd, in order to defend Holland against possible attack by state troops or even by Prussians. After weeks of political consultations between England, Prussia, and the Orangists, Prussia sent an ultimatum on September 9. The States of Holland had to admit blame,

A war of caricature during the republic's crisis. Left, English satirical print of 1787, when Wilhelmina of Prussia was insulted and the Prussians intervened: we see those involved, a Prussian, Englishman, Dutchman, and Frenchman.

punish those responsible, and invite the princess to The Hague under threat of war. On September 12 the States rejected the ultimatum, and the morning after a Prussian army of 20,000 crossed the republic's borders.

The prince restored

The main attack of the Prussians was aimed at South Holland, particularly The Hague. The small Patriot units had no chance against the trained invaders who easily cut through the country. On the night of September 15 the Patriots fled from Utrecht en masse toward Amsterdam. The roads were crammed, the boats overloaded, and in the villages on the way Orange flags were flying. On September 20 William entered The Hague with the English envoy next to him in the coach. Before the end of the month, the stadholder's side was in control again, except in Amsterdam. The Orangists had plenty of scope for vengeance. With the Prussians watching or even helping, they began to plunder homes and businesses and abuse people. In The Hague, the American Embassy was daubed orange. The beating up of "lightning Patriots" became so violent that the authorities had to call for moderation. In the "democratized" towns the same thing happened. Patriot officials resigned, free companies and societies were dissolved, and all Patriot decisions annulled. The old rulers returned. Amsterdam alone held out. The Prussians were not anxious for a siege since the purpose of the campaign had been achieved: the prince was restored. The city had good defenses, but her troops were badly trained. The Prussians took surrounding small towns and closed a ring around Amsterdam, which began negotiations. But when there seemed no hope of a French army of relief, these ran out. The heads of the Patriot movement left, Patriot newspapers were forbidden, riots broke out, and the old council took over again.

After the surrender was signed, Orange banners suddenly abounded while all Patriot decorations disappeared quickly. Makers of banners and pins did well in these revolutionary years. The free companies were disarmed and near the Leyden Gate 150 Prussians made camp, and at the request of the re-

Opposite above right, anti-Orangist beaker with engraved keeshond, *the canine symbol of the Patriots, at one time the Dutch boatman's mascot, urinating on an orange tree (Rotterdam, Museum Boymans-van Beuningen).*

Below right, a pacifist print showing a soldier who has reaped only mutilation. Above, English caricature of 1787: among frogs, Dutch burghers practice shooting at the Prussian drawn on the wall. Top,

caricature of William V's departure from Holland on January 18, 1795: the last stadholder leaves the country never to return, and people dance around the tree of liberty.

stored rulers, the prince's troops came to the city to forestall uprisings. The Patriot fires were utterly dampened and the republic's last years were at hand.

The last years, 1787-1795

The Orange side won completely. Early Patriot successes were due to their courage in arms in the face of an irresolute prince. Their defeat was caused by the forces supporting the prince: English diplomacy, Prussian hussars, and a strong-willed Princess Wilhelmina. The Patriots had overestimated their own power, they were disunited, they had limited political experience, and they had placed unrealistic hopes in French help.

A reaction set in. Government offices, guards, guilds, and even church councils were swept clean of Patriot elements. The prince was too frightened to come to Amsterdam so that he could purge the law as his father had done 40 years before. Instead, two delegates performed that task. Stricter censorship befell press and pulpit, while mail for France, where thousands of Patriots had fled, was watched. The courts were severe—simply signing a petition could entail prosecution. Throughout the republic at least 450 anti-Patriot trials were held, mostly for anticonstitutional behavior (at best a vague concept), breaking military oaths, or lèse-majesté.

The last years of the republic were repressive. The country was under the guardianship of England and Prussia, both guarantors of the stadholder's position. Those Patriots who had not fled lived discreetly, meeting secretly in reading circles in coffeehouses hired at night. Calling each other by numbers, they read papers and correspondence from France. Their hopes were fixed on an army of liberation.

On February 1, 1793, ten days after Louis XVI had been guillotined, the National Convention in Paris declared war on the English king and the stadholder. The French armies broke through into the republic but were beaten back by the Austrians. Still, clearly the Dutch could not resist for long because the army had been badly neglected. The Orangists lost courage. "I see that the republic is weak and small, and the total disorder at our gates," sighed the last grand pensionary of Holland, the faithful van der Spiegel, in a letter to the princess in February 1794. In December the French occupied North Brabant and East Flanders. The Patriot exiles in France planned a new state, though they lacked unity and clear ideas. Within the country, Patriot reading circles spread. Of the rather robust Amsterdam reading circle *Doctrina et Amicitia* we know that in 1791 and 1792 political lectures were held on "Swiss freedom" and "The need for revolutions." From this circle Patriots made contact with colleagues exiled in France. A French secret agent who visited the republic in 1794 estimated that in Amsterdam alone there were 34 clubs of 60 to 80 members each. On July 31, members of Holland clubs met at Haarlem and decided to send two representatives to the French to counsel speed and ask for Dutch independence in case of conquest. The French responded favorably but did not act at once. The Patriots carried out their plans for revolution from within: secret presses produced pamphlets and stores of arms were set up.

In October, when the French were in Brabant, Amsterdam Patriots handed the city administration a request signed by 3,600 burghers; it asked that no floods be released nor English troops encamped. Although the administration saw that resisting the French was pointless and would cause bloodshed, they reacted rather formally. Some signatories were arrested, some had to go into hiding, and others fled. An arms dump was discovered with hundreds of rifles, powder, and bullets, and the city decided to forbid the closed reading circles. These were the last convulsion of a dying administration. Only the neutral Felix Meritis could remain open, although concerts were forbidden. The city administration re-

Above, entry of the Prussians through the Leyden Gate, October 10, 1787. Below left, Prussian attack on Weesp, September 30, 1787. Below right, Prussian hussars camping at the Leyden Gate in November.

January 19, 1795; the French enter Amsterdam through the Utrecht Gate, in a print by J. Cats.

garded musical entertainment as inappropriate to the serious circumstances.

The Velvet Revolution

In December 1794 frost had set in. The Waterline, instead of being a reliable defense, became a level access road. In January 1795 the French troops easily crossed the rivers Maas, Waal, and Lek. The demoralized state army hardly resisted, and the English auxiliaries retreated eastward plundering as they departed. On January 16, Utrecht surrendered.

In Amsterdam, on Sunday, January 18, a revolutionary committee met in the coffeehouse "Het

Left, parade of Amsterdam's civic guard in 1786, print by N. van der Meer. Right, French revolutionary armies crossing the river Waal, January 10, 1795.

Wapen van Embden" on the Nieuwendijk, to plan a revolution from within and set up a revolutionary administration so that the French might enter not as conquering enemies of an aristocratic regime but as liberating brothers of the Amsterdam burghers in favor of the revolution. Boxes and baskets full of red, white, and blue cockades stood ready. Meanwhile the panic-stricken burgomasters consulted on whether to prepare defenses by hacking open the ice on the Amstel and the Ij, or to send a deputation to the French. In the afternoon the physician Krayenhoff appeared at the Weestergate clad in a French uniform. The previous October he had been forced to flee as a suspected Patriot, and he had joined the Dutch contingent in the French army. Krayenhoff, in the name of the revolutionaries, asked for the command of the city. To this end he sought out the garrison's commander, Golowkin, who, seeing how things stood, amicably invited the visitor to dinner. However, Golowkin had no power to decide and after dinner Krayenhoff hurried to the house of burgomaster Straalman, where all the burgomasters had assembled. Under pressure from a noisy crowd around the house and the reality of the situation, they decided to resign the next day and, in order to prevent bloodshed, to transfer command to Krayenhoff. At midnight by torchlight, his appointment was proclaimed from the steps of the Waag. At the same moment, 38 miles away, from the beach at Scheveningen, a fishing boat left for England with William V, the republic's last stadholder, who never returned.

The following morning, Amsterdammers wearing red, white, and blue cockades assembled by the Hoge Sluis (High Lock) on the ice of the Amstel to scan the southern horizon, and soon the first French hussars appeared. Some rode into the city over the opened Weestergate bridge. At nine, the burgomasters, council, and jurors appeared at the town hall. After an hour's reflection, they called for the Revolutionary Committee's delegates to enter. Chairs stood ready for them in front of the open fire because it was bitterly cold. The committee's president thanked the rulers for their services to the city and declared them relieved of office in the name of the people of Amsterdam. Their offices were abolished,

and without protest they agreed and were allowed to go home in peace. Some left by the back door.

Thus, in snow-covered Amsterdam, centuries-old administrative institutions came to an end. Formal occupation by the French was prevented while their presence could be construed as a liberation. In front of the town hall, where 60 hussars had meanwhile posted themselves, a freedom tree was raised, a pine the French had cut from the Watergraafsmeer, now provisionally held up by cables. For, as the preacher C. Rogge recalled a year later, "the frozen ground was so hard that they could not plant the tree, because it would have meant hours of work." While bells were ringing people danced round this unstable symbol of freedom, a foretaste of an exuberant freedom feast.

For the moment Amsterdam was governed by 21 "Provisional Representatives" whose president, the lawyer R. J. Schimmelpenninck, took a very sober view. In his first address he warned that "the same applause by which the people, hearing our names, made the air reverberate, can be replaced by grumbles, contempt and dissatisfaction." There were as yet no grumbles. Revolutionary elation slowly engulfed the city. Political prisoners were freed from the workhouse and triumphantly led to "Revolution Square," as the Dam had been rebaptized.

In other cities of the republic the governmental change followed similar lines. Revolutionary committees removed the old rulers without a shot being fired or a drop of blood spilled. It was a "Velvet Revolution," a term coined on February 21. On that day the ex-secretary of Amsterdam's ex-mayor wrote to a Patriot who had fled to France in 1787: "Our revolution is a revolution of velvet."

Burdens of fraternization

In the wintry days of that January, "Liberty, Equality, and Fraternity" were the ubiquitous watchwords; a tricolor flowed from the roofs and citizens walked about with red, white, and blue cockades on their lapels or on hats pulled over their ears. On January 20 the representatives of the French people and the army issued a proclamation "to the Batavian people," in which they warned, as is usual for occupying armies in foreign towns, against "mischief" and "excesses" and promised to respect Dutch independence. "The Batavian people through its supreme authority alone shall be able to alter or improve the arrangement of its government." The citizens should be sovereign; this was now in black and white, and it inspired confidence.

French soldiers, in tatters, sometimes barefoot and wrapped in rags and blankets, evoked fraternal sympathy, although many hostels did not know what to do with the French paper money, the *assignats,* and the burghers wondered how long the billeting would last, while the poor became restless because of the rising prices. Perhaps, people thought, these were infantile diseases of the new freedom.

Early on March 4 the burghers planted a new and definitive freedom tree in Revolution Square, this time made from a genuine Kattenburg ship's mast. It was the beginning of the Feast of Revolution. In the morning, 26,000 armed burghers drew up between the butter market and Revolution Square and at midday began a long procession of Amsterdammers who in some way had contributed to the Patriot cause. Guns boomed, bells rang, and flags fluttered. Speeches full of pathos were made about the "sun of freedom," and young and old danced round the freedom tree along with French generals and brand-new representatives. The *Marseillaise* resounded, as did the popular revolutionary dancing song *"dansons les Carmagnoles, vive le son des canons."*

With all this festive noise, one wonders what the Velvet Revolution in the Netherlands had achieved. A full answer would be difficult, but a brief one is possible. The three political forces that had determined the life of the republic for over two centuries simply vanished. The office of stadholder and grand pensionary were abolished and the power of city rulers as closed oligarchies disappeared. Henceforth, every citizen was equal before the law, so that disadvantaged groups like Catholics, Jews, and Dissenters were gradually emancipated. Consequently, the electoral system was changed, giving more citizens some say in political matters. Moreover, church and state became separate and the guilds were abolished.

A state some centuries old is not transformed from one day to the next with impunity, nor can a new arrangement be conjured out of thin air. The shaping of the new Batavian republic was laborious and never final. Soon there appeared violent clashes between the supporters of a unitary state and those of a federal one. Coup followed coup, reflecting the changes of power in France—for the French kept a firm grip on Dutch political and economic life, indeed, so firm that in 1806 they replaced the republic by the Kingdom of Holland with a brother of Napoleon as king. Three years later the whole country was simply annexed. In these French years, centralization grew apace. In many fields, such as administration, taxation, education, health care, and postal services, the ground was laid for the Kingdom of the Netherlands, which would be proclaimed in 1815. The king of this independent unitary state, which until 1830 included the southern Netherlands, was the son of the last stadholder, thus symbolizing the considerable continuity of Dutch politics. Only well into the 19th century did the kingdom, functioning through an enterprising middle class, acquire such stability and wealth as to recall the Golden Age.

For Amsterdam the revolution had far-reaching consequences. The city's dominant position in the country since the 16th century was lost. The already declining prosperity further fell. The French siphoned off money and goods; shipping decreased, which caused the staple market to decay; the Exchange Bank forfeited confidence; the West and East India companies formally ceased to exist in 1792 and 1799 respectively; and industry dwindled, all of which, in sum, produced dreadful poverty. The economic coup de grâce came just after 1810, and recovery not until well in the 19th century, but by then Rotterdam had overtaken the city on the Ij.

Politically, too, Amsterdam had to relinquish its brilliant role. In the federalist republic it had been dominant in Holland and therefore in the whole country. But after 1795, when the outlines of a unitary state began to become sharper and voting was by heads and not by towns, this dominance ended. No longer was the country's policy determined by the interests of a small group of powerful ruler merchants from Amsterdam, but by the voice of the king and by the consensus of delegates from the whole country assembled at The Hague. Amsterdam ceased to be a state within a state; it became one city in the kingdom, albeit an important one.

In spring 1795 no one could foresee all this. The civic administrations were overrun with petitions and proposals of the most diverse kinds, aimed at giving some shape to their new task. Arduous negotiations took place between French and Dutch diplomats. On May 16 the Treaty of The Hague was signed, a dictate rather than a treaty. The price of liberation seemed high. French fraternity was rather asphyxiating for the republic. The two states entered an offensive and defensive union, so that the Dutch henceforth had to fight throughout Europe alongside the French. The Dutch had to feed and clothe 25,000 French soldiers, which the French exploited by always sending "fresh" starved soldiers to the fraternal Batavian land. Moreover, the Dutch had to cede southern parts of their territory and pay an indemnity of 100 million guilders.

None of this prevented the celebration of a great feast of alliance on the first day of Messidor (June 19, 1795). Throughout the city small freedom trees were erected and everywhere one heard shouts like "Long live freedom" and "Down with tyranny." The French marched alongside the Dutch, and Dutch horsemen paraded with French hussars. From the House of the Community, formerly the town hall, a combined French-Batavian flag flowed. Most impressive were the decorations several feet in height, which represented revolutionary ideas such as "Destruction of the Aristocracy," "National Virtue," and, on the Amstelveld, "The People's Power Confirmed." In Revolution Square the symbols of the ancien régime were burned: coats of arm from churches and public buildings, Orange decorations, and the wigs of former rulers. In the evening, the representatives of the people of Amsterdam dined in the House of the Community. The fraternal feast was

At the top of this print for the meeting of Batavian clubs (1795) we read in Dutch and French: "Long live the two united republics." The union between the Batavian and French revolutionary republics did not last long. A new history had begun and that of Amsterdam, metropolis of the world, had ended. We conclude with Descartes's dictum, which the city had engraved on the façade of Westermarkt 6, where he had lived: "Where else in the world could one choose a place where all life's commodities and all the curiosities one could wish for are as easy to find as here? In which other country can one enjoy such utter freedom . . . ?"

grandiose, but with some hitches: a seafight on the Ij at midday was a complete failure, and in the evening during the illuminations many lampions would not light, some of them hung upside down while others lacked fuel. Was this deliberate, as one eye-witness cautiously suggested? Or was it merely the rough weather and the strong wind? Or perhaps a presage of dark clouds gathering over the country? In his speech in the morning, Schimmelpenninck had said that "Often conflicting interests, the new order of things, the most salutary change can work against the most sensible measures."

Few Amsterdammers dancing and celebrating long into the night in the streets or in the civic hall of the opened town hall would have foreseen through what difficulties the city would have to go in the years to follow.

Chronology,
special topics,
index

Chronology of the Netherlands and Amsterdam

The Romans: 1st century B.C.
When Caesar conquered Belgium in 57 B.C., the Rhine was the approximate border between the Celts and Germans. In this region lived three Germanic peoples, the Batavians, around the estuaries of the Rhine and Maas rivers; the Caninefates (mentioned by Tacitus in connection with the Batavian revolt, which they joined and whose name survives in the place name "Kennemerland") in Holland; and the Frisians farther north. These coastal peoples of the North Sea were subjugated by Drusus in 12 B.C. and, in spite of some rebellions, remained Roman for some four centuries. The Romans pushed their frontier to the Rhine and defended it with military camps, the most important being Lugdunum Batavorum (Leyden), Trajectum ad Rhenum (Utrecht), and Noviomagus (Nijmegen).

The Batavians, 1st century A.D.
"Of all these peoples the Batavians excel in valor," wrote Tacitus in his book on Germany. They "inhabit the island of the Rhine," the land between the estuaries of the Maas and Rhine rivers. They were conquered by Drusus and provided auxiliaries for the Romans. He continues: "At one time they were part of the Catti, but later, because of internal struggles, they went to these regions where they were to become part of the Roman Empire. They retain the notable honor, witness the old pact of alliance: they are neither humiliated by tribute nor does the tax collector ravage them; exempt from contributions and excise, they help only in war." Pliny the Younger was in the garrison there in A.D. 50, in the fort at the mouth of the Rhine whose remains can be seen at low tide; he was not inspired by the site and the landscape seemed sordid. The Batavians were attacked and absorbed by the Franks about A.D. 300, but their name remained: when the Dutch founded their post at Djakarta on Java they called it Batavia, a name that persisted for three centuries until Indonesian independence when it became the new capital. When in 1795 the Republic of the Seven United Provinces disappeared after the French Revolution, for a brief period there was a Batavian Republic.

Julius Civilis and the Batavian revolt, A.D. 69
Tacitus, in books IV and V of the *Histories*, speaks of this. Indeed, what remains of the work begins where Civilis and the Romans meet to make peace. "Civilis, of royal blood," sent to Nero in chains, freed by Galba and again in great danger under Vitellius (whose army wanted to kill Civilis), "was more than commonly astute for a barbarian" and raised his men with the seeming purpose of helping Vespasian. "Civilis, under pretext of a banquet, united the most prominent citizens and the most resolute men of the people in a sacred wood; when he saw them, excited with the enchantment of the night and the banquet, exalting the glory of their tribe, he began to enumerate the injuries, depredations and other evils of slavery: 'No longer allies as before, but slaves. When does a legate ever come among us, even with a strong following or with the arrogance of power? Today we are in the hands of prefects and centurions. When they are sated with our spoils and blood, others follow and there are new imposts found, these are but different names for robbery. Today there is the levy which tears sons from parents, brothers from brothers, like a supreme parting, and yet, never was Rome in as bad a way as today. In winter quarters there are only veterans and booty. Raise your sight and fear of these phantom legions will vanish. With us are forces of foot and horse, the Germans through blood ties, the Celts through common goals. Nor is our war against Vitellius unfriendly to Rome, which with doubtful outcome will always be like a title of merit near Vespasian; if we win he will not have to give account of himself.' Heard with great applause, Civilis bound them to himself by the patriotic oath acceding to the rite of barbarians" (Tacitus, IV, 14-15). This is the oath later painted by Rembrandt for the new Townhall of Amsterdam; Julius Civilis became a great hero of Holland, and the Batavian revolt was later likened to that against Spain.

Willibrord, bishop of Utrecht, A.D. 695
From the 3rd century, the Batavians were gradually absorbed by the Franks. Saxons settled east of the Ijssel, and Frisians further south round the Maas and Rhine estuaries. From the 7th century the Frisians came in contact with the Merovingians, but initial attempts at conversion by English monks were strongly resisted. A little before 650 the Franks of Utrecht founded a chapel dedicated to St. Martin, but the Frisian king Radbodo staged something of a national revolt. When South Frisia was conquered by Pepin of Heristal, conversion would proceed under Frankish arms. Toward 690, Willibrord came to Frisia, an Englishman born in Northumberland about 657 and later a monk in an English monastery and then in Ireland. In 695 he was consecrated bishop of Utrecht. A new reaction set in after Pepin died, but in 719 Willibrord would return. Founding churches and monasteries, he organized his bishopric, and it became a center of Christian influence. Willibrord, considered the apostle of Frisia, died in 739 in the abbey of his foundation at Echternach in Luxemburg.

The county of Holland, 10th century
Charlemagne had firmly conquered the pagan north; among his gifts to the caliph Harun-al-Rashid there were Frisian cloths. Dorestad on the Rhine, not far from Utrecht, was the first port in Holland. After Charlemagne died, his empire was divided and the Vikings infiltrated and destroyed Dorestad among other places. The only seat of power remaining was the bishopric of Utrecht. In 922, the French king Charles the Simple (879–929) assigned church lands in North Holland to the Frisian count Theoderic I (Dirck I); his son Dirck II obtained other lands from the German emperor and became a rival to the bishop of Utrecht; his grandson Dirck III built a castle on the bishop's lands from which he could control traffic on the rivers Maas and Waal, and exact a toll. There was constant warfare between the bishop of Utrecht and the counts of Flanders.

In the 12th century the county of Holland was able to enlarge its rule at the bishop's expense. The contested area was the border strip between the two territories, of which Amstelland, where Amsterdam rose, was part.

The first mention of Amsterdam: 1275
This occurs in a tax-exemption document given by Count Floris V of Holland in 1275 to the *homines manentes apud Amestelledamme,*" the dike on the Amstel, Amsterdam. When the marshy site was first settled is unknown. It was carefully reclaimed at great risk. Archaeological excavations have revealed an inhabited nucleus going back to about 1225. A dike or dam on the Amstel probably had been built in 1270 to protect the land behind it from the seawater brought in by the Ij. At that time, Amsterdam had dwellings of wood and mud with straw roofs, housing a handful of craftsmen, peasants, and boatmen.

The first charter of Amsterdam: 1300

Count Floris V of Holland was assassinated in 1296, his heir died two years later, and the line of Dirck I died out. The county passed to a cousin, John of Hainault, against whom the bishop of Utrecht rose. The bishop was defeated and killed, and John managed to have his own brother Gwijde of Hainault elected bishop of Utrecht, to whom he gave Amstelland. Gwijde awarded Amsterdam its first charter (1300), which made its inhabits "burghers" with certain privileges as to jurisdiction and commerce in return for imposts, one of them on beer. The place was administered by a mayor (*schout*) and jurors (*schepenen*). Shortly after there was more warfare: the city was taken by Jan van Amstel (the Amstels were feudal tenants of the bishops of Utrecht) and his followers, and then besieged. This is described in Vondel's drama *Gijsbrecht van Amstel*, much beloved by Amsterdammers: it gives a picture of medieval Amsterdam, somewhat based on its later prosperity, and misnames the hero, Jan. From 1317 when Gwijde died, Amstelland was part of the county of Holland held by the house of Hainault. In 1342 the city obtained a second charter enhancing its privileges and fixing its boundaries.

The miracle of the Host: 1345

On the Tuesday before Palm Sunday in 1345, a man living in Kalverstraat in Amsterdam, being on the point of death, received viaticum. A few hours later, he had an attack of vomiting. The following morning one of the women of the household discovered the Host lying intact among the burning embers of the fire, where the man's vomit had been thrown. Placed in a casket and taken to the Oude Kerk, the foremost parish church of the city, where it became an object of veneration, the Host disappeared and turned up elsewhere. The city authorities brought it back in a solemn procession to the church. The following year, Bishop Jan van Arkel declared that these strange events, whose authenticity had been verified, constituted a miracle. The house in Kalverstraat was demolished and a chapel was built on the site, which came to be known as *Heilige Stede,* the Holy Place. Its fame spread and for a long time it became a place of pilgrimage for the devout.

The Venetian galleys return to Bruges: 1374

In 1374, galleys belonging to the Venetian state once more embarked on the "Flanders route" and headed for Bruges. The route had been suspended for some time by the authorities because of the Anglo-French wars and other circumstances, leaving the way free for private enterprise. This event coincided with the Flemish city's greatest period of prosperity, which lasted from the mid-14th to the mid-15th century, when it competed with Venice for commercial supremacy in Europe. As early as the 11th century Bruges was actively involved in commerce with England, Denmark, and northern Germany, acting as an entrepôt. It was the only city in the area with access to the sea, via the Zwyn estuary. During the 14th century it was the main port of call for Venetian and Genoese galleys trading with Flanders, and it was one of the stations of the Hanseatic League. Its prosperity, however, declined for a number of complex reasons, as is revealed by, among other things, the silting-up of its harbors in the Zwyn estuary, a phenomenon seen by some as a cause and others as an effect. Bruges' role as the great commercial center was taken over by Antwerp, which in turn was supplanted by Amsterdam.

Burgundy: 1428

The duchy of Burgundy had been established in the 9th century. In 1363 it was vested in Philip the Bold, fourth son of John II of France. In 1384 he acquired by marriage Flanders, Artois, and Franche Comté. His son John the Fearless, taking advantage of the madness of the French king Charles VI, tried to gain dominion over France by allying himself with the English (at the time of the Hundred Years' War) and was finally murdered. After his death, his son Philip the Good, the new duke, at first pursued the same policy of alliance with the English, but later joined up with the French king, with whom he signed the Treaty of Arras, gaining exemption from all obligations of vassalage. Having become, for all practical purposes, independent, Philip the Good considerably enlarged his dukedom by the acquisition of the county of Namur (1421), the duchy of Brabant-Limburg (1430), the counties of Hainault, Holland, Zeeland, and Friesland—forcing his cousin Jacoba of Bavaria, who had inherited these counties, to cede them to him (1428)—the duchies of Luxemburg (1433) and of Liège (1467). In this way, the Low Countries, which were one of the most urbanized and industrially and commercially prosperous areas of Europe at the time, entered in the Burgundian sphere of influence.

The marriage of Mary of Burgundy: 1477

Attacked by the French king Louis XI and by the Swiss, Charles the Bold, the new duke of Burgundy, suffered serious defeats at Granson (1476) and Morat (1477) at the hands of the Swiss infantry and died while trying to gain possession of Nancy (January 5, 1477). This marked the end of Burgundian power and of the elegant, learned, and cultured Burgundian court. The heir to the duchy was the young Mary of Burgundy, only child of Charles the Bold. On February 3, her 20th birthday, there was a meeting at Ghent of the States General, the feudal assembly that had been used by the dukes to impose taxes and levies. Mary was obliged to sign the *Groote Privilegie* (Great Privilege), whereby, in return for support, money, and soldiers, she restored to the cities all the rights and privileges taken from them by the rulers of Burgundy in pursuit of their policy of centralization. On August 18 she married the son of the Emperor Frederick III, Maximilian Habsburg. Two years later, Maximilian routed Louis XI, who was hoping to restore Burgundy to the French kingdom, at the Battle of Guinegate (August 17, 1479), thereby rescuing the dowry of his young wife. In fact, Burgundy proper reverted to France as a male fief, with Alsace, Lorraine, Guelderland, Zutphen, and Liège becoming separated from the duchy. But the other territories of Charles the Bold that Mary had brought to her husband as a dowry (Brabant, Limburg, Luxemburg, Franche Comté; the counties of Flanders, Hainault, Namur, Artois, Zeeland, and Holland; the marquisate of Antwerp; and the seigneury of Malines) passed to the Holy Roman Empire. Once again, Amsterdam had a new master.

The vroedschap of Amsterdam: 1477

Amsterdam's city council (*vroedschap*), the mouthpiece of the wealthiest sections of the middle class, which had already enjoyed consultative status during the earlier part of the century, now assumed its definitive form as a result of the *Groote Privilegie* granted by Mary of Burgundy: the city had thus finally completed the process of asserting its independence from feudal authority. The election, without the participation of the feudal overlord, of a college of four councilors, later known as burgomasters, had first taken place in around 1400, after which its power had grown rapidly, while at the same time the authority of the mayor (*schout*), acting as agent of the feudal lord, diminished. The nomination of the jurymen, who made up the judiciary college, remained the prerogative of the feudal lord, but the names had to be selected from a list drawn up by the council.

The crown of Maximilian in the Amsterdam coat of arms: 1489

Maximilian Habsburg, at that time king of

Germany and shortly afterward Holy Roman emperor, in 1489 granted the burghers of Amsterdam the privilege, at little cost to himself, of placing the crown over their city's coat of arms. Much graver consequences lay in store for Amsterdam and the Low Countries in his matrimonial politics. His own marriage to Mary of Burgundy had already brought the Low Countries within the Habsburg orbit, but by marrying off his son Philip the Fair in 1496 to Juana the Mad, daughter and heiress of Ferdinand II of Aragon and Isabella of Castile, not only did he pave the way for the birth of a grandson, Charles V, destined to have a profound effect on European history, but he also determined that link between Spain and the Low Countries that was to have such baleful effects on the second half of the following century. Philip the Fair inherited the Low Countries from his mother at the age of four (1482), but did not become their king until 1494; he died in 1506.

The Sound and the Baltic: 1497

The thin strip of water separating Sweden (Skåne Province) from the Danish island of Sjaelland (which also contains the Danish capital Copenhagen) and known as the Sound, was, like the Straits of Gibraltar and of Malacca, and the Bosphorus, one of the gateways of international trade. It is the corridor that links the Baltic with the North Sea, through which passed the raw materials from the Baltic countries on their way to the manufacturers of Western Europe, who in turn used it to transport their merchandise, mainly manufactured goods, back to the countries along the Baltic seaboard. This exchange of products was carried out by the German merchants of the Hanseatic League, whose western terminal was the Low Countries, where this trade route joined up with the east-west route that linked England with the countries of the Rhine. Since 1429 ships passing through the Sound had paid a toll to the Danish king, who ruled over both its shores. The toll statistics of 1497 show that 70 percent of the ships passing through came from the northern part of the Low Countries, and that 75 percent of those, or more than half of the total, were Dutch, mainly from Amsterdam and the Waterland, the homeland of the sailors who put to sea in the pay of that city. This information shows that Dutch merchants had or were about to replace the Hanseatic League, which no longer had a monopoly on Baltic trade, and that Amsterdam had seized the economic opportunities offered her by geography.

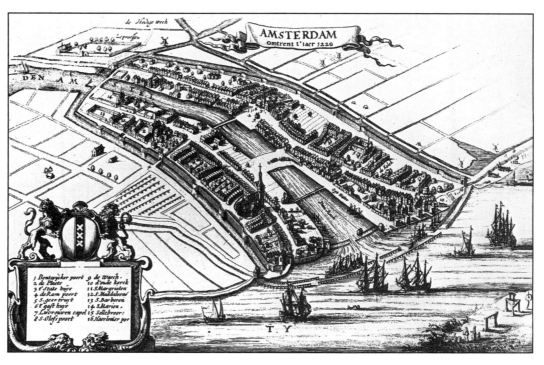

"Enkomion morias seu laus stultitiae": 1509

Desiderius Erasmus, the Augustinian scholar from Rotterdam, traveled through France, England, and Italy. He was a follower of the Italian humanist Lorenzo Valla. After returning from Italy, he wrote his most famous work, the *Enkomion morias* or *In Praise of Folly*, in which he indicted in bitterly satirical tones the presumption of theologians and scholars, the scandalous life style of the clergy, and the unworthiness of the curia, working from an intensely Christian, humanist viewpoint. His cultural influence on the intellectual community was enormous, and although, in a sense, he anticipated the Reformation (to which, however, never subscribed, indulging, instead, in polemical discussions with Ulrich von Hutten and Martin Luther between 1523 and 1527) by virtue of his critical attitude towards scholasticism and the "barbarized religious forms" (Giorgio Spini) of the late Middle Ages, he opposed it because of his ideal concept of humanistic completeness. A believer in gradual, rational, and peaceful reform, he was the spiritual master of the tolerance that characterized Dutch society. As Johan Huizinga has pointed out, despite recurrent bouts of Protestant strictness, the voice of Erasmus expresses the character of Dutch life much better than that of the Geneva reformer. The link between devotion and scientific and cultural awareness, which had lain at the heart of the great Rotterdam philosopher, had already put down its roots in

Plan of the city of Amsterdam in 1220, as seen in a 17th-century reconstruction.

Holland before Calvin, in the year of Erasmus' death, pronounced his granite words. Humanism, in a typically Nordic form that differs markedly from the French, Italian, and German forms, has always provided the ground in which the civilization of the Low Countries has developed.

Albuquerque, Antwerp, and the spice trade: 1509

In 1509, Alfonso de Albuquerque replaced Francisco de Almeida as viceroy of the Portuguese Indies. By conquering Goa and Malacca (1511), launching two expeditions against the Moluccas, and occupying Hormuz in the Persian Gulf (1515), he laid the foundations of Portugal's mercantile prosperity. Rather than working to the advantage of Lisbon, however, this favored Antwerp. The city on the Scheldt already enjoyed considerable prosperity, its commercial success having started with the grain trade during the 13th century, while because of its accessibility to England, France, and the areas along the Rhine, it became, during the first half of the 15th century, the most important entrepôt for the English wool trade.

During the next century, following the shift in trade from Bruges to Antwerp, and the city's development as a center for the distribution of spices equal to Lisbon, to the availability of finance from its own and Augsburg's bankers, the merchants of the Hanseatic League also began to use it as a center for all their Baltic trade. Antwerp, with a population of 40,000, as opposed to Amsterdam's 13,000 (in 1514), thus became the greatest marketplace of the known world.

The Anabaptists in Amsterdam: 1535
The beginning of the Reformation was marked by Martin Luther nailing his 95 theses to the door of Wittenberg Cathedral in 1517, and by 1530 the ideas of the Reformation were circulating among the *haute bourgeoisie* of Amsterdam, stimulated by trading contacts with Lutheran areas. The city's governing body, however, showed considerable moderation in applying the edicts (*Placards*) against the "heresy" published in Brussels by Margaret of Austria, who was acting as regent for her brother, Emperor Charles V. In 1533, the Anabaptists of John of Leyden peacefully took over Münster, creating there a "New Zion," but after a siege of 15 months, the city fell (June 1535). In the meantime, in May 1535, shortly before the fall of Münster, the Anabaptists tried to turn Amsterdam into another "New Zion" by storming the town hall. The social radicalism of this Protestant sect, which had made a certain amount of headway among the populace of Amsterdam, was unable to influence the solid mercantile bourgeoisie that held the reins of power, however tolerant it may have been of the Lutherans. The 40 or so Anabaptists who had seized the town hall in a surprise assault, were evicted the following day, and the gallows on the Dam became the scene of numerous executions. This episode made it impossible to pursue a policy of religious tolerance; the administration was purged by Margaret of Austria contrary to the privileges of the city, and the governing group installed at this point remained in power until the *alteratie* of 1578.

The Diet of Augsburg: 1548
On June 26, 1548, Emperor Charles V, born at Ghent and Flemish by language and education, obtained an agreement from the Imperial Diet that all his provinces in the Low Countries, which formed part of the Empire, should form a single administrative unit. The following year, the states of each province ratified a "pragmatic sanction," which guaranteed that all the provinces were to remain united under the same authority and same institutions after the emperor's death. Charles V had increased his Burgundian inheritance,

received on the death of his father Philip the Fair, by the addition of East Friesland (1515–1524), the bishopric of Utrecht (1528), whose temporal powers he abolished, Groningen and Drenthe (1536), and Gelderland and Zutphen (1543). They represent the "seventeen provinces," or Low Countries, corresponding to present-day Holland, Belgium, and Luxemburg, plus a few small areas of northern France. In 1555, when he abdicated, Charles V left this "princely, oligarchical republic of municipalities and feudal seigneuries, under the bland government of a dynasty too firmly wedded to the medieval past to have either the inclination or ability to give birth to a modern, absolutist state" (Giorgio Spini), to his son Philip, who the following year became king of Spain, while the Empire and the hereditary domains of the house of Austria passed to his own brother Ferdinand.

Het Wonderjaar, the Annus Mirabilis: 1566
The policies of Philip II, who aimed to create a centralized, absolutist power structure in the Low Countries, combined with his unyielding Catholicism in a land steeped in Erasmian ideals and also partly Protestant, led to open rebellion. The Low Countries were now being governed from Brussels by Philip II's sister, Margaret of Austria (or Parma): the king issued harsh *Placards* against heresy, and formed a new ecclesiastical organization of 14 bishoprics headed by Cardinal Granvelle, who was created archbishop of Malines. The general discontent, particularly strong among the nobility, whose most outstanding member was William ("the Silent") of Orange, persuaded Philip to withdraw the Spanish garrisons (1561) and leave the country to Granvelle. Still the popular agitation of the Calvinists continued, as did the conflict between the centralizing policies of the king and the aspirations of the townspeople and the nobility. In April 1566 the nobles presented the regent with a petition for the abolition of the *Placards*. It was then that the name of *gueux* (beggars) was first applied to them, by a disparaging courtier. In the meantime, there were widespread outbreaks of iconoclasm (aimed at Roman Catholic churches) by the Calvinists, who were becoming increasingly well organized.

The Sea Beggars capture Den Briel (Brielle): 1572
Philip II thought that he would be able to suppress the rebellion of the Low Countries and stamp out all heresy by dispatching the duke

of Alba and a number of experienced Spanish regiments to the area. The duke used terror as a weapon; the *conseil de troubles,* immediately dubbed the *bloedraad* (council of blood), issued death sentences, ignoring legal processes and local privileges. In June 1568, the count of Egmont, who had fought bravely for Philip II in the decisive Battle of St. Quentin against the French, and the count of Horn were both executed (this date marks the beginning of the Eighty Years' War). William of Orange, stadholder of Holland and prince of Nassau, gathered together an army but was defeated. The rebels turned their attention to the sea, becoming *watergeuzen* (sea beggars), attacking the duke of Alba's supply ships and the ones containing coin to pay the soldiers. The imbalance between the cost of armies and the amount of money that could be raised by fiscal means was one of the key features of the 16th and 17th centuries, because it forced monarchs to borrow from bankers in order to make up the deficit; Philip II himself went bankrupt on several occasions. Alba now found himself short of money and imposed two *alcabalas* (excise duties) without consulting the States General (1571), thereby bringing the middle classes nearer to the Calvinist minority. Taking advantage of an opportunity, one of the Sea Beggars, Willem van der Marck, conducted a surprise raid on the port of Den Briel at the mouth of the Maas (April 1572) and captured it. From the Protestant town of La Rochelle, Ludwig of Nassau, the brother of William, attacked Vlissingen (Flushing), while others occupied bases on Walcheren; in Holland, Friesland, Gelderland, and Utrecht, the cities rose up against the Spaniards acclaiming the House of Orange.

Leyden University: 1574
In agreement with the states of Holland and Zeeland, Leyden University was founded by William the Silent as "a solid pillar and support of liberty and of the good and legitimate governments of the country, not only in religious matters, but also in what concerns the community and the well-being of the citizenry." Leyden and the other universities subsequently established by the republic, were centers of Calvinism and, as such, were attended by students from Germany, Scotland, England, and Poland: they were "new" universities, to a certain extent detached from the medieval tradition, and therefore able to provide opportunities to study not only theology, but also classical and Eastern disciplines, as well as astronomy, anatomy, botany, physics, and chemistry.

The Reconciliation of Ghent: 1576

The war took a heavy toll. Ludwig of Nassau was forced to surrender at Mons. A *conseil des troubles* decimated the population. Alba gained control over the southern Low Countries and moved northward. There were massacres at the capture of Zutphen; Naarden negotiated its surrender, but, despite the negotiations, further massacres ensued; the siege of Haarlem cost the Spanish half their forces and culminated in a slaughter of the garrison and the inhabitants. This was the duke of Alba's last success: at Enkhuizen (1573) the Dutch destroyed the fleet of Philip II of Spain and Alba's troops remained unpaid. Mutiny broke out. Alba was replaced by Don Luis de Requesens, who first tried making peace and then launched an offensive in Zeeland. He was thwarted by the same obstacles as Alba—the intentional flooding of the land, the coastal blockade of the rebel fleet, and mutinies among his own forces, who still had to be paid. In March 1576 Requesens died, and chaos erupted. The rebelling Spanish troops took to massacre and plunder: the sacking in November of Antwerp, a city which had remained faithful to the king, was particularly horrific, going down in history as the "Spanish Fury." The way to agreement seemed to be opening up for the rebels, however: bourgeois cliques and aristocrats, Calvinists and Catholics, together came to an agreement at Ghent (November 8, 1576) to rid the country of foreign garrisons, abolish the repression of heresies, and restore their rights of independence.

The alteratie at Amsterdam: 1578

Amsterdam had remained like an oasis of calm in the midst of the whirlwind, but from an economic point of view it paid a high price. While many cities in Holland had taken the part of William the Silent and supported the rebellion, Amsterdam had remained faithful to the Spanish king. At the siege of Haarlem, for example, Alba's soldiers had received reinforcements and provisions via the city. From 1567, following the news of Alba's imminent arrival, many of its Protestant merchants had emigrated to places such as Emden, and this, combined with the activities of the Sea Beggars, had a dire effect on the city's economic life. With Holland and Zeeland firmly on the side of William, Amsterdam was isolated and forced to negotiate with the States of Holland and the prince. On February 8, 1578, the Treaty of Satisfaction was signed, which was a compromise agreement that allowed for the resumption of trade, the restoration of the civil guard—which had been previously disbanded because of doubts as to its trustworthiness—and the return of exiles—among them many Calvinists—while the government of the city continued to remain independent. This state of affairs was not to last for long, however. In the words of a document in the city archives, "in the year 1578, certain differences arose between the deputies of the States of Holland and the magistrates of this city . . . and since the aforementioned magistrates could not be moved to reason, a sudden change occurred on the day of May 26 in the aforesaid year, in the form of a riot, but without any blood being spilled, which resulted in the majority of the aforementioned magistrates being expelled from the city." This event came to be known as the *alteratie* (alteration). The representatives of the regime that had been overthrown were taken outside the confines of the city, the clerical members in one boat and the secular in another. The civil guard nominated a new council and new burgomasters; the latter were all Protestants, while the council also contained Catholics. After the *alteratie,* which really was a revolution, there was a sudden explosion of commercial and manufacturing activity in the city.

The Union of Utrecht: 1579

The reconciliation of Ghent in 1576 brought about a union of the "seventeen provinces," but it was a union undermined by the religious conflicts between the Catholics and Calvinists. Its members began to look for a king, the choice being between Matthias Habsburg and François d'Alençon, a member of the French House of Valois, both of whom were already in the country. William the Silent, however, favored neither of these candidates, nor did he like John of Austria, the natural son of Charles V, the victor of Lepanto who had been appointed governor general by Philip II. John of Austria, who put forward the totally unrealistic proposal that all Spanish troops would be withdrawn in return for the whole country's reversion to Catholicism, then attempted a military solution and died a disappointed man (1578). His successor was Alessandro Farnese, duke of Parma and son of Margaret of Parma (or Austria), the woman who had acted as regent in Brussels until the arrival of the duke of Alba. Farnese, playing on Catholic fears of Protestant expansion, succeeded in restoring the southern provinces to the rule of the Spanish king (the Union of Arras, January 6, 1579), thereby splitting the Union of Ghent and decisively breaking up the "seventeen provinces." Immediately the seven northern provinces (Holland, Zeeland, Gelderland, Utrecht, Fries-land, Overijssel, Groningen, and Drenthe) formed the Union of Utrecht (January 23, 1579). In practical terms, this event marks the birth of the republic of the United Provinces, even though Philip II still had not renounced his claim to them. In addition, his nephew Alessandro Farnese was an experienced general.

The "Invincible Armada": 1588

The Union of Utrecht of 1579 had also been joined by a number of Flemish cities such as Ghent, Tournai, Ypres, Bruges, and Antwerp, but over the next six years Farnese had recaptured the whole of western Flanders. The fall of Antwerp following a siege (August 16, 1585) proved to be a fatal blow for this city that had once been the "marketplace of the world." The return of Antwerp to Spanish sovereignty had two basic consequences for the northern provinces: the closure of the Scheldt made a hole in the world trade system, which Amsterdam was quick to fill, and the emigration of the Calvinists, who were generally well educated and often rich in terms of both finance and professional skills, whom Amsterdam strove to attract with considerable success. Meanwhile, in July 1581, at a meeting in The Hague, the deputies of the States of all the northern provinces had proclaimed Philip II's forfeiture of all his sovereign rights. This produced a constitutional problem unusual in Europe at the time, namely the lack of a monarch. William once again called on François d'Alençon, but he proved unpopular with his potential subjects (Antwerp expelled his French soldiers by popular acclaim) and died unexpectedly in 1584. Shortly afterwards, in Delft, a Catholic fanatic assassinated William the Silent (July 10, 1584). His post as stadholder for Holland and Zeeland was taken over by his son Maurice (already stadholder for Utrecht, Gelderland, Overijssel, Groningen, and Drenthe), who proved to be one of the greatest soldiers of his day. The crown was then offered to Henry III of France, who turned it down, and to Queen Elizabeth of England, with whom the Treaty of Nonsuch was signed (August 20, 1585), and who dispatched a small armed force and her favorite, the earl of Leicester. He was created governor general of the States General (February 1586), but he quarrelled with the Dutch, and showed himself to be militarily incapable; he returned home unmourned (December 1587). In the meantime, the influence of Johan van Oldenbarnevelt, at that time grand pensionary of Holland, had grown considerably; after Leicester's departure, he made the States

THE REPUBLIC OF THE SEVEN UNITED PROVINCES

Aurich

Emden

EAST FRIESLAND

Leer

Dokkum

GRONINGEN

Vlieland

Franeker   Leeuwarden   Groningen

Harlingen   FRIESLAND

Texel   Bolsward   Assen

Workum   Sneek   DRENTE

Marsdiep   Hindeloopen   IJlst

Staveren

Sloten

Meppen

Medemblik   LINGEN

Enkhuizen   Kampen   BENTHEIM

Alkmaar   Hoorn   Zwolle   Lingen

Edam   Elburg   OVERIJSSEL   Nordhorn

Purmerend   Hattem

Haarlem   Monnikendam   Harderwijk   Bentheim

Amsterdam   Deventer   Burgsteinfurt

HOLLAND   Amersfoort   Zutphen   Lochem

GELDERLAND   Groenlo

Leyden   Utrecht

The Hague   Gouda   UTRECHT   Doesburg

Delft   Montfoort   Rhenen   Arnhem   Doetichem   Stadtlohn

Schiedam   Rotterdam   Schoonhoven   Wijk   Wageningen

Brielle   Tiel   MÜNSTER

Gorkum   Nijmegen

Dordrecht   Bommel   Kleve   Rees

's Hertogenbosch   KLEVE   Wesel

Zierikzee   Goch   Recklinghausen

Breda   Tilburg   Dortmund

Veere   Tolen   Roosendaal   Mörs   Essen

Middelburg   ZEELAND

Flushing   Goes   THE GENERALITY   Venlo   ARCHBISHOPRIC OF COLOGNE

Düsseldorf

BERGENLAND

Bruges   Antwerp   Weert   Roermond

FLANDERS   Lier   Echt   DUCHY OF JÜLICH   Cologne

Gent   Jülich

Dendermonde   Brühl

Aalst   Maastricht   Bonn

Kortrijk   Brussels   LIMBURG   Aachen

Oudenaarde   BRABANT   Neerwinden

Landen

General acknowledge that the United Provinces should form a republic. This took place in 1588, the same year that also saw the launching of Spain's *Armada Invencible*. Perhaps Farnese would have been able to win the war against the United Provinces, but Philip II certainly prevented that by ordering Farnese to prepare his troops to embark on the fleet due to arrive from Spain for the invasion of England. The three hundred ships with their three thousand men and two thousand four hundred pieces of artillery, which assembled in the Tagus estuary opposite Lisbon, were doomed for destruction. The English sailors, with the help of the Dutch, ensured that Philip II's great strategic plan was thwarted; storms did the rest.

Willem Barents and the Northeast Passage: 1594

A Friesian by birth, Willem Barents was a cartographer in the Mediterranean. By now the Dutch were preparing everywhere for their trading expeditions. His fame, however, rests on the three voyages he undertook in Arctic waters in the hopes of finding a northern route to China—a route that we now know does exist, but which was not navigated completely until the 19th century and is free of ice for only a short period of the year. In his first voyage (1594), Barents reached as far as 70° north latitude and touched the coast of Novaya Zemlya. He then made a second attempt in 1595, reaching as far as the Kara Straits. Undaunted, he made a further attempt the following year, visiting Bear Island, Spitsbergen, and, once again, Novaya Zemlya. This time his ship became trapped in the ice, and he was forced to spend the winter in the bitter conditions of the Arctic. The brief account of his winter spent in a hut on the coast of Novaya Zemlya (1596-1597) was rediscovered *in situ* some three hundred years later. In attempting to return home in boats with no decks, the explorer finally met his death.

The way to the Indies: 1595

Every European merchant was well aware of how much money there was to be made in the spice trade: the Venetians had grown rich by buying from the Arabs of the Levant, while the Portuguese, who a hundred years earlier had discovered the route to the Spice Islands via the Cape of Good Hope, had themselves grown rich on the proceeds, as, to an even greater extent, had their financial backers in Antwerp and Augsburg. The Dutch obtained their supplies of spices from Lisbon, but a number of Dutchmen had worked for the

Portuguese in the Far East. One of these men was Jan Huyghen van Linschoten, who, having left home at the age of 17 and having spent 13 years in the Indies, in 1595 published a book in which he listed his own experiences, the trading techniques of the Portuguese, and the weaknesses that existed in their dominions. In March 1594, nine merchants in Amsterdam set up the *Compagnie van Verre* (Afar Company), with the aim of sending two trading expeditions to the Indies. The first was not very fortunate: composed of four ships, led by Cornelis de Houtman, it reached Madagascar, Bantam, and Bali, but it also lost one ship and a large number of men. But the cargo of pepper they brought back from Bantam covered their investment when they returned to Texel in August 1597 after two years' absence. The second expedition, commanded by Jacob Cornelis van Neck, visited Bantam and the Moluccas. This was the famous "second voyage." Four ships returned in July 1599, after 15 months' absence, and the bells of Amsterdam rang out in joy; when the other ships that had fallen behind also returned home, it was realized that a 400 percent profit had been made. In the exultant words of the poet Vondel, "those that took the risk have received four in exchange for one; everyone is pleased and offers thanks to the Lord." The year after Houtman's return, no fewer than 22 ships, the property of at least five different, independent, and competing companies, set sail for the Indies. One sailor from Rotterdam, Olivier van Noort, took the route via South America and the Pacific, thereby becoming the first Dutchman to sail around the world in the same way as had Magellan and his expedition.

The fluit, a nimble instrument of trade: 1595

The type of ship known by the Dutch as a fluit, which was first built at Hoorn in 1595 and soon passed into general service, proved to be a formidable weapon for Dutch traders plying the European sea routes, particularly in the Baltic; it was not, however, used for oceanic trade, which called for heavily armed vessels. A fast-moving three-master, with remarkable cargo capacity, needing only a modest crew, and possessing a shallow draught that enabled it to enter shallow-water harbors, the fluit allowed the Dutch to transport their European tradegoods—which, it should be remembered, were far less valuable, weight for weight, than the precious merchandise of the Orient—at prices below those of their competitors. One curious feature of the fluit was its inward-sloping sides, which gave it a reduced deck area, but one of

the advantages of this was that the tolls levied at the sound were based on the size of a ship's bridge.

The last witches are condemned to death: 1595

It is significant that capital punishment for witchcraft should have been stopped in Holland, as Huizinga stresses, roughly a hundred years before anywhere else in Europe. The last great trial of witches, complete with torture and the death penalty, took place in Utrecht in 1595. Elsewhere, there were a number of extremely bloodthirsty trials of witches during the 17th century (the witches of Loudun in France, Salem in America, and the Valtellina in Italy) and the practice continued even into the 18th century.

The Archdukes: 1600

Philip II's last attempt at resolving the problem of the Low Countries was undertaken in 1600. The Infant Isabel was married to a Habsburg of the Austrian branch, the Archduke Albert, and the Spanish king announced that he was prepared to renounce his sovereignty over the Low Countries in favor of his daughter and son-in-law, who were to hold court in Brussels; if Maurice and the United Provinces would agree to be their subjects and to stop fighting, then they would be granted religious freedom. They refused. In any case, the independence of the archduke and his wife, which was bolstered by the Spanish ambassador and Spanish troops, was an illusion. Maurice of Orange, an extremely able strategist, had already captured Breda (1590), Nijmegen (1591), and Groningen (1594), and on July 2, 1600, assisted by troops sent by Queen Elizabeth of England, he was also able to defeat Archduke Albert at Nieuwpoort.

The Dutch East India Company: 1602

There was a sudden explosion of trade with the East Indies. Even though of the 22 ships that left in 1598, only 14 returned, 1601 saw the departure from Dutch ports of 65 ships, divided into 14 expeditions. There were a number of rival active companies, and the rivalry between the provinces of Holland and Zeeland was particularly acute. There was now a danger that this method of operating would lead to a rise in prices in Asia and a lowering of prices in Europe. In January 1598 the States General asked the various companies that had been set up for the purpose of overseas trade either to join together or cooperate. The grand pensionary of Holland, Johan van Oldenbarnevelt, pursued a series of long and difficult negotiations, finally succeeding in obtaining a merger of the various companies into a single East India Company (*Verenigde Oostindische Compagnie, or VOC*), with a capital of six and a half million florins and a charter (dated March 20, 1602) that granted it a monopoly over maritime trade with the Orient. It was one of the great instruments of Dutch prosperity; it built up a colonial empire in Indonesia that lasted until the end of the republic. In 1611, Hendrik Brouwer discovered the Roaring Forties, the strong prevailing west winds that blow between 40° and 50° south latitude; six years later, the company authorized the use of this faster route through southern seas for the journey out to the Indies.

Oriental porcelain: 1603
In 1603 the Dutch captured a Portuguese carrack off St. Helena, part of whose cargo consisted of Chinese porcelain, and the following year they captured another Portuguese carrack off the coast of India, again with a cargo of Chinese porcelain. The auction of the cargoes of the two ships, the *Santiago* and the *Santa Catarina*, was a great success, and the term *kraak-porcelein* (carrack porcelain) was used for several decades to describe Ming blue-and-white porcelain. It has been estimated that during the next 60 years the Dutch imported more than three million pieces of Chinese porcelain, while many more millions were taken to Batavia and sold through the markets of Indonesia, Malaysia, India, and Persia. The potteries of Delft imitated Chinese porcelain, even though what they produced was not true porcelain, and their wares, with a characteristic decoration that combined Japanese, Chinese, and Indian elements, remained in fashion for more than a century and a half. In fact, at one point Japanese potters imitated the Delft pattern, which had itself derived ultimately from the Far East.

The draining of the Beemster: 1607-1612
Fifteen businessmen requested a license for this drainage operation from the provincial States in the spring of 1607; it is an example of the intensive land-reclamation activities that took place between the mid-16th and mid-17th century in the province of Holland. Using a system that involved a chain of windmills (*molengang*) to pump out the water, a lake was drained measuring some 17 acres in area, with water to a depth of 10 feet. In this context, mention should be made of Jan Leeghwater, a builder of windmills and one of the greatest hydraulic engineers in Holland, whose work resulted in the reclamation of vast areas of land in the province. Leeghwater also drew up a plan for the draining of the lake at Haarlem, a project that was not undertaken until two centuries later.

The Truce of Antwerp: 1609
The war between Spain and the United Provinces dragged on, proving to be a costly affair for both sides. From 1602, Maurice of Orange had to contend with Ambrogio Spinola, a member of the great Genoese banking family, who used his own money to make good the chronic lack of money in Spanish possession: the war was costing Spain five million florins a year, plus the premium owed to the bankers who lent the money and transferred it from Spain to the Low Countries. The Genoese leader did achieve certain brilliant successes, such as the capture of Ostend in 1604, but no single battle had a decisive effect on the war as a whole; Spinola himself was to tell the Spanish king in 1628 that "the experience of sixty years of war with the Dutch has shown how it would be impossible to conquer those provinces by force." The United Provinces were also feeling the financial strain of the struggle: from an annual sum of five million florins in the final decade of the 16th century, the military budget of the republic had risen to ten million florins during the period 1604-1606. In April 1606, Spinola received instructions from the king, Philip III, to inform the Dutch that Spain was willing to negotiate. Discussions were speeded up by a major naval victory on the side of the United Provinces in 1607, when Jacob van Heemskerck of Amsterdam, who had been with Barents in Novaya Zemlya and then with Van Neck on the famous "second voyage," attacked the Spanish fleet in the Bay of Gibraltar and, with the loss of 150 men out of 2,000 (Heemskerck himself died), destroyed it completely. As one Englishman commented at the time, "such a brave enterprise has certainly never been carried out before." Spain now seemed to be prepared to recognize the independence of the United Provinces (one Rotterdam burgomaster remarked at the time: "What other purpose could there be for waging war, since even if we were to continue for another forty years, what more could we have than the recognition of a free republic?"), but it also wanted an explicit guarantee of tolerance for the Catholics, the end of the blockade of the Scheldt and of the Flemish coast, as well as a cessation of Dutch trade with the East and West Indies. These conditions, however, were not acceptable to Holland and Zeeland, and all that was achieved was a truce, the Twelve Year Truce or the Truce of Antwerp, signed on April 9, 1609.

Hudson, an Englishman in the service of the Dutch East India Company: 1609
The hope of finding the Northeast Passage to the Indies did not die easily. In 1609 the Dutch East India Company tried with the English navigator Henry Hudson, who in the two previous years had already completed two sailings on behalf of the English Muscovy Company, reaching 80° north latitude and calling at Greenland and Spitsbergen and, on the second voyage, Novaya Zemlya. On his third voyage, which was financed by Dutch merchants, he set off once again in search of the Northeast Passage, but was stopped by ice; he then turned west, exploring the coasts of North America and sailing down the river which now bears his name. It was a voyage that failed to fulfill its original purpose, which was in any case impractical. Hudson completed a fourth voyage (1610), this time on behalf of a group of London merchants, when he sailed along the coasts of Greenland and

The founding charter of the Dutch East India Company, 1602.

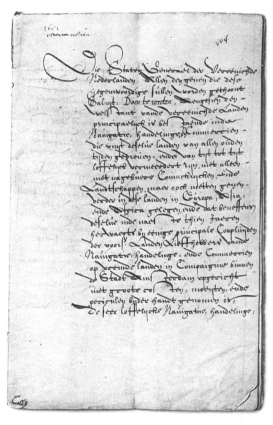

Labrador, finally entering what is now known as Hudson Bay, where he became ice bound. He was unable to proceed until June the following year, but his crew mutinied and set him adrift with eight others; he died in Hudson Bay.

The Muider-kring: 1609-1647

This was a circle of learned figures who met periodically between 1609 and 1647 in the Castle of Muiden, the bailiff of which was Pieter Hooft, son of a famous Amsterdam burgomaster. The circle, which played a very important role in the literature and general culture of Holland during its Golden Age, included Hooft, himself a poet, and such personalities as Grotius; Laurens Reael, former governor general of the East Indies and correspondent with Galileo on scientific matters; the organist J. P. Sweelinck; the poet Constantijn Huygens, secretary to two successive princes of Orange; Vondel; Vossius; Barlaeus; Roemers-Visscher; and his two daughters Anna and Maria. The *Muider-kring* was contemporary with the Hôtel de Rambouillet salon satirized by Molière in his *Précieuses ridicules*, but "whereas madame de Rambouillet conducted an elegant court, the *Muider-kring* was the expression of a new democratizing direction linked to humanism" (Deric Regin).

Remonstrants and Counter-remonstrants: 1610

The Twelve Year Truce, concluded at Antwerp in 1609, was primarily the work of Johan van Oldenbarnevelt, grand pensionary of Holland, a champion of the great capitalist and mercantile bourgeoisie of the cities and substantially, in so far as these terms are applicable, head of a republican faction that favored peace and civic autonomy, that is to say, government by the ruling classes, the patriciate. The opposition was provided by an Orangist faction, in which Maurice of Orange played on the intransigence of the Calvinists, many of whom were refugees from Flanders, and of the lower classes in the ports and industry: it was a faction that supported the continuation of the war and a centralized form of government. This antipathy was also tied up with religious disputes. The middle classes were mainly followers of the theologian Arminius, a moderate man in the Erasmian tradition, who tended to play down the dogma of predestination within Calvinism. By contrast, the theologian Gomarus, a refugee from southern Flanders, was an ardent defender of the doctrine. This theological question carried with it certain egalitarian implications, which meant that Gomarus gained a wide following

among the lower classes, but it also created an unbridgeable gap between Catholics and Calvinists, leading inevitably to a resumption in hostilities. Gomarus sought to have the matter settled by a synod, while the followers of Arminius (who had died in 1610) expressed their opposition in 1610 by means of a *remonstratie* (hence the name Remonstrants, with the followers of Gomarus being called Counter-remonstrants), maintaining that the problem should be dealt with and settled by the civil authorities of each province, the governing patriciate. The theological dispute, with its obvious political ramifications, was fueled by the publication of pamphlets, violent sermons from the pulpit, and civil agitation.

The Amsterdam Stock Exchange: 1611

The commercial enterprise of the merchants of Amsterdam, the historical and geographical circumstances that favored the rapid and large-scale development of trade, and the city's ensuing prosperity (which was deprecated by certain contemporary figures: one 17th-century Calvinist described Amsterdam's driving force as *naar winst! naar winst!*, "just profit!") encouraged the establishment of practical institutions. A public weigh house had existed at the center of the Dam since 1556, the first price list for all the markets dates from 1585, and a chamber of insurers had opened in 1598. The city, however, now felt the need for a place to conduct its commercial and financial transactions, and so in 1608 a decision was taken to build an exchange. The architect Hendrick de Keyser was sent to London to study the exchange building there, and in 1611 the Amsterdam Exchange was opened. From 1609 onwards, the town hall housed an exchange bank, a peculiar public banking organization *sui generis*, whose mysterious wealth became almost legendary. In 1617 a special grain exchange was set up.

The expansion of the city of Amsterdam: 1613

From the Middle Ages up until the 19th century, almost every European city consisted of a protected area surrounded by a ring of fortifications, initially walls and turrets, but later ramparts and bastions. The expansion of any city was always a costly operation because it involved the replacement of these defensive elements. Amsterdam was no exception, although it did possess certain topographical peculiarities. In the famous map of Cornelis Anthoniszon, executed in 1544, the city appears as an almost perfect rectangle, surrounded by walls and canals, with one of the

shorter sides facing onto the Ij and divided lengthwise almost in half by the lower reaches of the Amstel. At the end of the republic, in the late 1700s, the city, surrounded by bastions, ramparts, and canals, seems like a semicircle, its chord represented by the Ij, with the old heart of the town almost at the center and with semicircular canals in the expanded section. The population of the city rose from thirty thousand inhabitants in 1570 to one hundred thousand in 1620 and two hundred thousand in 1660, particularly as a result of immigration. The year 1613 is especially significant because it was then that the city council decided to start work on the first third of the characteristic belt of canals on the western side of the city, an act which marked the first decisive step towards the realization of the full semicircle (there had already been expansion schemes carried out at the end of the 16th century). The final expansion took place later in the century, the land being acquired in 1663, but contrary to expectation, the territory embraced by the plan remained undeveloped because population levels began to stagnate, with the result that a vast area to the east of the city was given over to a public park, the Plantage (1682).

The Greenland Company: 1614

This company was founded in 1614 and had a monopoly on travel in the Arctic seas, the main objective of which was whaling. Even though, like its sister organization, the Dutch East India Company, it was divided in a number of chambers that represented the interests of the various ports, half its working capital came from Amsterdam. The Greenland or Northern Company did not enjoy the same success as the mighty East India Company or, for that matter, the West India Company, which was set up a few years later. In 1642, its monopoly charter was not renewed. In fact, the whaling industry only developed after the company's demise, when lively competition broke out among private Dutch entrepreneurs, as well as between themselves, the English, and the Danes.

De Spaanse Brabander by Brederode: 1618

De Spaanse Brabander (The Spanish Brabander), is a comedy that reflects contemporary Amsterdam society and the contradictory feelings of its people toward immigrants from the southern Low Countries. It was performed in 1618, the year of its author's death, in the wooden theater on Keizersgracht, which preceded the *Schouwburg*. Gerbrand Adriaensz. Brederode (Amsterdam, 1585–1618), a poet and comedy writer, was the author of the *Boertigh amoureus en aendachtigh groot lied-boek* (The Great Comic, Love and Religious Song-Book), of realistically witty farces written in the language of the people, such as *De klucht van de koe* (The Farce of the Cow, 1612) and *De klucht van den moelenaer* (The Farce of the Miller, 1613) and of comedies inspired by Spanish chivalrous romances or based on French models, but his best-known works are his last two great comedies *Het moortje* (The Brown-Haired Man, 1616) and the *Spaanse Brabander*.

Batavia: 1619

The Dutch merchants who were trading in the Orient on behalf of the East India Company, soon felt the need to have a base where they could assemble their ships for arrival or departure, where their cargoes could be loaded or unloaded, and where goods destined for markets in Asia could be either stored or prepared for transshipment. It also became clear that such a base ideally should be situated near either the Straits of Malacca or the Sunda Strait. The eyes of Jan Coen then fell on the small port of Djakarta on the island of Java. He took the town by force (May 30, 1619), defying both the Sultan of Bantam and the *Heeren XVII* who ran the company from Amsterdam and would have liked the base to have been acquired by negotiation. On the ruins of Djakarta there arose the Dutch town of Batavia. Some years earlier, in fact, Jan Coen had written to the directors of the company (1614): "Your Honors must know from experience that trade in Asia has to be conducted and maintained under the protection and favor of your Honors' arms, and that arms have to be paid for by trade; we therefore cannot sustain trade without war, nor war without trade."

The Synod of Dordrecht and the execution of Johan van Oldenbarnevelt: 1618-1619

On November 13, 1618, the synod sought by the Counter-remonstrants was assembled at Dordrecht. It was also attended by representatives of the Reformed Church in Switzerland, Scotland, England, and Germany. Arminianism was condemned and Arminians were banned from taking communion. The Dutch Reformed Church, which followed the teachings of Calvin, emerged from the synod as the official church. It gained it certain privileges, although it never became the state church. Only the Erasmian philosophy of the cities' ruling classes, who followed the practice of subordinating ecclesiastical powers to civil ones, could create the climate of tolerance

Immigration into Amsterdam from the Low Countries
(from the city's marriage registers)

	17th century	18th century
North Holland	15,140	10,388
South Holland	12,668	12,591
Overijssel	10,515	14,937
Friesland	7,975	5,608
Gelderland	7,395	18,637
Utrecht	6,987	8,755
Groningen	2,701	2,986
Zeeland	2,637	1,173
North Brabant	2,465	3,467
Drenthe	1,359	2,398
Limburg	1,211	1,497

Immigration into Amsterdam from Europe
(from the city's marriage registers)

	17th century	18th century
Germany, East Prussia, and Silesia	51,591	66,681
Belgium	8,617	2,374
Norway	7,784	4,085
France	5,382	3,228
England, Scotland, and Ireland	4,331	1,087
Denmark	3,458	3,589
Sweden	3,143	2,861
Poland and Danzig	1,291	1,601
Russia and Königsberg	460	728
Portugal	325	150
Italy	315	408
Spain	233	148
Switzerland	142	498
Finland, Hungary, Greece, Yugoslavia, Malta, and Iceland	61	49
Czechoslovakia	40	134
Austria	23	57

Statistics relating to immigration into Amsterdam, taken from marriage registers.

that allowed virtual freedom of religion for other Protestant sects and, albeit in secret, for Catholics as well. Maurice, certainly not for any deeply held religious beliefs, took advantage of events to get rid of Oldenbarnevelt and his party: he dismissed all Arminians in positions of power in the main cities, while the grand pensionary himself, accused of conspiracy with the enemy, was beheaded in The Hague on May 13, 1619, even before the synod had ended (May 29). Huig van Groot (Grotius), the advocate of Utrecht Province, who was also an Arminian, was sentenced to life imprisonment, but he subsequently escaped and fled to France.

The West India Company: 1621

Modeled on its counterpart, the East India Company, the *West-Indische Compagnie* or *WIC* was instituted with a charter granted by the States General on June 3, 1621. The Twelve Year Truce between the United Provinces and Spain was now over, and the company, which had a monopoly of trade with America and West Africa, had clearly hostile intentions toward the Atlantic trade and colonial empire of the Iberian peninsula (Spain and Portugal were united under the same crown at the time). It achieved a brilliant success when Piet Heyn captured a Spanish fleet laden with Mexican silver in the Cuban port of Matanzas (1628), but in practice its efforts were aimed at the sugar of Portuguese Brazil and the gold, ivory, and slaves of the Portuguese settlements in West Africa. In fact, it operated in Brazil, as we shall see in greater detail later, on the Gold Coast (capture of Elmina, 1638), and in Angola (Luanda, captured in 1641, was retaken by the Portuguese a few years later). In the Caribbean, its most important prize was the capture of the island of Curaçao in 1634. The company also administered Guyana, where the Dutch had had a settlement since as early as 1580.

The Brazilian venture: 1624-1654

This was the most spectacular enterprise of the West India Company, but it was short-lived, since the Portuguese had already put down deep roots in Brazil. An expedition under the leadership of Admiral J. Willekens, with 26 ships, 300 pieces of artillery, and 3,200 men, captured San Salvador de Bahía. The Dutch were immediately driven out, but they established more permanent settlements further to the north at Recife (1630–1654), Paraíba (1635–1654), and São Luis do Maranhão (1641–1644). In 1637 the company nominated John Maurice of Nassau as governor general and overall captain of the fleet and army; he conquered the great Guinea slave station of São Jorge de Mina (Elimina, 1683). Brazil and sugar, Guinea and slaves: the two were complementary. When, in 1640, Portugal regained its independence from the

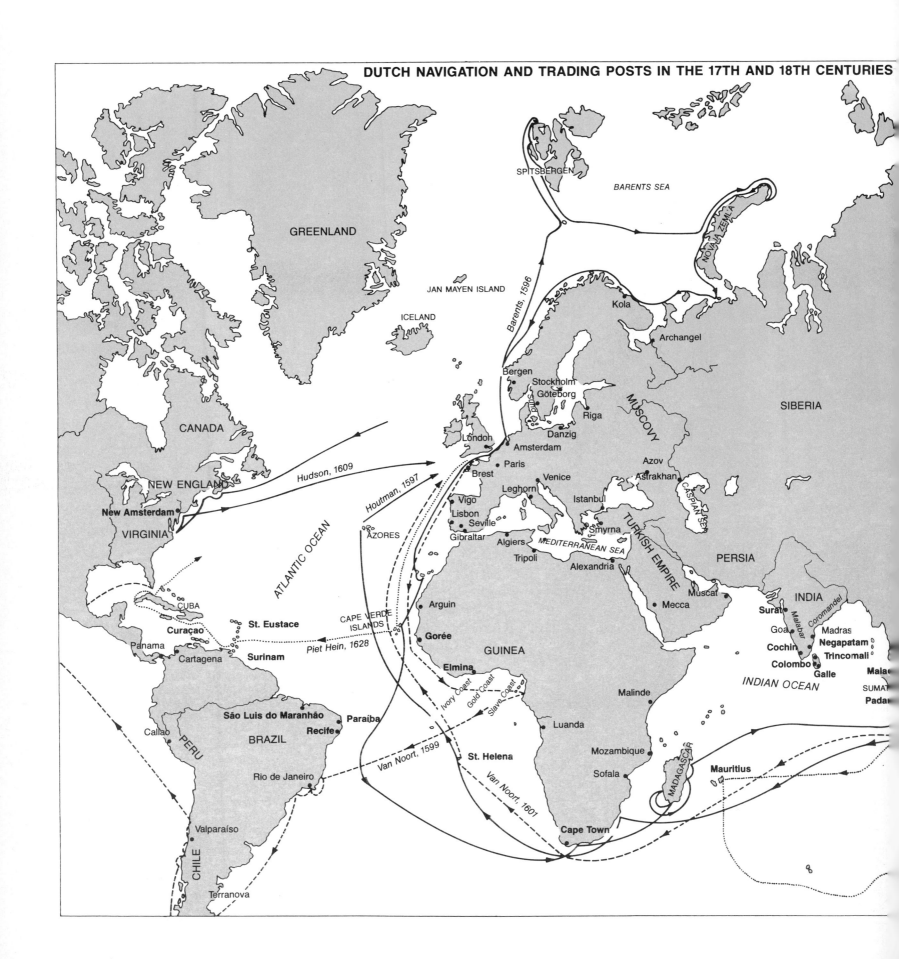

DUTCH NAVIGATION AND TRADING POSTS IN THE 17TH AND 18TH CENTURIES

SPITSBERGEN

BARENTS SEA

NOVAJA ZEMLA

GREENLAND

JAN MAYEN ISLAND

Kola

Archangel

ICELAND

Barents, 1596

Bergen

Stockholm

Göteborg

SIBERIA

MUSCOVY

Riga

Danzig

London

Amsterdam

Azov

CANADA

Paris

Astrakhan

Brest

NEW ENGLAND

Hudson, 1609

Houtman, 1597

Vigo

Venice

Leghorn

Istanbul

CASPIAN SEA

New Amsterdam

Lisbon

Seville

Smyrna

TURKISH EMPIRE

PERSIA

VIRGINIA

AZORES

Gibraltar

Algiers

MEDITERRANEAN SEA

INDIA

ATLANTIC OCEAN

Tripoli

Alexandria

Muscat

Surat

CUBA

Mecca

Malabar

Coromandel

St. Eustace

CAPE VERDE ISLANDS

Arguin

Goa

Madras

Curaçao

Panama

Piet Hein, 1628

Gorée

GUINEA

Cochin

Negapatam

Colombo

Trincomali

Cartagena

Surinam

Elmina

Galle

Mala

INDIAN OCEAN

SUMAT

Ivory Coast

Gold Coast

Slave Coast

Malinde

Pada

São Luis do Maranhão

Paraíba

Callao

Recife

Luanda

BRAZIL

PERU

Van Noort, 1599

St. Helena

Mozambique

Mauritius

Rio de Janeiro

Van Noort, 1601

Sofala

MADAGASCAR

Valparaíso

Cape Town

CHILE

Terranova

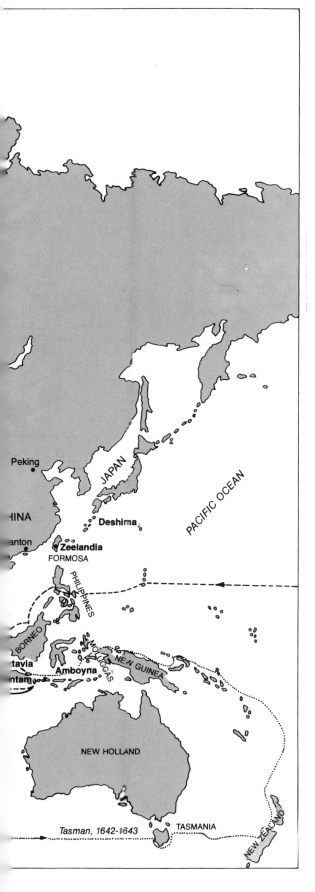

On the map opposite, the Dutch commercial bases appear in boldface.

Spanish crown, to which it had been subject for 60 years, King John IV of Braganza formally acknowledged the Dutch occupation of the northeastern coast of Brazil, but in reality he incited the Portuguese colonists to revolt. The revolt broke out in 1645, shortly after Nassau returned home; the company had failed to renew his contract. The revolt lasted for nine years and the Dutch were finally expelled, but the trade in slaves, who were needed for the sugar plantations, continued to flourish.

De iure belli ac pacis: 1625

Huig van Groot, better known under the Latinized name of Grotius, a native of Delft and friend of the grand pensionary of Holland Johan van Oldenbarnevelt, was himself advocate general of Holland, and in 1609 he had anonymously published, under the title *Mare liberum,* a chapter of his treatise *De iure praedae.* It is obvious how precious the freedom of the sea would be to Dutch merchants in their struggle against the colonial monopolies of Spain and Portugal, but not everyone was convinced of the willingness of the Dutch to live by that principle. Downing, English ambassador to The Hague during the period leading up to the second war with England, wrote: "It is *mare liberum* in British waters, but *mare clausum* along the coast of Africa and in the East Indies." A supporter of Arminius, Grotius had been condemned to life imprisonment after the victory of the Counter-remonstrants at the Synod of Dordrecht, but he was able to escape after two years and died in exile. His treatise *De iure belli ac pacis,* published in 1625, played an important role in the formulation of international law and in the juridical regulation of war.

The Palamedes of Joost van den Vondel: 1625

Joost van den Vondel (1587–1679), whose poetic oeuvre succeeded in blending Renaissance classicism with baroque grandeur, is held to be the most outstanding representative of Dutch culture during that country's Golden Age. "We Dutch are firmly convinced that Vondel is one of the greatest poets of all time. We also know, and we accept it as a fact, that the world does not know him, and never will" (Johan Huizinga). His parents were Anabaptists who fled from Antwerp to Cologne, where Joost was born, and then to Amsterdam. There he devoted himself to working in his father's shop, which he later took over. The business went bankrupt (1656), however, and the poet went to work in a pawnshop. He gained his early intellectual training in the heady atmosphere of the *rederiijkerskamers* (rhetoric chambers) and wrote a great amount of occasional verse, commenting on almost every event in the city and the republic. He translated Seneca, Sophocles, Euripides, and Virgil, and wrote 24 plays in Alexandrine verse. His *Palamedes* (1625), which used a classical theme to conceal an allegorical reference to the tragic death of Johan van Oldenbarnevelt, led to his being prosecuted, while his *Gijsbrecht van Amstel* (1637), based on a medieval episode in Amsterdam's history, was the first play to be performed at the Schouwburg, despite attempts to suppress it by the church, who mistrusted Vondel because of his known Catholic tendencies (in 1641, in fact, he converted to Catholicism).

The surrender of Breda (1625) and the capture of 's Hertogenbosch (1629)

After the Twelve Year Truce expired, the war between Spain and the United Provinces was resumed. The Dutch fought the Spanish along the borders that existed when hostilities ceased in 1609, as well as overseas. At home, the resumption of the war did little to alter the situation, but in the meantime the Thirty Years' War—which was to ravage Europe—had broken out. The stadholder Maurice failed to achieve any further successes, and shortly after his death on April 23, 1625, Spinola, after a year's siege, obtained the surrender of Breda (May 25, 1625), which Velázquez made the subject of a famous painting. Maurice was succeeded by his brother Frederik Henry captured 's Hertogenbosch United Provinces. In vain the Spanish laid siege to the fortress of Bergen op Zoom, a powerful stronghold on the Scheldt, while Frederik Henry captured 's Hertogenbosch and Wesel (1629) and then Maastricht (1632).

Nieuw Amsterdam: 1626

In 1626, Pieter Minnewit paid a group of American Indians 60 florins for the island of Manhattan, situated at the mouth of the Hudson River, and built a fort there, which he called Amsterdam. Around this fort there developed a commercial center (Nieuw Amsterdam) and a colonial settlement peopled by Protestant refugees from Europe and from the more populous and prosperous areas of New England that had already been colonized by the English. The government of the colony by the West India Company cannot have been very popular, to judge by the fact that some forty years later the colonists forced the governor, Pieter Stuyvesant, to give himself up to an English expeditionary force (1664). Thus Nieuw Amsterdam became New York.

The Athenaeum Illustre: 1632
Amsterdam had no university: university education took place at Leyden, in the university founded by William the Silent less than thirty years earlier. In order to ensure that the youth of Amsterdam obtained adequate instruction prior to attending Leyden University, since the preparation that they received in the city's Latin schools was insufficient, and also to ensure that Amsterdam had a seat of higher learning for those who did not want to go away to study, in 1632, following lengthy negotiations with Leyden, the *Athenaeum Illustre* was founded, offering courses in philosophy, history, medicine, law, rhetoric, Greek, Latin, Oriental languages, and mathematics. The school was situated in a chapel of the convent of St. Agnes on Oudezijds Voorburgwal, which had been confiscated after the *alteratie* of 1578 and used as an Admiralty warehouse. Among its most brilliant teachers were Caspar Barlaeus and Gerardus Vossius. The *Athenaeum Illustre* was the direct forerunner of the modern Amsterdam University.

Tulip fever: 1634-1637
Frenetic speculation, a malaise that typically affects the financially naive, broke out in the United Provinces almost a hundred years before the extravagant débâcles of John Law in Paris and the South Sea Company in London, and although this type of financial speculation was also to affect Holland and Amsterdam, the speculative commodity there was tulip bulbs. The tulip, a flower from the Middle East that had been cultivated by the Turks and Persians, first arrived in the northern Low Countries via Flanders and in 1590 was being grown at Leyden. Bulb merchants offered their merchandise by means of *Tulpenboeken,* a series of beautiful watercolor illustrations of the flowers. The speculative boom was sudden and short-lived: it started in western Friesland and spread to Amsterdam, Alkmaar, Rotterdam, Utrecht, Leyden, and many other cities. Prices rocketed: for a bulb of a medium-priced variety it rose from 30 florins in 1634 to 48 in 1635, and 75 in 1636. At the beginning of 1637 people began to go mad: for another variety, the price rose from 120 florins on January 15 to 385 on the 23rd of the same month, reaching 1,400 and 1,500 florins on February 1 and February 2. Then came the inevitable collapse, with the cancellation of

contracts being decided upon by agents from the centers of production, and finally intervention by the authorities. One person to go broke as a result of these events was the famous painter Jan van Goyen, who, as a result of having speculated just before the bubble burst, remained in debt for the rest of his life.

Anton van Diemen: 1636
Anton van Diemen, one of the architects of Dutch power in the Indies, was 25 years old when, like many of his fellow countrymen, he set sail for the East (1618). In 1636 he became governor general of Batavia, the commercial heart of the East India Company. He succeeded in winning Ceylon and Malacca from the Portuguese (1641) and in extending trade as far as Japan. He was not, however, always in agreement with his masters in the republic. C. R. Boxer noted that when the Delft chamber of the East India Company was bewailing the losses and expenses caused by the conquest of Malacca and Ceylon, it observed that van Diemen would do better to use his talent honorably and dispatch rich cargoes from Asia to the Low Countries than to embark on costly territorial conquests better suited to crowned heads and powerful monarchs than merchants in search of profit. Van Diemen replied that there was a great difference between the general and the particular, and between one kind of trade and another. He also maintained that experience had shown that trade in Asia could not exist without territorial conquests.

The recapture of Breda (1637) and the naval battle of the Dunes (1639)
Johan Huizinga has written that after 1635 the capture of Antwerp was a very feasible proposition from a military point of view, but that any decision to forego the opportunity would not have been solely the result of opposition by Amsterdam; since the United Provinces' alliance with France, their foreign policy had become an altogether more subtle affair. This alliance with France was the first occasion on which the Dutch had dealt as equals with a European power, and it also meant that their war with the Spanish became part of the much greater scenario of the Thirty Years' War. Although Frederik Henry, the third stadholder, was not allowed to capture Antwerp, as he had planned in 1630 and 1635, he was able to recapture the city of Breda for good in 1637. Two years later, Maarten Tromp, the first in a long line of great Dutch admirals who were to fight with such skill in the two wars against the English, inflicted a heavy defeat on the second great Spanish Armada at the Dunes

(October 21, 1639), thereby asserting their maritime supremacy. And yet nine more years were to pass before the two countries finally concluded the peace treaty that had eluded them at the Truce of Antwerp 30 years earlier.

The Statenbijbel: 1637
One of the decisions taken by the Synod of Dordrecht had been to entrust a commission of 18 theologians, Orientalists, and historians with the task of translating the Bible into Dutch, because the existing translation, based on Luther's German translation, was judged to be inadequate. The *Statenbijbel* (States Bible), so called because it was financed by the States General, was published in 1637 and had a remarkable influence on the Dutch language, soon becoming used throughout the United Provinces.

The Discourse on Method: 1637
Having abandoned his military career and traveled to a number of different countries, the French philosopher René Descartes (La Haye, Turenne, 1596–Stockholm, 1650) settled in Holland at the end of 1628. In Amsterdam, he lived in a house at 6 Westermarkt. In a famous letter to Jean Louis Guez de Balzac, he wrote: *"en cette grande ville où je suis, n'y ayant aucun homme, excepté moi, qui n'exerce la marchandise, chacun y est tellement attentif à son profit, que j'y pourrais demeurer toute ma vie sans être jamais vu de personne."* ("I am the only person in this large city I find myself in who does not follow the profession of tradesman and everyone is so intent on making his own profit that I could live here all my life without anyone ever noticing me.") In fact, the philosopher had come to Holland in search of the intellectual peace and quiet that he feared losing amid the distractions of Paris, and he remained in the country, apart from a few visits to France, until the final weeks of his life. His great admirer, Queen Christina of Sweden, sent a ship to Amsterdam to take him back to Stockholm, but the rigors of the Swedish winter soon brought on a fatal lung infection. His most famous work, the *Discours sur la méthode,* had been published in Amsterdam in 1637.

The Dutch in Ceylon: 1638
This island, known to ancient geographers as Taprobane or Serinda, is now called Sri Lanka. Ceylon, its name until a few years ago, comes from the Singhalese Selan, which in turn derives from the Sanskrit Sinhaladnipa (Island of Lions). The Portuguese, who had first gained a foothold on the island in 1505,

were opposed by van Diemen, the head of the East India Company at Batavia, who entered into an alliance with the king of Kandy. The first intervention by the Dutch (1638) in support of the local monarch (but with an eye on the island's cinnamon plantations), concluded with the complete expulsion of the Portuguese. The Dutch then gained control over the coast and deprived the king of Kandy of all access to the sea. The island remained under Dutch control until 1795, when it was conquered by the English.

The Schouwburg, the city's first theater: 1638
Midday, Sunday, January 3, 1638, saw the opening of the inaugural performance in Amsterdam's first independent and permanent theater, called the Schouwburg (meaning, quite simply, "theater"), situated on Keizersgracht, although there had obviously already been theatrical performances in halls or on temporary platforms erected for the annual fairs. The new theater was run by two social institutions, the city orphanage and the old people's home, which shared the profits. The first performance had, in fact, been scheduled for December 26, 1637, but the Reformed Church had intervened in order to ensure that "the representation of Papist superstitions such as the Mass and other ceremonies" would not be allowed. The burgomasters had to examine the text that was due to be performed and reassure the church: the work was Vondel's *Gijsbrecht van Amstel*, based on an episode in the city's medieval past that had taken place at the beginning of the 14th century, and which finished with the appearance of an angel who prophesied Amsterdam's future greatness. It was a great success, being performed by male actors exclusively, even in the female roles. The first actress did not appear on the stage until 1655: her name was Ariana Noozeman and she was paid four and a half florins for roles such as Chimène in *Le Cid*.

Deshima: 1641
The Dutch East India Company also followed in the footsteps of the Portuguese in respect to trade with Japan. But in the fourth decade of the 17th century, the shogunate of Tokugawa broke off all contacts with Westerners. The Dutch, however, were the sole, tiny exception: the company's agency, situated on an islet less than two hundred meters long in the Bay of Nagasaki, to which they were confined in 1641, continued to trade Chinese silk for Japanese silver and copper. Between 1641 and the middle of the 19th century, something of

the science and technology of the West still managed to filter into Japan via Deshima, making a significant contribution toward that country's sensational transformation during the succeeding century.

The Night Watch: 1642
The most famous painting by Holland's greatest painter, Rembrandt van Rijn (1606-1669), who was born in Leyden but belonged to Amsterdam in spirit, life, and work, is in reality a portrayal of Captain Frans Banning Cocq's company. It is a *Doelen-stuk*, or a group portrait — of a division of the civil guard — a genre of painting that has immortalized a great many of the characters who lived in Amsterdam and has transmitted something of the spirit of one of its most characteristic institutions, the civil guard. In this masterpiece, Rembrandt succeeded in taking the genre to new heights. His fame as an artist had already been established by another well-known work, also closely connected to the life of the city: *The Anatomy Lesson of Doctor Nicolaes Tulp* (1632). In the year that Rembrandt completed *The Night Watch*, his wife Saskia van Uylenburgh died, an event that marked the start of an unhappy and troubled period in the artist's life, culminating in the enforced auction of his house and goods to pay his debts (1658). In 1662, however, Rembrandt was to paint another famous work, a very vivid reflection of the middle-class life of the city, a group portrait of the *Staalmeesters* (five syndics of the Amsterdam Guild of Drapers).

Tasman and New Zealand: 1642-1643
Abel Tasman, in the service of the governor general of the East Indies at Batavia, Anton van Diemen, carried out a great voyage (1642-1643) that has ensured him a place in history as the greatest oceanic explorer after Magellan. The aim of his voyage was the ambitious one of finding a route from the Indies to South America through the southern Pacific. Leaving Batavia with two ships, Tasman sailed westward to Mauritius, turned south, and then ventured toward the east. He there discovered the island today known as Tasmania, but which he christened van Diemen's Land. Then he pressed on, discovering an unknown land that he called New Zealand, following the coast toward its northernmost point, which he named after the governor's wife, Maria van Diemen. Quite rightly convinced now that the route to South America was a possibility, he returned to Batavia, passing the north coast of New Guinea, which the Dutch believed formed part of a single land

mass together with Australia, even though the Spaniard Luis Vaez de Torres in one of his voyages (1605-1607) had already sailed through the strait between New Guinea and Australia that bears his name.

Work begins on Amsterdam's new Town Hall: 1648
In as early as 1639, a communication from the burgomasters to the city council noted that the old medieval town hall was in a state of extensive disrepair and that some kind of accident was bound to occur sooner or later. However, it was not until January 1648, after the necessary studies, plans, and expropriations had been carried out, that work began on driving in the thousands of wooden piles needed for the foundations; the ceremony of laying the first stone was conducted later in the year. While construction work was underway, the old town hall burned down (1652), and for three years the city had to be governed from a temporary site. The architect of the new building was Jacob van Campen, who had studied Palladio's drawings in Vicenza, but who built very little else in Amsterdam, working mainly for the court of Orange. The fact that the rulers of Amsterdam had selected this project for completion, combined with the grandeur of the actual building and the nature of its decoration, may be seen as an indication of the way in which they saw their own function and also of the ambitions that they possessed for their city.

The Treaty of Münster: 1648
The Treaty of Münster, concluded in 1648 (together with the Peace of Westphalia and the Treaty of Osnabrück, also signed in the same year), brought to an end the 80-year-long war between Spain and the United Provinces and the more general Thirty Years' War, as well as marking the end of Habsburgs' imperial dream. For the republic of the United Provinces, it signaled the end of their struggle for independence, and on extraordinarily favorable terms: Spain renounced her claims to the seven provinces and recognized the republic as a free and sovereign country, while the Scheldt was to remain closed and the Spaniards undertook not to sail in the waters of the territories conquered by the Dutch East India Company. In a letter written from The Hague to his king by the Portuguese ambassador, Francisco de Sousa Coutinho, we read that the peace was proclaimed in Holland simply by reading the clauses of the treaty in the supreme court of justice at ten o'clock on the morning of June 5, 1648, that particular day and hour being chosen because it coincided

exactly with the time, 80 years earlier, when the counts of Egmont and of Hoorn had been executed in Brussels by the duke of Alba. The States General wanted their own freedom to start on the same day and at the same hour as those on which these two men had died in its defense.

Amsterdam and William II: 1650
On the death of Fredrik Henry in 1647, his 22-year-old son William II had become stadholder. He had many grounds for conflict with the states of Holland, who were dominated by Amsterdam. He would have liked to continue the war with Spain in deference to Holland's alliance with France, but the Treaty of Münster was rushed through. In addition, being married to King Charles I's daughter, Henrietta Maria Stuart, he would have liked to have waged war against Cromwell's England, following the execution of his father-in-law, but the States General prevented him. Once the Treaty of Münster had been signed, the states of Holland were of the opinion that they ought to be able to reduce military spending in order to restore a budgetary balance. Negotiations on the matter dragged on, until the States of Holland suspended part of the payment for the troops. The prince got the States General to agree to send a mission to the principal cities in order to get these measures rescinded, but none of the cities, including Amsterdam, would receive the delegation. It was then that William attempted to take the city by surprise, and it was only because of the alarm raised by the postal courier from Hamburg — who had seen suspicious troop movements on the road during the night of July 30, 1650 — that his surprise attack failed. Amsterdam prepared for a siege, but nothing came of the incident because the prince died of smallpox before the year was out. His son, the future William III (William of Orange, king of England), was born after his death, and there began the first period with no stadholder or, in the opinion of the anti-Orange faction, the period of "true freedom." One citizen placed in an offertory box, along with his coins, a piece of paper with the words "the prince is dead, my spirit soars; no such welcome news for eighty years." Three years later, the government of the city obtained from the States of Holland repayment of the 54,000 florins spent during the "siege," and two years later the *vroedschap* (city council) moved the fair (*kermis*), which was normally held in September, to the first week in August, in order to celebrate annually the so-called victory of William II. This episode of the prince's attempted move

against Amsterdam is symptomatic of the basic political conflict that pervades the whole history of the Republic of the United Provinces, which was, in a sense, an anomalous political system within a Europe dominated by monarchical absolutism: on the one hand, there was the monarchical impulse of the Orangist faction, while on the other there were "the liberties," basically of medieval derivation, but sustained by the commercial and manufacturing prosperity of the patriciate who governed the cities. This patriciate governed the country for the next 22 years without the counter-balance of the stadholder, and the man who personifies that period is the grand pensionary of Holland, Johan de Witt, de facto "prime minister" of the republic.

The first Anglo-Dutch War: 1652-1654
War broke out following an incident in May 1652 off Dover between ships of the English fleet under Admiral Blake and the Dutch fleet under Admiral Tromp: a presumed slight, an exchange of gunfire, a loss of ships. The real cause, however, was the commercial rivalry

The destruction of Amsterdam's old town hall by fire (1652), from an engraving by J. de Baen.

between the two powers, and particularly Cromwell's *Navigation Act* (1651), which worked to the detriment of the Dutch. It stipulated that no goods could be unloaded in England unless transported by English ships or ships from the country of the goods' origin (the carrying of merchandise from its country of origin to its country of destination was one of the mainstays of Dutch prosperity). The war was a naval one, waged by two fleets, of which the Dutch was the largest, but the British the more powerful, having larger vessels and greater fire power. Their two strategies were mirror images of each other: the duty of the Dutch admirals was to protect the Baltic and North Sea routes, to escort home ships from the East Indies and to protect the fishing industry, while the job of the English was to disrupt trade and capture the greatest possible number of ships. The Dutch succeeded in getting their silver fleet safely back to port: these were the ships that carried the proceeds of Holland's trade with Spain and her colonies, which were the linchpin of the world's economy, since the silver was used to buy spices in the Orient and raw materials in the Baltic region. Tromp attacked Blake off Dungeness and routed him, but in March the following year (1653) he was defeated in the English Channel, with the Dutch suffering a

further defeat at the Gabbards off the Naze. The English had now regained their domination of the sea and blockaded the Dutch coast. The republic was forced to yield and enter into peace negotiations with Cromwell, to the irritation of certain sections of the English public, who wished for the war to be continued. England, however, had achieved a brilliant success, while the Dutch had been forced to face up to a weak spot in their mercantile success story.

The Dutch at Cape Town: 1652

The small Dutch colonial settlement at the southern tip of Africa, later to become Cape Town, was founded on behalf of the East India Company by Jan van Riebeck in 1652. The original intention of the *Heeren XVII* had been for the settlement to act as a supply station providing fresh food and water for ships to and from Batavia. It did indeed fulfill this function, both for the Dutch and also for the ships of other countries, which called in regularly at the bay lying at the point where the Indian and Atlantic oceans converge. Only later did the agricultural colonization of the hinterland begin, mainly with a view to making the station self-sufficient in food. During the 1680s groups of Huguenots arrived from France, fleeing their homeland following the revocation of the Edict of Nantes (1685), along with Dutch families and young girls of marriageable age from orphanages in the United Provinces. Later on, colonists from Germany also arrived. Unrestricted by neighboring colonies of other nationalities, as had been the case in North America, the colony developed slowly but surely. During the first decade of the 18th century, the term *Afrikaner* began to be used to describe whites born in the colony.

The second Anglo-Dutch War: 1665-1667

England now declared war on the republic for the second time on March 4, 1665. England was now no longer ruled by Cromwell, but by Charles II, following the Restoration. The war was fought in the North Sea, but also in North America, the West Indies and off the coast of Guinea. The English were unable to repeat the success that they had enjoyed a dozen years earlier, and thanks to the work of the grand pensionary of Holland, Johan de Witt, and his brother Cornelis, the Dutch navy had rapidly built up its forces, with its ships being increased in both strength and fire power. The English won a victory off Lowestoft (June 3, 1665), but failed in an attempt to capture the East India fleet, which had put in at Bergen (1665). The next spring, the Battle

of the Four Days ended in a resounding victory for the Dutch admiral de Ruyter, who, although subsequently beaten off the North Foreland (July 19, 1666), gained a great success with his incursion into the Medway on June 11 the following year. The English failed to blockade the Dutch coast, and the Dutch showed that they were capable of taking the offensive. At the Peace of Breda (1667) it was established that the Navigation Act would no longer be applied to goods carried up the Scheldt and the Rhine—which marked a softening of England's protectionist measures—and that both countries would retain their overseas acquisitions. England held Nieuw Amsterdam, conquered in 1664, which became New York, while the Dutch kept Surinam.

Nil volentibus arduum: 1669

The society with the Latin name *Nil volentibus arduum* ("Nothing is hard for those with the will") was founded in Amsterdam in 1669 with the aim of making the French classics and the classical taste a part of the city's cultural life. The works of Racine, Corneille, Molière, and many other lesser writers were translated and performed at the Schouwburg. The taste for all things French also spread beyond culture: the English ambassador William Temple wrote a few years later of how the Dutch were striving to imitate the French in their appearance, their clothing, their speech, and their food, as well as in gallantry and vice. He commented that they were none the better for this sort of affected refinement: in fact, they often ended up as poor copies, whereas they could have been good originals.

Swammerdam's insects: 1669

Jan Swammerdam (Amsterdam, 1637-1680) was a celebrated naturalist, a researcher on the anatomy and biology of invertebrates, a skilled dissector and preparer, and a famous microscopist, one of the founders, in fact, of entomology. His work and his collections attracted the interest of the grand duke of Tuscany, Cosimo de' Medici, who offered twelve thousand florins for the naturalist's scientific cabinet. The matter was never concluded because Swammerdam was unwilling to move to Florence. Swammerdam published during his lifetime a natural history of insects (1669) and a life of the ephemera. Later, however, he underwent a religious crisis and tried to burn his manuscripts, but these fortunately were saved, and his works were subsequently published by Herman Boerhave under the title *Bijbel der Natuure* (1736).

Spinoza's Tractatus theologico-politicus, 1670

Baruch (Benedictus) Spinoza (Amsterdam, 1632–The Hague, 1677) belonged to the Sephardic Jewish community, which was Portuguese in origin. He had been expelled from the community because of his religious views, which ran counter to those of the orthodox establishment, and he earned a modest living manufacturing optic lenses. In his *Tractatus theologico-politicus*, published anonymously in 1670, "interpreting the spirit of the industrious and liberal Dutch middle class, the philosopher combined a deep love of his homeland with an equally warm sense of individual freedom and a courageous defence of religious freedom." (Giorgio Spini) *"In hac enim florentissima republica et urbe praestantissima omnes cujuscumque nationis et sectae homines summa cum concordia vivunt"* ("In this highly flourishing republic and most outstanding city, all men, of whatever nation or sect, live together in the greatest harmony."), wrote Spinoza in his *Tractatus*, the publication of which, however, aroused such ill feeling that he suspended publication of his greatest work, the *Ethica ordine geometrico demonstrata*, which came out after his death in *Opera posthuma* (1677).

The murder of the de Witt brothers, the third Anglo-Dutch War and Louis XIV's attack on the United Provinces: 1672-1678

On the death of Philip IV of Spain (1665), Louis XIV, husband of Maria Theresa of Spain, the dead king's daughter by his first marriage, had claimed the Spanish Netherlands. His claim was based on an article of Brabant law that barred the hereditary succession of children from a second marriage (the Law of Devolution), which was the case with the new Spanish king, Charles II. Louis XIV's advance toward the borders of the republic was halted not so much by the Spanish forces, whom the French had easily defeated (War of Devolution 1667-1668), as by the Triple Alliance, which, following the end of the second Anglo-Dutch war with the Peace of Breda (1667), had been set up between England, Sweden, and the United Provinces (1668). Having concluded the Treaty of Aix-la-Chapelle with the Spanish (1668), in which he restricted himself to the acquisition of a part of Flanders, Louis XIV prepared to attack the Netherlands, his old and trusted ally. Following the republic's political isolation by French diplomacy, the attack was suddenly launched on land by Louis' armies— which in three months had overrun almost the whole country (1672)—and despite the Alliance of 1668, on sea by the fleet of Charles

II of England (the third Anglo-Dutch War 1672-1674), who was fighting with the financial assistance of the French so as not to have to ask Parliament for the necessary funds. In addition, forces from Cologne and Münster also invaded the republic. In mortal danger, the Dutch placed themselves in the hands of the 22-year-old William of Orange, who in February 1672 had been made leader of the army and in July was elected stadholder (the end of the first period without a stadholder). Johan de Witt, the grand pensionary of Holland, who had been in charge of the republic's foreign policy, was accused of not having been able to foresee the French invasion and was publicly censured. On July 24, his brother, Cornelis, was arrested and charged with having intended to assassinate the stadholder, and on August 4 Johan tendered his resignation. On August 20, both brothers were killed in The Hague by the Orangist mob, who tore them limb from limb. The Dutch held out against the French, who had occupied Naarden, some twelve miles from Amsterdam, from behind the Waterline, while William III succeeded in drawing up a coalition of Spain, Austria, Denmark, and a number of German principalities to oppose Louis XIV. Charles II withdrew from the war under the pressure of English public opinion, which was against the alliance with France (1674), and only four years later the Treaty of Nijmegen was signed (1678), which assured the United Provinces of their independence.

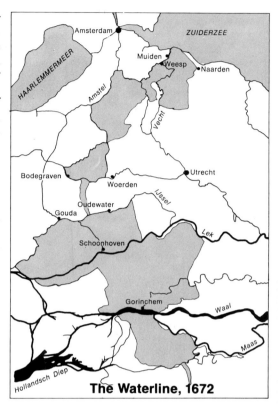

The Waterline, 1672

In gray, the lands flooded in order to create a defensive line.

Amsterdam was able to take advantage of, but it also increased the hostility of the Protestant countries towards France's expansionist policies. In 1686 the League of Augsburg was set up: it consisted of both the Austrian and Spanish branches of the Habsburg empire (Spain was concerned about her possessions in the Southern Netherlands), the United Provinces, Sweden, and numerous German principalities, and its aim was to halt Louis XIV's aggressive policies. In 1688 the stadholder William III of Orange, who was married to Mary Stuart, the daughter of James II of England, landed in England and, as a result of the Glorious Revolution, received the crown of England, Ireland, and Scotland. Louis XIV's alliance with England was thus ended, and the diplomatic policies so carefully nurtured by Mazarin, which had ensured France's dominant position in Europe, lay in ruins. The ensuing war (the War of the League of Augsburg, 1688–1697), bitterly fought in the Pyrenees, in Piedmont, on the Rhine, in the Low Countries, in the American colonies, and in the seas of Asia, demonstrated both the unrivaled military might of the French, which was able to compensate for Louis XIV's total isolation, and also the naval superiority of the English. In the Peace of Ryswick (1697), Louis XIV was forced to give up all the cities and territories occupied since the Treaty of Nijmegen (1678), except for Strasburg and Saarlouis, and to recognize William III as the rightful king of England.

Locke in Holland: 1683-1688

John Locke (1632–1704), the great English thinker, advocate of the Enlightenment, critical investigator of the nature of human knowledge, and staunch advocate of liberal government, arrived in Holland in 1683, following in the wake of the earl of Shaftesbury, whose secretary he had been. In Amsterdam, inspired by Jean le Clerc's *Bibliothèque universelle et historique,* he published his first manuscripts at the age of 54, including an extract of his reflections on psychological matters later republished as *Essay Concerning Human Understanding.* His famous *Epistula de tolerantia,* published anonymously in 1689, one of the great documents of the Glorious Revolution in England, was also formulated in Holland. As Charles Wilson has pointed out, Descartes, Spinoza, and Locke, three philosophers whose thoughts are inextricably linked to one another, and not just only where they coincide, but also where they diverge, could never have produced their works without the freedom and intellectual

stimulus that they were able to enjoy in the republic.

Locke visits Leeuwenhoek: 1685

In his diary, the English philosopher Locke records a visit, on June 22, 1685, to Antony van Leeuwenhoek (Delft, 1632–1723). The earthly fortunes of this brilliant pioneer of biological research did not extend beyond a modest job with the council of his native city, but using microscopes of his own devising (the instrument was probably invented in Holland), he made innumerable observations and discoveries, including that of the red corpuscles in the blood, infusoria, and spermatozoa, which were of great importance in furthering biological knowledge.

The War of the League of Augsburg: 1688-1697

The revocation of the Edict of Nantes (1685) by Louis XIV provoked the emigration of large numbers of Huguenots to the Republic of the United Provinces, a phenomenon that

Huygens and the ondulatory theory of light: 1690

In 1690, after discussions with Isaac Newton, Christiaan Huygens (The Hague 1626–1695), the most important Dutch scientific figure, published his *Traité de la lumière.* In opposition to Newton, Huygens expounded the ondulatory theory of light, which did not become universally accepted until the 19th century. A fellow of the Royal Society in London and a member of the Académie des Sciences in Paris, he already had a number of important scientific researches to his credit, which make him one of the founders of mechanics and optical physics. In 1655, using a telescope of his own construction, he identified Saturn's rings and discovered its satellite, Titan, in 1656. He had written his *De ratiociniis in ludo aleae,* the first treatise on the laws of probability, in 1673, and in his *Horologium oscillatorium* he had elaborated the theory of the compound pendulum and the first theorems of rigid-system mechanics; while many years earlier (1657) he had created a pendulum clock.

The visit of Peter the Great: 1697

Peter Romanoff arrived in the spring of 1697 from Riga at Zaandam, the town near Amsterdam where there was a flourishing shipbuilding industry, the czar's main field of interest at the time. Later, worried by the public's interest in him, he moved to Amsterdam, where he was looked after by the burgomaster, Nicolaes Witsen, a man with scientific interests and also administrator of the East India Company. Peter visited Jacob de Wilde's collection of Greek and Macedonian coins and Frederik Ruysch's collection of anatomical samples; he attended a performance at the Schouwburg, a splended festival with water effects and fireworks on the Amstel, and witnessed naval reviews and even the execution of two criminals in the Dam. He departed with a great load of books and curiosities after engaging 740 Dutch technicians, engineers, shipbuilders, mathematicians, and seamen for his future fleet. Nevertheless, in his instructions for the Russian navy, drawn up under his supervision in 1720, there was a warning that "the Dutch do not possess the art of geometrical perfection in their shipbuilding." Dutch naval technology was no longer supreme.

The War of the Spanish Succession: 1702-1713

William III of Orange, stadholder of the United Provinces and king of England, was killed in a riding accident in March 1702, thereby precipitating the second period without a stadholder. But the great anti-French alliance (the Grand Alliance), established the year before, was active during the fearful War of the Spanish Succession. The ultimate victor was Great Britain, who established her maritime supremacy and gained important commercial advantages. The republic threw all its resources into the war effort and emerged exhausted: its great era of power was over. The cause of the war had been the death without heirs of Charles II, the last of the Spanish Habsburgs, and the selection, after much French diplomatic maneuvering, of Louis XIV's grandson as his successor, who ascended the Spanish throne as Philip V (1701). The most outstanding figures of the war were the duke of Marlborough and Prince Eugene of Savoy on the side of the Alliance. The Netherlands achieved its last great naval victory when it defeated the French in the Mediterranean (Battle of Malaga, August 1704), but the country suffered severe casualties fighting the French under Villars at the Battle of Malplaquet (September 11, 1709). The death of the Austrian Emperor Joseph I

and the succession of his brother Charles VI, who was the rival candidate to Philip V for the Spanish throne, ran the risk of creating a union between the Habsburg Empire and Spain. This would have caused an imbalance of power similar to that resulting from the dynastic union of France and Spain, and so a number of new treaties were signed: the ones affecting the republic were those of Utrecht (April 11, 1713) and of Antwerp (also known as the Barrier Treaty, November 15, 1715). As a result, the Spanish Netherlands passed to Austria, creating a buffer between France and the republic, which, in accordance with the Treaty of Antwerp, obtained the right to maintain garrisons there (in the fortresses along the frontier).

Hollandsche Spectator: 1731

August 20, 1731 saw the publication by the learned Justus van Effen, a native of Utrecht, of the first issue of the *Hollandsche Spectator,* a cultural periodical inspired by Addison and Steele's *Spectator,* "an English journal that I propose not to translate, but instead to copy in my mother tongue," as its author vowed from the outset. The magazine lasted until April 8, 1735, and enjoyed a great success among the republic's middle classes, fulfilling a function similar to that of the many 18th-century magazines, which during that period widened the scope of intellectual debate to include an ever-greater range of topics.

The War of the Austrian Succession and the Amsterdam riots: 1747-1748

Emperor Charles VI left as his sole heir the young Maria Theresa, which provoked another European war (1740–1748) since the French rejected the Pragmatic Sanction, whereby Charles VI had tried to obtain international guarantees to ensure his daughter's succession. During the course of this war, in which Great Britain and the United Provinces alone supported Austria, the French, following their victory at Fontenoy (May 11, 1745), occupied the Austrian Netherlands and then also invaded the United Provinces (1747–1748). The war ended the second period without a stadholder. William IV of Nassau, from a cadet line of the House of Orange, already stadholder of Friesland, Groningen, and Gelderland, was also made stadholder of the other provinces, and the office was declared hereditary. This was a moment of crisis for the powerful urban oligarchies: there was an insurrection in Amsterdam, which also spread to other localities, in protest both against the monopoly of appointments held by the re-

stricted governing class and also against the tax farmers. After the riots in Amsterdam of June 24–28, 1747, the States of Holland debated the abolition of the tax-farming system. Faced with further demands of a political nature, aimed at restricting the power of the local governing bodies, William IV, who had been invited to Amsterdam, replaced the burgomasters and renewed the council. It was, however, merely a change of employees, not of system, and it was the latter that had been put into doubt. Merchants who had never had a place on the council were now admitted, and the mercantile element also became stronger among the burgomasters. The oligarchical system continued, and the middle class opposition of the *doelisten,* which had placed its hope in the House of Orange, was disappointed.

Neutrality: 1748-1780

After its involvement in the War of the Austrian Succession and up until the outbreak of the Fourth Anglo-Dutch War, the republic of the United Provinces was able to enjoy a period of peace, the fruits of its policy of neutrality. It was a period that the Dutch historian Johan Huizinga has likened to an afternoon's nap on a long summer's day, "when the coffers were full of gold coin." In particular, the republic managed to keep out of the great Seven Years' War (1756–1763), while at the same time profiting from it, despite considerable interference in its maritime trade on the part of the English. The stadholder William IV died in 1751, and his son William V, who at the time was only three years old, took over the office in 1766: therefore, in practice, there was another period of dominance by the ruling oligarchy. The country possessed an abundance of capital, and there was a tendency to deal in financial investment rather than in commercial or manufacturing entrepreneurship. Many invested overseas: in 1737 it was said in the House of Commons that the Dutch held 22.7 percent of the British national debt, while in 1758 it appears as though Dutch investors possessed a third of the shares in the Bank of England, the East India Company, and the South Sea Company. In 1762, one Rotterdam banker maintained that the Dutch held a quarter of the British national debt, which then stood at £121 million, and some twenty years later, the grand pensionary, Van de Spiegel, calculated that Dutch overseas investments totalled 335 million florins, of which 280 was in England and the rest in other countries. C. R. Boxer, in referring to these figures, comments that their accuracy has been questioned and mentions the fact that modern research would seem to suggest that only a small number of Dutch capitalists invested heavily overseas, and even this group invested more than half their wealth in their own country. Contemporary visitors to the United Provinces were unfavorably impressed: James Boswell, writing from Utrecht in 1764, noted that many of the Dutch cities were in a sad state of decline, and that instead of finding everyone busily employed, there were large numbers of poor people languishing in wretched conditions. He remarked that if Sir William Temple (the author of *Observations on the United Provinces*, 1673) were to have revisited the country, he would hardly have believed the extraordinary changes that had taken place in it.

The American War of Independence and the Fourth Anglo-Dutch War: 1780-1784
The American struggle for independence was sympathetically viewed in the United Provinces: for the enlightened middle classes, it acted as a political catalyst, while the mercantile sector anticipated the opening-up of a great new market, conducting, in the meantime, a lucrative trade in contraband goods with the American insurgents via the island of St. Eustace in the Antilles. Nevertheless, the republic hoped to weather the storm though its by-now traditional neutrality, even though the French intervened on the side of the recently acclaimed American republic in January 1778. The English declared war on the United Provinces (it was the fourth war between the two countries), both in order to stamp out the trade in smuggled goods from St. Eustace and also to detach the Dutch from the League of Armed Neutrality organized by Russia. The pretext for this act was the discovery by the English, during a maritime search, of a secret agreement negotiated between the American agent William Lee and the banker Jean de Neufville on behalf of the Amsterdam burgomasters. Great Britain declared war on December 20, 1780. There was a naval encounter on August 5, 1781 in the North Sea, near the Dogger Bank, which was of little strategic importance, and then the English captured St. Eustace; but the main effect was on Dutch trade. Because the English were blockading the Channel, ships arriving from the East Indies were obliged to sail around the north of the British Isles, and even then there was no guarantee that they would reach their port of destination, because the English fleet was also in control of the waters off the Dutch coast. In 1784 the two countries made a peace agreement, which historians

The bodies of two hanged men dangle from the weigh house at the Dam in Amsterdam, while the civil guard fire on the crowd during the disorders of 1748: drawing by Simon Fokke.

have defined as being ''reasonably generous'' to the republic. But the whole war had been a disaster for the Dutch.

Princess Wilhelmina's carriage: 1787
The traditional anti-Orangism of the middle class and the governing patriciate of the republic finally split into two factions as a result of the events of the American War of Independence and the Fourth Anglo-Dutch War, whose consequences had proved disastrous for Dutch colonial trade. These two groupings can be categorized as democratic and conservative, respectively, with the first being inspired by the political ideals of the Enlightenment and the second by the ''true liberty'' of the periods without a stadholder. The stadholder William V was held responsible

for the outcome of the war against the English, and the Patriots armed themselves. At Amsterdam, on April 21, 1787, nine members of the council were forcibly replaced by Patriots in the face of armed threats; on July 5, two burgomasters were replaced. William V had been expelled from The Hague, and outbreaks of plundering occurred, with conflicts between Patriots and Orangists. Seen in retrospect, the situation appears to represent Europe's first revolution, anticipating the one in France. It was, however, a failure. The stadholder had the support of Great Britain, while a minor incident provoked the armed intervention of Prussia on his behalf. Three provinces had been ''democratized,'' three were Orangist, and a third was split between the two factions, when the stadholder's consort, Princess Wilhelmina, while trying to return to The Hague, found her carriage's progress blocked by a body of armed volunteers. The Princess was, in fact, the sister of the king of Prussia, who demanded satisfaction from the States of Holland for this affront. When his ultimatum was rejected, twenty thousand Prussians crossed over the republic's frontiers (September 13, 1787), whereupon the Patriots either fled to France or went underground.

The new seat of the Felix Meritis society: 1788

The new building specially constructed by Jacob Otten Husly to serve as the *Felix Meritis* society's new headquarters, was opened in 1788. The society, a typical product of the Enlightenment and strictly apolitical, was the most famous of the many that sprang up during the 18th century—all of which possessed different yet analogous aims and provided a focal point for Amsterdam's cultural life during the final period of the republic. It had already been in existence for several years prior to the inauguration of the new building in 1788, and it was divided into five sections (commerce, physics, design, literature, music), which together provided a significant catalog of the interests of the late 18th-century middle class.

The Velvet Revolution: 1795

The final confrontation between the republic of the Seven United Provinces and the oligarchical regime of Amsterdam's patriciate was destined to be touched off by the French Revolution. The Convention declared war on Great Britain and the republic on February 1, 1793. At the end of the first year, following the French victory over the Austrians in the southern Low Countries, the Scheldt was reopened, a measure to which the republic had always been energetically opposed ever since the time of the Peace of Münster. On March 18, the French revolutionary army, at whose side a "Batavian legion" also fought, was defeated at Neerwinden, northwest of Liège. It was only a brief respite. During the summer of 1794, the Patriots, while preparing for a revolution within the republic, sent messages to France asking for assistance and guarantees of independence. In October, the French were in Brabant: the only thing that could now save the regime was the Waterline, the traditional means of water defense that had saved Holland during other times of crisis. The winter freeze, however, spelled the end. Utrecht surrendered on January 16; on January 19, the burgomasters of Amsterdam agreed to hand over their powers to a revolutionary committee and returned home. A crowd wearing red, white, and blue cockades applauded the French hussars as they entered from the Westerpoort. The stadholder, William V, had already set sail for England from the beach at Scheveningen. At the Dam, the flag of freedom was raised.

Willem van Genth, sectional view of a warship, mid-18th century.

The Eighty Years' War, 1568-1648

The war fought by the northern provinces of the Low Countries against Spanish rule, is known as the Eighty Years' War. It was, in fact, a series of continually interrupted military clashes. The conflict involved an intricate network of religious, political, and economic elements toward which each province or city in the Low Countries reacted in a different way. But its outcome was the establishment of an independent republic, recognized as such by all the European powers.

Philip II had succeeded his father Charles V in the Low Countries (1555) and in Spain (1556), and, like his father, he dreamed of turning the Low Countries into a modern, centrally governed state. But in this he encountered resistance from the provinces, where the traditions of self-government were firmly rooted. The situation was further aggravated by the harsh persecution of heretics, high taxation, and the influence of Spanish advisers in the court at Brussels. In addition, economic conditions were poor, with frequent famines.

After the outbreak of violent religious insurrections in Holland and Flanders in 1566, Philip II sent the duke of Alba to the Low Countries in order to restore order and eradicate heresy. Under Alba's strict government, rebellion became inevitable, with Prince William of Orange, the stadholder of Holland and Zeeland, becoming its de facto leader.

With his strategical expertise and well-drilled Spanish regiments, the duke of Alba subdued the majority of the rebel provinces: the only ones to hold out were Holland and Zeeland, who were favored by their abundance of water, which hindered the enemy's military operations. In Holland and Zeeland diehard Calvinists represented probably three percent of the population, but these provinces were the focal point of resistance, and in 1575 they united, granting William considerable

powers. Before Alba had succeeded in completing his task of suppressing the rebellion, Philip II was forced to lessen the pressure due to the secondary threat posed by the Turks in the Mediterranean.

Hostilities diminished in 1574, with both sides finding themselves in serious financial difficulties. Mutinies by the unpaid Spanish soldiers created panic, especially in the southern provinces, and it was against this background that an alliance was forged between Holland and Zeeland and the provinces that had been returned to Spanish rule (the Union of Ghent, 1576). This was accomplished without the knowledge of Philip II because no new governor had been appointed since the death of the old one, Don Luis de Requesens. The aims of this union were to ensure the expulsion of Spanish troops and to find a peaceful solution to the religious conflicts between Catholics and Protestants. Philip II, however, refused to recognize the Union of Ghent, while, on the other hand, the political, religious, and economic differences between the various provinces proved to be too great. Following the outbreak of violent religious disturbances, certain of the rich southern provinces nervously joined together in a defense pact (Union of Arras, 1579), while the northern provinces followed their example and created their own Union of Utrecht as a counterbalance in the same year.

Philip II regarded William of Orange, who was a staunch supporter of religious freedom for both Catholics and Protestants, as the source of all his troubles in the Spanish Netherlands, and in 1580 he exiled him, declaring him to be an outlaw. As an extreme consequence of the increasing ill will between the Spanish king and his subjects, the northern provinces revoked their oaths of loyalty to Philip (1581). To contemporaries, the rejection of a sovereign was not unacceptable, especially in the case of misgovernment, but to remain without a sovereign was something else completely. For this reason, up until 1588 the rebellious provinces looked for a seigneur in England and France, only then deciding to take their fate into their own hands, with power in the various provinces resting not in the hands of a single individual, but in the already existing provincial states. Around 1580, a new phase in the war had opened up: Philip II had acquired a new source of revenue in the silver from the Americas, while his wars with the Turks were now over. Alessandro Farnese, duke of Parma, displayed great military skill and political ability and rapidly reconquered new areas of the Low Countries

for Spain. In all probability, every single one of the provinces would have fallen, had Philip II not forced Farnese to prepare an abortive landing in England and to turn his attentions towards France. Because of their lack of finance and military organization, the rebel provinces would have been able to make very little headway against Farnese. Following his departure, Maurice of Orange, William's son, being stadholder of most of the republic's provinces, was able to organize an effective counteroffensive. For the first time, the republic used modern military techniques, while at the same time, thanks to its increasing trade, it gained access to the necessary funds.

By the beginning of the 17th century, both parties had tired of the war, and in 1609 a treaty was hammered out (the Truce of Antwerp or the Twelve Year Truce). The next few years saw the emergence of all the new-born republic's seething troubles: the difficulty in harmonizing different traditions and idiosyncrasies, the problems of sharing the costs, the maintenance of the balance of power, and the reconciliation of the conflict between local and collective interests. And yet these difficulties, like the religious disputes, were finally settled.

In 1621, following the breakdown of the truce, hostilities were resumed under very different conditions from those prevailing in 1568. Spain had been irrevocably weakened, whereas the United Provinces had grown into a major economic power. The war was conducted on both sides by skilled military strategists, but the frontiers established before the truce did not alter much, and most of the battles were fought in the areas along the republic's southern boundaries. In 1635 the republic signed a treaty of alliance with France against Spain: this was the first time that the Dutch had negotiated as equals with a foreign power.

The war dragged on. The northern provinces did not really want union with the ones in the south, whose economic competition they feared, and they became increasingly loath to invest ever-greater sums of money in a pointless war. Finally, in 1648, the Treaty of Münster was signed: the republic obtained the recognition of the Spanish king and the Empire, while both sides retained all territories in their possession at the time, including those overseas.

The beginnings of social security: the Amsterdam experience

Elsewhere we have referred to the rise in Amsterdam's population during the 16th and 17th centuries, which was the result of a wave of immigrants from both inside and outside the country, actively encouraged by the city's rulers. The reservoir of labor created in this way made possible the city's commercial and industrial expansion during the last quarter of the 16th century and the first half of the 17th, but there also was another side to the rise in population: there was not enough work for all the immigrants, and many activities, such as the whaling and building industries, were seasonal. Widows and children often found themselves with no means of support; the guilds looked after their master craftsmen, but not their apprentices; there were invalids who were no longer able to work, and all those living close to poverty who during periods of increase in the cost of living found themselves in difficulties. There were also large numbers of discharged soldiers and impoverished, vagabond peasants, who survived by begging and even stealing, wandering from city to city and making the countryside unsafe. From the 16th century, the problem of helping the needy and of fighting poverty became more pressing than ever.

In Amsterdam, the care of the poor had long been the job of the authorities: in as early as 1350, the councilors, later burgomasters, were obliged to look after widows and orphans. Around 1400, the *huiszittenmeesters,* special civic functionaries, were entrusted with the task of distributing bread, butter, cheese, and peat, which before had fallen to the two parish churches. Churches, convents, and private individuals had, from the outset, contributed towards the alleviation of suffering among the poor and infirm; religious confraternities, for example, founded hospices for elderly and sick strangers. During the 15th century, special homes were set up for lepers and plague victims.

During the Middle Ages, evangelical poverty (the renunciation of worldly goods in order to live in humility off alms) was regarded as worthy. However, during the 16th century the rise in the number of paupers as a result of the increase in population and inflation, made it necessary to adopt a new conceptual approach to the problem, already exacerbated by the growing abuse of "Christian charity." Luther, for example, regarded beggars as social parasites. Anyone capable of work ought to become an active member of society: the poor, therefore, should work, and only receive assistance when they were incapable of labor. Luther also believed that the care of the poor should be centrally organized by the secular authorities and inspired by the church.

Working from a completely different, humanist viewpoint, Juan Vivés, a Spaniard who spent part of his life in the Low Countries, reached similar conclusions. In his *De subventione pauperum* (1526) he wrote that material decline, of which the poor were innocent victims, led to moral decline. Education was one of the means of improving the lot of the poor, every one of which should be provided with a suitable job. Orphans should be housed in orphanages. In cases where a person refused to work, their behavior should be altered by means of carefully administered discipline. It is no coincidence that the first measures against begging were taken in the highly industrialized areas of Flanders. In 1525, Ypres banned beggars and at the same time centralized the system of helping the poor. In his far-reaching decree against begging, which applied to the whole of the Low Countries, Charles V (1531) drew inspiration from, among other things, the example set by Ypres: begging was prohibited and help for the poor was centralized and also restricted to those in real need.

Thirty years later, Calvin gave a new interpretation to the word "charity": the rich had to give to the poor because his earthly goods were his to administer, not to command. For this reason, the rich man should share his possessions with the poor and invest money in things that would ease unemployment. The care of the poor fell within the domain of the church, which would provide for them through specially selected members (deacons). These principles were adhered to by a relatively restricted group of people, mainly because of the difficulty of their practical application, but there are echoes of them in the care of the poor in Amsterdam during the 17th and 18th centuries: the distinction between the truly poor and the malingerers, the centraliza-

tion of assistance, the preoccupation with creating new jobs, and the need for better education and an efficient system of punishment.

The ideas of Juan Vivés found an echo in the late 16th-century humanist intellectuals of Amsterdam. During his period in prison at the time of the duke of Alba's repression, Dirck Volckertsz. Coornhert, a native of Amsterdam, wrote his *Boeven-tucht, ofte Middelen tot minderingh der schadelijcke ledighgangers* (Disciplines for Robbers, or the Means of Diminishing the Numbers of Harmful Lay-abouts, 1567), in which he pointed out the importance of teaching a trade to those with no work and also the role played by work in the creation of good citizens; the corporal punishment of delinquents, particularly the very young, would only exacerbate the situation. His follower, the poet Hendrick Spiegel (1549–1612), and the Amsterdam burgomaster Sebastiaen Egbertszon Spiegel elaborated these ideas in their proposals for the institution of a juvenile prison. Spiegel, in particular, was ahead of his time in his ideas on rehabilitation, but the theory that there was good in all men, even the delinquent, aroused little response. The Reformed Church, for example, considered that everyone's destiny was preordained.

In the prison, founded in 1589, inmates had the chance of learning how to make woolen velvet and how to weave, under the supervision of a master weaver, but very soon they began to concentrate on the grating of wood in order to obtain colorants for the dyeing industry; in 1602, the prison, known as the Rasphuis, obtained the monopoly for supplying powdered wood dye to Holland and western Friesland, except for those cities where there were already prisons. The Rasphuis and the Spinhuis, founded shortly afterward for women, became one of the city's tourist attractions, and other cities founded prisons along the lines of the one in Amsterdam. Among the inmates were people who had been caught begging, a practice that had been banned in 1585 by the States of Holland, except among those who possessed a license, and outlawed completely in Amsterdam in 1613. Between 1596 and 1598, however, the specially registered "poor wardens" arrested 4,489 beggars: the restrictions had clearly not solved the problem of poverty.

The system of help for the poor that already existed in Amsterdam favored members of the citizenry or those who had lived for some time in the city; since 1568 it had been decreed that the goods distributed by the *huiszittenmeesters* should go only to the needy who had possessed citizenship for at least three years or had been resident for five, while the deacons of the Reformed Church took care only of members of their church. In a city that was attracting large numbers of outsiders, it was inevitable that poverty would be an enormous problem, which could be resolved neither by the existing measures nor by prisons.

In 1631, the city instituted a college of six almoners (*aalmoezeniers*), who were called on to carry out certain specific functions for the care of the poor. First and foremost, they had to seek out beggars, which they did with the help of a chief guard, assisted by ten helpers authorized to arrest beggars throughout the city and take them back to the *Aalmoezeniershuis* to beat hemp. The number of those arrested rose so quickly that by 1650 a *Werkhuis,* workhouse, had been founded, in which beggars made sails and carpets, beat hemp, and wove and spun. Both men and women stayed there for varying lengths of time, with a considerable number of outsiders among the inmates: in 1654, a third of those arrested came from the empire, with only an eighth coming from Amsterdam itself. The supervision of beggars became even more efficient when the heads of the various neighborhoods had to register them and list the parents that sent their children out to beg instead of getting them to learn a trade.

The almoners only looked after the poor who were citizens or residents for three consecutive years. They distributed bread, butter, cheese, and sometimes in the summer when there were no other welfare handouts, money. They placed orphans and foundlings with adoptive families (from around 1520 there was an orphanage in the city, but the conditions of entry were particularly restrictive), they helped women in labor, arranged paupers' funerals and obtained coffins for them, and also took care of young boys who had come to the city to learn a trade from a master craftsman. Usually the master craftsmen did not provide board and lodging for these apprentices, who were, therefore, forced to beg, and the city acted repeatedly on their behalf.

The numbers of orphans and foundlings increased greatly during the 17th century, while admission to the city orphanage and to the ecclesiastical ones remained limited. The almoners, therefore, acquired a new Aalmoezeniershuis (1662) in which to house the children rather than boarding them out. In 1683, the home was already housing 1,100 children, and in 1714, almost 1,500, after which the numbers decreased, only to rise again in the final quarter of the century; when

the French entered Amsterdam, there were more than 2,400. Their activities on behalf of orphans took up so much of the almoners' time that in 1682 the government of the city relieved them of their other duties, passing them over to the administrators of the hospices (*huiszittenmeesters*).

In 1611, according to the huiszittenmeesters, the number of families receiving assistance was 2,511, of which fewer than two hundred were Dutch. The city historian Jan Wagenaar states that this number rose from 2,795 to 5,860 in the period between 1655 and 1673. In the winter of 1764–1765, there were 1,800 in Oude Zijde (the part of the city to the east of the Damrak) and more than 5,000 in Nieuwe Zijde (the part to the west).

In the mid-17th century, the city tightened up the process of selecting who was eligible to register with the administrators of the hospices, using the heads of the neighborhoods to assist them: the basic precondition was to have lived in the city for at least six consecutive years, which was later changed to seven. Long queues waited for weeks in front of the offices in Oude and Nieuwe Zijde to register, and strict controls were exercised: those deemed to be ineligible were childless people under 40 and able to work, and families with a single child; the wives of sailors had to prove their status by means of a certificate, and those who were rejected were put on a register to ensure that they did not present themselves again. Checks were also made to ensure that claimants were not already being helped by some corporative fund or ecclesiastical institution, in which case they were only given peat.

The daughters of assisted families aged between 7 and 14 inclusive, had to go and work in the Zijdewindhuis rolling up skeins of raw silk; if their parents prevented it, the girls were excluded from the winter assistance.

The city was not prepared, it is clear, to extend this type of assistance to actual beggars, even when the care of the poor became better regulated. They continued simply to be rejects: the city gave them free passage on the haulage boats. Nevertheless, the almoners and the huiszittenmeesters directed their activities to the neediest sections of Amsterdam's population. The inmates of the oldest social institutions, such as the Burgerweeshuis (civic orphanage) and the Oude Mannen-en Vrouwenhuis (old people's home), were not completely without means: in the latter institute, people had to bring certain things with them in order to gain admission (a bed with a sheet and blankets, a cup, jugs, chamber pot, etc.), and the food was

almost luxurious in comparison with that of other charitable institutions: there was meat regularly, game, and sometimes wine.

After 1578, the various small hospitals of the city were brought together in Sint Pietersgasthuis, a large building with two separate departments for men and women, in which two doctors and two surgeons worked. The city had also expressly decided that people of all religions could be admitted. Soldiers and sailors of the Admiralty enjoyed a discount on the cost of their treatment, and in return the Admiralty handed over to the hospital a part of the goods that they had taken as plunder or confiscated. In the hospital, too, there was probably a large number of outsiders during the first half of the 17th century: in 1623 there was only one citizen in it.

Victims of the plague were housed in the Pestenhuis, outside the city; the mentally ill were confined in the Dolhuis, which dated from the mid-16th century and could be visited on payment. For the poor, the vagabond, and the homeless, there was the so-called Bayerd, a hospice that had always been linked to the hospitals: vagabonds were granted shelter there for three nights and could only return after six weeks.

After 1578, a vast network of ecclesiastical assistance developed. The Reformed Church was regarded as the official church, but a number of different sects were soon able to hold services and organize help for their own communities. This was even true of the Catholic Church, which was officially banned but nevertheless able to operate clandestinely.

The Reformed Church organized the diaconate; the city was divided into small neighborhood areas in which two deacons were entrusted with the selection of those in need of assistance. Initially, there were no limits, but the deacons did check to see if the applicant belonged to a guild and was receiving charity from that source. The assistance offered by the Reformed Church mainly took the form of distributions of cheese, bread, peat, and money. The figures speak for themselves: in 1731, the diaconate distributed 166,600 loaves to people's homes, 43,612 in the orphanage, 53,428 in hospices for the aged, and 744 to the residents of a *hofje*. The bread came from the diaconate's central bakery, which had six ovens and produced 720 loaves a day during that year.

The easily acquired right to assistance probably contributed to the growth of the Reformed Church. Around 1580, only 10 percent of the republic's population was Protestant; the majority were undecided, neither fanatically Catholic, nor fanatically Protestant, but the poorest sections of the Protestant population were undoubtedly attracted to the Reformed Church by the assistance it offered. The Reformed Church also took care of children, founding schools for the poor and placing orphans with private families. In 1656 it created an orphanage and in 1681 a hospice for the elderly. Unrestricted eligibility for assistance became impracticable: in 1625, a condition was imposed of six months' membership of the church, which had risen to six years by the middle of the next century. Conditions for entering the hospice were also strict: women had to have lived in the city for at least 15 years, belonged to the church for ten, received assistance for at least two, and not possess children under the age of 25. Men had to be over 60 (50 in the case of invalids), to have lived in the city for 20 years, been a member of the church for 15 and to have received assistance for a year. Both men and women had to be single or widowed. The Reformed Church also condemned beggary: it was possible to receive assistance, but not to beg, and beggars were denied admittance to their institutions.

The Mennonites, Lutherans, Episcopalians, and others also organized help for the poor, and this is equally true of the Catholic Church, which in 1628 had been given permission to set up an orphanage for girls and, later in the century, one for boys as well. Bearing in mind that in 1770 a fifth of the population was still Catholic, this permission was probably urgently needed. As has already been mentioned, the ecclesiastical assistance was independent of the civic authorities, but when a church found itself short of money, the city would make a contribution. This happened in the case of the Walloon Church, which after 1685 had to deal with the problems of French refugees. The city also put building sites at the disposal of the charitable institutions, as well as making financial contributions toward the cost of building. It was in the best interests of the city, which could never have dealt with the requirements of all the needy by itself, to ensure that the churches assisted the poor in the best possible way.

Financing these charitable institutions was difficult. Part of their income derived from the money obtained from the sale of the goods that they produced. After the *alteratie* in Amsterdam (1578), a great part of the possessions belonging to convents were handed over to the charitable institutions: some of them, such as the civic orphanage and the hospital, were actually moved into convent buildings. They also obtained money from collections in churches and on the streets, from poor boxes

and from legacies, while the city itself also gave them various sources of income. Other funds were derived from a variety of taxes on wine, grain, and funerals that took place in the evenings, and there were also the proceeds from fines, such as the ones payable by those arriving late at the Stock Exchange and those who failed to stretch a rope out in front of their house on the canal, in the event of fog, to prevent anyone from falling into the water.

The financial running of the social institutions was carried out by their respective governors, who were chosen by the city's rulers from among the wealthy middle class. It was an unpaid job, but it often helped in advancing a person's career. The governors, both male and female, met every week or fortnight in the luxurious and specially designated room that each institution possessed: on the walls there hung group portraits of the preceding council and carved wooden plaques bearing the coats of arm of the governors in charge, while fresco paintings on the ceiling or over the door paid tribute to the charitable nature of the administrators.

The day-to-day running of the institutions called for the employment of executive and supervisory staff: someone had to supervise the smooth running of the kitchen, the bakery, and the laundry, while there was also the everyday care of the inmates and the general maintenance of the building. There was always a school attached to the orphanages and also a place where the girls learned to cook and sew, which called for schoolmasters and cooking and sewing teachers. There was also a lot of work to be done outside, in supplying fuel, flour, milk, peas, beans, and other food.

The construction of institutions also entailed large-scale building activities, often involving famous architects. The city and the church strove to complete imposing buildings, with great refectories and high-windowed dormitories, broad archways, courtyards, flower gardens, and sometimes even orchards.

The help given to the needy could never have been so comprehensive without the city's prosperity and the fact that the old sense of charity still lived on; by and large, the citizens regarded donations as a Christian duty, an investment in the hereafter. On the offertory boxes in the Mennonite orphanage there were the following words: "Give a part of your property to our poor orphans; with us your money is secure, profitably employed; God will return it to you in great quantities, both here and in the hereafter."

The rich satisfied their sense of charity by bequeathing money for the establishment of a

hofje, an institution in which poor single women could find shelter in little individual houses, as well as receiving food, peat for heating, and on holy days, money distributed by the governors. Often the founder would also lay down the rules of the institution, stipulating that the little houses should be kept clean, that the street outside should be swept, that no alcohol be drunk and no outsiders accepted, that the residents all live peacefully together and that the main entrance gate be shut at ten in the evening. Through this main entrance, over which hung a plaque bearing the name of the founder, one entered into a courtyard around which were arranged the little houses for the inmates. The hofjes were often very simple, but during the 18th century some were founded along monumental architectural lines, with exteriors resembling those of luxurious merchant's houses. By the mid-18th century, there were 28 hofjes in the city, some of which were the result of initiative by the ecclesiastical or civic authorities and were, like other social institutions, administered by a college of governors.

A certain number of 16th-century ideals had been put into practice, but the problem of poverty had not been solved decisively; nor was that an eventuality envisaged by the city. In contemporary eyes, poverty was inevitable, almost a natural phenomenon; all that could be done was to make it bearable for the deserving. The overwhelming concern of the civic authorities was order: assistance was seen as a means of preventing poverty from leading to mass insurrection. And, in fact, they succeeded in this: foreigners made much of the way in which the poor were cared for, and how scarce beggars were on the streets. The situation elsewhere must clearly have been worse.

Beggars, vagabonds, and those unwilling to work had no right to assistance: both the church and the civic government regarded them as criminals. When in the first half of the 18th century, poverty reached vast proportions and the countryside was full of beggars, they became subject to actual physical harassment; only after the mid-18th century, as a result of the Enlightenment influences, was there a different attitude toward the problem of pauperism and assistance, and different solutions were attempted.

Amsterdam's civic orphanage

Orphanages are among the very earliest charitable institutions, being founded as early as the beginning of the 16th century by rich citizens. A municipal hospice for orphans, situated in a house on Kalverstraat, had been set up around 1520. Over the course of the century, the number of orphans grew, which is not surprising in view of the enormous growth in population. By the middle of the century, the orphanage was no longer able to exist on private donations alone, and it also lacked space. After the *alteratie* of 1578, the city confiscated the property of the Catholic institutions, with the civic orphanage being assigned to the buildings of the neighboring convent of St. Lucian. The nuns were housed elsewhere, and their maintenance became the orphanage's responsibility for the rest of their lives. A drawing of 1631 (page 168) shows the old buildings of the convent ranged around a courtyard to the right. In 1599, the orphanage had a new wing built by the famous architect Hendrick de Keyser as one of his first commissions, but this was not the only time that a great architect was employed: the rebuilding of 1634, which resulted in the almost total disappearance of the old monastery, was carried out in the classical Italian style, in all probability in accordance with a plan by Jacob van Campen, who later became municipal architect.

These costly building works would not have been possible without an improvement in the institution's financial position. In addition to the St. Lucian buildings, the orphanage had come into possession of the convent's property and the property belonging to the Carthusian monastery: houses and land, both inside and outside the city, which provided an important source of revenue. There were, in addition, the offerings taken in the Nieuwe Kerk and private donations. In as early as 1553, a messenger dressed in a half-red, half-black cloak (the colors of the orphans' uniforms) went round from house to house collecting money. Finally, the governors of the orphanage, together with those of the hospice for the aged, administered the Schouwburg, the city's theater, dividing the profits in the ratio of two thirds to the former and one third to the latter. On a tablet above the entrance to the orphanage were written the following lines by Joost van den Vondel, encouraging passers-by to contribute: ''We grow in number and we are needy. / Our second parents sigh and grieve. / Do not pass before this great door / without giving a small contribution.'' The only children admitted to the orphanage were those of citizens, a status obtained by heredity, marriage, or the payment of a considerable sum of money. Children from families of the Dutch Reformed Church had priority; Lutheran and Mennonite orphans could find a place in the orphanages of their respective churches. Children were admitted up to the age of ten years; the orphan's inheritance was administered by the orphanage up until the moment of his or her departure at the age of 18. Orphans were released each year on the first Sunday in May, and each of them left with a farewell present of a ''trousseau'' and a sum of money.

The orphanage was an almost self-sufficient community, with a bakery, a kitchen, and a shoemaker, as well as a school where the children were taught to read, write, and do arithmetic. The girls were then prepared for the domestic life, while the boys learned a trade from some master craftsman in the city, the choice of which was left up to them to a certain extent. It was, however, impossible for them to take courses in the Athenaeum Illustre. Every day that they left for their apprenticeship training, the boys had to show the custodian a special piece of paper bearing a representation of two orphans and the city's coat of arms; tools and personal effects were kept in lockers in the boys' court-yard (page 168). The number of orphans in residence varied from two hundred in the mid-16th century, seven hundred in 1629 and a thousand in 1664.

The orphans all wore a uniform (half red and half black), a practice that lasted up until the 20th century. The earliest representation of this uniform dates from 1581; a later one, taken from a register in the archives, shows that in 1636 the boys were wearing white trousers, while an engraving from 1680 shows that the color of the trousers was blue.

Like all the other charitable institutions, the orphanage was run by governors of both sexes, members of the upper middle classes, who carried out their job without pay. The six male and four female governors, however, were not concerned with the day-to-day running of the institution, which was performed by a paid staff of, among others, cooks, nurses, seamstresses, masters, a tailor, and a cobbler.

The girls' courtyard in the orphanage, 1663.

Place names

Amstelland: historical administrative district on both sides of the Amstel, in medieval times under the bishop of Utrecht; the van Amstel nobles ruled there as vassals to him. Amsterdam lay in this territory.

Bocht van de Herengracht: part of the Herengracht between Nieuwe Spiegelstraat and Leidsestraat, laid out in the 17th century as part of the third urban expansion. Some houses of rich merchants rose in this the most expensive part of town.

Bolwerken: the bastions. The city was girded by fortified walls with pentagonal defensive bastions protruding at regular intervals. On each bastion stood a windmill. The bastions were removed in the 19th century.

Brug: bridge over water. In the 17th century the city had several hundred bridges. Stone bridges were also called ''sluis'' (q.v.), which really means ''lock.''

Burgwal: the word ''burg'' means town or shelter, and the burgwal is the wall around it. Later the name extended to the street behind the wall, and the name remained when the wall was removed for urban expansion. Later still, the water ditch along the original wall was called by this name, too, for example, the Kloveniersburgwal.

Dam: the heart of Amsterdam. Here stood the Town Hall, the Waag, the New Church, the Stock Exchange, and the fish market. Originally there were two squares: the true Dam was called Middeldam, and the western part Plaetse, until the 16th century.

Damrak: ''rak'' originally meant a straight stretch of water. The Damrak is thus the channel from the Ij to the Dam, now mainly filled in and a busy road between the Central Station and Dam.

Dijk: a dike, usually an earthen wall, often reinforced with wooden stakes or with stone cover, along or around an area of water as protection against flooding. The oldest dikes near the mouth of the Amstel were Warmoesstraat and the New Dike.

Doelens: targets which stood at the end of the shooting range behind a depot where the guards met and practiced shooting with bows or muskets.

Dwarsstraat: a transversal side street, particularly frequent in the Jordan (q.v.).

Eilanden: islands, in Amsterdam a number of artificial islands. The oldest are Marken, Uilenburg, and Rapenburg, which came to lie within the city in 1593. During the expansion of 1658, Kattenburh, Oostenburg, and Wittenburg were built in the eastern area of the port. Much shipbuilding went on here and the ships' carpenters or *Bijltjes* were the typical inhabitants. In the 17th century, artificial islands were built in the western area of the port, too, with warehouses and wharves: Prinseneiland, Realeneiland, and Bickerseiland.

Gang: passage, narrow lane between houses or walls.

Gracht: excavated canal in town, and the street along the bank.

Grachtengordel: the famous ring of canals dug in the 17th century, during the successive expansions that have given Amsterdam its typical half-moon shape.

Hofje: charitable house for old or single women, built round an inner courtyard (hof). Each was a foundation with its own income and rules.

Houttuinen: timber yards, where timber merchants stored their stocks, as in the Haarlemmer Houttuinen, Joden Houttuinen (Jewish timber yards), and Niewezijds Houttuinen.

Ij: sea inlet of the Zuiderzee cutting deep into Holland. Amsterdam lies where the Amstel flows into the Ij.

Jordan: western part of Amsterdam, which came to lie inside the city at the expansion of 1612. Unlike the canal belts, the street plan here follows the original division into fields.

Kade, Ka, or Kaai: stone-clad bank where ships can tie up for loading and unloading and along which land traffic can run.

Kalverstraat: now a busy shopping street between the Dam and the Mint. The name recalls the time when cattle were driven from the country to the market on the Dam (''calf street''). In the Middle Ages the calf market was probably held at the end of the street. In the southern part, the ox market took place.

Kattenburg: one of the artificial islands built in the eastern port area in the 17th century. Site of the East India Company wharf, and the Admiralty store (still extant and now a maritime museum).

Kolk: space between two lock gates. The Niewezijds Kolk and Oudezijds Kolk are reminders of this.

Lastage: in the Middle Ages, areas outside the city walls; northeast of the town, site of many ship-repair yards, rope-walks, and saw-mills. Toward 1600, the area came to lie within the new city walls.

Lijnbaan: rope-walk. The old ones were within the city walls. The canal running along the wall was the Lijnbaansgracht, which can still be traced over long stretches.

Markt: market, of which Amsterdam had many. The biggest were the Noordermarkt (northern), Westermarkt (western), Botermarkt (butter), Nieuwmarkt (new), Kalkmarkt (lime), and Turfmarkt (peat). Except for the Dam, site of the fish market, all markets took place along the canals: markets for fruit, flowers, pipes, etc. Water was important for bringing the goods to market.

Nieuwe Zijde: new side, as against the Oude Zijde (q.v.), west of the Amstel, where after 1400 the second parish church, the Catherine Church, was built, also called the New Church. Hence, also names such as Nieuwendijk, Nieuwe zijds Voorburwal, Nieuwezijds Kolk, etc.

Nieuwmarkt: new market, also called St. Anthony's market after St. Anthony's Gate, arose in 1614 when part of the Kloveniersburgwal was filled in and covered. Some years later St. Anthony's Gate was set up as a weighing station. Several markets were held round it.

Oude Zijde: old side; after the foundation of the New Church, the first parish church, St. Nicholas Church, was called the Old Church. The part of town east of the Amstel, where the church stands, was called the old side from the 15th century. Hence names like Oudezijds Voorburgwal and Oudezijds Achterburgwal.

Palen: stakes or poles. Since the 14th century the harbor front of Amsterdam was closed by a double row of stakes, which had a defensive function. At regular intervals there were gaps that could be shut with booms where ships could enter to their anchorage inside. At night these gaps were shut.

Plantage: a park; the new quarter of town east of the Amstel, laid out in 1658, was not much needed because the population was no longer growing so fast. Part of it was therefore set aside by the burgomasters as a park in 1682. Lanes were built and trees planted; recreational facilities, gardens, and summer pavilions arose. It was a splendid place for walks.

Poort: gate. At the city walls there were gates for access. In the 18th century there were eight, of which only the Muiderpoort survives.

Rokin: distortion of "rak-in." A rak is a straight stretch of water, and the rak-in is the stretch of water on the inner side of the dam. Originally part of the Amstel which flowed through a lock in the Dam and the outer channel (Damrak) into the Ij.

Schans: entrenchment; a defensive position thrown up on the terrain, but in Amsterdam used also for part of the city wall, as in Oude Schans.

Singel: a canal on the outside of the city, or the path along it; literally "enclosure." After 1450, the Singel was the city boundary of Amsterdam, and the name remained.

Sloot: in general, excavated watercourse in grazing land, or a small canal. In Amsterdam the Recht Boomsloot and Krom Boomsloot ("straight" and "curved") are called after the 16th century ships' carpenter Cornelis Pieterszon Boom. He had these ditches dug to link his wharf on the Lastage with the surrounding waterways.

Sluis: a lock. A device for regulating water flow by at least two doors. Used also for passage of ships between stretches of water at different levels.

Spui: a place where water is released by means of locks. The Spui is the name for a watercourse between Singel and Rokin filled in in the 19th century.

Steeg: a narrow street.

Straat: either street, or straits.

Trekwaart: a straight canal dug specially for towing barges. Often named after their destination, such as Haarlemtrekvaart, Weesptrekvaart.

Vaart: an excavated watercourse, such as the Nieuwe Vaart along the eastern islands in the port.

Wal: generally a mound, or more particularly, a stone or stone-clad rise along a watercourse. In Amsterdam also, the canal along this wall and the bank near it, as in the Kloveniersburgwal.

Walen: anchorages behind the double stake barrier in the harbor, protected by rows of stakes on all sides.

Waterland: region north of Amsterdam on the far bank of the Ij. Economically always closely linked with the Amstelland.

Zaanstreek: region north of Amsterdam on the river Zaan. In the 17th century one of Europe's most industrialized areas.

Bibliography

d'Ailly, A.E. *et al. Historische Gids van Amsterdam,* Amsterdam, 1971.

Assaert, G.; Bosscher, Ph.M.; Bruyn, J.R.; Hoboken, W.J. van; eds. *Maritieme geschiedenis der Nederlanden,* 4 vols., Bussum, 1976–1978.

Barbour, V. *Capitalism in Amsterdam in the 17th century,* Baltimore, 1950.

Boxer, C.R. *The Dutch Seaborne Empire, 1600–1800,* London, 1965.

Blok, D.P.; Prevenier, W.; Roorda, D.J. *et al.,* eds. *Algemene geschiedenis der Nederlanden,* 15 vols., Haarlem, 1977.

Brugmans, H. *Geschiedenis van Amsterdam,* 6 vols., Utrecht, 1972–1973.

Burke, G.L. *The making of Dutch towns. A Study in urban Development from the tenth to the seventeenth Centuries,* London, 1956.

Burke, P. *Venice and Amsterdam; a study of seventeenth century élites,* London, 1974.

Carasso-Kok, M. *Amsterdam Historisch, een stadsgeschiedenis aan de hand van de collectie van het Amsterdams Historisch Museum,* Bussum, 1975.

Carter, A.C. *The Dutch Republic in Europe in the Seven Years War,* London, 1971.

Christensen, A.E. *Dutch Trade to the Baltic about 1600,* The Hague, 1941.

Cotterell, G. *Amsterdam: the life of a city,* Boston, 1972.

Dillen, J.G. van. *Van Rijkdom en Regenten; handboek tot de economische en sociale geschiedenis van Nederland tijdens de Republiek,* The Hague, 1970.

Elias, J.E. *De Vroedschap van Amsterdam, 1578–1795,* 2 vols., Haarlem, 1903–1905.

Fremantle, K. *The Baroque Town Hall of Amsterdam,* Utrecht, 1959.

Gelder, H.A. Enno van. *Getemperde vrijheid. Een verhandeling over de verhouding van Kerk en Staat in de Republiek der Verenigde Nederlanden en de vrijheid van meningsuiting in zake godsdienst, drukpers en onderwijs gedurende de 17e eeuw,* Groningen, 1972.

Glamann, K. *Dutch-Asiatic Trade 1620–1740,* Copenhagen-The Hague, 1958.

Haley, K.H.D. *The Dutch in the 17th century,* London, 1972.

Houtte, J.A. van. *An economic History of the Low Countries, 800–1800,* London, 1977.

Lambert, A.M. *The Making of the Dutch Landscape; an historical geography of the Netherlands,* London-New York, 1971.

Leeb, I.L. *The ideological Origins of the Batavian Revolution. History and Politics in the Dutch Republic 1747–1800,* The Hague, 1973.

Murray, J.J. *Amsterdam in the Age of Rembrandt,* Norman, 1967.

Parker, G. *The army of Flanders and the Spanish Road, 1567–1659; the logistics of Spanish victory and defeat in the Low Countries' wars,* London, 1972.

Parker, G. *The Dutch Revolt,* London, 1977.

Price, J.C. *Culture and Society in the Dutch Republic during the 17th Century,* London, 1974.

Regin, D. *Traders, artists, burghers; a cultural history of Amsterdam in the 17th century,* Assen, 1976.

Rosenberg, J.; Slive, S.; ter Kuile, E.H. *Dutch Art and Architecture, 1600–1800,* Harmondsworth, 1966.

Rowen, H.H. *John de Witt, Grand Pensionary of Holland, 1625–1672,* New Jersey, 1978.

Schama, S. *Patriots and Liberators; Revolution in the Netherlands 1780–1813,* New York, 1977.

Smith, J.W. *The Netherlands and Europe in the 17th and 18th Century,* in J.S. Bromley and E.H. Kossmann, eds. *Britain and the Netherlands in Europe and Asia,* London, 1968.

Taverne, E. *In 't land van belofte: in de nieue stadt; ideaal en werkelijkheid van de stadsuitleg in de Republiek, 1580–1680,* Maarssen, 1978.

Temple, W. *Observations upon the United Provinces of the Netherlands,* 1673; new edition, Oxford, 1972.

Vries, J. de. *Barges and capitalism. Passenger transportation in the Dutch economy, 1632–1839,* Utrecht, 1981.

Vries, J. de. *De economische achteruitgang der Republiek in de archttiende eeuw,* Leyden, 1968.

Vries, J. de. *The Dutch rural economy in the Golden Age, 1500–1700,* London, 1974.

Wagenaar, J. *Amsterdam in zijne opkomst, aanwas, geschiedenissen, voorregten koophandel, gebouwen, kerkenstaat, schoolen, schutterijen, gilden en regeeringe, beschreeven,* 13 vols., Amsterdam, 1760–1768.

Wilson, C. *The Dutch Republic and the civilisation of the seventeenth century,* London, 1968.

Wilson, C. *Profit and Power; a Study of England and the Dutch Wars,* London, 1957.

Zumthor, P. *La vie quotidienne en Hollande au temps de Rembrandt,* Paris, 1959.

The Dutch Cityscape in the 17th Century and its Sources, Bentveld, 1977; exhibition catalogue.

The Dutch Republic in the days of John Adams, The Hague, 1976; exhibition catalogue.

Index

(Numbers in *italic* refer to illustrations.)

Photo Credits

The abbreviations t, b, c, l, r, (top, bottom, center, left, right) refer to the position of the illustration on the page.

Amsterdams Historisch Museum, Amsterdam 8b (Dienst Openbare Werken), 9b (Dienst Openbare Werken), 12tr, 12rc, 12b, 13bc, 13br, 18t, 31lb, 34l, 36l, 36r, 37b (Dienst Openbare Werken), 37t, 38t, 38b, 39, 40t, 42b, 55tl, 56, 59, 62b, 63, 67, 68, 76b, 80tr, 84b, 86tl, 87tl, 88br, 94, 98–99, 102b, 103, 104l, 104c, 106t, 109t, 110l, 114, 115, 117t, 119tr, 119br, 123b, 125t, 125b, 128tl, 131l, 131r, 134l, 140br, 143t, 143tr, 143rc, 143br, 145br, 146t, 147l, 150b, 160b, 166, 167, 171tr, 172t, 172b, 173, 191br, 194, 195t, 197, 198l, 198r, 199, 201, 202b, 204b, 206l, 210, 211l, 211r, 212c, 214b, 217, 223t, 223b, 224t, 225t, 226t, 230t, 231, 233tr, 233b, 234tl, 234tr, 238, 240t, 244.

Archivio fotografico Arnoldo Mondadori, 212b.

Arctisch Centrum, Groningen, 86b (Ben Bekooy).

University Library, Warsaw, Stanislaus Potocki Collection, 130l.

Biblioteca Laurenziana, Florence, 80br (Sansoni), 83t (Sansoni).

Bibliothèque Nationale, Paris, 51bl (Lalance).

British Museum, London, 80l.

Bymuseum, Elsinore, 87b (Carsten Møller).

Het Catharina Gasthuis, Gouda, 30r.

Centraal Museum, Utrecht, 89bl, 129.

The Cleveland Museum of Art; gift of Harry D. Kendrick, Cleveland, 62t.

Private collection, 73 (Pegorini).

Devonshire Collection, Chatsworth; reproduced by permission of the Chatsworth Settlement Trustees, 58b.

By kind permission of the William Fehr Collection, Cape Town, 78t.

The Fitzwilliam Museum, Cambridge, jacket illustration, 154b.

Frans Halsmuseum, Haarlem, 163 (Tom Haartsen).

The Frick Collection, New York, 144.

Gemeentelijke Archiefdienst, Amsterdam, 13bl, 19, 29t (Tom Haartsen), 58c, 62–63, 64, 65, 66, 69l, 72, 90l, 90r, 97, 100l, 100r, 101bl, 101r, 104r, 105r, 106b (Tom Haartsen), 108t, 134r, 135, 146–47, 146b, 147r, 145tr, 148b, 154l, 154c, 155, 161, 168t (Tom Haartsen), 168c, 168b, 175, 180bl, 180br, 180–181, 181, 184, 185t, 185c, 191tl, 191bl, 192l, 195bl, 200b, 203t (Tom Haartsen), 203b (Tom Haartsen), 205tl, 205tr, 205b, 207b, 213t, 215, 218t, 219t, 219b, 222, 226b, 227, 232, 241t, 241bl, 241br, 260, 264, 270.

Groninger Museum voor Stad en Lande, Groningen, 177b.

Gruuthusemuseum, Bruges, 44 (M. Platteeuw).

Hamburger Kunsthalle, 120.

Herzog August Bibliothek, Wolfenbüttel, 29b.

Historisch Museum, Rotterdam, 42–43, 208l.

Historisch Museum, Rotterdam; Atlas van Stolk, 54, 55tr, 55b, 69r, 108b, 111b, 123t, 158br, 191tr, 192r, 195c, 200t, 202t, 208r, 214t, 233l, 235, 237br.

By permission of the Houghton Library, Harvard University, 26r.

KLM Aerocarto, Schiphol, 6, 8t.

Koninklijke Bibliotheek, The Hague, 26l, 142b.

Koninklijk Instituut voor de Tropen, Amsterdam, 182.

Koninklijk Oudheidkundig Genootschap, Amsterdam, 40b (Rijksmuseum, Amsterdam).

Kunsthistorisches Museum, Vienna, 46b, 49 (Meyer).

Louvre, Paris, 165 (Lalance).

Maritiem Museum Prins Hendrik, Rotterdam, 128tr.

Mauritshuis, The Hague, 107.

The Metropolitan Museum of Art, New York; Bequest of Mrs. H. O. Havemeyer, 1929; The H. O. Havemeyer Collection, 105l.

Musées Royaux des Beaux-Arts de Belgique, Brussels, 82b (ACL), 160t (ACL).

Szépművészeti Múzeum, Budapest, 153.

Museum Boymans-van Beuningen, Rotterdam, 81t, 91, 112 (Dick Wolters, Ovezande), 213c, 236tr.

Museum Bredius, The Hague, 148t (Tom Haartsen).

Nationaal Scheepvaartmuseum, Antwerp, 28.

National Gallery, London, 154t.

National Gallery of Ireland, Dublin, 206r.

The National Maritime Museum, London, 87tr, 114–115.

The National Trust Polesden Lacey, 162l.

Nederlandsch Historisch Scheepvaart Museum, Amsterdam, 33r, 70l, 70tr (Costa), 70bc (Costa), 71l, 71r, 75l, 78bl, 79t, 81b (Costa), 88t, 89br, 117b (Costa), 118tr, 145l, 183t, 186, 187, 228t, 253, 265.

Toni Nicolini, Milan, 2, 10, 18b, 21, 24,

31r, 35, 41, 45, 58t, 85t, 85b, 96, 111t, 122, 132, 133, 136, 137, 149, 169, 174r, 178, 193, 228b, 239.

Raccolta delle Stampe Achille Bertarelli, Milan (Saporetti), 32t, 32b, 70br, 224bl, 225bl, 225bc, 225br.

Rijksarchief, Haarlem, 204t (Engel).

Rijksarchief, Haarlem; Provincial Atlas, 9t (Engel), 17b.

Rijksmuseum, Amsterdam, 11, 12tl, 20, 22, 23, 27, 30l, 31tl, 34r, 43, 46t, 46b, 47t, 50, 74t, 74b, 75r, 76t, 77, 83b, 84t, 86r, 89t, 92–93, 109b, 110r, 113t, 116, 118l, 118br, 119rc, 121, 124, 128b, 130r, 138, 139r, 140l, 140tr, 141l, 142t, 151b, 152b, 152r, 158t, 158bl, 159, 162r, 170l, 171tl, 171bl, 171br, 174l, 183bl, 183br, 185b, 188, 189, 195br, 196l, 196c, 196r, 207t, 209, 216, 218b, 220, 221, 229, 236l, 237t, 237b, 240bl, 240br.

© Rijksvoorlichtingsdienst, The Hague, 101t, 102t (Bart Hofmeester), 113b, 141r (Bart Hofmeester).

John and Mable Ringling Museum, Sarasota, Florida, 151l.

Salvat, Barcelona, 48.

Sotheby Parke Bernet & Co., 119l.

Staatliche Kunstsammlungen. Kupferstichkabinett, Dresden, 82t.

Staatliche Museen, Gëmaldegalerie, Berlin, 95l (Ralph Kleinhempel).

Staedelisches Kunstinstitut, Francoforte, 180r.

Stedelijk Museum, Amsterdam, 157.

Stedelijk Museum "Het Prinsenhof," Delft, 51tl.

Stichting De Oude Kerk, Amsterdam, 14.

Stichting Het Catharijneconvent, Utrecht, 13t, 150t, 176.

Teylers Museum, Haarlem, 224br, 234b.

The Toledo Museum of Art; gift of Edward Drummond Libbey, 139l.

Universiteits-Bibliotheek, Amsterdam, 33l, 78br, 79b, 126, 127, 142l, 177t, 212t, 213b, 230b, 248.

Vrije Universiteit, Amsterdam Kaartenverzameling, 17t.

The Warden and Fellows of All Souls College, Oxford, 51r.

Zaanlandse Oudheidkamer, 190 (Drukkerij Meijer Wormerveer bv).

Some illustrations and graphics have been adapted from the following sources: Eurobook Productions, Amsterdam, for the illustration pp. 16–17; H. Zantkuyl, Amsterdam, for the illustrations on pp. 60, 61; Algemene Geschiedenis der Nederlanden, for the map on p. 78; H. Van Dijk and D. J. Roorda, for the graphics on pp. 120, 121; J. de Vries, California, for the table on p. 147.

Acknowledgments

The authors would like to thank the institutions and individuals who facilitated the research and collection of the illustrations, and in particular the Amsterdams Historisch Museum, the Amsterdamse Gemeente Musea and the Historisch Topografische Atlas of the Gemeentelijke Archiefdienst. The authors would also like to thank Messrs. D. G. Carasso, M. Broekhuysen, R. Daalder, F. van Erpers Royaards, B. Haak, S.A.C. Dulok van Heel, W. G. Heeres, P. C. Jansen, P. H. J. van der Laan, M. Jonker, H. F. K. van Nierop, L. Noordergraaf, K. Vermeulen, L. J. Wagenaar, for their expert revisions of parts of the text.